Names in the Economy

Names in the Economy: Cultural Prospects

Edited by

Paula Sjöblom, Terhi Ainiala and Ulla Hakala

CAMBRIDGE SCHOLARS PUBLISHING

Names in the Economy: Cultural Prospects,
Edited by Paula Sjöblom, Terhi Ainiala and Ulla Hakala

This book first published 2013

Cambridge Scholars Publishing

12 Back Chapman Street, Newcastle upon Tyne, NE6 2XX, UK

British Library Cataloguing in Publication Data
A catalogue record for this book is available from the British Library

ISBN (10): 1-4438-4945-6, ISBN (13): 978-1-4438-4945-6

CONTENTS

Preface viii

Part I: Global Trends and the Westernisation of Names

Lumia by *Nokia*, *iPhone* by *Apple*: Global or Local Features in Commercial Names?
Paula Sjöblom 2

Catering to Tastes Beyond Cultural Frontiers: Branding and the Supervening Challenge of Globalisation
Kanavillil Rajagopalan 15

Thailand's Exported Food Product Brand Naming: Semantic and Pragmatic Perspectives
Nithat Boonpaisarnsatit and Jiranthara Srioutai 26

The Price of Home: Names and Prestige of Domicile in Japan
Kyoko Takashi Wilkerson and Douglas Wilkerson 55

Romanian Brand Names as Cultural Mediators
Alina Bugheşiu 73

Restaurant Names in the City of Bucharest: Cross-cultural and Sociolinguistic Perspectives
Adriana Stoichiţoiu Ichim 89

Part II: Local Separation and Cultural Identity

Names in Italian Slogans
Paola Cotticelli-Kurras and Enzo Caffarelli 108

Bread Packages as Verbal and Visual Signs
Irma Sorvali 136

The Touchy Subject of the Place Name: Contemplating Municipality Names and Branding in Merging Situations
Ulla Hakala and Paula Sjöblom 152

Stadi and *Hesa*: Helsinki Slang Names as Commercial Names
Terhi Ainiala 173

Part III: Names in the Era of the Internet

Abbreviation Tendencies in Company Names Deriving from Internet Addresses and Logos
Fabian Fahlbusch 186

The Co-creation of Brand Names
Nicholas Ind 201

User Names in the Online Gaming Community Playforia
Lasse Hämäläinen 214

Part IV: Changing Name Use and Naming Processes in the Changing World

Preferred Sound Shapes of German Brand Names
Elke Ronneberger-Sibold and Sabine Wahl 232

Notes on the Syntax of Commercial Names in Italian
Maria Chiara Janner 250

Tu y yo: Aspects of Brand Names Related to Interaction and Identification
Antje Zilg 269

How Names Reflect the Culture of Competition: An Example from Sugar Beet Harvesting Technology
Sabina Buchner 282

From Car Brands to their Legends
Marcienne Martin 300

An Extended Typology for Product Names: Examples from Yoghurt Names of the German and Swedish Market
Dina Heegen 311

The Lady Gaga Economy: How Paragons Conquer Today's Business Discourse
Angelika Bergien 332

Contributors 345

Index 349

PREFACE

Names are a pervasive part of human culture. We are continuously reminded of their existence by our surrounding environment. Names always come about and are used in interaction between people and in a language community. We give names to referents worth naming, that is, to objects that are meaningful or valuable to us. Moreover, organisations – companies in particular but also public organisations – are increasingly aware of the importance of naming; brands and their names are powerful tools in today's commercial environment.

The approval of names for common use requires a community with a fairly similar vision of the surrounding world, a shared culture. Cultures, in this context, can be conceived as the surrounding environments – international or national – where companies operate, or they can be seen as cultures of the organisations themselves. Culture produces names and names produce culture. Commercial names forge cultures, on the one hand, and changes in cultures may affect commercial names on the other. The world of economy and business has created its own culture, the perspectives of which must be taken into account when constructing commercial names.

The economy has a powerful role in the contemporary global world. Scholars of many fields have had to take this into consideration and search for new angles in scientific studies. There has also been a growing interest among onomasticians towards names that reflect the new commercial culture. Brand names, product names and company names play an important role in business and in the economy, but commercial culture also affects many other names, such as names of rock bands, names of race horses, and even traditional name types such as place and personal names.

The present volume, *Names in the Economy: Cultural Prospects*, contains articles that are based on contributions made to the fourth Names in the Economy symposium (NITE 4) that took place in Turku, Finland in June 2012. The financial support for this conference by the Foundation for Economic Education, the Federation of Finnish Learned Societies and the Turku University Foundation, indirectly promoted the publication of this book. The series of NITE symposia began in 2006 in Antwerp and continued a year later in Vienna. The third one was held in Amsterdam in

2009. All these symposia have led to publications (see Kremer and Ronneberger-Sibold 2007; Wochele, Kuhn and Stegu 2012; Boerrigter and Nijboer 2012). The goal of all four publications has been more or less multidisciplinary: they contemplate names that appear in the economic world, especially from the viewpoints of linguistics and onomastics as well as marketing and branding research.

The 20 articles in this volume have been developed from a collection of papers presented in NITE 4. They have been double-blind reviewed. The theoretical background of the articles is varied: there are traditional onomastic standpoints as well as newer linguistic theories, sociological and communicational views, multimodality theory, brand research etc. The range is also geographically vast: the authors come from ten different countries and from three continents.

All the articles more or less deal with names in the changing environment. The change has, in many cases, been utmost rapid, and the change is global; there is hardly any corner of the world that has not been reached by international culture. We have divided the book into four thematic sections: (1) global trends and the westernisation of names, (2) local separation and cultural identity, (3) names in the era of the Internet and (4) changing name use and naming processes in the changing world.

The first section casts a glance into the impact of globalism. As PAULA SJÖBLOM notes in her article, globalisation can be seen as a process of a world-wide cultural and economic homogenisation. As a counterpoint, the phenomenon may cause a rise of local culture and local identity. Sjöblom contemplates how both global and local goals may be taken into account in commercial naming. The theme continues with the article by KANAVILLIL RAJAGOPALAN who searches for answers to the question of how to make brand names appealing to world-wide and increasingly fragmented audiences whose tastes and trends are still culture-bound. These dilemmas are concretely approached in the article by NITHAT BOONPAISARNSATIT and JIRANTHARA SRIOUTAI. These researchers examine food brands exported from Thailand. They have noticed that many Thai exporters still export their products without brand names or under foreign-owned brands. The authors remark that a good brand name is essential in the introduction of a new product, and show properties of preferable brand names.

Global trends often refer to trends adopted from the Western world – in the economy, mainly from the English-speaking parts of the world. KYOKO TAKASHI WILKERSON and DOUGLAS WILKERSON provide us a view to names and prestige for physical spaces which can be bought: condominiums, assisted-living condominiums and burial sites in Japan. They demonstrate that the names of these commercial spaces employ non-

Japanese words, especially Western loanwords and pseudo-Western neologisms. However, westernisation concerns also commercial naming in Eastern Europe. The articles by ALINA BUGHEŞIU and ADRIANA STOICHIŢOIU ICHIM shed light on commercial naming in Romania from two different angles: Bugheşiu approaches brand names as cultural mediators both before and after the Revolution of 1989, and Stoichiţoiu Ichim analyses restaurant names of Bucharest in contemporary, post-communist society and shows both similarities and peculiarities in comparison to West European naming cultures.

The second section consists of articles that focus on commercial naming in local cultures. Names are important bearers of local identities and they consist of many features that evidently are targeted on local consumers. PAOLA COTTICELLI-KURRAS and ENZO CAFFARELLI describe company names in Italian advertising slogans and create an argument for a linguistic analysis of the names that most slogans are created for the local people. IRMA SORVALI takes a multimodal approach to Finnish bread packages and the bread names found on them. She also compares her data to smaller corpuses collected from Estonia, Sweden and Belgium. The relationship between a place and a brand, on the one hand, and between name and identity, on the other, is the theme of ULLA HAKALA and PAULA SJÖBLOM's article on place branding in municipality merging situations and of TERHI AINIALA's article about the commercial use of slang variants of the name *Helsinki*.

The third section applies to the question of the e-era. The Internet has probably been the most important instigator of the rapid change of cultures in the entire world. FABIAN FAHLBUSCH argues that the development of German company names towards simpler and shorter forms has especially been driven by their use on the Internet. Furthermore, social media has altered our habits: it has given new opportunities for ordinary people to take part in, not only in political issues but also in business. In his article, NICHOLAS IND discusses a new, consumer-oriented and participative approach to brand creation. Consumers and other stakeholders have, via social media, opportunities to influence brands through their active involvement. The Internet and social media have also created quite new types of names. New environments with a commercial aspect have emerged, as well. LASSE HÄMÄLÄINEN analyses user names found in one particular online gaming community. This study concerns one fairly new name type that has not extensively been studied before.

The last section focuses on articles that touch upon questions concerning the use of commercial names, the creation of names and naming processes in the changing world. The subject of the article by

ELKE RONNEBERGER-SIBOLD and SABINE WAHL concerns German brand names and their sound shapes. They compare new brand names with a large corpus of historical brand names and state that there are certain tendencies in the diachronic development of the names. The syntactic structure of commercial names is discussed in MARIA CHIARA JANNER's article. She presents a corpus-based morpho-syntactic analysis of commercial names in Italian and theoretically ponders whether the names are proper or common nouns. ANTJE ZILG approaches brand names from a communicative perspective. She argues that in the contemporary environment, one important function of a brand name is to generate a tie between the product and the consumer, and shows how this relationship is linguistically established.

SABINA BUCHNER describes in her article a special range of business, sugar beet harvesting technology, and searches for an answer to the question on how the names in this industry may reflect the culture of competition. Technology is, in a way, also the subject of MARCIENNE MARTIN, who ponders how the nicknames of two famous car brands have developed a legend. DINA HEEGEN presents in her article a typology of the structure of product names. She compares yoghurt names in German and Swedish markets, and finds naming tendencies motivated by e.g. the respective culture. Last but not least, ANGELIKA BERGIEN illuminates the concept of *paragon* which, in cognitive linguistics, refers to an individual member of a category representing an ideal or its opposite. She analyses two paragon names in business discourse: *Lady Gaga* and *Lehman*. Bergien shows that the paragon primarily indicates the writer's attitude towards the referent rather than helping the receiver to identify complex economic issues. A shared socio-cultural background is especially important in the comprehension of paragons.

The 20 articles in this volume represent the manifold world of names, cultures and economics. At best, they capture the spirit of commercial and other names at the beginning of the 21st century. The interdisciplinary perspectives comprising the theme of this book may lead us to new insights on names in the economy.

Finally, we would like to give acknowledgements to the persons and organisations that have made this book possible. First of all, we thank the authors of this collection and the anonymous reviewers for their prompt collaboration on this project. The Department of Marketing and International Business and the Department of Finnish and Finno-Ugric Languages at the University of Turku have supported our work in many ways. We are most grateful to MA Leonard Pearl, a translator and onomastician, for language consulting and for his many valuable improvement proposals. Special thanks are directed to our editorial secretary Louna Karjalainen, a Finnish language graduate student, who proved to be a thorough, flexible and skilful assistant in the transformation of variegated article manuscripts into a consistent book. Thanks to Cambridge Scholars Publishing for approving our book in its publications and to Ms Carol Koulikourdi for her support.

Paula Sjöblom, Terhi Ainiala and Ulla Hakala

References

Boerrigter, R. and Nijboer, H. (eds.). 2012. *Names as language and capital. Proceedings Names in the Economy III, Amsterdam, 11-13 June 2009*. Amsterdam: Meertens Instituut. Electronic publication: http://depot.knaw.nl/12899/.

Kremer, L. and Ronneberger-Sibold, E. (eds.). 2007. *Names in commerce and industry: past and present*. Berlin: Logos.

Wochele, H., Kuhn, J. and Stegu, M. (eds.). 2012. *Onomastics goes business. Role and relevance of brands, company and other names in economic contexts*. Berlin: Logos.

PART I:

GLOBAL TRENDS AND THE WESTERNISATION OF NAMES

LUMIA BY *NOKIA*, *IPHONE* BY *APPLE*: GLOBAL OR LOCAL FEATURES IN COMMERCIAL NAMES?

PAULA SJÖBLOM
UNIVERSITY OF TURKU, FINLAND

Abstract

Globalisation is often seen as a process of world-wide cultural and economic homogenisation, as well as a change from national identities to more diverse identities. Localism, on the other hand, emphasises local production and consumption, local culture and identity. However, local and global are not antipodes but rather different perspectives to interpret different socio-cultural phenomena. The term *glocal* describes the co-presence of both universalising and differentiating processes.

This paper will focus on global and local features of language in commercial names: what is it in language that particularly makes us consider a name global or local? Linguistically, global features are such structural and semantic features of language that promote and maintain the economic and cultural process of globalisation, whereas local features of language are perceived and interpreted only by a local language community and by a local culture.

The question will be approached with help of some examples. Finally, a proposal is made on how to combine local and global goals for commercial naming as well as two important functions of commercial names, i.e. bearing identity, on the one hand, and producing a good image, on the other.

Introduction

When Nokia in October 2011 presented its new Windows phone models, Lumia 800 and Lumia 710, chief executive officer Stephen Elop stated: "Lumia is light; it is the new dawn for Nokia" (Reuters, 26 October 2011). While stressing the importance of the new model for Nokia, Elop, in a way, interpreted the name of this product as well. *Lumia* is reminiscent of the Latin word *lumen* 'light' – and it probably is associated the same way all over the Western world, regardless of language.

Right after the phone was released, information about the "right" meaning of the name started to spread in social media. The tabloids in Finland screamed: "The new Nokia phone is actually a hooker!" (Mäkinen 2011, my translation). Someone had found that some online Spanish dictionaries had the word *lumia* as having the meaning 'prostitute'. Apparently, it is not a very familiar word, because none of the Spanish people interviewed by the newspaper knew it. Nevertheless, when they were told this meaning, they believed that they would not like to buy a phone with a name like this – and so said even the one who had said that the name reminds him of lightness. A negative association was easily attached to the name.

Lumia is a typical name in the contemporary global market: it is made of a quasi-word which is not meant to be any language. It is not informative – it does not describe the product – but the phonetic form has been carefully thought of by linguistic experts: the word form must not mean anything negative or cause pronunciation difficulties in any language, but instead awake similar kinds of images in the consumers' minds (Volpe 2011). These linguistic features make the name global, i.e. easy to use everywhere in the world.

However, at the same time, a global name like *Lumia* will be interpreted locally. Presumably, most Spanish-speaking people do not think about the uncommon Spanish word. Instead, Finnish consumers are likely to think of the Finnish word *lumi* 'snow' as well and its plural partitive form *lumia*. As for snow, it is reminiscent of purity, lightness and whiteness. And these images fit well into the more universal way of interpreting the name.

In this paper, I will discuss and clarify which linguistic features, if any, make us consider commercial names as global or local. The question is mainly theoretically approached, and illustrated with case examples. The purpose is to stimulate ideas and to provoke some interdisciplinary dialogue about the multifaceted phenomenon of globalism in commercial naming.

Complex Concept of Globalisation

Global, globalism and globalisation can be understood in many ways (see a broader discussion in Garret 2010). The terms *globalism* and *globalisation* can be ideologically charged: they have the meaning of a process of cultural and economic homogenisation, and *globalisation* is often combined with the "Americanisation" of consumption, mass media and culture. Sometimes *globalism* is a counterpoint to regionalism as well. (E.g. Söder 2010: iv.) Globalisation can also be seen as a historical economic change characterised by, for instance, increasing complexity of global supply chains and internationalisation of finance, and it can be seen as a change from national or social class identities to more diverse identities based on ethnicity, religion, lifestyle, hobbies or occupational interest (Hess 2009: 3–4). *Localism*, on the other hand, emphasises local production and consumption, local culture and identity. *Local* can be used as an equivalent for *domestic* or *national*, but also, on a smaller scale, it can be used to refer to a neighbourhood in a larger region (Hess 2009: 11). According to Robertson (1995: 31), local is a relative concept: a village community is local relative to region, as well as a society is local relative to a civilisational area.

Actually, local and global are not antipodes but rather different perspectives to interpret socio-cultural phenomena, two sides of the same coin. The term *glocal* in some way captures the complex local–global relationship (Hess 2009: 4). Global does not necessary mean only the homogenisation of cultures but also heterogenisation. *Glocalisation* means that global and local features reach their meaning and identity only in relation to each other. Local is not a counterpoint to the concept of global but rather an aspect of globalisation, and globalisation is a kind of hybridisation process. (Robertson 1995: 30, 40–41; see also Nederveen Pieterse 1995.)

There are three dimensions to globalisation: economic, political and cultural. They all have an influence on each other. Technological development, political and economic interdependence between different countries and interaction across large distances may give us the impression of living in a global village where our activity is first and foremost local. Global is not experienced uniformly, nor universally. It is a phenomenon of difference as well as uniformity emerging in relation to each other. (See Garret 2010: 448–449; Coupland 2010: 5.)

Skutnabb-Kangas and Phillipson (2010: 81) argue that linguistic glocalisation has to be conversed in a framework that reckons with political and economic issues and the global and local power relations of languages. Without going any deeper into their arguments concerning language politics in general, I accept the wide contextual view as a starting point for the examination of linguistic features in the world of global economy. Many researchers see language as a resource and a commodity in the economy (see e.g. Heller 2010: 352), and taking advantage of this economic value of language demands an understanding of the relations of languages in local and global contexts.

In this paper, I will focus on special features of language in commercial names: what is it in language that especially makes us consider a name global or local? Linguistically, I see global as such structural and semantic features of language that promote and maintain the economic and cultural process of globalisation, whereas local features of language are perceived and interpreted only by a local language community and by a local culture – the speakers of one dialect or a language. I will approach the question with help of some examples.

Does Language Choice Make a Name Global or Local?

It is common knowledge that English has become the universal language of business. International trading is basically managed in English and companies recruit new staff members more and more with job advertisements written in English – even if the recruitment process focuses on a non-English-speaking country. Regardless of the local clientele, TV and press advertisements contain English. In many countries, English is quite commonly regarded as a universal language that everybody understands, although this insight in reality does not hold true (Gerritsen et al. 2000: 18). It has been argued that English is not a lingua franca in all contexts and for all users (Skutnabb-Kangas and Phillipson 2010: 81).

As David Crystal (2002: 70) puts it, "the world has never had so many people in it, globalization processes have never been so marked; communication and transport technologies have never been so omnipresent; there has never been so much language contact; and no language has ever exercised so much international influence as English." According to him, the position of English as the language of business has been confirmed not least by the dominance of the United States in the world of marketing and advertising (Crystal 1998: 53, 86).

Thus, it is reasonable to claim that English is a global language, and choosing it as the language of a commercial name is a statement for the international and multilingual use of the name. However, the question is not as simple as it may seem to be. English as the language of a name has different motives of choice and different interpretations depending on the surrounding culture and language situation. Similarly, it is oversimplified to claim that other languages would bring a local feature or an association of some special country to the name.

One should remember that English is also a local language to millions of people. A bus driver in Nottingham or an insurance agent in Canberra hardly pays any attention to the language of the name *Apple* when tapping his iPhone. *Apple* is just the name of the company that produces, for example, mobile phones and it is associated to the familiar fruit that is also represented on the sign of the company. Whereas a Finnish phone owner pronounces the name /ɑplɛ/, which means nothing in his own language. He probably knows that it is English and that the company the name refers to is from the English-speaking United States. If he knows English, he understands the meaning of the word in the name, and if not, he anyhow associates the name with an apple because of the symbol connected to the name. *Apple* is a global name because the company acts globally, but the mere name form, the fact that the name is in English, is probably not as noticeable to English-speaking people as it is to other language speakers. In other words, English may be a sign of a global name just in those areas where English is not the dominant language.

The brand name *iPhone* provokes a bit more complicated associations even in English-speaking areas. *Phone* is understandable, it describes the product at least somehow (it is still a telephone as well), but there is no such appellative in English as *iphone*, which – in case there were – might not even be pronounced /aɪfon/ but perhaps in some other way such as /ˈɪfən/ or /ˈɪfəni/[1]. The speaker may think that perhaps the idea of *i* is to emphasise individuality – this is the phone that is like me. On the other hand, according to pronunciation, the name could be associated to 'eye'. Or maybe the *i* is an abbreviation of *intelligence*. All these kinds of different associations awakened by the name may be combined in the language speaker's mind. The name form is targeted more to global rather than local markets because of its obscurity: it will function similarly regardless of the language or country it is used in.

Let us take one more example of the complexity of language choice. For Finnish-speaking people the company name *Nokia* is a Finnish name. The name of the global telecommunications company is based on an old toponym: the first factory *Nokia Ab*, which at that time manufactured wood pulp, was incorporated in the 1860s on the bank of the *Nokianvirta* 'Nokia river' and on the grounds of the Nokia Manor. The name includes a relic of an ancient Finnish word that meant 'sable'. Even though Finns do not know the old word any more, their common cultural knowledge is to connect the name to the town of Nokia, an industrial town that has grown from the paper mill village, and therefore they regard the name as being Finnish. To other people in the world, however, *Nokia* is a name without any other meanings but those that are connected to the company.

[1] I am grateful to Leonard Pearl for this information (e-mail 12 February 2013).

The form of the name does not connect it to Finland – on the contrary, some people still think that it is Japanese. It is usually interpreted as a global name because of its global use.

As already described in the introduction, Nokia's phone model *Lumia* has a name that is framed for global use. It is not any language but it nevertheless arouses similar associations around the world. At the same time, the name form has local interpretations as well. Finnish speakers, who know the Finnish background of the named object, tend to also recognise the Finnish word for 'snow' in the name.

In a comprehensive study of Finnish company names (Sjöblom 2006), attention is also paid to the language of names. The names are analysed synchronically; in other words, the interest is not in the etymology and the original language of the words in the names. Instead, the question is discussed from a Finnish language speaker's view: how is the language to be interpreted by Finnish people? The study shows that Finnish company names include elements from several languages. The names are divided to three main groups: monolingual names, multilingual names and universal names. *Monolingual names* contain only one real language, mainly Finnish or English but also Latin or Swedish. *Multilingual names* consist of combination of elements of two or more languages. Again, the typical combination is Finnish and English, but many other languages, such as French, Italian, and Chinese can be combined – usually with Finnish or English. *Universal names* are divided to three subgroups: *international* names that contain only words that appear in several languages in nearly the same form and meaning (such as *pizza*, *kebab*, *café*, *supermarket*), names that contain words of no real language, i.e. *quasi-linguistic* names, and names that *consist only of a personal name* – in practice, the name of the owner or the founder of the company. (Sjöblom 2006: 303–304; Sjöblom 2009: 291–293.) The same results can probably be applied to product names as well.

Accordingly, from a local point of view, the language of commercial names can be categorised in the above-mentioned way. We can look the names through the eyes of one language community and analyse how the speakers of this language conceive the lingual origin of the names that they deal with. From this angle, local or global features in names can be rethought and pointed out. The context where the name is used is crucial. A Finnish element can be considered to be local, and an English element can be considered to be global in commercial names in the Finnish environment – in some other language community, the same features may be interpreted differently.

Linguistic Features of Commercial Names

What are the local and global features that a commercial name can include? As stated earlier, local features are such linguistic features that can be understood and interpreted only by the local language community, such as people of a country or a village. Locality in a name first of all appears in elements that are dialectal, either words or morpho-phonological characteristics. For example, in Frisian areas in the Netherlands, it has been found that dialectal names have become more common as a response to globalisation (van Langevelde 1999: 58–59). On the other hand, Johnstone (2010: 387, 401) argues that it is oversimplified to claim that using regional dialects is a response to globalisation. Instead, she considers that dialect indexicality is a result of globalisation: local linguistic forms get new ideological values, they become the focus of differentiation and they are culturally noticed.

Naturally, the use of the main language(s) of the country or the region as well (such as Finnish and Swedish in Finland or French in the Walloon region of Belgium) can be seen as a local feature. Elements that include a local toponym or the name of a locally known person or just a local personal name are local features as well; for instance the use of *Hesa* or *Stadi* in company names in Helsinki (see Ainiala in this book), and the names of *Sandels* beer[2] or popular *Reino* slippers[3] in Finland. Locality can also be seen in elements that refer to local history or mythology, such as the names from the Finnish national epic Kalevala (e.g. *Kalevala Koru* 'Kalevala jewellery').

Global features in commercial names are linguistic elements that promote the process of globalisation in one way or another and, at the same time, are spread all over the globe with the help of the political, economic and cultural globalisation process. These elements can be interpreted all over the Western world in the same way. One of the features that can make a name global is the choice of language, which has already been discussed earlier. As previously mentioned, the meaning of language regarding the globality or locality of name depends on the context where the namc is used. I will now continue with considering what kinds of language choices in general could make a commercial name globally functional.

---

[2] According to the web pages of the manufacturer (Olvi), the name originates from the famous military hero, colonel Johan August Sandels, who led the Swedish troops into victory against the Russians in the Finnish War of 1808.

[3] *Reino* is the Fennicised form of the German male name *Reinhold* (Saarelma 2007: 65).

As previously mentioned, the most conventional way of integrating companies or products into the whole world is to use English parts in the names or make names that are completely English, but it is not the only way. The dead language Latin and ancient Greek are regarded as universal languages as well. They are languages that have given a great deal of vocabulary not only to Indo-European but to many non-Indo-European languages as well and therefore, are comprehensible to at least most of Western peoples. These languages can be considered to be politically neutral because they are not directly connected to any contemporary country. These are the reasons why Latin and ancient Greek without a doubt function globally in commercial naming. (Ainiala et al. 2012: 240.)

Names that consist of quasi-linguistic words which – on the other hand – often are made of parts of words from English, Latin or some other known languages are also globally functional. However, like the Finnish name *Nokia*, many names that seem to be quasi-linguistic are, in fact, words of some language. This may lead to awkward coincidences: a product name that was meant to be quasi-linguistic can mean something embarrassing in some language. For instance, a French company called *Laho Équipement* which sells technical equipment and materials for building trade has quite an inconvenient meaning in Finnish: as *laho* means 'rotten' in Finnish, it may be wise for the company not to expand its operation to Finland with that name.

Internationalisms, words that appear in many languages, are linguistic elements that make commercial names globally functional. Like quasi-words, these words can also be risky – *Volkswagen Polo* is 'poor Volkswagen' for Finns, for example. Most abbreviations as elements of names, e.g. *IBM*, *BMW*, *LG*, *MTV* and *HSBC,* which are amongst the world's most powerful brand names (Forbes.com), are equally globally vague. And, finally, any allusions to internationally known persons, places, history, and mythology can be seen as global features in commercial names – for instance *Nike* which includes the name of the Greek goddess of victory, Nike.

Studying Glocal Names

In the world of globalisation, language communities overlap and locations, i.e. places, are inhabited by an increasingly multilingual population. It might be quite reasonable to ask, what is actually local, if the local community consists of long-time local inhabitants speaking one or perhaps several languages, and also having immigrants from all over the world.

There has been an increasing scholarly interest in linguistic landscapes (e.g. Shohamy and Groter 2009; Edelman 2010), and in these studies, proper names, especially commercial names, are also sometimes taken into consideration. Names of shops, brands and products are very common in the texts that show up in the linguistic landscape (Edelman 2010: 23). Eliezer Ben-Rafael (2009) has created a sociological framework for linguistic landscape research, and it may be applied to name research as well. According to him, there are four principles that guide the use of different languages in such situations: 1) presentation of self, 2) good reasons, 3) power relations, and 4) collective identity. *Presentation of self* relates to identity, and this principle aims at showing uniqueness and dissociation. *Good reasons* refer to the fact that the actors, in this case the name givers, adapt to the values of the audience and aim at solutions that generally are positively valued by the public. As a principle, *power relations* aim at imposing certain models by force of dominant position. And finally, there is *collective identity* which, as the first principle, relates to identity and aims at showing likeness, similarity to a certain part of the public.

I will make an effort in developing Ben-Rafael's framework to apply to commercial naming. The four-field table in table 1 is more or less a sketch of ideas and it has not been tested with actual company or brand names. Nevertheless, it is an attempt to combine local and global goals for naming in the economy and to combine two important functions of commercial names: bearing individual and social identity, on the one hand, and making a good image, on the other.

Table 1. The four dimensions of commercial naming.

	Identity	**Image**
For local people	Collective identity	Good reasons
For global markets	Presentation of self	Power relations

In regard to what has illuminated previously, the choice of a linguistic feature may have different status in different situations and to different audiences, i.e. to the four dimensions as described in table 1. This will be clarified through one name example. The Finnish engineering company called *Kone*, which is among the leading manufacturers of elevators and escalators worldwide, has a name consisting of the Finnish word *kone* 'machine'. The name dating back to 1910 probably was chosen for good reasons, in other words, for making a good image in the eyes of the

Finnish public: at that time, Finnish nationalism was gaining strength, but many companies in Finland had Swedish names and Finland was an autonomous part of Russia. Choosing a Finnish word for the company name was a comment on national values and appealed to the local people. In Finland nowadays, the Finnish word in the name *Kone* reflects a collective Finnish identity and Finnish people interpret the name first and foremost as local. At the same time, in the global markets, the name *Kone* presents uniqueness and dissociation and thus reflects the company's identity. Therefore, it represents presentation of self. The meaning of the word included is not internationally known. For global markets, *Kone* is a leading name that sounds quasi-linguistic and as such, is also a naming model for others. Therefore, it represents power in relation to competing companies.

A name can be glocal in many ways. This will be illustrated with a few more examples from the list of most valuable brands. They are names which are global not only because of the global use of them: *Pizza Hut*, *Kraft*, *Marimekko* and *Google*. *Pizza Hut* is an example of an English name which also includes an internationalism, i.e. the word *pizza*. For the local (American) people, the name probably carries a familiar image through the word *hut*. Instead, in non-English speaking countries around the world, the name may be connected to the similar kind of word *hat* because of the image reminiscent of a hat in the logotype. For global markets, the name is first and foremost a representation of the unique personality of the company. The German name *Kraft* and the Finnish name *Marimekko* function globally as names without any special meaning, as well as *Google* which can be considered to be a quasi-lingual name[4]. Globally, the associations connected to these names are based only on their phonetic form and the characteristics of the companies themselves. Locally, the name *Kraft* is associated to 'power', and the name *Marimekko* to 'Mari[5] dress'. The last example of a name that can be considered to be glocal is *Stadin Pizza ja Kebab*. It is a restaurant located in Helsinki, Finland. The name is very local because of the word *Stadin* which is the genitive form of a local slang name for *Helsinki*. At the same time, the name is quite international – *pizza* and *kebab* are international words and

[4] The story behind the name is somewhat more complex. The founders, Larry Page and Sergey Brin, wanted to find a name that was related to the indexing of an immense amount of data. They got the idea of the word *googol*, which refers to a specific large amount of numbers. Because of a spelling mistake, the name was registered as *Google*. (Koller 2004.)

[5] Finnish female name originating from *Maria*.

Stadin is understandable at least to Nordic people who have the word *stad* 'city' in their languages.

Conclusion

We are indisputably living in a global world of business. Our economies and cultures encounter one another even within one country or one town, and even the smallest businesses in small villages can operate in the international markets and their potential clients may be found anywhere in the world. Inevitably, commercial nomenclature in particular has to respond to the challenges and change. Companies have to take local as well as international stakeholders and interest groups into account and design their naming policy bearing these both directions in mind. The names we started with – *Nokia*, *Apple*, *Lumia* and *iPhone* – are all appropriate globally, but they are global in a different way in relation to locality. The name and brand researchers have an interesting assignment to find out in what way commercial names are made glocal – as functional in the local as well as in the global markets.

References

Ainiala, T., Saarelma, M. and Sjöblom, P. 2012. *Names in focus. An introduction to Finnish onomastics*. Leonard Pearl (trans.). Studia Fennica Linguistica 17. Helsinki: Finnish Literature Society.

Ben-Rafael, E. 2009. A sociological approach to the study of linguistic landscapes. In *Linguistic landscape: Expanding the scenery*, E. Shohamy and D. Gorter (eds.), 40–54. London: Routledge.

Coupland, N. 2010. Introduction. In *The handbook of language and globalization*, N. Coupland (ed.), 1–27. Chichester: Wiley-Blackwell.

Crystal, D. 1998. *English as a global language*. Cambridge: Cambridge University Press.

—. 2002. *Language Death*. [e-book] West Nyack: Cambridge University Press. Available through http://site.ebrary.com.

Edelman, L. 2010. *Linguistic landscapes in the Netherlands. A study of multilingualism in Amsterdam and Friesland*. Utrecht: LOT.

Forbes.com = http://www.forbes.com/powerful-brands/ (retrieved 3 December 2012).

Garret, P. 2010. Meanings of 'globalization': East and west. In *The handbook of language and globalization*, N. Coupland (ed.), 447–474. Chichester: Wiley-Blackwell.

Gerritsen, M., Korzilius, H., van Meurs, F. and Gijsbergs, I. 2000. English in Dutch commercials: not understood and not appreciated. *Journal of advertising research*, July–August 2000, 17–31. New York.

Heller, M. 2010. Language as a resource in the globalized new economy. In *Handbook of language and globalization*, N. Coupland (ed.), 349–365. Oxford: Oxford University Press.

Hess, D. J. 2009. *Localist movements in a global economy: Sustainability, justice, and urban development in the United States*. Cambridge MA: MIT Press.

Johnstone, B. 2010. Indexing the Local. In *Handbook of language and globalization*, N. Coupland (ed.), 386–405. Oxford: Oxford University Press.

Koller, D. 2004. Origin of the name "Google". http://www.webcitation.org/68ubHzYs7 (retrieved 3 December 2012).

Langevelde, A. van 1999. What's in a Frisian business name? Regional identification in private enterprise in the Netherlands. In *Bilingualism and regional economic development. A Dooyeweerdian case study of Fryslân*, A. van Langevelde (ed.), 57–73. Rijksuniversiteit Groningen.

Mäkinen, V. 2011. Nokian uutuus onkin ilotyttö! [The new Nokia product is actually a hooker!]. *Ilta-Sanomat* 27 October 2011: 6–7. Helsinki.

Nederveen P. J. 1995. Globalization as hybridization. In *Global modernities*, M. Featherstone and R. Robertson (eds.), 45–68. London: Sage.

Olvi = http://www.olvi.fi/web/en/products/beers/sandels (retrieved 17 April 2013).

Pearl, L., quote from the e-mail, 12 February 2013.

Reuters, 26th Oct. 2011. http://uk.reuters.com/video/2011/10/26/nokias-new-dawn-with-windows-phones?videoId=223917315 (retrieved 4 June 2012).

Robertson, R. 1995. Glocalization: Time-space and homogeneity-heterogeneity. In *Global modernities*, M. Featherstone, S. Lash and R. Robertson (eds.), 25–44. London: Sage.

Saarelma, M. 2007. *Nimi lapselle* [A name for a child]. Helsinki: Minerva.

Shohamy, E. and Gorter, D. (eds.) 2009. *Linguistic landscape: Expanding the scenery*. London: Routledge.

Sjöblom, P. 2006. *Toiminimen toimenkuva. Suomalaisen yritysnimistön rakenne ja funktiot* [A firm name's job description. The structure and function of Finnish company names]. Helsinki: Suomalaisen Kirjallisuuden Seura.

—. 2009. The lingual origin of company names in Finland. In: *People, products, and professions. Choosing a name, choosing a language*, E.

Lavric, F. Fischer, C. Konzett, J. Kuhn and H. Wochele (eds.), 289–295. Frankfurt aM: Peter Lang.

Skutnabb-Kangas, T and Phillipson, R. 2010. The global politics of language: Markets, maintenance, marginalisation, or murder? In *Handbook of language and globalization*, N. Coupland (ed.), 77–100. Oxford: Oxford University Press.

Söder, H.-P. 2010. Foreword: From space to place and the spatial turn within the 'global age'. In *Language and the moulding of space. An interdisciplinary discussion*, N. Jänicke and F. Lenehan (eds.), iii–v. Magdeburg: Meine Verlag.

Volpe, J. 2011. What's in a name? Nokia's new Lumia and Asha line explained. http://www.engadget.com/2011/11/02/ (retrieved 28 November 2012).

CATERING TO TASTES BEYOND CULTURAL FRONTIERS: BRANDING AND THE SUPERVENING CHALLENGE OF GLOBALISATION

KANAVILLIL RAJAGOPALAN
STATE UNIVERSITY AT CAMPINAS, BRAZIL

Abstract

There is a long tradition of regarding tastes and trends as essentially culture-bound. It is held that cultural differences determine our colour and taste preferences, dress codes, musicality and so forth. The dictum "De gustibus non est disputandum" is interpreted as implying that any cross-cultural evaluation of tastes is simply pointless and preposterous. Names, as onomasticians tell us, are likewise characteristically regarded as culturally sensitive. Indeed, marketing experts and advertisers have long known this for a fact. A product name that sounds enticing and appealing in one culture or one language, may sound like a profanity or at least invoke one in another culture, triggering an instinctive and totally unintended consumer repulsion. Here we come to the most challenging of all the many vexing questions in respect to naming brands in our globalised world: what factors must be taken into account while making our choices when it comes to naming brand new products for a worldwide market and/or renaming, or at least "rehashing", already existing brand names so that they are capable of being appealing to wider and more heterogeneous audiences, and apt to be marketed in new and completely alien settings? The answer is far from being either simple or straightforward.

Introduction

The central argument of this paper is that, from a philosophical standpoint, branding is an activity that is riddled with all manner of tensions, many of them leading to gruelling tie-ups or even crippling mental stalemates. Consider, for example, the commonplace remark that what makes a fresh brand name "click" in popular imagination, and thus guarantees its afterlife for years to come, is newness. People adore novelty and abhor what they perceive as passé. They prefer the out-of-the-ordinary and are enticed by what they see as nothing like what they are used to. Nevertheless, while novelty is indeed the soul of a successful brand name being introduced on the market for the first time and possibly the key to its ultimate success, it is equally true that in order for it to be easily memorable and readily recognisable (we are here referring to two important attributes that it can ill afford to dispense with, on pain of being consigned to the dustbin of oblivion), its novelty must not be allowed to go too far. Novelty not tempered with some amount of "familiarity" (sounds, permissible clusters of letters in a spelling system and so on) runs the risk of sliding into bizarreness, of smacking of something exaggeratedly weird or outlandish. The situation here is analogous to what the old adage says about liberty: namely, liberty not restrained by adequate means, can easily degenerate into licence.

In this paper, I intend to take a closer look at another looming paradox in the realm of branding and naming. Once again, it is all too often pointed out that names that stick in mind and are constantly spinning around in one's head long after being exposed to them for the first time, are precisely those that somehow appeal to one's aesthetic sensibilities. And it is further held that all too commonly one's aesthetic sensibilities are not the outcome of one's unique temperament or idiosyncratic developmental history or something like that. One may not even be consciously aware of them or be able to spell them out with any amount of clarity. Instead, one has the aesthetic sensibilities that one has because of the societal factors that play a decisive role in shaping one's tastes. Put simply: we are all inescapably products of the society in which we were raised, and society is the ultimate determinant of our likes and dislikes.

Such an attitude has encouraged many purveyors of the scene to conclude peremptorily that tastes and trends are basically or even definitively culturally driven. Such a conclusion has, in turn, sometimes been interpreted to mean that it is completely pointless to even try to sell one's brand name beyond one's cultural bounds. The fact that a given product name has been a roaring success in one society or setting does not in itself guarantee that it will do equally well in another. In fact, if it does succeed in another culture, that will be purely happenstance.

But then, we have every reason to wonder what happens in our age of globalisation, when products get passed around the globe. Can one at all market one's products under the same brand name in another cultural environment or is one naturally obliged to market them under a new brand name under these conditions? That is to say, is it absolutely necessary to *adapt* already established brand names (or, maybe, replace them with more attractive ones) to better suit, say, the phonological structure of the host language? Researchers such as Klink (2000) and Bao et al. (2008) seem to be inclined to think so. Moreover, they invariably seek their inspiration from Edward Sapir's (1929) classic paper on phonetic symbolism. To be sure, there are a number of concrete cases that seem to recommend this strategy.

But what about truly global, highly successful brand names? Doesn't their very existence call the bluff of the time-old argument that there can be nothing transcultural about tastes? Besides, if the thesis of cultural insularity were an inviolable truth, all those internationally successful brand names, of which glaring examples are legion, would not be anything but glorious exceptions to the rule. And what can one conclude about a putative rule to which exceptions only keep proliferating as the world shrinks by the day, thanks to the relentless advance of globalisation?

In what follows, I intend to hone in on the crucial question of how brand names can cross cultural boundaries and aspire to a universal or at least transnational, transcultural status. I ask this question on the basis of the assumption that, with the process of globalisation implacably and, from the looks of it, irreversibly in progress today, experts in marketing must somehow find ways to break the gridlock of the alleged cultural confinement of tastes and trends.

The Thesis of Cultural Specificity in Tastes

"De gustibus non est disputandum," says a celebrated Latin maxim, possibly of mediaeval origin. This maxim has been frequently invoked in order to discourage all attempts to compare tastes and trends across different cultures. For tastes, according to the maxim, are a law unto themselves; every society, every culture has its own unique tastes that cannot and should not be judged by using outside criteria (Bungarten 1999). A more recent amendment of the maxim that says "De gustibus et coloribus non est disputandum" adds one more ingredient to it. And, to be sure, colour preferences are notoriously known to be culture-specific.

Colour symbolism is one area that has been most looked at in this regard. Black, as it is well-known, is typically associated with political conservativism in Austria and Germany, but has patently unsavoury associations in, say, China and many other cultures. On the other hand, in India and China, white is associated with death and mourning in sharp contrast with the West where it symbolises purity, among other things. We may go on adding to this list.

Names, as onomasticians tell us, are likewise characteristically regarded as culturally sensitive. An oft-cited example is that of the Sony Corporation, an internationally recognised Japanese manufacturer of electronic products. Founded in 1946 by Masaru Ibuka and Akio Morita under the name of *Tokyo Tsushin Kogyo K. K.*, it did not take very long for the company to realise that it had better rename itself with a more attractive and easy-to-remember brand name or fizzle out from the world market. Indeed, marketing experts and advertisers have long known this for a fact. A product name that sounds enticing and appealing in one culture or one language may sound like an expletive, or at least invoke one, in another culture, triggering an instinctive and completely unintended consumer repulsion. Experts in phonotactics would argue that while the phonetic sequencing of syllables in brand names might make or mar the product, there are many other language-bound restrictions one is allowed to take liberties on in exercising creativity when it comes to naming. (Frisch et al. 2000; Bailey and Hahn 2001).

Cultural Rootedness of Tastes and the Danger of Relativism

Taken to its logical extreme, however, the thesis of cultural specificity of tastes and values can lead to some veritable mind-bogglers. To begin with, it can help create the impression that, as sentient beings, we are all, as it were, lost on an island in the middle of the ocean, cut off and completely isolated from the rest of mankind. To make matters worse, there is no prospect whatsoever of making contact with the rest of the world. In other words, the island becomes a metaphor for a mental and cultural prison. However, Eriksen (1993) convincingly argues that the island metaphor is not only misleading but, in the final analysis, pernicious and leads to a complete mental paralysis. Here is what he has to say about the metaphor's tremendous appeal:

> […] an image of nearly totemic stature and significance in modern biogeography and evolutionary theory is that of a literal archipelago, namely the Galàpagos islands, which played a pivotal part in the development of Darwinism. In anthropology, too, island metaphors have had a strong attraction on the discipline's practitioners, and for similar reasons. Modern social anthropology was, as we are all aware, founded on an island, Kiriwina in the Trobriand archipelago, which is in many ways what the Galàpagos islands are biology. (Eriksen 1993: 133–134)

Moreover, he goes on to point out how outmoded such disciplinary outlooks have become over the years:

> The notions of societies and cultures as closed and symbolic systems have been severely criticised in recent years. It has been stressed repeatedly that no society is entirely isolated, that cultural boundaries are not absolute, and that webs of communication and exchange tie societies together everywhere, no matter how isolated they may seem at first glance. Nevertheless, the idea of societies, groups and cultures as entities which can meaningfully be isolated for analytical purposes has not been discarded in practice. (ibid.)

Universalism as the Answer to Cultural Relativism

Traditionally, the thesis of cultural relativism, as embodied in the maxim "De gustibus non est disputandum", has a powerful rival, enshrined in the famous Shakespeare quote:

> What's in a name? That which we call a rose
> By any other name would smell as sweet.

As an antidote to cultural relativism, Romeo's words point to cultural universalism. However, we must hasten to note that Shakespeare did get it wrong here. For, not having lived to see the age of advertising and marketing in the sense in which we know them today, he failed to perceive that a name can make or mar a product to a considerable extent. Here is a case in point. Several years ago, Volkswagen launched a car under the name *Voyage* in Brazil (the same that had earlier or near-simultaneously been introduced in the US and Canada under the brand name *Fox*). In a survey conducted in the country before the carmaker launched its new product, a surprising discovery had been made that the would-be customers showed an overwhelming preference for a 'Frenchified' pronunciation of the word *voyage* to its English counterpart. This was contrary to all expectations, based as they were on the growing prestige of the English language and the diminishing role of French in Brazilian society. One can easily imagine how valuable the opinion poll must have been in ensuring the success of the new brand in the Brazilian market. To go back to the famous line from the bard, it should be perfectly in the fitness of things to venture that if he had a foretaste of things to come, Shakespeare would have certainly rewritten it to say something like "A rose by some other name could even smell foul"!

However, jocosity aside, what Shakespeare did succeed in capturing in that memorable and oft-quoted line is the familiar idea that what matters in the final analysis is the product itself, the *Ding an sich*, and not the appellative that is attached to it and by which it gets referred to. Such a position, let us not forget, is deeply rooted in our time-honoured metaphysical beliefs about language and, more specifically, in the idea of the names of objects being of secondary importance when compared to the objects themselves which they name. It is not for nothing that advertising and marketing are eyed by many with suspicion, even today. Klein (2008) points out that

> Consumers pay a higher price for brand name products than for products that do not carry an established brand name. Because this involves paying extra for what some consider an identical product that merely has been advertised and promoted, brand names may appear to be economically wasteful. This argument was behind the decision to eliminate all brand names on goods produced in the Soviet Union immediately after the 1917 Communist revolution.

This shows that, for all its revolutionary thrust, the Soviet version of communism was very much wedded to the age-old belief that names had no role whatsoever to play in a product's appeal, being at best capable of confounding the judgment of a would-be consumer.

Between the Scylla of Outright Relativism and the Charybdis of Stock-in-trade Universalism

Going back to Eriksen, it is important to stress that he is not throwing his weight behind universals by way of making an apology for essentialism as an escape from the slippery slope of cultural relativism either. If anything, the thrust of his paper points to a need to redefine universals, not in essentialist terms as is customarily done, but as a tendency of otherwise diverse phenomena to converge, thanks to the presence of powerful centripetal forces at work.

Among these centripetal forces at work in the contemporary world scenario is globalisation. Now, there are many scholars who balk at the very idea of globalisation as some sort of a steamroller of uniformisation levelling everything in its way across the world. In her recent book *Identity Formation in Globalizing Contexts*, Higgins (2011) invokes Arjun Appadurai's (1990) concept of "scapes" and their increasing interconnectedness in order to buttress her thesis that in our times, *ethnoscapes*, *technoscapes*, *finanscapes*, *mediascapes* and *ideoscapes* all crisscross to form new kaleidoscopic possibilities of self and identity. Higgins' point is valid insofar as the multiplicity of the parameters she identifies and discriminates yield multifarious possibilities, thanks to the mathematical operations of permutation and combination.

Although, once again, the situation portrayed by Higgins may underscore a random and somewhat chaotic 'scattering' of new identities, one should not lose sight of the fact that there are supervening forces that contain the process and prevent the resultant new possibilities from, as it were, 'going berserk' and out of control. In the case of globalisation, it seems to me, these supervening forces of convergence lead to what we may well consider universal trends and tendencies that are nevertheless fundamentally non-essentialising and, hence, subject to constant and unpredictable evolutionary changes.

The two types of universalising trends can be illustrated by the following sets of partially overlapping circles:

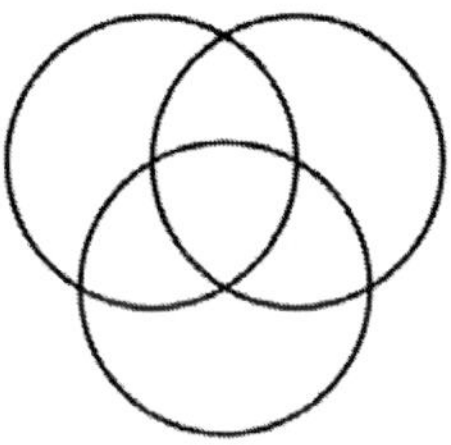

Figure 1. Three overlapping circles.

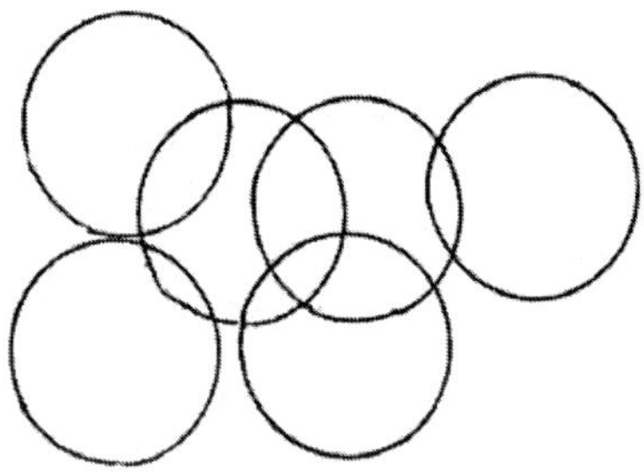

Figure 2. Six circles partially overlapping.

Figure 1 depicts a set of three overlapping circles all of which share a common area – the area that symbolises the essence and the only criterion of set membership. Figure 2, on the other hand, depicts a set of six circles that are only partially and haphazardly overlapping. Whereas in the first case, membership in the set is equally and evenly distributed among the individual circles (in the sense that each one of the circles is entitled to an equal claim to the set membership), in the second case it is distributed unevenly, allowing for the possibility that membership could be regarded as graded and one may speak of a given circle (the one that overlaps four of its neighbours) as being "more of a member" of the set than another (say, the one the on the extreme right, which, as it were, only "latches on" to the set rather tenuously). In the first case, membership in the set is a matter of all or nothing; in the second it is one of 'more or less'.

It is my claim that it is much more productive to think of the spread of brand names across national and cultural boundaries along the lines represented in figure 2, which the philosopher Wittgenstein called 'family resemblance' i.e. similarity among the various elements, guaranteed not by essences but by some likeness which is difficult to pin down with any amount of precision.

The Challenge of Branding Products for the Global Marketplace

Of course, global branding is one area that forces us to put contending principles of international marketing of goods and services to the test (Bungarten 1999; Zilg 2011). Branding or giving attractive names to new products and services being launched to the world market requires extra sensitivity to cultural norms that still hold out as well as requires an eye for detecting trends that sweep across national boundaries and take the world stage by storm. As Zilg (2011) puts it:

> The name is almost considered as a cognitive anchor representing a whole set of values, thus providing orientation for the consumer [...]. A suitable brand name has become the *conditio sine qua non*, the strategic success factor [...].

In the words of Hernández (2011: 369):

> Successful brands are among a company's most priceless assets. They are essential in identifying the maker or seller of a product or service and they result in brand equity (i.e. the value a brand name adds to the product), thus positioning companies at a vantage point against their competitors.

The success story of Lexicon Branding, a company founded in 1982 in Sausalito, California, USA, says it all. Among their trophies are global brand names such as *Pentium* (for Intel), *Swiffer* (for Procter & Gamble), *Power Book* (for Apple) and *Dasani* (for Coca-Cola). On their website (Lexiconbranding.com), the company declares:

> Why do some brands resonate with consumers more than others? Why do some brand names generate interest and excitement and others simply go unnoticed? The answer lies in the way words or phrases are used to connect thought and emotion and deliver a relevant but unexpected new idea.

Nothing Succeeds like Success

The truth of the matter is that there is no ready-made recipe for success, valid for all times and climes. As elsewhere in the world of marketing, there is no silver bullet either. What can be found is a set of strategies that have been tried and tested and proved useful. Colapinto (2011) wrote a piece titled 'Famous Names. Does it matter what a product is called?' in the *New Yorker*, wherein he noted:

> Most projects at Lexicon start off with free-associated Mind Maps – large diagrams of words that spread out like dendrites from a central concept. Lexicon employs two in-house linguists and consults with seventy-seven others around the world.

Colapinto thus gives the lie to Hernández's somewhat sweeping assertions such as that "[r]esearch on the creation and effectiveness of brand names has been mostly carried out by marketing scholars" and that "despite the inherently verbal nature of brand names, studies on linguistic aspects of branding are scarce" (Hernández 2011: 369).

There is however some important truth to Hernández's suggestion maintaining that focus on narrowly linguistic aspects of naming such as the phonetic, the orthographic, the morphological or even the strictly semantic (truth-functional) aspects has yielded precious little by way of providing any fresh insight into what makes a given brand name 'click' where another fails miserably. This is because, in dealing with marketing and advertising, we are no longer in the territory of certainty or an area where rules of a fully deterministic nature are operative. In other words, there simply are not nor can there ever be any hard and fast rules that guarantee success in marketing. Moreover, the fact that a given recipe worked once does not authorise one to take it for granted that it will succeed on a subsequent occasion. If anything, the chances are that "audience weariness" will only thwart any blind repetition of an already attempted strategy.

The Constant Need for Novelty and Innovation

As regards the longevity of a brand name and its secrets, once again we are faced with two opposing and apparently contradictory factors. Names that stick and are readily recognised by people do so, thanks to the regularity and constancy of exposition. Product names that stand the test of time and survive intact sit well in the esteem of consumers. They help foster brand loyalty. In many cases, they become so much a part of the day-to-day experiences of the consumers that they often cease to function as proper nouns and assume the grammatical function of common nouns. Words such as *aspirin*, *band-aid*, *chapstick*, *hoover*, *jacuzzi*, *kleenex*, *vaseline*, and *xerox* are among the best-known examples.

But there is an old saying stating that familiarity breeds contempt. Besides, immutability can often been seen as resistance to change and innovation. The line dividing the two is a tricky one indeed. On the one hand, we would ideally wish the constancy of the brand, its name along with the lettering and design, to stand for customer fidelity. But one would be wise to constantly remember that refusal to innovate runs the risk of being seen as a sign of outmodedness. This is the challenge faced by many newspapers of mass circulation around the world as they change their mastheads (also called nameplates).

To illustrate this point, consider the case of the mastheads of famous newspapers such as *The Times* (of London). If one were to compare it to the Gothic/calligraphic typeface of the masthead that appeared on its edition of December 4, 1788, one would be struck by the sea change that has occurred over the years. The contrast between the two is very telling indeed. Some interesting remarks are in order here. The change of the typeface is, to be sure, a sign of changing times. Mastheads do evolve over time; in fact, it is incumbent upon them to keep abreast of the times, lest they should appear “stale” or “out of date” (or, worse still, out of touch with popular tastes). But change can by no means become synonymous with a complete overhaul. Something, it would seem, has to remain constant or, at the very least, hark back to the original. This is exactly what we see in the case of the crest or the logo that represents the brand. (Notice, incidentally, that newspapers elsewhere in the world, across continents, have been through similar experiences of “updating” their mastheads while keeping their trade mark crests intact).

Does this mean that the crest would be the quintessence of the brand? Well, in the case of the specific newspaper and its masthead, there are grounds for us to conclude that this might indeed be the case. The question is: does it *have* to be that way? With globalisation steaming ahead at this breakneck speed and cultural inter-animation also occurring at a rate unimaginable up until very recently, we can only make wild guesses at what the future may hold for us. One thing is for sure: the very idea of there being absolute essences across cultures may stand in need of close investigation.

Acknowledgements

I wish to thank the CNPq, a funding agency maintained by Brazil’s Ministry of Science and Technology for financing my research under grant no. 301589/2009-7.

References

Appadurai, A. 1990. Disjuncture and difference in the global cultural economy. *Public Culture* 2: 1–24.

Bailey, T. M. and Hahn, U. 2001. Determinants of wordlikeness: Phonotactics or lexical neighborhoods? *Journal of Memory and Language* 44: 568–591.

Bao, Y., Shao, A. T. and Rivers, D. 2008. Creating new brand names: effects of relevance, connotation, and pronunciation. *Journal of Advertising Research* 48: 148–162.

Bungarten, T. 1999. *Sprache und Kultur in der interkulturellen Marketingkommunikation*. 2nd edn. Tostedt: Attikon.

Colapinto, J. 2011. Famous Names. Does it matter what a product is called? *New Yorker*. October 3, 2011. Available on http://www.newyorker.com/reporting/2011/10/03/111003fa_fact_colapinto#ixzz1sPHaP03X (retrieved in April, 2012)

Eriksen, T. H. 1993. In which sense do cultural islands exist? *Social Anthropology* 1 (19): 133–147.

Frisch, S., Large, N. R. and Pisoni, D. B. 2000. Perception of wordlikeness: Effects of segment probability and length on processing nonwords. *Journal of Memory and Language* 42: 481–496.

Hernández, L. P. 2011. Cognitive tools for successful branding. *Applied Linguistics* 32 (4): 369–388.

Higgins, C. (ed.) 2011. *Identity formation in globalizing contexts: Language learning in the new millennium*. Berlin: De Gruyter Mouton.

Klein B. 2008. Brand Names. *The Concise Encyclopedia of Economics*. Library of Economics and Liberty. http://www.econlib.org/library/Enc/BrandNames.html (retrieved 22 June 2012).

Klink, R. R. 2000. Creating brand names with meaning: the use of sound symbolism. *Marketing Letters* 11 (1): 5–20.

Lexiconbranding.com = www.lexiconbranding.com/index.html (retrieved on 1 March 2010).

Sapir, E. 1929. A study in phonetic symbolism. *Journal of Experimental Psychology* 12: 225–239.

Zilg, A. 2011. *That's amore*: brand names in the Italian food market. *International Journal of Applied Linguistics* 21 (1): 1–25.

THAILAND'S EXPORTED FOOD PRODUCT BRAND NAMING: SEMANTIC AND PRAGMATIC PERSPECTIVES

NITHAT BOONPAISARNSATIT
AND JIRANTHARA SRIOUTAI
CHULALONGKORN UNIVERSITY, THAILAND

Abstract

This paper explores the semantic and pragmatic properties of 175 exported food brand names from Thailand. The study results indicate that both semantic and pragmatic meanings of brand names can significantly influence brand communication in the export market. The study also confirms that all brand name owners have specific intentions underlying the use of certain words or phrases for their brand names. Nevertheless, intended information of the brand name could be perceived by customers only when the *sense* and *reference* of the brand name are conventional and relevant enough to the customer's encyclopaedic knowledge. Brand names with appropriate semantic and pragmatic properties should make brand name communication less complicated and less costly to conduct. It is suggested that the exporters pay more attention to the semantic and pragmatic properties of their exported products' brand names.

Introduction

It is widely recognised that brand names play a very important role in marketing products or services and in their acceptance by the public. A study by Kotler and Armstrong (1997) suggests that brand names contribute significantly to the success or failure of new products. A brand name seems to be the first thing that conveys product information to consumers. It is likely that consumers use brand names as a means to recognise product information such as product type; for example, the brand name *Coca-Cola* allows consumers to recognise quickly that the product under that name is a cola-flavoured drink (Kohli and Suri 2000). Dawar and Parker (1994) also points out, in their study, that customers normally use brand names as one of their evaluative tools to justify the quality of a product. The choice of a brand name is, therefore, an important strategy a company needs to take into consideration at the beginning stage of its business development. As Ellwood (2000: 139) suggests, "creating, selecting and testing brand names should not be left to a minor meeting long after new product development has begun; it needs to be thought of at the start of the business, as it is powerful to highlight and shape the information of the business structure".

Choosing a proper brand name is a very essential point in the introduction of a new product. A wisely chosen brand name can create a favourable image and help in creating and enhancing brand awareness (Keller, Heckler and Houston 1998). Brand name scholars propose that a brand naming system consists of three basic components: the marketing component, the legal component, and the linguistic component (Chan and Huang 1997, 2001; Klink 2001; Ellwood 2000). Among the three, the linguistic component seems to be the most fundamental, thus more crucial than the other two. As Charmasson (1988) points out, the degree of marketing promotion and legal protection of brand names is derived from the use of a brand name, which depends almost entirely on the intrinsic characteristics of its syllables, words and phrases.

Brand name scholars such as Chan and Huang (1997) point out that the linguistic component of a brand name is often explained by the fact that it involves the choice of linguistic elements which consists of three parts: phonetic choice, choice of morphological process and semantic choice. It seems that there is a lack of the term *pragmatics* in the previously mentioned literature. However, by investigating the three basic components of brand names carefully, it is quite obvious that the marketing and the legal component of brand names involve the context of brand name use. As pragmatics is often defined as "the study of language in use" (Cruse 2006), it can be assumed that the marketing and legal components are parts of the pragmatics of brand names. The basic components of brand names may thus be refined to involve only the language aspect, or the linguistic specification, and the use aspect, or the communicative specification of brand names.

Previous studies on brand names, e.g. Kohli and LaBahn (1995), Klink (2001) Yorkston and Menon (2004), etc., often focus on the phonetic and morphological aspects of brand names, which are considered to be a part of the linguistic specifications of brand names. Although the aspects of linguistic meaning or the semantics and the aspects of communicative meaning or the pragmatics of brand names seem to be significantly essential; only a few studies have paid attention to the semantics and pragmatics of brand names. It is likely that there is very little knowledge on the semantics and pragmatics of brand names. A few researchers have proposed that a brand name should convey positive connotations and avoid negative ones (Ellwood 2000; Zhang et al. 2004; Hong et al. 2002; Boonpaisarnsatit 2009). To our knowledge, there was only one study, by Klink (2001), that indicates the importance of semantics of brand names. He points out that "the semantics, or meaning of a brand name word, could enhance both product liking and positioning" (Klink 2001: 27). Despite these few studies, there is still a lack of clear and systematic explanation for the nature of the semantics and pragmatics of brand names or brand name meanings. This study thus aims to reveal the semantic and pragmatic properties of brand names, which might be useful for both business operators as well as linguists whose works are related to brand naming.

Realising the importance of brand names in the global market, the Department of Export Promotion of Thailand has encouraged its exporters to export their products under their own brand names. A programme, among others, called *Thailand's Brand: Diversity and Refinement* has been launched to support the manufacturers or exporters who export quality products to the international market under their own brand names. According to the programme's official website, www.thailandsbrand.net retrieved on 30 October 2011, *Thailand's Brand* is a symbol licensed by the Department of Export Promotion and given to Thai-branded products in order to assure their quality and originality. The programme helps promote Thailand's branded products to be recognised among international importers. According to the Department of Export Promotion, the branded products that carry the *Thailand's Brand* symbol not only enjoy the recognition of international consumers but also benefit from superior marketing opportunities since the consumers tend to be more confident when buying products with brands.

Despite the good support from this government organisation, many Thai exporters still export their products without brand names or under the brand names of foreigner-owned companies. This phenomenon makes Thailand's export value lower than it should be. For example, in 2008, the total export value of Thailand's food products was USD 25935 million, according to the National Food Institute of Thailand. However, if Thailand's exporters had exported more brand name food products, Thailand's Department of Export Promotion believes that the food export value would have increased by 10 to 20 per cent. One example is rice products. There are a total of 497 companies of rice exporters in Thailand, but only 90 companies export rice under their own brand names. In 2008, the total export value of Thai rice products was USD 6775 million. According to Thailand's Department of Export Promotion, the value could have been approximately USD 7453 million to USD 8129 million if the exporters had exported more branded products. This is apparently the loss of economic opportunities of the country as the branded products often generate more profit margin than the unbranded ones.

As Thailand positions itself as "Kitchen of the world" and "Food Hub of Asia", its food industry seems to be outstanding in the global market. Food products from Thailand are also various, ranging from simple agricultural produce such as rice, fresh fruits and vegetables, fresh meat, etc. to sophisticated processed food such as instant meals, modern snacks, ready-to-eat microwavable food, etc. The brand names of these exported products exhibit a wide variety of brand naming traditions in Thailand. They are thus considered worth studying.

Semantics and Pragmatics of Brand Names

In this study, the semantics and pragmatics of brand names refer to the linguistic and communicative components of brand names. Based on literature in the field of lexical semantics and lexical pragmatics, i.e. Cruse (1986), Blutner (1998; 2002), Carston (1999), Bach (1999), Wilson (2003) and Jaszczolt (2005), it can be generalised that the semantics of a brand name is relevant to the linguistically encoded information in the brand name. The pragmatics of a brand name pertains to how the brand owners intend their brand names to mean in communication acts, and to how consumers infer or interpret the brand names in their conceptions.

Regarding the roles of brand name owners and consumers, it can be observed that both parties perform tasks in both semantic and pragmatic domains. The brand name owners have an intention of using a brand name. This process occurs in the pragmatic domain. Then, they encode certain linguistic information in the brand name to convey their intention; this action occurs in the semantic domain. For consumers, they play roles in decoding the linguistic form of the brand name. This takes place in the semantic domain. Then, the consumers make an inference of the brand name from the pragmatic environment. This semantics-pragmatics boundary can be summarised in figure 1.

<table>
<tr><th colspan="4">Brand name</th></tr>
<tr><td rowspan="2">Pragmatic domain
Intention to use a brand name</td><td colspan="2">Semantic domain</td><td rowspan="2">Pragmatic domain
Pragmatic inference process</td></tr>
<tr><td>Linguistically encoding process</td><td>Linguistically decoding process</td></tr>
<tr><td colspan="2">Brand owners</td><td colspan="2">Customers</td></tr>
</table>

Figure 1. The semantics-pragmatics boundary of brand names.

Since the nature of brand name communication is normally not face-to-face, the semantic and pragmatic information used by the brand name owners and by the consumers may be different. It is possible that the brand name owners use one set of conceptual and contextual information when they intend to use a brand name, while the consumers use another set of information for decoding and making an inference of the brand name.

Study Design

This study investigates the semantic and pragmatic properties of Thailand's exported food product brand names in order to find out some factors that might affect brand name communication in international markets and to establish guidelines for the brand naming of exported products. The study addresses the two following questions:

1) What are the semantic and pragmatic properties of the brand names of Thailand's exported food products?
2) Which semantic and pragmatic factors affect the communication of brand names in export markets?

To answer these questions, we designed our study as shown below.

The Data

As brand naming apparently involves product owners, brand names and customers, the data used for this study comprise three sets of information. The first set of data involves 175 brand names of Thailand's

Brand[1] awarded products listed in the Food Category of *Thailand's Exporters Directory 2009–2010*[2]. These brand names include 30 brand names of rice products, 23 brand names of frozen and chilled food, 35 brand names of canned and instant food, 29 brand names of snacks and candies, and 58 brand names of ingredients and seasonings (Table 1).

Table 1. The brand name data.

Product	Brand names
Rice products (30 brand names)	*Golden Crane, Golden Pearl, Golden Earth, Imperial Taste, Royal Elephant, Royal Umbrella, Super Dragon, URC, Golden Diamond, Jasmine Gold, Q-Rice, Golden Phoenix, Golden Globe, Royal Orchid, Great Harvest, Golden Horse, Smart Chef, Double Elephants, Golden Lotus, Golden Rabbit, Golden Tub, Royal Dancer, Kaset, Mah Boonkrong, Ponglarp, Surin Tip, Swat-D, Love Farmer, Young Elephant, Sun*
Frozen and chilled food (23 brand names)	*Sea Fresh, KC Fresh, Surapon Foods, Vitafood, Ventuna, PFP, PTN, CMR, CNV, AMS, U.F.P, TSF, CSF, Chef's Choice, Excel Fruit, Ocean Star, Little Chef, Fruit King, Fruit Cellar, May, Aroy-D, KISS, PAM*
Canned and instant food (35 brand names)	*Ocean Taste, Royal Sea, Pan Asia, KC, O&P, UFC, Asian Bowl, Yum Yum, Mama, Three Lady Cooks, Prochef, King Bell, Queen Bell, Delight, Hi-Q, Star, Smiling Fish, Madame Wong, AMPRO, Double Dragon, Trofco, Battleship, Roza, Twin Elephant & Earth, S.Khonkaen, Pine, Nautilus, Bamboo, Kin Dee, River Kwai, Benjamas, Pigeon, Bean, Wai Wai, Pichaya*

---

[1] Thailand's Brand is an icon licensed by the Department of Export Promotion under the Ministry of Commerce. The logo comprises the wordings: THAILAND and Diversity & Refinement inside an oval shape which encapsulate the distinctive image of Thailand as the land of diverse productions of goods with originality, quality, refined craftsmanship and distinction. The Thailand's Brand logo is highly recognised as assurance that the quality of products and services of Thailand are up to the standard of the world's market.

[2] Thailand's Exporters Directory is available in two formats, hard copy and online, each containing the same content. This study uses the online version found at http://application.depthai.go.th/Center_Public/thailand_export_directory.html for it is more convenient to access than the hard copy.

Product	Brand names
Snacks and candies (29 brand names)	*Flower Food, Nut Candy, Mr. Squid, Jumbo, Potato, Softline, My Mint, Wafruit, Capuno, Fisho, Bigga, Euro, Crusty, Yofruit, One More, Durio, Khao Shong Nuts, Tong Garden, Nut Walker, Otari, Classic, Koh-Kae, Manorah, Richo, Taro, Cougar, Pillo, Tao Kae Noi, Jeed Jard*
Ingredients and seasonings (58 brand names)	*Sun Sauce, No 1. Choice, Oyster, Classic Thai, Siam Kitchen, Oriental Chef, Cook Yim, Golden Coins, Desert Rose, Gold Label, 3 Chefs, Flying Rabbit, Flying Tiger, Thai Choice, Neo Suki, Shoice, Pegasus, Golden Fish, Golden Boat, New Grade, King, Chao Thai, Hand No.1, Star Lion, Alfa One, Megachef, Thai Dancer, Talad Thai, Foodex, Thai Smile, Red Spoon, White Elephant, Oleen, Morakot, Ramwong, Lobo, Suree, Pantainorasingh, Rizi, Razor Clam, Fuang Fah, Rose, Three Triangles, Mae Pranom, Kangaroo, Mae Krua, Ruamros, Golden Boy, Gogi, Jade Leaf, Chao Koh, Mae Ploy, Mae Sri, Arroza, Tree, Raitip, Moradok, Juthathip*

The second set of data involves intentions to use the brand names of the brand name owners. E-mail and telephone interviews were used as the method for data collection. Initially, the interview questions were sent to the companies' contact persons via the e-mail addresses given in *Thailand's Exporters Directory 2009–2010.* The deadline for e-mail response was two weeks after the e-mail had been sent. In case any company failed to respond to the e-mail interview within the set deadline, a telephone interview was conducted to complete the data collection. The main purpose of the interviews with the brand name owner was to obtain the meanings of the brand names as intended by their creators.

The third set of data contains customers' interpretations of the brand names. To collect the data, 125 selected consumers of Thailand's exported food products were asked to interpret the brand names based on their own understanding. During the interviews, the interviewees were given pictures of the product packages where the brand names appeared. One interviewee was asked to interpret five brand names. The interviews were conducted at the resting area provided at ThaiFEX-World of Food Asia, the largest food exhibition in Thailand held by Thailand's Department of Export Promotion. These interviewees were customers of Thailand's exported food products who were quite familiar with products from Thailand. The majority of these customers came from the United States, Australia and the United Kingdom. The rest came from Brazil, China, Argentina, Indonesia, India, Malaysia, Taiwan, New Zealand, Japan, South Korea, Singapore, Canada, France, Vietnam, the Netherlands, and Myanmar. Importantly, these international customers were considered fluent in English.

Data Analysis

The analysis of data was processed quantitatively and qualitatively. Regarding the quantitative dimension, percentage and frequency analysis was adopted in the investigation of the brand name data. As for the qualitative dimension, content analysis was used in the investigation of the linguistically encoded meanings and the intended and interpreted meanings of the brand names. The quantitative investigation of brand names involves the frequency and percentage of brand name presentation methods, brand name categories and brand name intended-interpreted meaning matches. The qualitative analysis emphasises the linguistic and communicative aspects of the brand names, which include sense, reference, cooperativeness of brand name owners, customers' comprehension of brand names and brand name relevance.

The main focus of quantitative analysis is placed on the frequency and percentage of three main aspects of brand name communication: 1) brand name presentation methods, 2) categorisation of brand names and 3) the match between intended and interpreted meanings of the brand name data.

Firstly, the way the brand names were presented in the markets, e.g. translation, transliteration, borrowed words, etc., were investigated in order to understand the nature of brand name communication in the export markets. Secondly, the lexical items used as the brand names were examined and categorised. It is expected that lexical categories with high frequency and percentage may reflect certain properties of Thailand's exported food brand naming. Thirdly, the match and non-match between the brand name meaning as intended by the brand name owner companies and the meaning as interpreted by consumers were investigated in order to make generalisations about certain properties of brand names in the two groups.

The qualitative analysis of brand name data was conducted to reveal the sematic and pragmatic factors that might influence communication of brand names in the export markets. For semantic dimension, the focus is placed on *sense* and *reference* of the brand names as adapted from Frege (1892) and Lyons (1977). In terms of pragmatics, the analysis is focused on the cooperativeness of brand name owners, customers' comprehension of brand names and brand name relevance.

Regarding reference, both *original reference* and *brand name reference*, where an original reference refers to a referent in possible worlds, and a brand name refers to the product labelled by that brand name, were analysed. As for a brand name's sense, both literal sense and contextual sense of the brand name were investigated. For example, the original reference of the brand name *Sun* is the star at the centre of the Solar System, and its brand name reference is the product it is labelled on. The literal sense of the brand name *Sun* can be a hot and bright object, and the specific contextual sense of *Sun*, where *Sun* is a chili sauce, can be hot and spicy flavour. The analysis of sense and reference of brand name was aimed to determine how the sense and reference of a brand name might influence the communication of brand names in the market.

As for the cooperativeness of the brand name owners, the analysis was based on Grice's (1975) "Cooperative principle". According to Grice (1975), if one would like to communicate successfully, he/she is required to be cooperative in that communication situation. The level of cooperativeness can be indicated by a good observation of so-called communication maxims which consist of four sub-maxims: quality, quantity, manner and relation. In this study, the analysis of cooperativeness was conducted by considering the members of brand names in the intended-interpreted meaning matched groups and the members of brand names in the intended-interpreted meaning non-matched groups. The aim of this analysis is to consider if the brand name owners observed which communication maxims and violated which maxims.

To further the analysis of brand name communication maxims, the level of relevance of the brand names was also analysed. Based on Sperber and Wilson's (1986) "optimal relevance", the analysis of brand name data was conducted to find out how the brand name relevance affected the customers' comprehension of brand names in the export markets. To do this, both brand names in the intended-interpreted meaning matched group and brand names in the intended-interpreted meaning non-matched group were investigated in order to reveal different factors that might affect the comprehensibility of brand names in the two groups.

Results and Discussions

Brand Name Presentation Methods

The investigation of the brand name data shows that seven types of brand name presentation methods were used. These methods include: 1) direct translation, 2) adapted translation, 3) transliteration, 4) abbreviation, 5) borrowing, 6) lexical deviation and 7) hybrid method. Each method is prominently used to present the brand names of each product type, as shown below.

Direct translation is the word-for-word rendering of the Thai original brand names to English, e.g. รักชาวนา [rʌ́kʃāwnā:] *Love Farmer*. It was found to be one of the primary techniques used to present brand names of rice products, canned and instant food as well as ingredients and seasonings. The study results show that 40 per cent of rice product brand names, 28.57 per cent of canned and instant food brand names and 24.14 per cent of ingredient and seasoning brand names are presented by direct translation method. However, this method was not found used in the presentation of frozen and chilled food brand names and snack and candy brand names.

Adapted translation is defined here as "the method by which an original brand name in Thai is expressed in a different way that is familiar or appropriate to English language culture" (McArthur, 1992), e.g. ม้าบิน [má:bīn] *Pegasus*. Interestingly, the adapted translation method was also found to be used only in three product categories: rice product, canned and instant food, and ingredients and seasonings. The majority of adapted translated brand names, 23.33 per cent, were found in the presentation of rice products. 17.24 per cent were found in the presentation of ingredients and seasonings, and 2.86 per cent were found in the presentation of canned and instant food.

The transliteration of brand names in this study refers to the method used for converting brand names in the Thai originals into phonetically equivalent ones in the English language, e.g. เกษตร [kàsèt] 'agriculture' *Kaset*. Transliteration was found to be used in the presentation of the five product categories studied. The majority of transliterated brand names, or 29.31 per cent, were found used in the presentation of ingredients and seasonings. The method was also used to present 17.14 per cent of canned and instant food brand names, 16.67 per cent of rice product brand names, 13.79 per cent of snack and candy brand names, and 4.34 per cent of frozen and chilled food brand names.

Abbreviation is known as a shortened form of a word or phrase. It can be considered one of the popular methods used for presenting Thailand's exported food brand names, as it was found to be used in every product category studied. There are three types of shortened forms found in the case of Thailand's exported food product brand names, including 1) alphabetical abbreviation, 2) acronyms and 3) clipping. In this study, an alphabetical abbreviation refers to a group of initial letters used as an abbreviation for a brand name, e.g. *AMS, CNV, PFP*, etc. An acronym is an abbreviation that can be pronounced as a word, e.g. *PAM, KISS*, etc., and clipping refers to the method which consists of the reduction of a word to one of its parts (Marchand, 1969), e.g. *Euro* (European), *Capuno* (Cappuccino) etc. The analysis of brand name data reveals that 3.33 per cent of rice product brand names, 52.17 per cent of frozen and chilled food brand names, 20 per cent of canned and instant food brand names, 13.79 per cent of snack and candy brand names and 1.73 per cent of ingredient and seasoning brand names are presented as an abbreviation.

Borrowing, or an adoption of lexical items from other languages as brand names, is considered quite popular among the Thai food product exporters, as it is found to be used in the presentation of all the product categories studied. The highest percentage, 48.28 per cent, is found in the presentation of snack and candy brand names. The percentage of brand names presented by lexical borrowing is also high in the presentation of frozen and chilled food brand names, 34.78 per cent, and in canned and instant food brand names, 28.57 per cent. Rice product brand names and ingredient and seasoning brand names presented by borrowing are not quite so high in percentage. There are 13.34 per cent of borrowings found used in the presentation of rice product brand names and 17.24 per cent in the presentation of ingredient and seasoning brand names.

Lexical deviation is the process by which the brand name owners create entirely new words or deviate from the regular norms of words that already exist. Brand name creators may play with spellings; for example, he/she may change the initial letter 'c' in the word *choice* to letter 's' to make the brand name *Shoice*. Or, he/she may add extra letters to words that already exist, for example, adding letter 'o' to the word *fish* or *rich* to make the brand names *Fisho* and *Richo*. In the case of Thailand's exported food product brand names, lexical deviation was found to be used in two product categories only: snacks and candies, and ingredients and seasonings. It was found that 17.24 per cent of snack and candy brand names and 8.62 per cent of ingredient and seasoning are presented by lexical deviation.

The hybrid method refers to the use of the combination of two different brand name presentation methods. There are only two types of hybrid found. The first one is abbreviation + borrowing or vice versa, and the second one is transliteration + borrowing or vice versa. This brand name presentation method was found to be used in every product category studied, but the frequency and percentage of use are not high. The analysis shows that 3.33 per cent of rice product brand names, 8.70 per cent of frozen and chilled food brand names, 2.86 canned and instant food brand names, 6.90 per cent of snack and candy brand names, and 1.73 per cent of ingredient and seasoning brand names are presented by the hybrid method.

The percentage of each presentation method used in the five product categories studied can be summarised in Table 2.

Table 2. Percentage of brand name presentation methods.

Product categories	Direct translation	Adapted translation	Transliteration	Abbreviation	Borrowing	Lexical deviation	Hybrid
Rice products	40%	23.33 %	16.67 %	3.33 %	13.34 %	0	3.33 %
Frozen and chilled food	0	0	4.34 %	52.17 %	34.78 %	0	8.71 %
Canned and instant food	28.57 %	2.86 %	17.14 %	20%	28.57 %	0	2.86 %
Snacks and Candies	0	0	13.79 %	13.79 %	48.28 %	17.24 %	6.90 %
Ingredients and seasonings	24.13 %	17.25 %	29.31 %	1.73 %	17.23 %	8.62 %	1.73 %

Categorisation of Brand Names

The investigation of products and brand name categories shows that owners of each product category tend to use certain lexical items from certain conceptual categories as the brand names of their products. For example, most of the rice product brand names, e.g. *Golden Crane, Golden Pearl, Golden Lotus*, etc. tend to be something in gold or in golden colour, so they can conceptually be grouped together in the category [[GOLDEN ENTITY]]; the majority of ingredient and seasoning brand names, e.g. *Classic Thai*, *Thai Choice*, *Thai Smile*, etc. appear to be concepts relating to the category [[THAINESS]]. The categorisation of brand names of each product type interestingly reveals the nature of Thailand's exported food product brand naming, as shown below.

Rice products:

[[GOLDEN ENTITY]]: *Golden Crane*, *Golden Pearl*, *Golden Earth*, *Golden Diamond*, *Jasmine Gold*, *Golden Phoenix, Golden Globe*, *Golden Horse*, *Golden Lotus*, *Golden Rabbit*, *Golden Tub*
[[ROYAL ASPECT]]: *Imperial Taste*, *Royal Elephant*, *Royal Umbrella*, *Royal Orchid*, *Royal Dancer*,
[[PROPER NAME]]: *Mah Boonkrong*, *Ponglarp*, *Surin Tip*, *URC*
[[ANIMAL/CREATURE]]: *Super Dragon*, *Double Elephants*, *Young Elephant*
[[AGRICULTURAL ACTIVITY]]: *Kaset* 'agriculture', *Great Harvest*
[[PROFESSION]]: *Smart Chef, Love Farmer*
[[HEAVENLY BODY]]: *Sun*
[[GREETING]]: *Swat-D* 'hello'
[[GRAIN]]: *Q-Rice*

Frozen and chilled food:

[[PROPER NAME]]: *PFP*, *PTN*, *CMR*, *CNV*, *AMS*, *U.F.P*, *TSF*, *CSF*, *KISS*, *PAM*, *May*
[[FOODSTUFF]]: *Surapon Foods*, *Vitafood*, *Ventuna*, *Fruit King*, *Excel Fruits*
[[FOOD'S ATTRIBUTE]]: *Sea Fresh*, *KC Fresh*, *Aroy-D* 'delicious'
[[CHEF THEME]]: *Little Chef, Chef's Choice*
[[HEAVENLY BODY]]: *Ocean Star*
[[FOOD STORAGE]]: *Fruit Cellar*

Canned and instant food:

[[PROPER NAME]]: *Madame Wong*, *Pichaya*, *Mama*, *S.Khonkaen*, *River Kwai*, *Pan Asia*, *UFC*, *KC*, *O&P*, *Hi-Q*, *Ampro*, *Trofco*
[[FOOD'S ATTRIBUTE]]: *Delight*, *Ocean Taste*, *Kin Dee* 'good for eating', *Yum Yum* 'yummy', *Wai Wai* 'quick'
[[ANIMAL/CREATURE]]: *Double Dragon*, *Nuatilus*, *Twin Elephant & Earth*, *Smiling Fish*, *Pigeon*
[[PLANT]]: *Bamboo*, *Pine*, *Bean*, *Benjamas* 'chrysanthemum'
[[ROYAL STUFF]]: *Royal Sea*, *King Bell*, *Queen Bell*
[[PROFESSION]]: *Prochef*, *Three Lady Cooks*
[[KITCHEN UTENSIL]]: *Asian Bowl*
[[HEAVENLY BODY]]: *Star*
[[NAVAL FLEET]]: *Battleship*
[[RITE]]: *Roza* 'Islamic Fasting'

Snacks and candies:

[[FOODSTUFF]]: *Flower Food*, *Nut Candy*, *Potato*, *My Mint*, *Wafruit* 'fruit wafer', *Capuno* 'cappuccino', *Khoa Shaong Nuts*, *Yofruit* 'fruit yoghurt', *Fisho* 'fish', *Durio* 'durian'
[[FOOD'S ATTRIBUTE]]: *Jumbo*, *Sofeline*, *Classic*, *Crusty*, *Bigga* 'bigger', *Jeed Jard* 'sour', *Richo* 'rich'
[[PLACE]]: *Tong Garden*, *Euro* 'Europe', *Otari* 'a village in Japan'
[[PERSON]]: *Tao Kae Noi*, *Koh Kae*, *Taro*
[[PERSONIFIED ENTITY]]: *Mr. Squid, Nut Walker*
[[SPEECH ACT]]: *One More*
[[ANIMAL]]: *Cougar*
[[BEDDING]]: *Pillo* 'pillow'
[[LOCAL ENTERTAINMENT]]: *Manorah* 'Manorah performance'

Ingredients and seasonings:

[[THAI MATTER]]: *Classic Thai*, *Siam Kitchen*, *Thai Choice*, *Chao Thai*, *Thai Dancer*, *Talad Thai*, *Foodex*, *Thai Smile*, *Ramwong* 'Thai circle dance'
[[PROPER NAME]]: *Suree*, *Pantainorasingh*, *Mae Pranom*, *Chao Koh*, *Mae Ploy*, *Mae Sri*, *Juthathip*
[[ANIMAL/CREATURE]]: *Flying Rabbit*, *Flying Tiger*, *Pegasus*, *Star Lion*, *White Elephant*, *Razor Clam*, *Kangaroo*

[[HORICULTURE]]: *Desert Rose, Oleen* 'palm olein', *Fuang Fah* 'local flower', *Rose, Jade Leaf, Tree, Raitip* 'sacred farm'
[[FOODSTUFF]]: *Sun Sauce*, *Neo Suki*, *Foodex*, *Rizi* 'rice', *Arroza* 'rice', *Oyster*
[[GOLDEN ENTITY]]: *Golden Label*, *Golden Coins*, *Golden Fish*, *Golden Boat*, *Golden Boy*
[[PROFESSION]]: *Oriental Chef*, *Cook Yim*, *3 Chefs*, *Megachef*, *Mae Krua* 'lady cooks'
[[SHAPE/SYMBOL]]: *Alfa One*, *Hand No.1*, *Three Traiangles*, *Red Spoon*, *Lobo* 'globe'
[[HIGH QUALITY]]: *New Grade*, *No.1 Choice*, *Shoice* 'choice'
[[VALUABLE OBJECT]]: *Morakot* 'emerald', *Moradok* 'inheritance'
[[FOOD'S ATTRIBUTE]]: *Ruamros* 'mixed taste'
[[NOBILITY]]: *King*
[[LINGUISTICS]]: *Gogi* 'word meaning'

Considering the frequency of brand name categories found in each product category, it is noticed that certain conceptual categories can be dominant in the brand naming of certain product types. The top five categories used are [[PROPER NAME]], [[FOODSTUFF]], [[FOOD'S ATTRIBUTE]], [[ANIMAL]] and [[GOLDEN ENTITY]], respectively. This may show a current trend of brand naming of Thailand's exported food products. It seems that the brand naming focus is placed mainly on three aspects, namely the manufacturers or owners of the products, types of products and quality of the products. This brand naming practice may also be used as a guideline for future brand naming tasks.

For rice products, the concept relating to product quality is significant, and it was found that the words *golden* and *royal* are normally used to convey such concept. For frozen and chilled food products, the exporters tended to focus on the concept relating to product types, as most brand names contain lexical items that show product types, e.g. *fish*, *seafood*, *frozen food*, *tuna*, etc. However, the brand names of frozen and chilled food are mostly abbreviated in order to make the brand names easy to remember. It is also the aim of these abbreviated brand names to show the concept of modern product brand naming in international markets. Canned and instant food brand name owners tend to emphasise the product properties or qualities, as the lexical items used, such as *high quality*, *delight*, *yummy*, *universal*, etc. can say something about the properties of the product. Snack and candy brand name owners also seem focused on product types and product properties. The lexical items used in snack and candy brand names, e.g. *potato, nut candy*, *nut walker*, *jumbo*, *classic*, *crusty*, etc., all communicate types and/or properties of the products. The ingredient and seasoning brand name owners tend to use lexical items together with the word *Thai* such as *smile*, *classic*, *choice* and Thai personal names such as *Suree*, *Mae Pranom*, *Mae Ploy* to communicate the properties of being Thai original products. All in all, it can probably be claimed that the brand names of Thailand's exported food products were created based on similar concepts even though choices of lexical items used may be different.

Intended-interpreted Meaning Matching

Each brand name tends to be different on the level of intended-interpreted meaning match. As one intended meaning of a brand name is matched with its five interpreted meanings, the level of intended-interpreted meaning match can range from one to five. This number means that if the five interpreted meanings of a brand name are matched with its intended meaning, the match level is five. If four, three, two and one interpreted meaning(s) of a brand name is/are matched with its intended meaning, the match level is four, three, two and one, respectively. When the number of intended-interpreted meaning match is zero, the brand names are categorised in the meaning non-matched group.

It was found that for the brand names of rice products, the total number of brand name intended-interpreted meaning matched is 22 brand names, which account for 73.33 per cent of the rice product brand names studied. The total number of brand name intended-interpreted meaning non-matched of the rice products is 8 brand names, or 26.67 per cent. For frozen and chilled food brand names, it was found that the total number of brand name intended-interpreted meaning matched is 19 brand names, or 82.61 per cent. The total number of brand name intended-interpreted meaning non-matched is 4 brand names, or 17.39 per cent. For canned and instant food brand names, it was found that the total number of brand name intended-interpreted meaning matched is 15 brand names, or 42.86 per cent of the canned and instant food brand names studied, and the total number of brand name intended-interpreted meaning non-matched is 20 brand names, or 57.14 per cent. For snack and candy brand names, it was found that the total number of brand name intended-interpreted meaning matched is 20 brand names, or 68.97 per cent of the snack and candy brand names studied, and the total number of brand name intended-interpreted meaning non-matched is 9 brand names, or 31.03 per cent. For ingredient and seasoning brand names, it was found that the total number of brand name intended-interpreted meaning matched is 27 brand names, or 46.55 per cent of the ingredient and seasoning brand names studied, and the total number of brand name intended-interpreted meaning non-matched is 31 brand names, or 53.45 per cent.

Considering the brand names in the brand name intended-interpreted meaning matched group, it can be noted that all brand names are, at least, meaningful in English. The brand names in level five, e.g. *Imperial Taste*, *Sea Fresh*, *Royal Sea*, *Flower Food*, *Sun Sauce*, etc. are English borrowings. The translated brand names, e.g. *Golden Crane*, *Golden Pearl*, *Oyster*, etc., simple clippings, e.g. *Wafruit*, *Capuno*, etc., and simple lexical deviations, e.g. *Fisho*, can show a good match between their intended meaning and interpreted meanings. It is understood that the alphabetical abbreviations, e.g. *URC*, *PFP*, *CNV*, *KC*, *UFC*, etc. are abbreviated for something. Although the customers do not know what the full forms of these abbreviated brand names are, they seem to be ready to receive information about the full forms of the brand names. All in all, it can be generalised that English lexical items and abbreviations tend to be effective and powerful for brand name communication in the international markets.

On the contrary, brand names in the brand name intended-interpreted meaning non-matched group, e.g. *Kaset*, *Ponglarp*, *Mae Sri*, *Gogi*, *Rizi*, *Roza*, etc. are mostly Thai transliterations or foreign language borrowings. These brand names are not meaningful in the English language, so they tend not to be interpretable by the customers. The acronyms, e.g. *Trofco*, *PAM*, *KISS*, etc. and the complex lexical deviations, e.g. *Lobo*, *Oleen*, etc. are also found in the brand name intended-interpreted meaning non-matched group. Although these brand names are pronounceable as a word in English, their pronunciation may lead to a non-preferred interpretation. There are also English borrowings and translated brand names, e.g. *Sun Sauce*, *Tree*, *Cougar*, *Pigeon*, etc. found in the brand name intended-interpreted meaning non-matched group. However, these brand names tend not to be directly related to the products found on their labels. For example, the brand name *Pigeon* seems to have nothing to do with canned food. Therefore, it can be concluded that in addition to being meaningful in English, a brand name for the international market must be directly or somehow related to the product found on its label.

More importantly, it was also found from the study of brand name intended meaning, that the intentions of the brand name owners were crucial for the match and non-match between the brand name intended meaning and the brand name interpreted meaning. If the brand name owners' intentions are well conveyed by the lexical items used, the interpretation of the brand name tends to match its intended meaning quite well. For example, brand names such as *Sun Sauce*, *Potato*, *Oyster*, etc.

seem to convey the brand name owners' intentions to the target customers quite well, so the five customers who interpreted these brand names could get the brand name meanings as they are intended in order to communicate.

In conclusion, the match and the non-match between the brand name intended meaning and the brand name interpreted meaning tend to depend on three main aspects, including 1) the meaningfulness of brand names in the target markets, 2) the relationship between the brand names and the products they label, and 3) the possibility that the brand names convey the owners' intentions to target customers. These three aspects are specifically concerned with the semantic and pragmatic properties of brand names.

Sense and Reference of Brand Names

As the term *reference* is semantically defined as an object in the world, the reference of a brand name is the set of products the brand name on its label is. For example, the reference of the brand name *Potato* is a snack product labelled by *Potato* on the package. The term *sense* is defined as ideas, thoughts or concepts associated with words. In the case of brand names, *sense* can generally be referred to the ideas, thoughts or concepts that customers have about certain brand names. In other words, it is the ideas or concepts that form a link between the brand names and the products found on their labels. For example, the sense of the brand name *Ocean Taste* is the concepts that form a link between the brand name and the canned seafood which carries the *Ocean Taste* label. However, the lexical items used as the brand names normally have senses that can be linked to the products. The phrase *ocean taste*, for example, contains an idea or concept of the flavour of the sea. When the word is used as a brand name for canned seafood, it seems that the concept of *ocean taste* can easily be transferred to the brand name *Ocean Taste*. Therefore, when considering the sense of a brand name, it may be necessary that we consider the sense of the words used as the brand name in order to investigate an association between the two senses.

From the investigation of Thailand's exported food product brand names, it can be noted that the reference and sense of the brand names do, as expected, influence brand name communication. The successful cases of brand name communication show that the reference of brand names should be directly related to the reference of the lexical items used as the brand names. Also, the sense of the brand name should easily be associated with the sense of the lexical items used as the brand names.

Regarding the direct relationship between the reference of a brand name and the reference of the lexical items used as the brand name – although the brand names with this feature, e.g. *Potato*, *Oyster*, etc. are quite effective for communication – they also have limitations when they are used as the brand name for other product types. Their power of communication may not remain the same. For example, if *Potato* is used as a brand name for canned seafood, the communication of the brand name may not be as effective as when it is used as the brand name for a potato snack. For sense association between the brand name and the lexical items used as the brand name, it is necessary to note here that if a brand name consists of more than one lexical item, the sense of one lexical item may dominate the senses of others. That is, when one lexical item is more closely associated with the sense of the brand name or product than other lexical items, it seems that the lexical item will be dominate the senses of other lexical items. See, for example, the abovementioned cases of *Golden Earth* and *Golden Lotus*.

In conclusion, both the reference and sense of the brand names tend to play an important role in brand name communication, so when creating a new brand name, the creators of brand names have to think about how to select a lexical item that can convey effective reference and sense to customers in the target markets.

Cooperativeness of Brand Name Owners

The cooperativeness of brand name owners can also be considered to be an important factor that influences brand name communication in international markets. As adapted from Grice's (1975) Cooperative principle[3], it can be generalised that the brand name owners are expected to be cooperative in the communication of brand names. Although the nature of brand name communication is not exactly the same as general conversation, the communication of brand names and conversation seem to be more or less similar. In other words, when comparing brand name communication with conversation, the brand name owner can be compared to the speaker in a conversation, the brand name itself is the massage, and the target customer can be compared to the hearer. To exemplify, the owner of the brand name *Sun Sauce*, who intended to communicate the fact that his chili sauce is very hot or very spicy, intended to convey the

[3] "Make your conversational contribution such as is required, at the stage at which it occurs, by the accepted purpose or direction of the talk exchange in which you are engaged" (Grice 1975: 26).

idea that "This chili sauce is hot like the sun". As the brand name owner wanted his brand name to be easy to remember, he then shortened his expression to *Sun Sauce*. From this example, it is quite clear that a brand name is created to convey a certain message from the brand name owner to the target customers.

As Grice's (1975) Cooperative principle normally concerns the four maxims of conversation, brand name communication tends to concern something similar to the four conversational maxims which researchers shall refer to as brand name communication maxims. Adapted from Grice's (1975) conversational maxims, the first maxim, or maxim of quality, can supposedly be the requirement suggesting that brand name owners say something true about their products. The second maxim, or the maxim of quantity, can be that the brand name owners give enough information about the products. The third maxim, or the maxim of relation, can be that the brand name owners make their brand names relevant enough to the products and customers' experiences. The last maxim, or the maxim of manner, can be that the brand name owners make their brand names clear enough for customers to be able to comprehend. It is noted that these adapted maxims are used to investigate and explain the phenomena where the brand names are successfully or unsuccessfully communicated.

The investigation of Thailand's exported food product brand names shows that the brand names in the intended-interpreted meaning matched group can meet the requirements stated in the four brand name communication maxims. For example, the brand name *Nut Candy* can well exemplify the brand name owner's observation of the four maxims. That is, the brand name owner intended mean, "This product is made from nuts and it can be eaten like candy", which seems to be true (maxim of quality) and informative (maxim of quantity) enough. The brand name *Nut Candy* is used for a kind of nut coated with flavoured sugar. It can be noticed that both *nut* and *candy* are directly relevant to the product. Also, the customers are expected to have some kind of knowledge and experience about *nut* and *candy*. The brand name *Nut Candy* can be considered relevant (maxim of relation) enough to both the product and the customers' background knowledge. In terms of clarity (maxim of manner) of the brand name, it can be said that *Nut Candy* is clear enough to be understood.

Nevertheless, most brand names in the intended-interpreted meaning matched group tend to lack certain maxims. For instance, the brand name *Sea Fresh*, which is intended to say, "This product is from the sea, and it is fresh", seems to lack the maxim of quality (be truthful), since we cannot be so sure that the seafood is fresh. Normally, seafood has to travel for many hours before it reaches the factory. Therefore, the seafood may not be as fresh as the brand name owner thought. The alphabetical abbreviated brand names e.g. *URC*, *PFP*, *PTN*, *CMR*, *UFC*, *AMS*, etc. obviously lack the maxim of quantity (be informative) and the maxim of manner (be clear). These brand names can be considered truthful due to the fact that they are intended to communicate abbreviations of the brand name owners' companies. The abbreviation itself may not be relevant to the product until the full form of the abbreviation is given. For example, the brand name *PFP* can be relevant to the situation of brand name communication when the full form, *Pacific Fish Processing*, is given. Clipped brand names, such as *Wafruit*, *Yofruit*, *Ventuna*, *Euro*, *Capuno* etc. and lexical deviated brand names, such as *Fisho*, *Bigga*, etc. also lack an informative maxim. However, these brand names seem to be quite relevant to the situation of brand name communication. For example, the brand name *Capuno*, which is intended to say, "This candy has cappuccino flavour" can be considered to be relevant enough since it is used as the brand name for cappuccino flavoured candy.

As for brand names in the intended-interpreted meaning non-matched group, it was found that most of them lack the maxim of relation. That is to say, the brand names are not relevant enough to the situation of brand name communication. For example, the transliterated brand names e.g. *Aroy-D*, *Jeed Jard*, etc. may be relevant to the situation of brand name communication in the Thai market, but irrelevant in international markets because the brand names are meaningless in English. Other meaningful brand names such as *Cougar*, *Kangaroo*, *Sun*, *Pigeon*, *Tree*, etc. also tend to lack the maxim of relation. These brand names seem to have nothing to do with the products that bear their labels. That is, in the situation of brand name communication, the brand name such as *Kangaroo* tends not to be relevant to either the product (tapioca flour) or the customers' experiences.

In conclusion, it can be generalised that if the brand name owners can meet the requirements of all maxims, i.e. be truthful, be informative, be relevant and be clear, they tend to be successful in communication of their brand names. However, it seems to be quite difficult for the brand name owners to follow all the maxims, so some maxims may be occasionally ignored. The effectiveness of brand names in communication tends to be less and less when a greater number of maxims is violated. From the observation of Thailand's exported food product brand names, it is suggested that the brand name owners have to keep their brand names relevant enough to the situation of brand name communication if they want the brand name to be effective. When the brand name owners do not observe the maxim of relation, it is likely that the brand names cannot convey their intended meanings to their target customers. This is one of the important factors the brand name creators have to keep in mind when giving a brand name to a new product.

Brand Name Relevance

Adapted from the two principles of relevance, i.e. the Cognitive principle of relevance and the Communicative principle of relevance, it can be generalised that certain brand names convey relevance of a certain level, and the brand name relevance allows customers' cognition to comprehend information conveyed by the brand name. As Sperber and Wilson (1985/1995) states in their Relevance Theory, *relevance* is a property of inputs (e.g. a sight, a sound, a linguistic expression, a memory, etc.) to cognitive processes. Thus, the relevance of a brand name can be seen as any linguistic or non-linguistic element which provides an input to customers' cognitive processes; and the input should be relevant to the customers so that they can process the input without difficulties.

Adapted from Sperber and Wilson's (1985/1995) Relevance Theory, it can be concluded that the relevance of a brand name to a customer concerns cognitive effects and a processing effort. That is, the relevance level of a brand name is considered high if: 1) the brand name is relevant enough to the cognitive system or background information of customers that allows them to perceive the right interpretation, and 2) the brand name requires less processing efforts from the customers. When a brand name possesses a high level of relevance, it is likely that the customers can comprehend the intended information conveyed in the brand name.

Considering brand names in the intended – interpreted meaning matched group, it can be noticed that the brand names have different levels of relevance since they seem to contain different cognitive effects and require different amounts of processing efforts. Brand names such as *Flower Food*, *Oyster*, *Potato*, *Nut Candy*, *Mr. Squid* etc. can be considered to possess a high level of relevance because these brand names tend to, when processing in the relevant context (a brand name of certain product), yield positive cognitive effects. That is, they tend to fit the background information stored in customer's cognitive system. In addition, it seems that these brand names require little effort for processing. For instance, to comprehend the fact that the brand name *Flower Food* means "This snack product is made from flowers", customers tend not to spend much effort. From these brand name cases, it can also be generalised that the more the brand name is directly related to its product, the higher the relevance level of the brand name is.

The brand names of rice products, e.g. *Golden Crane*, *Golden Pearl*, *Golden Earth*, etc. seem to have a higher level of relevance than the brand names such as *Golden Lotus*, *Golden Rabbit*, *Golden Tub*. This phenomenon can be explained that the first group of brand names may provide better cognitive effects than the second group. For example, customers who have knowledge about rice may compare the colour of the rice grain with a golden pearl when they process the interpretation of *Golden Pearl*. It is also likely that customers use little effort when comprehending *Golden Pearl* as "high quality rice". This is because the customers who interpreted the brand name *Golden Pearl* may have background information that gears their interpretation that way. On the contrary, a brand name such as *Golden Tub* may not fit the customers' background knowledge, so they seem to spend a great amount of effort in comprehending the brand name *Golden Tub* as "high quality rice".

In the case of abbreviated brand names, it seems that customers can comprehend alphabetical abbreviations, e.g. *URC*, *UFC*, *PFP*, etc. and clippings, e.g. *Wafruit*, *Yofruit*, *Capuno*, etc. better than acronyms, e.g. *PAM*, *KISS*, etc. It can be generalised that the alphabetical abbreviations and the clippings tend to fit customers' background knowledge better than the acronyms. That is to say, when customers see the brand name *URC*, their cognitive system tends to gear their interpretation to "abbreviation of something"; whereas, when customers see the brand name *KISS*, they tended to think that the brand name was derived from the word *kiss* in English. Many customers then gear their interpretation of the brand name *KISS* towards the lexical meaning of the word *kiss*. This example shows that customers tend to follow a path of least effort in comprehending a brand name.

Considering brand names in the intended – interpreted meaning non-matched group, it can also be noticed that these brand names tend to lack positive cognitive effects and require a great deal of processing effort. For example, the transliterated brand names such as *Jeed Jard*, *Manorah*, *Kin Dee*, etc. may not be relevant to any information stored in customers' cognitive system. In addition, customers may have to spend a great deal of effort in interpreting these brand names. According to the comprehension procedure suggested in the relevance theory, it can be generalised that customers tend to stop the interpretation since the transliterated brand names need too much processing effort. That is to say, these brand names exceed customers' abilities to comprehend. A similar situation can be observed in the case of foreign language borrowings, e.g. *Otari*, *Gogi*, *Roza*, etc.

Conclusions

Properties of Preferable Brand Names

There are four aspects to be considered about the properties of preferable brand names. They are, namely, 1) the brand name owners' intentions, 2) reference, sense and categories, 3) enrichable contexts and 4) the presentation of brand names.

First, a brand name can be preferable when the brand name owner intended it to communicate certain information to the target customer. The study results show that most preferable brand names are often intended to communicate something related to the branded products. Intentions to communicate product properties seem to be the most common property of most preferable brand names. Alternatively, the intention to communicate product origins and the intention to communicate product manufacturers are also possible for preferable brand names, but with the condition that the brand name owners are willing to work harder for the communication of such intentions. It can be expected that the right intention for brand naming can lead the product owners to the right brand names for communication in their target markets.

Second, a preferable brand name should have reference and sense that can be closely associated with the reference and sense of the branded product. That is to say, a brand name can be preferable if its original reference directly refers to an element of the branded product, e.g. ingredients of the product, purposes of product use, properties of the product etc. or if its sense is conventionally related to a certain idea attached to the branded product, e.g. "golden" items for premium product, etc. In addition, the preferable brand name should be a member of a category related to the branded product. For example, a member of [[FOOD ATTRIBUTE]] should make a preferable brand name for food products.

Third, a brand name can be preferable for communication if it is appropriately accompanied by enrichable contexts, i.e. logos, slogans, other additional texts and images. Brand name owners who want to make sure that their brand names will be comprehensible in the market should always consider creating the enrichable contexts to accompany their brand names. Even those brand names with less preferable sense and reference can be relatively preferable for communication when there are enrichable contexts appropriately accompanied with them.

Finally, a preferable brand name should be presented by the method that enables the brand name to be comprehensible for target customers in the target markets. In the case of exported products, for example, most preferable brand names tend to be presented by English borrowings, translations, lexical deviations, abbreviations and hybrid methods. This means that English tends to be now the most preferable language for most exported product brand naming. Not surprisingly, this finding is apparently compatible with the statement proposed by Professor Elwys De Stefani at the *Fourth International Symposium on Names in the Economy* in Turku, Finland on June 16, 2012 that "the English language will be more and more important for international product brand naming. As we can see, English has a leading role in today's international trade". However, this study suggests that the transliteration method is applicable for the communication of a curtain culture through brand naming.

Key Factors in Brand Naming

As brand naming is concerned mainly with the brand name creators, the target customers and to-be-branded products, the factors to be considered should be related to these three elements. Therefore, it can be generalised that the key factors to be considered in brand naming are: market environments, brand naming objectives and the comprehensibility of brand names.

As brand naming is firstly concerned with the pragmatic dimension of brand names, what the brand name creators have to take into consideration first is the target market environments. The information about the target markets, i.e. who the target customers are, what languages are used in the market, how other companies have named their products, etc., is expected to enable the brand name creators to make the right decision for their brand naming objective. In other words, with good information about the market, the brand name creator can gear their brand naming intention toward the target customers' preference. More importantly, the brand name creators will be able to avoid duplicating the brand names that have already been used by other companies.

As for semantic factors, the brand name creators are required to consider the linguistically encoded information of their selected brand names. As good linguistic encoding can lead to the high comprehensibility level of brand names, the brand name creators need to pay a great deal of attention to their lexical selection in brand naming. In other words, the brand name creators have to make sure that the selected brand name can conceptually be related to the branded product. Moreover, the brand name creators have to consider using the brand name presentation method that best presents their intentions to the customers in order to maintain the brand names' high level of comprehensibility.

Acknowledgement

This study is funded by the 90th Anniversary of Chulalongkorn University Fund (Ratchadaphiseksomphot Endowment Fund).

References

Allan, K. 1986. *Linguistic Meaning.* London: Routledge and Kegan Paul.

Alon, I., Littrell, R. F. and Chan, A. K. K. 2010. Branding in China: Global Product Strategy Alternatives. *The Multinational Business Review* 17 (November): 123–141.

Black, M. 1968. *The Labyrinth of Language*. New York: Praeger.

Blutner, R. 1998. Lexical pragmatics, *Journal of Semantics* 15: 115–162.

—. 2002. Lexical semantics and pragmatics. *Linguistische Berichte* 10: 27–58.

—. 2004. Pragmatics and the Lexicon. In *Handbook of Pragmatics*, L. Horn and G. Ward (eds.), 488–514 Oxford: Blackwell.

Boonpaisarnsatit, N. 2009. *Semantic Analysis of Thai Product Brand Names*. Berlin: VDM Verlag Dr. Muller Aktiengesellschaft & Co.

Carston, R. 1988. Implicature, explicature, and truth-theoretic semantics. In *Mental Representations: The Interface Between Language and Reality*, R. Kempson (ed.), 155–181. Cambridge: Cambridge University Press. Reprinted in S. Davis (ed.), *Pragmatics: A Reader*, 33–51. Oxford: Oxford University Press.

—. 2002. Linguistic meaning, communicated meaning and cognitive pragmatics. *Mind and Language* 17: 127–148.

Chan, A. K. K. and Huang, Y. Y. 1997. Brand naming in China – A linguistic approach. *Marketing Intelligence and Planning* 15, 5: 227–234.

—. 2001. Chinese brand naming: A linguistic analysis of the brands of ten product categories. *Journal of Product and Brand Management* 10: 103–119.

Chan, A. K. K, Huang, Y. Y. and Wu, D. X. 2009. Chinese Brand Names and Global Names: Implications from Two Corpus Analyses. A working paper presented at the Tenth International Business Research Conference, Dubai, UAE. 16–17 April 2009.

Charmasson, H. 1988. *The Name is the Game - How to Name a Company or Product.* Illinois: Dow Jones-Irwin.

Chiaravalle, B. and Schenck, B. F. 2006. *Branding for Dummies*. Indiana: Wiley Publishing Inc.

Cruse, D. A. 1986. *Lexical Semantics*. Melbourne: Cambridge University Press

—. 2006. *A Glossary of Semantics and Pragmatics*. Edinburgh: Edinburgh University Press.

Dawar, N. and Parker, P. 1994. Marketing universals: consumers' use of brand name, price, physical appearance, and retail reputation as signals of product quality. *Journal of Marketing* 58: 81–95.

Department of Export Promotion. 2010. *Thailand Exporters' Directory 2009–2010*. http://application.depthai.go.th/Center_Public/thailand_export_directory.html (retrieved 15 October 2011).

Department of Export Promotion. Thailand's Brand: Diversity and Refinement. http://www.thailandsbrand.net (retrieved 30 October 2011).

Ellwood, I. 2000. *The Essential Brand Book*. London: Kogan Page.

Evans, G. 1982. *The Varieties of Reference*. J. McDowell (ed.). Oxford: Oxford University Press

Frege, G. 1892. "Über Sinn und Bedeutung" *Zeitschrift für Philosophie und philosophische Kritik* 100: 25– 50. Translated as "On Sense and Reference" in *Translations from the Philosophical Writings of Gottlob Frege*, P. Geach and M. Black (eds.), 56–78. Oxford: Blackwell, 1952.

Grice, H. P. 1975. Logic and conversation. In *Syntax and Semantics* 3, P. Cole and I. Morgan (eds.), 41–58. New York: Academic Press.

—. 1978. Further notes on logic and conversation. In *Syntax and Semantics* 9, P. Cole and I. Morgan (eds.), 113–127. New York: Academic Press.

Hart, S. 1998. Developing New Brand Names. In *Brands: The new wealth creators,* S. Hart and J. Murphy (eds.), 67–89. London: Macmillan.

Hinton, L., Nichols, J. and Ohala, J. 1994. *Sound Symbolism.* Cambridge: Cambridge University Press.

Hong, F. C., Pecotich, A. and Schultz, C. J. 2002. Brand name translation: Language constraints, product attributes, and consumer perceptions in East and Southeast Asia. *Journal of International Marketing* 10, 2: 29–117.

Huang, Y. Y. and Chan, A. K. K. 1997. Brand Naming in China: A Linguistic Approach. *Marketing Intelligence and Planning* 15, 5: 227–234.

Interbrand. 2009. Best Global Brands 2009: The Definitive Guide to the World's Most Valuable Brands. www.interbrand.com (retrieved 29 September 2011).

Jain, S. C. 2001. *International Marketing*, 6th edition. Ohio: South-Western Education Publishing.

Jamil, S. 2010. Frege: The Theory of Meaning Concerning Proper Names. *Kritike* 4, 1 (June): 150–173.

Jaszczolt, K. M. 2005. *Default Semantics: Foundations of a Compositional Theory of Acts of Communication*. Oxford: Oxford University Press.

Keller, K., Heckler, S. and Houston, M. 1998. The Effects of Brand Name Suggestiveness on Advertising Recall. *Journal of Marketing* 62:48–57.

Klink, R. R. 2001. Creating meaningful new brand names: A study of semantics and sound symbolism. *Journal of Marketing Theory and Practice* 9, 2: 27–34.

Kohli C. S. and LaBahn, D. W. 1995. *Creating Effective Brand Names: A Study of the Naming Process*. Institute for the Study of Business Markets, The Pennsylvania State University.

Kohli, C. S. and Suri, R. 2000. Brand Names that Work: A study of the Effectiveness of Different Types of Brand Names. *Marketing Management Journal* 10, 2:112– 120.

Kotler, P. and Armstrong, G. 1997. *Marketing: An Introduction,* 4th edition. Englewood Cliffs, NJ: Prentice Hall.

—. 2004. *Principles of Marketing*, 10th edition. Upper Saddle River, NJ: Pearson Education.

Ku, H. and Zussman, A. 2010. Lingua franca: The role of English in international trade. *Journal of Economic Behavior & Organization* 75: 250–260.

Leclerc, F., Schmitt, B. H. and Dube, L. 1994. Foreign branding and its effects on product perceptions and attitudes. *Journal of Marketing Research* 31, 2: 263–270.

Li, F. and Shooshtari, N. H. 2003. Brand Naming in China: Sociolinguistic Implications. *Multinational Business Review* 11, 3: 3–22. Detroit.

Lowrey T. M., Shrum, L. J. and McCarty, J. A. 2004. Phonetic Symbolism in Brand Names. Working Paper. University of Houston. Presentation on 22 Oct. 2004.

Lyons, J. 1977. *Semantics*. Volume II. Cambridge: Cambridge University Press.

Marchand, H. 1969. *The Categories and Types of Present-Day English Word-formation: A Synchronic-Diachronic Approach*. 2nd ed. München: C. H. Beck.

McAuther, T. (ed.). 1992. *The Oxford Companion to the English Language*. Oxford: Oxford University Press.

O'Cass, A., Lim, K. and Julian, C. C. 2000. Brand classifications: identifying the origins of brands. In *Visionary Marketing for the 21st Century: Facing the Challenge: Proceedings of the Australian and*

New Zealand Marketing Academy (ANZMAC) Conference, Gold Coast, Qld.,28 November – 1 December, A. O'Cass (ed.), 871–878. Gold Coast: Griffith University School of Marketing and Management.

Peter, N. K. A. 1995. *Brand Association and Consumer Perceptions of Value of Products.* University of Nairobi.

Raskin, V. 1985. Linguistic and encyclopedic knowledge in text processing. *Quaderni di semantica* 6: 92–102.

Rosch, E. 1978. Principles of categorization. In *Cognition and Categorization,* E. Rosch and B.B. Lloyd (eds.), 27–48. Hillsdale, N. J.: Erlbaum.

Shipley, D., Hooley, G. J. and Wallace, S. 1988. The brand name development process. *International Journal of Advertising* 7: 253–266.

Shipley, D. and Howard, P. 1993. Brand-naming industrial products. *Industrial Marketing Management* 22, 1: 59–66.

Sperber, D. and Wilson, D. 1986. *Relevance. Communication and Cognition*. 1st edition. Oxford: Blackwell.

—. 1995. *Relevance. Communication and Cognition*. 2nd edition. Oxford: Blackwell.

Suri, R., Manchanda, R. V. and Kohli, C. S. 2000. Brand evaluations: a comparison of fixed price and discounted price offers. *Journal of Product & Brand Management* 9, 3: 193–207.

Wilson, D. 2003. Relevance and lexical pragmatics. *Italian Journal of Linguistics/ Rivista di Linguistica* 15: 273–291.

Wilson, D. and Sperber, D. 2004. Relevance theory. In *Handbook of Pragmatics*, G. Ward and L. Horn (eds.), 607–632. Oxford: Blackwell.

Yorkston, E. and Menon, G. 2004. A Sound Idea: Phonetic Effects of Brand Names on Consumer Judgments. *Journal of Consumer Research* 31 (June): 43–57.

Zhang, S., and Schmitt, B. H. 2001. Creating local brands in multilingual international markets. *Journal of Marketing Research*, 38 (August): 313–325.

Zhang, S., Schmitt, B. H. and Haley, H. 2004. Linguistic effects on consumer behavior in international marketing research. *The Chazen Web Journal of International Business:* 228–242. Columbia Business School.

THE PRICE OF HOME: NAMES AND PRESTIGE OF DOMICILE IN JAPAN

DOUGLAS WILKERSON
AND KYOKO TAKASHI WILKERSON
NAGOYA UNIVERSITY OF FOREIGN STUDIES, JAPAN

Abstract

This article examines the association between names and prestige for commercial commodities in Japan. The subject of this study is names for physical spaces which can be bought and occupied for 10–20 years or more: condominiums, assisted-living condominiums, and burial sites. Names of recently constructed condominiums and currently marketed plots in cemeteries are analysed with particular attention to script use and employment of non-Japanese words, especially loanwords and pseudo-Western neologisms; price is used as an estimate for levels of prestige. Responses to various naming characteristics (lexical items and grammatical constructions) were solicited from native Japanese speakers to clarify trends. Prestigious names for condominiums tend to copy recent developments in English syntax, use more Western words from non-English languages, and employ idiosyncratic pseudo-Western neologisms. Names for cemeteries demonstrate a tendency to copy naming conventions for domiciles.

Introduction

Research has shown that "Western" (usually English) words, borrowed directly from European languages or coined in Japan, have frequently been used to impart prestige to products, services, and places to increase their market value (Haarmann 1984; Takashi 1990; Rosenberger 1992: 117–119). This practice has been fairly common since the 1960s. However, as time passes, due to association with older products or other changes in cultural concepts, words once commonly used in commercial marketing often lose some of their prestige value.

Although the general use of foreign (English) words in marketing has been extensively examined, little has been done to explore which words are employed, how those words are written, and how and why the words in popular use change through time. This diachronic gap between perception at the time of naming and that at subsequent periods of marketing is paralleled by a potential synchronic gap between the intentions of those responsible for naming and the perceptions of potential consumers.

This study examines several aspects of these problems by looking at one segment of the Japanese market and asking the following questions: What foreign words are now used in commodity naming? Are they still primarily drawn from English? How are these words written? How well do the perceptions of potential consumers match the apparent intentions of those responsible for naming? The results indicate that, as the impact of simply using "Western" words diminishes through exposure and familiarity, Western words are manipulated in increasingly sophisticated ways to maintain and increase their prestige.

Methodology and Resources

To answer these questions we shall look at the naming of a commodity that usually requires a significant financial investment, the purchase of which would likely result in a lengthy physical (or geographic) association between consumer and commodity. The most appropriate commodity of this type was deemed to be geographic and physical space which the consumer typically purchases; this would include single-unit dwellings, condominiums, and assisted living homes. While most single-unit dwellings do not have unique names used in marketing (in Japan, mass-produced units are most often marketed under the name of the construction and building materials firm which produced them), multi-unit complexes most often are marketed using unique, often geographically explicit, names. The multi-unit complexes studied here include several types, as discussed below. Another commodity which also fits this description (i.e., significant financial investment and long-term physical association), one which has recently come to be marketed in a manner which resembles the marketing of commercial housing to a surprising degree, is the burial site or cemetery complex. Whether facing a grave site in a cemetery or before a Buddhist memorial altar in the home, many Japanese engage in very similar behaviour. The Japanese also frequently speak as though the deceased are not only cognizant of those addressing them at these sites, but are also aware of the physical surroundings of these sites, and potentially influenced by them. The lack of research on contemporary cemetery naming, their similarities to dwellings for the living, and references to cemeteries as "permanent homes" make them a valuable additional source of information on names and prestige.

This study examines names used in marketing these commodities in the largest urban areas of Japan (Tokyo, Nagoya, Osaka), and the prestige associated with these names. We shall look at various locations available for private purchase in the marketplace, using price and other factors to estimate prestige. Excluding hotels and temporary lodgings, we shall examine names for fixed (an estimated 10 to 20 years), long-term (estimated as more than 20 years), and "permanent" (burial) locations. We shall first examine 148 names for a relatively new option in mid-term living, "affordable" government-subsidised, assisted living quarters for the elderly. We will then look at 162 names for "upscale" mid-term living quarters, apartments targeted particularly at senior citizens (50 in Tokyo, 54 in Nagoya, and 58 in Osaka). These names are contrasted with those of 85 more expensive condominiums marketed to somewhat younger couples and families. In addition to the mid- and long-term options, we shall also attempt to uncover the qualities sought in an "ultimate home", by analysing the names of 136 cemeteries, 77 advertised as "sunny and park-like" and 59 touted as "historical and traditional".

Types of Living Facilities

Let us first explain the term "affordable" assisted living quarters for the elderly. In a revision of the Law Governing Housing for the Elderly, sponsored jointly by the Japanese Ministry of Land, Infrastructure, Transport and Tourism, and the Ministry of Health, Labor and Welfare, a new system was instituted beginning 20 October 2011. The new system provided for a national registry of facilities which "provide a certain required living space and facilities for the elderly, including a means of ascertaining the safety of individuals (and emergency response), and lifestyle counselling" (Sakoujuu.jp 2012). The 2 February 2012 edition of the magazine *Josei sebun* announced the results of a survey taken among the elderly in Japan with respect to facilities they desired in housing for the aged. Only 1% of the respondents indicated that they expected "elegant, hotel-like accommodations", while 49% chose "safety measures in case of emergency", and 24% accommodations similar to those in an apartment house (Josei sebun 2012: 73–80). Thus, it would appear that there is great interest in facilities for the elderly like these, which can be rented at a reasonable rate by the month, as one might an apartment. An examination of the 148 facilities listed on the registration system website (Satsuki 2012), reveals that monthly rents range from under ¥30,000 to just under ¥100,000. With key money (payable before occupancy) ranging from ¥0 to ¥400,000, rents are comparable to those of ordinary apartments.

Unlike the more affordable facilities described above, larger, fully-serviced care homes for the elderly require anywhere from a few million to several dozen million yen (Josei sebun 2012: 74). To examine the naming of this category of housing, we consulted www.sagasix.jp/search.php, a site used to search for housing marketed to the elderly. On 17 January 2012, the site listed a total of 162 properties in the major metropolitan areas: 50 in Tokyo, 54 in Nagoya, and 58 in Osaka. Many of them require entry fees of ¥30,000,000 or more; the site uses such slogans as, "A *premium second life* begins", "There is *only one* top-class home for you. An incomparable lifestyle, enjoying a superior *private room* and *service* brimming with *hospitality*. Your *premium* (unique) living begins with a home *one rank* higher, a feeling of luxury". While aimed at the elderly, the slogans make free use of phrases (italicised here) transliterated directly from English.

In order to compare the names of living quarters for the elderly with upscale condominiums for younger families, we shall also examine the names of new condominiums selling for prices ranging from ¥20,000,000 to ¥100,000,000. Some were taken from *SUUMO New Condominiums* (*SUUMO shinchiku manshon*) magazines: 35 condominiums in the Tokyo area (6 March 2012 Metropolitan edition), 32 in Osaka-Kobe (13 March 2012 Kansai edition). 33 others in Nagoya came from the Yahoo! Japan Real Estate site (Yahoo! 2012). A few "working names" were excluded as temporary, and the final sample analysed included 85 names.

Multiple Scripts

Before focusing on the words used in naming, we would like to say a few words about the scripts in which they are written. As shown in Table 1, contemporary Japanese commonly makes use of four different scripts. Sino-Japanese characters, *kanji*, are generally the same as Chinese characters, but read with Sino-Japanese or native Japanese pronunciation; these are frequently used in writing proper names and other important traditional vocabulary.

Table 1. Scripts used in Japanese names.

Script type	Examples	Translation
Latin Letters (LL)	NEXT LIFE MYM 1st STAGE	
Sino-Japanese (Sino-Jp)	和隠 愛桜園	'peaceful retirement' 'garden of cherry lovers'
Angular Syllabary (Ang Syl)	シニアライフサポートマンション	'senior life support mansion'
Cursive Syllabary (Cur Syl)	ゆめみぐさ	'cherry blossom'
LL + Sino-Jp	Soleado武庫之荘 愛SUNSUN	'soleado Mukonosou' 'love sunsun'
Sino-Jp + Ang Syl	プラチナ・シニアホーム足立川ノ塚	'platinum senior home Adachigawa-no-tsuka'
Ang Syl + Cur Syl	パートナーハイツいしかり	'partner heights Ishikari'
LL + Sino-Jp + Ang Syl	サンシティ銀座EAST	'sun city Ginza East'
Sino-Jp + Ang Syl + Cur Syl	にこにこハウス近川	'smiling house Chikagawa'

Japanese also uses two native syllabaries, an abbreviated, angular one (*katakana*), now used for transliterating foreign words, and a cursive syllabary (*hiragana*), used primarily for conjugations, particles, and native Japanese words. The fourth script in common use is Latin letters, used for foreign words and phrases, and for transliterations (Romanisation) of Japanese words. Japanese traditionally used Sino-Japanese characters for numerals; in many cases, these have been supplanted by Arabic numerals or occasionally Roman numerals.

Results

Naming Characteristics

We now proceed to an analysis of the names used for Affordable Assisted-Living Accommodations (*sakouju*), Premium Elderly-Care Facilities, and Newly-Built Premium Condominiums.

Table 2. Origin of Western words in domicile names.

	Assisted 89 Names	Assisted 159 Words	Care Homes 143 Names	Care Homes 233 Words	Condo 85 Names	Condo 164 Words
English [Pseudo -Eng]	85 (94.5%) [10 (11.2%)]	138 (86.8%) [10 (6.3%)]	89 (62.2%) [5 (3.5%)]	161 (69.1%) [5 (2.1%)]	69 (81.2%) [15 (17.5%)]	131 (79.9%) [15 (9.1%)]
French [Pseudo -Fr]	8 (9.0%) [3 (3.4%)]	10 (6.3%) [3 (1.9%)]	40 (28%) [26 (18.2%)]	47 (20.2%) [26 (11.2%)]	16 (18.8%)	25 (15.2%)
Italian	4 (4.5%)	5 (3.1%)	19 (13.3%)	20 (8.6%)	3 (3.5%)	4 (2.4%)
Spanish	3 (3.4%)	3 (1.9%)			1 (1.2%)	2 (1.2%)
German	3 (3.4%)	4 (2.5%)			1 (1.2%)	1 (0.6%)
Latin			1 (0.7%)	2 (0.9%)	1 (1.2%)	1 (0.6%)
Esperanto			2 (1.4%)	2 (0.9%)		

Only 60.1% (86/148) of the Affordable Assisted-Living Accommodations use Western words (with the exception of *saabisu* 'service', which is part of the Japanese name for this type of accommodation), while 88.3%

(142/162) of the Premium Elderly-Care Facilities and 100% (85/85) of the Newly-Built Premium Condominiums make use of them. A large number of names in all categories use Western words written in the angular syllabary followed by toponyms in Sino-Japanese (*kanji*), 26.4% (39/148), 40.7% (66/162) and 77.6% (66/85) respectively. The reverse order, Japanese toponyms followed by Western words, can be seen in only 1/148, 1/162, and 3/85 cases. Additional Western words following the first pattern, i.e. "Western words + J. toponym + Western words" (*City Life* Toponym *Hilltop Garden*, *Clivia* Toponym *East Side*) can be seen in 8.2% (7/85) of the condominiums, but in only one case, in each of the other categories. A transliteration of the English definite article, *the* (*za*), can be found in only one Care Facility, but in 5.5% of the condominiums. Western words in Latin letters, rather than transliterated into the customary Japanese syllabary, are seen in 3.4% (5/148), 0.6% (1/162), and 8.2% (7/85) respectively.

As we can see in Table 2, the vast majority of Western words come from English, but there is a smattering of words from other languages and of neologisms (pseudo-Western words) created in Japan.

What the Names Convey

Having analysed the names used in these accommodations, we then seek to find out what impression these names impart to the Japanese. Younger respondents (36 university students, aged 20 to 24) were asked to give their impressions by ranking the price, newness, and expected facilities and amenities on a scale of 1 to 3, and adding additional comments. The results are summarised in Table 3. This provided considerable quantitative data, but more qualitative and in-depth information was needed to explore the various cultural and other factors which play important roles in determining subjective reactions. To obtain this information an additional 6 older respondents (aged 45 to 55) were asked to complete the same survey, and were then interviewed concerning reactions and emotional responses, both to naming combinations and to individual naming elements, and were asked about the reasons for these reactions and responses. These latter qualitative responses are included in the discussion below, but, given the age difference, their responses were not included in the statistics.

Table 3. Ranking of domicile names (*PN = Proper name).

PRICE		NEWNESS		FACILITIES	
East Gate Square	2.67	East Gate Square	2.81	East Gate Square	2.61
Grand Créer, PN*	2.56	Grand Créer, PN	2.50	Grand Créer, PN	2.56
La Luce PN	2.06	La Luce PN	2.39	La Luce PN	2.22
PN Laurel Court	2.03	Leaf Court PN	2.08	PN Laurel Court	2.06
PN Sky Heights	2.03	PN Laurel Court	2.06	Leaf Court PN	1.97
Leaf Court PN	1.83	PN Sky Heights	1.92	PN Sky Heights	1.94
The PN Residence	1.72	The PN Residence	1.61	The PN Residence	1.75
PN Edifice #3	1.50	PN Edifice #3	1.11	PN Edifice #3	1.28

The only name written entirely in Latin letters, *East Gate Square*, was ranked most highly in all categories: price, newness, and facilities. Many respondents associated this name with luxury, contemporaneity, and hotels or apartments likely to have foreign occupants. But writing in Latin letters was not convincing for everyone, as at least 2 respondents associated this name with cheap one-room apartments for students.

Although the name ranked second in these three categories was *Grand Créer*, a Tokyo elderly-care facility, many younger respondents were impressed with the French "feel" and implications of the word grand. Other respondents felt the same name was stuffy, or implied a stiff, black building, or something otherwise very conservative. *La Luce*, generally ranked third, another elderly-care facility, this time in Osaka, sounded like an Italian restaurant to some, and like a chic French word to others. The ending *-ce* (*-che*), while implying 'petite' and 'cute', gave some the impression that the facility might be small and cheap. Most of the older respondents, however, felt these accommodations might be aging, outmoded apartments for single students.

Court is used both in *Leaf Court*, another Tokyo elderly-care facility, and in *Laurel Court*, condominiums to be found in several different cities. *Laurel* was found superior to the more frivolous *leaf* by many; but some also found *laurel* to convey a lack of durability.

The Residence Shirogane Suites, another elderly-care facility in Tokyo, employs both the English definite article *the* and the word *residence*, as does *The Clivia Residence*, a condominium in Nagoya. The pattern *The* + Toponym + *Residence* was thought to imply a slighter older building by at least 10 younger respondents, though 5 others thought it implied something new and rather splendid. That a company would include the definite article in an attempt to convey an image of superiority or splendor was seen as old-fashioned, dishonest, and cheap by 3 others. *Residence* generally was associated with luxury and superior facilities.

The image conveyed by the apparently dowdy Toponym + *Edifice #3* is quite interesting. This was the only name shown to the respondents which did not contain any Western loanwords. Almost all of the younger respondents felt it implied an older building, and ranked it last in all categories. The reasons given for this ranking included the exclusive use of Chinese characters (*kanji*), including an archaic clerical character for '3', suggesting to some a wooden structure built before the 1980s. Others, who also thought the building must be old, nevertheless inferred that it would be a Western-style building of very durable construction. In contrast, older respondents saw in it a high-class, possibly "retro-style" brick building of more conservative, but expensive, character, from perhaps two decades ago.

The name on which opinions differed most was the old/new Toponym + *Sky Heights*. To some, *sky* implied a 'sky tower', a very expensive high-rise apartment, while to others the use of *heights* paradoxically implied a cheap, two-story apartment house. Younger respondents ranked it sixth in "Newness", but more mature respondents ranked it at the top in all three categories.

Although there were exceptions, these results indicate that an English name written in Latin letters gives a strong impression of expense and luxury. Use of the definite article *the* was associated with slightly outmoded buildings that were upscale at the time of their naming, perhaps a decade or two ago, while names without any Western components were seen as even older. Use of the French *grand* was associated with luxury and quality, and the vaguely "European" *luce* with cuteness and modest size. When these eight names were presented as names of living accommodations, some associated them with one-person apartments, but none with facilities for the aged living alone or elderly-care facilities.

Looking at the frequency with which certain words are used in the naming of these accommodations, we find that *care* (*keea*), *life* (*raifu*), *senior* (*shinia*), *home* (*hoomu*), and *house* (*hausu*) are often found in names for assisted living facilities. Words used for both elderly-care facilities and condominiums include *garden* (*gaaden*) and *residence* (*rejidensu*), while condominiums frequently employed *city* (*shiti*), *court* (*kooto*), *park* (*paaku*), and *tower* (*tawaa*). We asked 42 Japanese to respond freely to 40 naming combinations which included these key words, and from which toponyms and other proper names (as independent indicators of price and prestige) had been removed. We will now discuss reactions to only those names which include *senior* (*shinia*), *care* (*keea*), and *life* (*raifu*), words often associated with assisted living and elderly-care accommodations.

Table 4. Reactions to names containing *senior*.

NEGATIVE	AMBIGUOUS	POSITIVE
Senior House	*Senior Pension*	*Senior Residence*
Platinum Senior Home	*Senior Living*	*Senior Mansion*

Senior: In contrast to traditional Japanese words meaning 'elderly' or 'aged' the euphemistic loanword *senior* implies a happier, more carefree life. However, as shown in Table 4, its use in set phrases related to homes for the aged has imparted a nuance of unfeeling, institutionalised care in some cases. Though the Japanese *manshon* ('mansion') means 'apartment' or 'condominium' rather than something like a Victorian mansion, it is usually associated with contemporary urban condominiums, currently at a premium in the Japanese market. *Residence* has come into popularity with a similar meaning and similar associations. Thus *manshon* and *rejidensu* bring out the positive connotations of *shinia*. The negative connotations of *shinia* are brought to the fore in association with such words as *house* and *home*. *Platinum* usually implies 'superior' or 'premium quality', so responses to the apparent oxymoron *Platinum Senior Home* were contradictory. *Living*, in this context, is relatively neutral, while *pension* in Japan carries connotations of a cozy European-style inn rather than a depressing collection of aged pensioners.

Table 5. Reactions to names containing *care*.

NEGATIVE	AMBIGUOUS	POSITIVE
Care Center	*Care Village*	*Care Residence*
Care House	*Care Park*	*Care Resort*
Care Home		
Care Community		

Care: *Keea*, like its English counterpart *care*, implies attention to the aged and infirm, has strong associations with hospital care, and is often a euphemism for psychiatric treatment. *Day-care* is a term rarely used in connection with children in Japan; rather it is used almost exclusively for facilities for the elderly who cannot care for themselves because of incontinence, immobility or impairment of cognitive function. Again, as shown in Table 5, *residence* and *resort* offset these negative connotations, while *center*, *house*, and *home* reinforce images of indigence. *Village*, an image taken from American nostalgia, and *park*, with associations of freedom and outdoor activity, result in cognitive dissonance when juxtaposed with *care*.

Table 6. Reactions to names containing *life*.

NEGATIVE	POSITIVE
Long Life	*Good Life Home*
Life House	*Best Life*
Life Senior House	*Second Life With*
	Next Life
	Royal Life

Life: *Raifu* is perhaps the most ambiguous of the three terms, having still tenuous associations both with desirable "lifestyle" and with the negative implications of "life insurance." Some respondents even made connections to its use in Evangelical Christianity and proselytisation. As shown in Table 6, *house* and *senior* work to emphasise negative connotations; *long life* implies great age and infirmity rather than happiness. Having one of the longest post-retirement expectancies in the world, Japan has managed to develop a positive image of the post-retirement transition, so *second* and *next* convey positive images. *Good*, *best*, and *royal* all serve to bring out positive connotations.

Permanent "Homes"?

The website *Tsui no sumika* (2012, 'eternal living-home'), relates that, due to the shortage of land in big cities such as Tokyo, Osaka, and Nagoya, most cemeteries are managed by Buddhist temples, with a few exceptions managed by the private sector. We compare the names of those advertised as "traditional cemeteries" and those promoted as "sunny and park-like cemeteries", not just in the major cities, but throughout Japan, though the great majority is in major metropolitan areas.

We first look at the part of the name identifying the facility as a public cemetery, the word meaning or implying 'a place for deposition of the deceased'. Nearly 60% (35; 59.3%) of the 59 "traditional" facilities used the Japanese equivalent of *cemetery*; 18.6% (11) used a variation of *graveyard*, nearly 7% (4; 6.8%) *garden* or *park*, while 5% used a word related to Buddhist temples, 5% a pastoral term like *country* or *forest*, and 5% transliterations from English: *Bird Hills*, *Cemetery*, and *Memorial Park*. Of the "sunny and park-like locations", 65% used *cemetery*, 8% *graveyard*, 13% *garden* or *park*, 9% *country* or *forest*. Only 3% used words related to temples, one a transliteration from English, *Memorial Square*, and one a transliteration of memorial together with the Sino-Japanese characters meaning 'villa of peace and happiness'.

Compared with the names for the types of housing described above, it comes as no surprise that names for cemeteries contained few Western loanwords; it was something of a surprise to find any at all included in the listing of "historical and traditional" cemeteries, names such as: *Minami Oosawa Bird Hills*, *Cemetery Tokorozawa*, and *Musashino Memorial Park*. Among the "sunny and park-like cemeteries" we find, with some frequency, *memorial*, combined with such words as *park* (*Memorial Park Yuukari Hallowed Ground*), *square* (*Memorial Square Unga*), and *green* (*Memorial Green Nagareyama Hallowed Ground*).

To better understand the images conveyed by names for cemeteries and graveyards, we asked our respondents to rank ten names in terms of price, maintenance (corresponding roughly to "facilities" used above), and whether or not the spot would be appropriate either for their own grave or for the graves of their ancestors (desirability). We also solicited other impressions. The results of the survey are summarised in Table 7.

Table 7. Ranking of cemetery names.

PRICE		FACILITIES		APPROPRIATE-NESS	
Sokushuu Monastery	2.50	*Sokushuu Monastery*	2.41	*Sokushuu Monastery*	2.32
Kanga Hermitage	2.50	*Kanga Hermitage*	2.33	*Kanga Hermitage*	2.28
Japanese Garden	2.50	*Japanese Garden*	2.33	*Japanese Garden*	2.28
Rinsen Temple	2.17	*Rinsen Temple*	2.25	*Rinsen Temple*	2.19
Morning Sun	1.89	*Prefectural Central*	2.22	*Prefectural Central*	2.08
Forest of Eternity	1.89	*Memorial Park*	2.08	*Morning Sun*	1.90
Bird Hills	1.89	*Bird Hills*	2.06	*Municipal Oubadai*	1.83
Memorial Park	1.89	*Morning Sun*	2.00	*Forest of Eternity*	1.69
Prefectural Central	1.69	*Municipal Oubadai*	1.83	*Memorial Park*	1.58
Municipal Oubadai	1.44	*Forest of Eternity*	1.80	*Bird Hills*	1.44

In the categories of price (most expensive) and suitability, the two names ranked consistently at the top were Gaun-zan Sokushuu Monastery (*Gaun-zan Sokushuu-in*) and Zuishi-zan Kanga Hermitage (*Zuishi-zan Kanga-an*). Some respondents suggested this was because the names were written in Chinese characters, and included some characters which are rarely used and difficult to read; at the same time such names also suggested that they might "be operated by a famous Buddhist temple", have "a calm, quiet atmosphere", have an impressive "pedigree", or have a notable history and traditions. Two of the middle-aged respondents suggested that the use of *-an* 'hermitage' was inappropriate for the name of a cemetery (as it implied the "living place" of a cultural/religious recluse), while others suggested it might be a profit-making enterprise operated by a secular company, a non-sectarian, non-religious cemetery for high-income city dwellers. Younger respondents said the same word, *-an*, suggested greater expense and a higher social class. Younger respondents also felt that *-in* 'monastery' implied a desirable and strong relation to an established religious body, while older respondents tended to associate it with bodies of dubious religious tradition.

CEMETERY NAMES IN FULL

- Sokushuu Monastery (*Gaun-zan Sokushuu-in*)
- Kanga Hermitage (*Zuishi-zan Kanga-an*)
- Japanese Garden Tombs (*Nihon Teien Ryuubo Kouyoutei*)
- Rinsen Temple Graveyard (*Rinsen-ji Bochi*)
- Country of the Morning Sun (*Asahi no Sato*)
- Forest of Eternity (*Towa no Mori*)
- Ousawa Bird Hills (*Ousawa Baado Hiruzu*)
- Memorial Park (*Memoriaru Paaku*)
- Prefectural Central Cemetery (*Kenritsu Chuuou Reien*)
- Municipal Oubadai Cemetery (*Shiei Oubadai Reien*)

Figure 1. Cemetery names in full.

The elaborately named Japanese Garden Tombs Autumn Foliage Pavilion (*Nihon Teien Ryuubo Kouyoutei*) suggested history, superior quality, admirable style, and careful attention to maintenance, but also greater expense, and possibly a restriction to persons of high social standing. Most of the younger group thought their ancestors could well rest "at their ease" in such a location. Older respondents felt a sense of history, and the possibility that important historical figures might be buried here, making it unsuitable for themselves, though others felt it might be appropriate in the event that the family had no ancestral grave at the temple with which the family is traditionally affiliated.

The word *-ji* 'temple' appears in the name of many cemeteries, as cemeteries traditionally were attached to Buddhist temples. Responses to the name Rinsen Temple Graveyard (*Rinsen-ji bochi*) suggested that it would be carefully tended, reliable, well shaded, and appropriate for ancestral graves. One respondent suggested that the old-fashioned *graveyard* (*bochi*) was a detraction, but that was balanced out by the use of *temple*. Generally, associations with the word *temple* were almost uniformly positive.

Names with considerably less traditional words, such as *country* (Country of the Rising Sun *Asahi no sato*) and *forest* (Forest of Eternity *Towa no mori*), widely elicited responses such as, "not a typical name for a cemetery" and "calls forth no images".

The more modern sounding *Oosawa Bird Hills* was seen as unlike a cemetery name, frivolous, of dubious character, or cheap, because of the Western loanwords (in Japanese syllabary), and inappropriate for one's ancestors; the negative images caused one respondent to suggest that the souls of one's ancestors could never rest in such a spot. Older respondents thought it might be out in the suburbs, probably attractive, with unusual grave stones, but also rather ambiguous in terms of (religious, etc.) orientation, and possibly even a crass scheme for making money.

Memorial Park, though also employing Western loanwords in the Japanese syllabary, had a more positive image, suggesting freedom, newness, and thorough maintenance. At the same time the use of Western words, as in *Bird Hills*, was seen as frivolous, not very "Japanese", and not suited for ancestral graves. Many even felt that such a name made light of the deceased, or was more appropriate for a pet cemetery. Others thought it might be a national cemetery for the victims of a large-scale disaster. In spite of this, two of the older respondents rated it very highly, and suggested that it would be an appropriate place for eternal rest.

Responses to *Central Prefectural Cemetery* and *Municipal Oubadai Cemetery* were quite similar. Many found the term for cemetery, "spirit/ghost garden" (*reien*) rather scary. Others thought the public ownership implied a more reasonable price and greater reliability; the other side of this coin was the image of a cheap, shoddily cared-for facility.

Discussion

From the information analysed above we can detect two trends. The first is the continued and evolving influence of English syntax. After a century and a half of actively importing Western words, Japanese exhibits several instances of the "grammaticalisation" of these imports, beginning, perhaps, with the formation of Japanese-conjugated verbs from foreign verbs and nouns, and extending to the adoption of the English definite article the as a nominaliser and intensifier, and adaptation of particles from French. The startling and once striking use of the definite article, in a language which does not traditionally employ articles, having been by now thoroughly domesticated, the form NOUN + ADJECTIVE (ADJECTIVAL NOUN) makes its appearance replacing the more traditional THE + ADJECTIVE + NOUN. As in English-speaking countries where *Team USA* replaces *the USA (Olympic) Team* and *Symphony Atlanta* vies with *The Atlanta Symphony Orchestra*, the use of toponym + EDIFICE NAME is gradually being supplanted by EDIFICE NAME + toponym, while the definite article is increasingly seen as outmoded.

PSEUDO-WESTERN NEOLOGISMS

Viequ **(viiku)**
VI- (Eng. 'vivid') + E- (Eng. 'especial') + QU (Eng. 'quality')

Sancleair **(sankureea)**
SAN (J. Sanyo) + CLE- (Eng. 'clean') + AIR (Eng.)

Lien-cier **(riansheeru)**
LIEN (Eng. 'ligament, bond') + -CIER (Fr. *concierge*)

Sakura-bia
Sakura (J. 'cherry blossom'/L. *sacra*) + BIA (L. *via*)

Werisu
WEL- (Eng. 'well/welfare') + LEASE (Eng.)

Eterno Teresa **(eteruno teresa)**
ETERNO (It.) + TE- (Eng. 'tend') + RE- (Eng. 'relax') + SA- (Eng. 'safety')

Amille **(amiiyu)**
AMI (Fr.) + -ILLE (Fr. *famille*)

Figure 2. Pseudo-Western neologisms.

The second trend is the use of pseudo-Western words, words formed in Japan ostensibly from Western elements. Several examples can be seen in Figure 2. Abbreviations and acronyms employing the first letter of Romanised Japanese words have been common since the nineteenth century; Japanese is also replete with neologisms formed, typically, from the first two mora of transliterations of Western words, a pattern similar to that used for centuries in the adaptation of Sino-Japanese words. Here, however, we see a new pattern emerging: the free adaptation of elements from Western languages, often unconstrained by traditions of abbreviation or the integrity of word roots. These elements are first freely combined in the form of Latin letters, and, in contrast to traditional practice, only then (if at all) transliterated into phonologically and morphologically recognisable Japanese names (and written in a Japanese syllabary). Because of this freedom in adaptation, most of these neologisms are neither immediately comprehensible (to native speakers of either Japanese or European languages), nor of clear and evident origin. Comprehension beyond the primitive level of association with a particular product (as a direct result of commercial advertising) requires reference to an explanation of the vendor's "concept", consistently provided on webpages and other publicity materials. The neologisms, thus, become a hermetic encoding of company philosophy, usually an attempt to combine a heterogeneous, and frequently contradictory, set of qualities in one product, seeking (vainly) to set it off from those of innumerable other producers attempting to do much the same thing.

The results of our examination of cemetery names make it clear that there continues to be a strong bias in favor of names which suggest a link with a temple or other traditional religious organisation. As one might expect, many facilities promise some form of perpetual care, both for the soul of the deceased and for the physical site of remembrance – the grave. But there is a growing tendency to think of these sites in human terms, in terms of the living rather than the dead, the rememberers rather than the remembered. Convenience of access for visitors, a pleasing aspect, and a "sunny and park-like" atmosphere are increasingly prominent in advertising, even in promotion of "traditional" gravesites. The use of such phrases as "eternal home", or, more literally, "eternal living house", in the title of a site dedicated to cemeteries is particularly suggestive. A prominent advertisement for the Memorial Rose Garden cemetery pictures a middle-aged man and woman in white, holding hands, with a red rose superimposed between them; the copy reads, "Even after I die, we will continue to date, right?" One of the most recent developments in the field of "perpetual care" is the heavily advertised Baikyuuin, a multi-story, completely enclosed facility, with gravestones stored in ranks, like the books in a library stack, but available for individual viewing when paying respects to the deceased. While the formal name (literally "Apricot Ancient Monastery") is reminiscent of Japanese Buddhist temples, the catchphrase for this facility is *o-haka no manshon* or 'apartment house for graves'. Though the pace of change is slow, with names employing such words as *Garden*, *Sun*, *Forest*, *Hills* and *Park*, we can surely expect even greater convergence of names for condominium, elderly-care, and perpetual-care facilities in Japan in the near future.

References

Haarman, H. 1984. The role of ethnocultural stereotypes and foreign languages in Japanese commercials. *International Journal of Sociology of Language* 50: 101–121.

Josei sebun. 2012. Chingin sukunai hito ga sattou! "Koureisha chintai juutaku" risuto [Hugely popular with those of modest income! "Rental Accommodations for the Elderly" List]. *Josei sebun* 4: 73–80.

Residences for elderly people with service. 2012. Saabisu-tsuki koureisha muke juutaku. Jouhou teikyou shisutemu [Assisted-living residences for the elderly. Information registration system]. https://www.satsuki-jutaku.jp/search/index.php (retrieved 22 January 2012).

Rosenberger, N. 1992. Images of the West: Home Style in Japanese Magazines. In *Re-made in Japan: Everyday Life and Consumer Taste in a Changing Society*, T. Joseph (ed.), 106–125. New Haven: Yale University Press.

Sagashikkusu. 2012. Yuuryou roujinhoomu kensaku sagashikkusu [Search site for fee-paying homes for the elderly Sagasix]. http://www.sagasix.jp/ (retrieved 17 January 2012).

Sakoujuu.jp. 2012. Sakoujuu (saabisu-tsuki koureisha-muke juutaku) no seido ni tsuite [About the Sakoujuu (Assisted-living Accommodations for the Elderly) system]. http://サ高住.jp/2-sakouju_system.html (retrieved 1 September 2012).

Satsuki 2012 = https://www.satsuki-jutaku.jp/search/index.php (retrieved 22 January 2012).

SUUMO Kansai. 2012. *SUUMO shinchiku manshon* [SUUMO New Condominiums]. Kansai edition. 13 March 2012.

SUUMO Metropolitan. 2012. *SUUMO shinchiku manshon* [SUUMO New Condominiums]. Metropolitan edition. 6 March 2012.

Takashi, K. 1990. A sociolinguistic analysis of English borrowings in Japanese advertising texts. *World Englishes* 9: 327–341.

Tsui no sumika. 2012. Tsui no sumika [Eternal living home]. http://www.tsuino-sumika.com/ (retrieved 24 January 2012).

Yahoo! Japan Real Estate. 2012. Yahoo! Japan fudousan [Yahoo! Japan real estate]. http://new.realestate.yahoo.co.jp/ansion/themelist (retrieved 16 March 2012).

ROMANIAN BRAND NAMES AS CULTURAL MEDIATORS

ALINA BUGHEŞIU
TECHNICAL UNIVERSITY OF CLUJ-NAPOCA, ROMANIA
NORTH UNIVERSITY CENTRE OF BAIA MARE

Abstract

This study explores the way in which brand names in the contemporary Romanian commercial environment function as cultural mediators. By considering the socioeconomic and cultural configuration of Romanian public space before and after the Revolution of 1989 (namely before and after the fall of the communist regime), Romanian brand names are analysed as translation acts that underlie a unidirectional and variable transfer of messages, facts, events, human values and behavioural patterns between the two aforementioned contexts. Their use is always based on an act of interpretation, a constructive process through which receivers (customers) interact with the senders (the advertising and/or marketing agents responsible for the choice of names), by trying to decode the subjective intention behind the naming process and the associations triggered by the names. While assenting to the viewpoint that naming is an act of power, the paper concludes that brand names in Romanian contemporary public space are employed to identify and advertise their bearers, especially when functioning as cultural mediators, i.e. as linguistically represented socioeconomic markers that can be indicative of the status and dynamic of the society in which they exist.

Globalisation, Localisation, Translation

Against the background of globalisation and localisation, this article explores the field of names in the contemporary Romanian commercial environment and aims at highlighting and analysing the use of brand names as cultural mediators. By taking into account the political, socioeconomic and cultural configuration of Romanian public space before and after the Revolution of 1989 (that is, before and after the fall of the communist regime), this study deals with brand names as translation acts. In this capacity, brand names ensure a variable transfer of messages (related to facts, events, human values and behavioural patterns) between two contexts of use: 1) an original one, in which the brands were established and their names were coined; 2) an adoptive one, where the embracement of globalising standards and the cultivation of localising ones (Boerrigter 2007: 56) occur simultaneously and symbiotically.

Romania has fallen under the incidence of globalisation since the 1990s, as borders have opened up not only to Romanians who wish to travel abroad for various purposes (study, work, or entertainment), but also – and more importantly – to foreign investors that see a potential profit in opening branches of their businesses in Romania. Nevertheless, despite the mobility and freedom that globalisation is known to promise, it has recently been blamed for denying and even cancelling identity. As a result, the field of commerce has started cultivating values that are believed to define Romanian local identity and that were rooted before 1989 but can only, in retrospect, be observed now. The values take the form of stereotypes: the prestige of local customs, the interest shown in tradition and authenticity, the connection between human beings and nature, as well as the quality, endurance and utility of Romanian products.

These principles were disregarded in the 1990s and early 2000s, as they were firmly linked to communist Romania and therefore connoted negatively. In the context of the deeply globalised, contemporary Romanian public space, there is a tendency to transfer them from that almost mythical past into today's polysemous world, where they give way to positive connotations. One of the fields that are subjected to such a process of interpretation comprises the names of brands[1] that were established before 1989 and that are trying to survive in the current particularly colourful landscape of trades. These brand names function as cultural mediators, as they underlie (and often trigger) acts of translation that try to solve the generation and cultural gap formed between pre- and post-revolutionary Romania and, naturally, between the people that represent these two periods.

---

[1] This paper is part of a more consistent study in the field of onomastics, developed within *Onomastics in Contemporary Romanian Public Space: Socio- and Psycholinguistic Research*, a project funded by CNCS in the "Human Resources" programme (PN II) meant for the stimulation of young independent research teams (TE), code 3/2010, contract number 57/2010, project manager: Associate Professor Oliviu Felecan.

Translation as Intracultural Communication

Terminological Remarks

Although the common perception of translation implies the transfer of language items and, implicitly, of the cultural load they carry from one linguistic code to another (i.e. from a source-language, SL, to a target-language, TL), on this occasion, my acceptation of the sociolinguistic process is broader. I agree with Lungu-Badea (2005: 5, orig. Romanian, my translation), who regards it as "a transfer of messages, facts, events, human relationships and behavioural patterns", perceived according to three variables: 1) the individuals involved, 2) the sociohistorical background, and 3) the situation of communication. This transfer is irrespective of whether it takes place between two distinct languages or at the level of a single language (cf. Steiner 1998: 49), between various sociocultural varieties (most often synchronically) or ages (diachronically). Whatever the orientation of the information sent may be, namely from an SL to a TL or at the level of the same linguistic code, a translation consists of an act of semiotic and pragmatic interpretation performed regularly, which is the essential constituent of any speech act:

> Any model of communication is at the same time a model of trans-location, of a vertical or horizontal transfer of significance. No two historical epochs, no two social classes, no two localities use words and syntax to signify exactly the same things, to send identical signals of valuation and inference. Neither do two human beings. [...] Thus a human being performs an act of translation, in the full sense of the word, when receiving a speech message from any other human being. Time, distance, disparities in outlook or assumed reference, make this act more or less difficult (Steiner 1998: 47–48).

Note that Steiner founded his statement on *speech*, not on *language*. Along the lines of Ferdinand de Saussure's distinction *langue – parole*, Steiner draws attention to the idiosyncratic dimension of communication, to its dependence on *context*. However, it is not just the source-context that matters, but also the (potential) target-context(s) in which the transferred elements will be used and activated. Therefore, the translator's job is that of a cultural mediator between two contexts of use, whereas the translation itself often tends to become a cultural adaptation, a "transfer of significance": "Through *cultural adaptation*, a message or a concept is subjected to modifications that make it meet the preferences and the taste of a certain target-audience, often defined by a particular cultural inheritance, a language, or an ethnic belonging" (Lungu-Badea 2005: 134, fn. 77, orig. Romanian, my translation).

Romanian Public Space as a Context of Cultural Mediation

The current perspective on translation derives from the analysis of contemporary Romanian public space as a diachronically bi-dimensional space on different levels: political, economic, social, technological, cultural and commercial (to mention only a few). Of these, the most conspicuous one is the political configuration since it is the Revolution of 1989 (as the threshold between communist and non-communist Romania) that allows for the analysis of brand names as mediators between two contexts of communication. Thus, as far as contemporary Romanian public space is concerned (by contemporary, I mean roughly starting from the mid-20th century on), the process of cultural mediation and the inherent transfer of values occur unidirectionally between the following two periods:

1) Before 1989: an inexpressive, insipid sociocultural tableau, in which the political communist colour dictated the course of events and people's personal or social existences were severely controlled by the state and party apparatus. This is the period of the famed "wooden language", implying desensitisation, revealing that the profession of one's individuality was discouraged, blamed and punished by communist authorities. Appreciation of Western values was thoroughly reprehended, since capitalist society was seen as the greatest enemy and threat to the diligence of the socialist man. There was an imposed feeling of national pride that pervaded every sector of the society and that, to the greatest extent, was induced by the political hierarchy. Put differently, Romanian public space before 1989 was *strictly* Romanian – from the arts, music, literature, technology and language, to commerce. The field of onomastics did not escape this standardisation, a fact that was notably salient in the case of trade names (brand names included). According to Rzetelska-Feleszko (2008: 595–596), this was the general picture of commercial onomastics before 1989 in the former "Eastern bloc", which, from this point of view, was defined by "colourlessness, blandness, and bureaucratic character, combined with a complete lack of advertising potential". Trade names were descriptive (Bergien 2008: 290), which is to say that the elements they comprised were semantically transparent. Likewise, businesses designated by such names stood out precisely because they were either the sole or the most visible option on the market.

2) After 1989: an outburst of Western influences that overthrew the structure of the society and made it almost unrecognisable. Completely unprepared for the tide of changes that occurred during the 1990s, Romanian public space showed itself very open to outer models of success and greedily consumed every suggestion in this respect without chewing (on) it. Ashamed of its recent past and angry at its silence, Romania heartily welcomed globalisation and the corresponding transformations on all the levels of public and even private space which now function under the sign of global networks of signification and hyperlinks. Politics, economy, technology and art have suffered fundamental modifications that derive from diverse cultural contacts favoured by internationalisation. Language has been Anglicised greatly[2], although it would probably be more legitimate to claim that it has been "Americanised", since globalisation promotes American values and mindsets. The evolution of commerce went hand in hand with that of the media and of marketing and advertising strategies. Therefore, trade names (and onomastics in general) became increasingly diverse (Felecan, O. 2008: 579), both as a result of the liberalisation of imports and as a result of the importance given to private property, market competition and distinctiveness (Schack 2008: 61). There were businesses that collapsed sooner or later after the 1989 moment, owing to the pressure exerted by large(r) foreign companies that opened subsidiaries in Romania (Dumitru 2011) and whose products/services were preferred by the Romanians as a form of rebellion against the restriction of having had to use only a certain local product/service and due to the repulsion that this restriction awoke in people in relation to that particular product/service (Panaitache n.d.). Moreover, a number of firms were taken over by more powerful, international companies whose marketing and advertising strategies had more impact on consumers; quite often, the products/services sold by a local business were kept under a different name. At the same time, there are brands that have managed to span these two phases in the evolution of Romanian public space. *BCR, Dacia, Guban, Napolact, Romtelecom, Ursus* etc. employ the values they stood for before 1989 (which were then highlighted for political reasons) and still strive to ensure their esteem not only with Romanians but also abroad.

[2] In this respect, as regards the presence and evolution of Anglicisms in Romanian, see especially Avram (1997), Pârlog (1971; 1999) and Stoichiţoiu-Ichim (2006; 2008), who not only quantify the influence of English on Romanian, but also (and more importantly) carry out a socio- and psycholinguistic analysis of the "digestion" of these borrowings by contemporary Romanian society.

Romanian Brand Names and (Intra)cultural Mediation

As regards the case analysed (i.e. Romanian brand names), we are dealing with a cultural transfer, an adaptation of messages (cultural values) that brands conveyed before 1989 to the current globalised landscape in which the same brands have to survive. To this end, cultural mediators try to remodel the discourse that these names create by consciously addressing two types of target receivers: 1) generations that can recall and have vivid memories of their experience of the period before the Revolution of 1989; 2) new generations that were either born shortly before the Revolution, or in the 1990s and even 2000s, who know what communism meant to Romanians from what they have heard from relatives, or from what they have seen or read in books and the media. Of the great variety of brands (of which international ones have a more significant impact than local/national ones), Romanian brands that span several generations and two major socioeconomic, political and cultural phases of Romanian public space need to convince both types of target receivers that they are worth their financial effort. Consequently, while global brands that become locally marketed generally underline how Romanians can become more international, more Western by wearing, drinking, eating, listening, reading, speaking *their way*, Romanian brands that were established before 1989 play on the prestige that age bestows on them, as well as on certain stereotypes that reveal various degrees of trustworthiness and empathy which the brands have been trying to convey since their coinage. These stereotypes point to the national identity of the Romanian people and manage to have individuals relate to one another by identifying common, shared experiences in their lives.

Romanian brands that function as cultural mediators are represented by marketing/advertising agents as well as by the brand names themselves, since customers seldom have any direct contact with advertisers and believe that names are invested with this quality of mediation, due to the associative meanings they trigger. It is one's *communicative competence* that ensures a proper decoding of the associative meanings that branding specialists design (or that initial name givers thought up when they created a certain name) and that advertisers explore in their employment of names, in their depiction of the (system of) values meant to capture the attention of potential consumers. This skill implies that, in the encoding and decoding processes, the language users' *linguistic competence* is supported by their *social knowledge* (Bell 2000: 128) which should be accessible to both ends of the chain of communication i.e. the sender and the receiver (as interchangeable positions).

Against a common linguistic background (globalisation works to somehow overcome language barriers), the cultural mediator has a two-fold role: to create a context of communication that would facilitate the addressees' proper identification of the message, and to educate his/her addressees in this respect, especially if their *social knowledge* runs thin on the object (an item of information and values related to it) that suffers the transfer. In other words, in promoting a brand, advertising agents consider first and foremost those aspects that potential consumers are sure to identify as characteristic in relation to a particular brand and that resonate with a community's social imaginary. Moreover, they care to shape these aspects in such a manner that younger individuals who are not familiar with the brand from any past experience (in the present situation, prior to 1989) are convinced of the information it conveys, which thus becomes part of their social knowledge.

The mediator must bear in mind the space of shared knowledge when constructing a brand's discourse since "A discourse is a socially accepted association among ways of using language, of thinking, believing, valuing, and acting that can be used to identify oneself as a member of a socially meaningful group or 'social network', or to signal (that one is playing) a socially meaningful 'role'" (Straniero Sergio 1998: 164[3]). The discourse built around Romanian brands such as *Arctic, BCR, Clujana, Dacia, Eugenia, Farmec, Guban, Murfatlar, Napolact* and *Ursus* aims to connect people together in a network that is a firm statement of their cultural identity (Felecan, D. 2011: 64), either by claiming to simply remind people of this identity or by attempting to develop it in those who only have the experience of a multicultural, global environment. The discourse in question results from the negotiation between localism and globalisation, from the transfer of values from one context of use to the other. This diachronic, (intra)cultural mediation is introduced and achieved, activated and re-activated through the brand name itself, in its capacity as the (onymic) constant of the illustrated instance of cross-generational, cross-contextual communication in Romanian public space.

Cultural Mediators in Contemporary Romanian Public Space: The Example of Romanian Brand Names

Although the widely accepted definition of *brand* explains the concept as "a class of goods identified by name as the product of a single firm or

[3] The original reference: Gee, J. 1990. *Social Linguistics and Literacies: Ideology and Discourse*. London: Falmer.

manufacturer" (Merriam-Webster Online, s.v. *brand*), due to the evolution of the concept in use and to the multiple perspectives that have been adopted in its study, it has suffered a semantic extension towards generalisation, as it also means "a particular identity or image regarded as an asset" (Oxford Dictionaries Online, s.v. *brand*). Therefore, since by *branding* one now understands "the process that helps develop and maintain a set of coherent, particular, distinctive attributes and values that are related to a brand and that are […] attractive to consumers" (Corbu 2009: 60, orig. Romanian, my translation), we can talk about brands not only in regard to products or services and distinct types of the two, but also in what concerns institutions or commercial establishments such as banks and companies that provide different kinds of services (e.g. telephone or television services) for the public. In Romania, an example in this respect is the case of business establishments that before 1989 were controlled by the government (i.e. they were marketed as "public goods") and that after the Revolution became private enterprises: *C.E.C.* (which became *CEC Bank*, a bank), *Romtelecom* (telephone company), *TAROM* (Romanian air transport company), and *TVR* (the Romanian national television company). These businesses initially had the monopoly on the services they produced, as the state practiced the programmatic manipulation of public space and, to the extent it managed, of the private, intimate space, as well. However, after the fall of the regime and once the economic modernisation of the state began in the 1990s, these companies were gradually privatised (either fully or partially), believing that they could thereby survive the tenacious competition that globalisation imposed on the economic market (*Wall-Street* 2007). What is essential is that these commercial establishments create an identity; one could claim that they virtually underlie myths, as "a brand is the performer and the carrier of a myth of identity" (Corbu 2009: 60, orig. Romanian, my translation).

The identity of a brand is firmly connected to its name; the way in which customers relate to a brand is linked to the associative meanings triggered by the brand name in use, which name givers and advertising agents try to make sure that customers will identify and activate whenever they hear, see and speak the name. Naturally, the audio-visual dimension of a brand's advertising potential is also vital (note the role of the emblem, logo or advertising slogans). Sjöblom (2008: 351) discusses the *multimodal potential* of company names, by underlining the collaboration of linguistic and extra-/para-linguistic elements in the establishment and interpretation of a company's identity: "Multimodality in communication means that the interpretations are provided not only by linguistic elements (writing and speaking) but also by other semiotic modes, e.g. image, sound and movement, which all are linked together in a socio-cultural context" (ibid.). Nonetheless, it is the name that establishes a special relation between product/service/company, on the one hand, and customers, on the other.

The types of associative meanings are not specific to brand names alone; they are common within the entire class of proper names. According to Van Langendonck (2007: 7), "Proper names do not have asserted lexical meaning but do display presuppositional meanings of several kinds: categorical (basic level), associative senses (introduced either via the name bearer or via the name form), emotive senses and grammatical meanings". Although the categorical meaning of a name (hinting at the basic level category to which the referent of a name belongs) can be suggested by the transparency of the lexical elements that underlie a brand name, this seldom happens in the case of brands, as their identity and success depend on their being distinguished from other similar products/services/companies. Moreover, "if all enterprises used the same sign or symbol in trade, no system of trademarks would exist" (Schack 2008: 61). Thus, the categorical meaning is normally established contextually, through use, just as the associative and emotive meanings are, and they are all promoted through emblems and slogans that advertise an object of trade and that aim to establish it as a brand.

The linguistic status of brand names is a debatable aspect, due to their semantic functionality and the variety of entities that the lexical elements they consist of may designate. In this respect, Schack (2008: 60) believes that brand names are closer to *terms* rather than *words*. Along the same lines, Teutsch (2008: 251) sees them as "crossbreeds between proper names and general terms". Van Langendonck (2007: 236) claims there are at least five categories of entities that can be distinguished in relation to trade and brand names. Based on his illustration of the *Ford* semantic model, here are the same five categories identified in relation to a Romanian commercial name (cf. Bugheşiu 2011: 537):

(1) The founder of a company (the lemma in the onymic structure has a proprial function and, in this context, the quality of a personal name): *Guban founded the famous Romanian shoe factory.*
(2) A company or subsidiary: *Guban is a shoe factory.*
(3) A brand: *Guban is an old Romanian brand.*
(4) A product: *Guban are very good leather shoes.*
(5) An exemplar of the product: *Maria has bought a pair of Guban last week.*

According to Van Langendonck (2007: 236), the uses in (2) to (5), like the uses of the corresponding *Ford* example, "can be derived from the previous one in the series by specific metonymical processes. The processes provide for the unity of the lexical item", which is a "multidenotative proprio-appellative lemma displaying proper name uses as well as appellative uses". Thus, when used to designate a company/subsidiary, a brand or a product, *Guban* has a proprial use, whereas when it is used to designate different exemplars of a product, the same lexical item functions appellatively (i.e. it is appellativised). Depending on the context, companies, brands and products may require the use of the corresponding categorical term for a clearer identification of the entity named.

As regards Romanian public space, not all five categories of entities can be distinguished in relation to every trade name. Sometimes, the first one (the founder of a company) is replaced by a toponym, the name of the city/region where the company is situated: *Azuga, Borsec*, *Murfatlar.* Conversely, this category may be missing altogether: *Farmec*. There are also cases when only the last three types of entities can be identified (these are the majority): *Brifcor, Doina, Mentosan, Mobra, Triumf,* and so on.

Semantically and economically, the Romanian trade names analysed throughout the present paper function mainly as brand names. The entities they designate belong to the following commercial categories:

(I) Companies that provide services and/or products: *Antibiotice* ('antibiotics'), *BCR (Banca Comerciala Română* 'commercial Romanian bank'), *C.E.C.* (*Casa de Economii şi Consemnaţiuni* 'house of economies and consignations', now CEC Bank)*, Plafar* (< *plante farmaceutice* 'pharmaceutical plants'), *Romtelecom* (< *Romania telecomunicaţii* 'telecommunications')[4], *TAROM* (*Transporturile Aeriene Române* 'Romanian Air Transport'), *TVR* (*Televiziunea Română* 'Romanian television').

[4] Stoichiţoiu-Ichim (2008: 42) states that in the period following World War II, Romanian acronyms based on noun phrases in which the head occupies the final position (as is the case of *Romtelecom*) can be explained by the increasing influence of English on Romanian, often mediated by French (in this case, *Romtelecom* follows the model of French *France Telecom*).

(II) Products:

(1) Vehicles: automobiles (*Dacia*[5], referring to the ancient Dacian Kingdom), motorbikes (*Mobra* < *motociclete/motor* 'motorbike/ engine' + *Braşov*, the city where engines for this motorbike were made), bicycles (*Pegas* 'Pegasus').

(2) Household appliances: refrigerators (*Arctic* < *arctic* 'arctic'), washing machines (*Albalux* < *Alba*, a Romanian county, + *lux* 'luxury').

(3) Domestic objects: ceramics (*Faimar* < *faianţă* 'earthenware' + *Maramureş*, a Romanian county).

(4) Clothing and shoes: *Braiconf* (< *Brăila*, the capital city of the homonymous county in the south-eastern part of Romania, + *confecţii* 'clothing'), *Clujana* (*Cluj* > *clujean, clujeană* 'related to Cluj-Napoca/Cluj; used to describe a person that is from this region' + feminine form of the enclitic definite article *-a* > **Clujana*), *Guban* (< *Guban*, the surname of the company's founder).

(5) Chemical products: detergents and cleaning agents (*DERO* < *Detergenţi România* 'Romanian detergents'; *Triumf* < *triumf* 'triumph', cooker cleaning agent), paints (*Policolor* < *poli-*, pseudoprefix, 'more, several' + *color* 'coloured').

(6) Pharmaceuticals and cosmetics: *Cheia* (< *cheie* 'key' + enclitic definite article *-a*, soap), *Cristal* (< *cristal* 'crystal', toothpaste), *Doina* (< *Doina*, Romanian female name), *Fares* (unknown origin, perhaps deriving from the founder's surname, *Farago*), *Farmec* (< *farmec* 'charm, magic, enchantment'), *Gerovital* (< *geriatrie* 'geriatrics' + *vital* 'vital').

(7) Food and beverages: dairy products (*Albalact* < *Alba*, a county in Romania, + *lactate* 'dairy products'; *Napolact* < *Napoca*, the name of an ancient region in Romania, then Dacia, + *lactate*);

[5] While models produced by *Dacia* in the communist period were designated by a numerical structure (e.g. *1300*), models made after 1989 bear sophisticated foreign names (e.g. *Solenza, Logan, Duster*, or *Lodgy*, in chronological order of their creation). Nowadays, Romanians have mixed feelings about the former. On the one hand, there are people who remember *Dacia 1300* nostalgically and they refer to the model by the brand name *Dacia* thus, aiming to highlight its reliability. On the other hand, there are Romanians who refer to the same product by the number underlying its name in order to clearly distinguish it from newer models; these people have a very poor opinion of the cars *Dacia* produced before 1989, mostly due to their being associated with life under the communist regime (Bugheşiu 2012: 396).

sweets (*Eugenia*[6] < *Eugenia*, Romanian female name; *Mentosan* < *menta* 'mint' + *sănătate* 'health'; *ROM* < *România*); mineral water (*Borsec* < *Borsec,* a city in Harghita County, Transylvania); soft drinks (*Brifcor* < *Băutura Răcoritoare Indigenă Fabricată cu Concentrat Original Românesc* 'autochthonous soft drink made from an original Romanian concentrate'; *CiCo* < *citrice* 'citrus' + *cola*); alcoholic drinks (beer: *Azuga* < *Azuga*, the name of the Romanian city in which the initial product was made; *Bucegi* < the Bucegi Mountains, situated in central Romania; *Timişoreana* < *timişorean, timisoreană* 'related to/from Timişoara' + feminine form of enclitic definite article *-a* > *Timişoreana*; *Ursus* < Latin *ursus*, *-i* 'bear'; wine: *Murfatlar* < *Murfatlar*, a town in Constanţa County, Romania).

(8) Cigarettes: *Carpaţi* (< *Carpaţi* 'Carpathians', a range of mountains forming an arc across Central and Eastern Europe), *Mărăşeşti* (< *Mărăşeşti*, a small town in Vrancea County, Romania, known for the battle that was fought nearby during World War I, in 1917, between the Kingdom of Romania and the German Empire), *Snagov* (< *Snagov*, a commune north of Bucharest).

The strictly grammatical (morphological, etymological and semantic) observations that can be made in relation to the names listed above are scarce, as the context in which these names were attributed encouraged the plainest organisation of public space. No interest was paid to language innovation before 1989 because it was believed to promote individuality, which was seen as the primary source of inequality and dissatisfaction. In general, the names illustrated above perfectly fit the pattern of the wooden language: they leave little room for publicly acknowledged connotations that could harm the systematic order of socialist Romanian public space. Most of the names are derived from nouns (both common and proper), either in full forms or as various types of acronyms (*Albalact, Brifcor, CEC, CiCo, DERO, Faimar, Napolact, ROM, TAROM*; initialisms: *BCR, TVR*). Before 1989, all these names conveyed associative meanings that were related to values which were imposed as the very definition of "Romanianness": authenticity, tradition and high quality. The compulsory

---

[6] Although it is a trademark, in everyday communication *Eugenia* became generic, as it can currently refer to products that resemble the original ones (biscuit sandwich cookies with cocoa cream filling). There was a similar tendency with *DERO*, too, as soon as the detergents market began to diversify after 1989, but it is less common today.

nature of these meanings made them less "edible" for the Romanians: there were only a few who actually believed in these qualities.

Nevertheless, after 1989, when individuality started being welcomed in spite of the uniformity quite often promoted by globalisation, advertising agents revitalised the brands above by keeping their names and the associative meanings they conveyed (and, thus, the values underlying "Romanianness" as well). It is both the context and the people that changed. Due to their continuity, the brands span generations. While they tickle the nostalgic ego of those individuals whose youth was overrun by communist Romania (cf. German *Ostalgie*, Ostalgia, the nostalgia for aspects of social life that defined East Germany, manifested especially by people who experienced the Democrat German Republic when they were young), they also aim to educate newer generations into preserving and cultivating local values. The brand names analysed borrow the function of cultural mediators: through their well-established associated meanings, they communicate diachronically a series of values that pertain to a brand's identity and facilitate the survival of the brand (at least) in the local market. As Steiner (1998: 489) argues, "The words we speak bring with them far more knowledge, a far denser charge of feeling than we consciously possess; they multiply echo. Meaning is a function of social-historical antecedent and shared response".

Conclusion

Semiotically, in Romanian public space, a brand name is "a mechanism capable of producing a discourse, giving it significance and communicating it to a receiver" (Corbu 2009: 60, orig. Romanian, my translation), namely to the potential customer. Besides ensuring identification, a brand name is "a vector of signification that contains a set of values and that proposes, at the same time, a contract to its consumers (readers)" (ibid.). In other words, brand names identify referents while also advertising them and communicating, through the associative meanings they trigger, certain qualities that define "Romanianness", the Romanian national identity. Due to this function, the brand names that were the subject of this study act as cultural mediators: they perform a unidirectional negotiation/transfer of information, from the context of use in which they were created and established as such (i.e. before 1989), into the post-communist context in which they have currently evolved.

Paradoxically perhaps, the very same brand names are socioeconomic markers of both contexts, of the "particular conditions in society" (i.e. the "zeitgeist", Teutsch 2008: 253, or "fashion", Kryukova 2008: 399) that are representative of the two phases identified in the development of Romanian public space. Thus, the Romanian brand names previously illustrated have the role of cultural mediators that bridge generations of customers and that diachronically translocate messages, events and information, through the reassessment of the micro- and macro-environment in which they occur (Knowles 1998: 105).

References

Avram, M. 1997. *Anglicismele în limba română actuală* [Anglicisms in contemporary Romanian]. Bucureşti: Editura Academiei Române.

Bell, R. T. 2000. *Teoria şi practica traducerii* [The theory and practice of translation]. C. Gazi (trans.). Iaşi: Polirom.

Bergien, A. 2008. Global and regional considerations in the formation of company names. In *I nomi nel tempo e nello spazio: Atti del XXII Congresso Internazionale di Scienze Onomastiche, Pisa, 28 agosto–4 settembre 2005, vol. II: Onomastica e Societá*, M. G. Arcamone, D. Bremer, D. De Camilli and B. Porcelli (eds.), 289–298. Pisa: Edizioni ETS.

Boerrigter, R. 2007. Identity reflecting business names. In *Proceedings of the 21st International Congress of Onomastic Sciences Uppsala 19–24 August 2002*, vol. 3, E. Brylla & M. Wahlberg (eds.), 53–61. Uppsala: Språk- och folkminnesinstitutet.

Bugheşiu, A. 2011. The politics of Romanian brand names: then and now. In *Name and Naming. Proceedings of the International Conference on Onomastics, 1st edition: Multiethnic Connections in Anthroponymy, Baia Mare, 19–21 September 2011,* O. Felecan (ed.), 535–544. Cluj-Napoca: Editura Mega.

—. 2012. On Brands and Branding in the Romanian Space. In *Name and Naming: Synchronic and Diachronic Perspectives*, O. Felecan (ed.), 388–400. Newcastle upon Tyne: Cambridge Scholars Publishing.

Corbu, N. 2009. *Brandurile globale. O cercetare cros-culturală* [Global Brands. A cross-cultural research]. Bucureşti: Tritonic.

Dumitru, E. 2011. Reinventarea brandurilor româneşti din "Epoca de Aur" [The reinvention of Romanian brands from the "Golden Age"]. *Adevărul*, March 7. http://www.adevarul.ro/dosar/Branduri_comuniste_vandute_in_capitalism_0_439156382.html (retrieved 5 May 2012).

Felecan, D. 2011. Observaţii referitoare la configuraţia semiotică a unor nume de firme (NF) din spaţiul public românesc actual [Observations on the semiotic configuration of some firm names (FN) in contemporary Romanian public space]. In *Limba română: ipostaze ale variaţiei lingvistice. Actele celui de-al 10-lea Colocviu al Catedrei de limba română (Bucureşti, 3–4 decembrie 2010), vol. II: Pragmatică şi stilistică* [The Romanian language: Instances of linguistic variation. Proceedings of the 10th Colloquium of the Romanian Language Department (Bucharest, 3–4 December 2010), vol. II: Pragmatics and stylistics], R. Zafiu, C. Uşurelu and B. Oprea (eds.), 63–76. Bucureşti: Editura Universităţii din Bucureşti.

Felecan, O. 2008. Nomi delle instituzioni romene dopo il 1989 [Names of Romanian institutions after 1989]. In *I nomi nel tempo e nello spazio. Atti del XXII Congresso Internazionale di Scienze Onomastiche, Pisa 28 agosto–4 settembre 2005, vol. II: Onomastica e Società,* M.G. Arcamone, D. Bremer, D. de Camilli and B. Porcelli (eds.), 579–594. Pisa: Edizioni ETS.

Knowles, F. 1998. "New" versus "Old". In *The Pragmatics of Translation,* L. Hickey (ed.), 103–113. Clevedon: Multilingual Matters.

Kryukova, I. 2008. Russian advertising names as a matter of linguistic fashion. *Onoma* 43: 397–410.

Lungu-Badea, G. 2005. *Tendinţe în cercetarea traductologică* [Tendencies in translation research]. Timişoara: Editura Universităţii de Vest.

Merriam-Webster Online. http://www.merriam-webster.com/ (retrieved 10 May 2012).

Oxford Dictionaries Online. http://oxforddictionaries.com/ (retrieved 10 May 2012).

Panaitache, M. (n.d.). Mărcile comuniste azi, nostalgia din care iese profit [Communist trademarks today, a nostalgia that is a source of profit]. *Historia.ro.* http://www.historia.ro/exclusiv_web/general/articol/marcile-comuniste-azi-nostalgia-care-iese-profit#comment_form (retrieved 5 May 2012).

Pârlog, H. 1971. Termeni de origine engleză în publicistica română contemporană [Terms of English origin in Romanian contemporary journalism]. *Analele Universităţii din Timişoara,* Seria Ştiinţe Filologice IX (1/1971): 55–68.

—. 1999. The Anglo-fashion. In *Seventy Years of English and American Studies in Bulgaria. Papers of the International Conference held in Sofia, 1–3 October, 1998*, Z. Catalan, C. Stamenov and E. Pancheva (eds.), 93–99. Sofia: St. Kliment Ohridski Press.

Rzetelska-Feleszko, E. 2008. Proper names of shops and firms (retail and services) in post-communist countries. In *I nomi nel tempo e nello spazio: Atti del XXII Congresso Internazionale di Scienze Onomastiche, Pisa, 28 agosto–4 settembre 2005, vol. II: Onomastica e*

Societá, M.G. Arcamone, D. Bremer, D. De Camilli and B. Porcelli (eds.), 595–600. Pisa: Edizioni ETS.

Schack, J. 2008. Distinctive names: constraints on brand name creation. *Onoma* 43: 57–72.

Sjöblom, P. 2008. Multimodality of company names. *Onoma* 43: 351–380.

Steiner, G. 1998. *After Babel. Aspects of Language and Translation.* 3rd ed. Oxford: Oxford University Press.

Stoichiţoiu-Ichim, A. 2006. *Aspecte ale influenţei engleze în româna actuală* [Aspects of the influence of English on contemporary Romanian]. Bucureşti: Editura Universităţii din Bucureşti.

—. 2008. *Vocabularul limbii române actuale: dinamică, influenţe, creativitate* [The vocabulary of contemporary Romanian: dynamics, influences, creativity]. Bucureşti: ALL.

Straniero Sergio, F. 1998. Notes on cultural mediation. *The Interpreters' Newsletter* 8: 151–168. http://www.openstarts.units.it/dspace/bitstream/10077/2497/1/20Straniero.pdf (retrieved 5 May 2012).

Teutsch, A. 2008. Trademarks as indicators of the zeitgeist. *Onoma* 43: 251–276.

Van Langendonck, W. 2007. *Theory and Typology of Proper Names.* Berlin/New York: Mouton de Gruyter.

Wall-Street. 2007. Cele mai longevive branduri româneşti [The most long-lived Romanian brands]. http://www.wall-street.ro/slideshow/Marketing-PR/32734/Cele-mai-longevive-20-de-branduri-romanesti.html (retrieved 5 May 2012).

RESTAURANT NAMES IN THE CITY OF BUCHAREST: CROSS-CULTURAL AND SOCIOLINGUISTIC PERSPECTIVES

ADRIANA STOICHIŢOIU ICHIM
UNIVERSITY OF BUCHAREST, ROMANIA

Abstract

The aim of the present paper is to analyse, from a multidisciplinary perspective, the most frequent strategies and patterns of naming public houses (restaurants, pubs, bars, cafés and tea rooms, generally designed as PHs).

The main premise of this synchronic approach is that the dynamics of such names is strongly influenced – in post-communist Romanian society – by the complex interplay of economic, sociolinguistic and cultural factors involved in the globalisation process.

Using examples taken from Yellow Pages, websites, advertisements and advertorials published in Romanian newspapers, we looked at the special status of such names among other commercial names. A cross-cultural approach showed similarities between Romanian and other West European cultures as well as peculiarities determined by specific cultural and historical heritage.

By adopting a sociolinguistic perspective, the present paper intends to emphasise the motivations and the functions of identification, individualisation and advertising of this category of commercial names. From an onomastic point of view, the structural (formal) and semantic characteristics of the names under discussion have been analysed, focusing on the generic and specific components of the most frequent naming patterns.

Introduction

The aim of this study is to analyse, from a synchronic perspective, the most frequent strategies of naming restaurants, pubs, bars, clubs, cafés and tea rooms (henceforth referred to as public houses – PHs) located in the capital of Romania.

The corpus examined, consisting of 360 names of public houses (NPHs), has been extracted mainly from several sources: Istodor 2011 (a tourist guide providing essential information on the PHs located in the Historical Centre or Old Centre of Bucharest, including Lipscani street, one of the oldest in the city); weekly guides (*Şapte seri* 'seven evenings', *Zile şi nopţi* 'days and nights', *24 – Fun*) presenting the main events in the town, which include a comprehensive list of PHs in Bucharest. Websites, the Yellow Pages, advertisements and advertorials published in Romanian newspapers and travel guides have also been used as additional sources for a synchronic approach accounting for a period of three years (2009–2012). For a brief comparative analysis of the current naming trends in Bucharest and in other European capitals, four travel guidebooks (registering NPHs in Athens, Paris, Rome and Wien) have been used (Davenport and Foster 2007; Morris 2007; Bramblett and Kennedy 2007; Leidig and Zoech 2011).

The specific purposes of my investigation have led to a tripartite organisation of the present paper. Starting from the premise that NPHs depend, to a large extent, on the dynamics of the society and the period in which they were created and used, the first part of my contribution proposes a diachronic comparative approach to the naming practices during two previous stages of the Romanian history: the 110 examples collected from history books (Doicescu 2008: 36–51; Zaman 2007: 125–172), as well as magazines and newspapers published in the 1920s and 1930s seem to differ considerably from the NPHs occurring in the communist epoch (1945–1989), on the one hand, and from those occurring in present-day Romanian, on the other hand.

In the second section, we bring forward a theoretical framework for a synchronic sociolinguistic and cross-cultural approach to NPHs, focusing on their particular status, motivations and functions among other commercial names.

The third part of the paper aims firstly to establish the linguistic profile of NPHs, analysed from etymological, formal and lexical perspectives and, secondly, to identify similarities and differences between Romanian and foreign NPHs.

Historical Overview

Unanimously considered as the most prosperous period of the Romanian economy (when Bucharest was known as the "little Paris"), the interwar epoch favoured free enterprise and private property. According to the local naming tradition, numerous PHs were identified by the full name (*Dragomir Niculescu, Iordache Ionescu*), the surname (*Oteteleşanu, Capşa, Riegler, Frascatti*) or the first name (*Mircea*) of the male owner, preceded by popular generic terms (such as *bodegă* 'tavern', *birt* 'eatery') or by neologisms (such as *restaurant, café, terasă* 'pub located on a terrace'). As a matter of fact, the tradition of non-Romanian NPHs began in the first decades of the 19th century, when the first French commercial names, such as *Café Royal* or *Moulin Rouge*, were mentioned in historical sources (cf. Tomescu 2011: 122).

The cosmopolitan "atmosphere" of the Romanian capital accounts for the locals' inclination towards using foreign toponyms in naming restaurants (*Berlin*, *Lido*, *Colorado*, *Germania*, *Atlantic*, *Bavaria*, *Monte Carlo*), ethnonyms (*Restaurantul American* 'the American restaurant', *La Elveţian* 'at the Swiss'), brand names (such as *Suchard*, for a shop that used to sell sweets) or simply French or English syntagms evoking favourable connotations linked with elegance, quality or refinement (e.g. *Mon Jardin*, *Café de la Paix*, *Mon Caprice*, *High-Life*, *Melody Garden*).

Mythological and literary names (such as *Mercur*, *Fântâna Blanduziei* 'Blanduzia's fountain'), former common nouns (*Pescăruş* 'seagull', *Cina* 'the dinner') or some amusing names (*Grădina Brotăcei* 'the little frogs garden', *Leul şi cârnatul* 'the lion [name of the Romanian currency] and the sausage') range among the most frequent NPHs which displayed an interesting combination of traditionalism and modernity[1].

During the communist regime (1945–1989), the state-owned economy, the full control of markets, and the specific "wooden language" aimed at manipulating the consumers explain the peculiarities of the naming process. Apart from a few traditional NPHs, tolerated as marks of national cultural identity (*Caru' cu bere* 'the brew carriage', *Hanu' lui Manuc* 'Manuc's inn') or due to the fact that they suggested a European setting (*Athénée Palace*, *Monte Carlo*, *Atlantic, Melody*), the vast majority of PHs

---

[1] My translation of Romanian NPHs into English respects the original patterns, determined by the rich nominal inflection and the existence of three genders (masculine, feminine, neuter). The Romanian definite article (*-ul* / *-u*' for masculine and neuter singular; *-a* for feminine singular nouns), equivalent to the English *the*, is agglutinated at the end of the word it refers to (e.g.: *leu* 'lion' – *leul* 'the lion'; *baladă* 'ballad' – *balada* 'the ballad').

were given politically-oriented names, motivated by the nationalistic obsessions of Nicolae Ceauşescu's regime. Foreign toponyms were strictly limited to several names of capital cities of (former) communist European countries (e.g. *Berlin*, *Budapesta*, *Varşovia*). Besides Romanian toponyms, such as the names of the historical provinces (*Moldova*, *Muntenia*), rivers (*Dunărea*, *Delta Dunării*), forests (*Codrii Cosminului*), vineyards (*Odobeşti*), one can also take note of historical anthroponyms (such as *Bucur*, the shepherd considered to be the founder of *Bucureşti* 'Bucharest'), names evoking Romanian folklore (*Mărul de aur* 'the golden apple' – title of a fairy tale, *Romanţa* 'the sentimental song', *Balada* 'the ballad') or common nouns used as proper names, which were not only completely inadequate for a PH, but also highly "politicised" (e.g. *Prietenia* 'the friendship', *Orizont* 'horizon' which has the metaphorical meaning of 'future', *Feroviarul* 'the railway employee').

The dissolution of the communist regime in 1989, which brought about the return to private property and free enterprise, the absence of political intrusion in naming practices, the abundance and variety of goods and services provided by the consumer society and, last but not least, the globalisation process have in various ways left their mark on the structure and use of NPHs. Although new denominating practices and patterns appeared during the last two decades, this topic has only recently drawn the attention of Romanian linguists (see Tomescu 2003 and 2011; Felecan, D. 2011; Felecan O. 2011).

Theoretical Background

If we accept the idea that NPHs, like other commercial names, are *complex conventional signs*, motivated not only linguistically, but also socially, economically and culturally, a sociolinguistic approach – based on the "close intertwining of linguistic and social facts" (Spolsky 2008: 4) – might throw light on the naming process and the values associated to certain naming patterns within a linguistic community. According to Baylon (2002: 25), sociolinguistics is interested in "tout ce qui est étude de la langue ou de la parole, ou du langage dans un contexte social, culturel ou comportamental" ('everything that involves the study of language or discourse, as well as in the investigation of language in a social, cultural or behavioural context'). A detailed discussion on the sociolinguistic and pragmatic meaning of proper names can be found in Vauxelaire (2005: 792–804). Sociolinguistics can also account for the impact of the relationship between locutor-owner and receiver-customer in selecting the appropriate naming patterns, according to several functions of company names identified by Sjöblom (2005: 268), besides those of *individualising* and *advertising* functions:

- The informative function refers to the (more or less adequate) knowledge the customer can get directly from transparent (motivated) NPHs or indirectly (implicitly) from non-transparent (non-motivated) names.
- The persuasive function is performed by means of positive images and various figurative, playful or ludic structures meant to attract the customer and sell the product.
- The sociocultural integrative function presupposes an implicit consensus between the owner and the customer, in terms of shared opinions, symbolic values and attitudes related to the sociocultural environment and, particularly, to the language in which the NPHs are coined. (For more comments on the role of the sociocultural context, behaviours, attitudes and prejudices, from a sociolinguistic point of view, cf. Baylon 2002: 54–57; Calvet 2009: 42–45; Spolsky 2008: 24–27.)

Since commercial names are coined and can function in a national-linguistic and commercial culture, a cross-cultural analysis of the current naming trends and inventories of NPHs in Bucharest and four other European capitals (Paris, Rome, Wien and Athens) may reveal not only peculiarities related to the history, geography and cultural traditions of a specific place, but also commonalities deriving from a large array of factors connected with the globalisation process and the homogenisation of human needs, goods and services in the consumer society, as emphasised in Baudrillard 2010 (for such comparative analyses, see, among others, Härmä 2000; Wochele 2007; Kolléca 1998).

From an onomastic perspective (taking into account the words incorporated), most company names are complex appositional structures including a specific component (a proper name, such as an anthroponym or a toponym) preceded or followed – according to the specific syntactic rules of an idiom – by a generic component (a common noun functioning as an appellative). The generic component can be omitted from the denominative patterns. According to a widespread opinion, proper names are monoreferential (they refer only onymically to a unique referent), are untranslatable and they aim first of all at identifying/individualising companies, shops, hotels, public houses, etc. In the current paper, appellatives (such as Romanian words *bar*, *bistro*, *club*, *han*, *restaurant* – see below) are seen as common nouns that designate and classify referents (while proper names nominate them). The mode of referring, in the case of appellatives, is semantic; consequently, they can be fully translated.

Sklyarenko and Sklyarenko (2000: 281–282) state that proper names with the highest degree of onomasticity have the lowest degree of lexical meaning, being characterised by an obvious social determination and the possibility of being subject to change anytime, following political or social changes (for instance, during the communist regime, a restaurant called initially *Perla* 'the pearl', changed its name to *Varşovia* 'Warsaw' and ended by being renamed, after 1989, as *Balcic*, the name of a city that used to be part of Romania and became part of Bulgaria, after the Second World War).

The Generic Component of NPHs

Despite their importance for the appropriate classification of PHs, generic terms that are frequently included in nominal designations (such as *Taverna Sârbului* 'the Serbian's tavern', *Waterloo Tavern*, *Trattoria Verdi*, *Ceainăria Tabiet* 'the settled habit tea house') have been neglected in Romanian onomastic studies. An inventory of such common nouns selected from my corpus and set against the list of NDU, NPR and OALD will throw light on the dynamics and diversity of this semantic field of great interest, not only from an etymological point of view, but also for historical and sociocultural information.

The terms discussed below illustrate, on the one hand, the hospitality of the Romanian language and its great force of assimilating both old (Slavonic, Serbo-Croatian, Bulgarian, Turkish) and neological loanwords (English, French, Italian, German). On the other hand, one can notice the clear predominance of suffixal derivation (especially in the traditional vocabulary, where the suffixes *-erie/-ărie* are the most productive), which denotes the creativity of Romanian language (for a detailed discussion on the correlative concepts of *hospitality* and *creativity*, see Avram 1993).

The dynamic and open character of the semantic field of common nouns (appellatives), used as generic terms in the structure of NPHs, is clearly proved by its continuous enrichment with loanwords, calques or derivatives and compounds from Romanian or foreign roots. I have identified a list of terms in Romanian dictionaries and in dictionaries of neologisms that can be grouped from an etymological point of view in the following categories (where the generic terms are presented in alphabetical order). Those preceded by an asterisk are not in active use any longer or are unsuitable in relation to modern standard Romanian:

- Neological loanwords: *bar* 'public bar' (< Fr. *bar*); *bistrou* 'eatery' (< Fr. *bistro*); *braserie* 'ale house/eatery' (< Fr. *brasserie*); *bufet* 'refreshment bar' (< Fr. *buffet*; It. *buffetto*); *cantină* 'canteen' (< Fr. *cantine*); *fast-food* 'fast food restaurant'; It. *gelateria* 'ice cream shop'; *locantă* 'public house' (< It. *locanda*; Gr. *lokanta*); Engl. *lounge*; *patiserie* 'pastry shop / bakery' (< Fr. *pâtisserie*); It. *pizzeria*; Engl. *(Irish) pub*; Engl. *public house*; *restaurant* 'exquisite public house' (< Fr. *restaurant*); *rotiserie* 'rotisserie'/ 'steak and grill' (< Fr. *rôtisserie*); Engl. *snack-bar*; Engl. *steak-house*; *terasă* (1) 'terrace'; (2) 'pub located on a terrace' (< Fr. *terrasse*); It. *trattoria* 'less formal Italian restaurant'.
- Old loanwords: **birt* 'less formal ale house/eatery' (< Srb. *birt*); **bodegă* 'public house / tavern' (< Germ. *Bodega*); *cafenea* 'café' (< Tk. *kahvehane*); Fr. *café (-bar)*; **cârciumă* '(popular) pub' (< Sl. *kručima*); Engl. *grădină* (1) 'garden'; (2) 'pub located in a garden' (< Bg., Srb. *gradina*); *han* (1) *'road side inn'; (2) 'traditional Romanian restaurant'; *tavernă* 'Greek informal restaurant' (< Fr. *taverne*; Germ. *Tavern*).
- Derivative nouns obtained from old roots: **berărie* 'beer / ale house' (< Rom. *bere* + *-ărie*); *ceainărie* 'tea room' (< Rom. *ceai* < Rus. *čajnyi* + *-ărie*); *cofetărie* 'confectioner's (café)' (< Rom. *cofet* < Gr. *ko(n)feta* + *-ărie*); **lăptărie* 'milk bar' (< Rom. *lapte* < Lat. *lacte(m)* + *-ărie*); *plăcintărie* 'pie shop' (< Rom. *plăcintă* < Lat. *placenta* + *-ărie*).
- Compound words: **autoservire* (< Rom. *auto-* + *servire*, cf. Engl. *self-service*); *bufet-expres* 'snack bar' (< Rom. *bufet* + *expres*).
- Lexical calques of structure following the pattern of recent loans: *clătitărie* 'pancake shop' (< Rom. *clătită* < Sl. *klatiti* + *-ărie*, cf. Fr. *crêperie*); *şaormărie* 'shawarma shop' (< Rom. *shaorma* < Arab *shawarma* + *-ărie*).

Interesting semantic changes can be identified in two cases: Rom. *casă*, inherited from Latin, has developed a specialised meaning in the field of NPHs, that is 'traditional Romanian restaurant' (e.g. *Casa Capşa* [surname of the founder], *Casa Veche* 'the old house', *Casa Gorjeană* 'the house from Gorj' [district in southwest Romania], *Casa cu Tei* 'the house with lime trees'). The same recent specialised meaning has been acquired by the word *han*, of Turkish origin, whose etymological meaning in the old and middle period of literary Romanian (i. e. from the 16th to the 18th century) was 'road side inn' (e.g. *Hanul lui Manuc* 'Manuc's inn', *Hanul Berarilor* 'the brewers' inn', *Hanul Voievozilor* ' the princes' inn').

As shown by the above mentioned generic terms, after the fall of the communist regime, the semantic field under discussion was seriously modified (with respect to both quantity and quality), because of the Romanian society's tendency towards attaining cultural homogenisation within an international globalising context. The most striking feature of this dynamic field – from the point of view of diaphasic (or stylistic) variation – is a rich synonymy between Romanian older words, typical of the standard language (such as *berărie*, *cafenea* or *bufet*) and recent loans of English origin (such as *pub*, *coffee house* or *snack bar*), which are favoured by the owners of such PHs, as a successful selling strategy, and by their potential or (already) loyal customers for their emotionally positive associations.

The Specific Component of NPHs

The specific components of PHs are given to single, specially discerned objects, not only in order to identify them, but also in order to be persuasive, convincing and even amusing, without excluding manipulation (according to Felecan, D. 2011: 65–66, in semiotic terms, a company name can be seen as a message sent by the locutor-owner to the receiver-customer). Yet, in time, what started as a unique designation was soon to be acknowledged as a generally accepted name, by means of some echoing techniques that are connected to autonymous use (for further details on autonymy, see Roibu 2010: 69–85).

Generally, this category of names can be classified according to different criteria, such as the degree of motivation and transparency (cf. Ainiala 1998: 44; Vauxelaire 2005: 161) or their relation to different onomasticon domains (cf. Akselberg 2005: 74). Following Sjöblom (2005: 268), who stated that "the meaning of proper names should first and foremost be considered in terms of the functional meaning of the names", three main categories of specific NPHs can be found:

a) Specific names meant to identify the referent in an objective way, by using proper Romanian or foreign names, such as toponyms evoking a specific cuisine (*Valencia*, *Santorini*, *Persia*, *Pekin*), or the owner's name (*Jerry's Pizza*, *Edgar's Pub*).
b) Specific names with additional connotative values that are supposed to have a strong persuasive effect on the target customers. Such names are based on associations and allusions, referring to historical and cultural heritage (*Trattoria Verdi*, *Van Gogh Grand Café*, *La Bucur* 'At Bucur's' [*Bucur* is considered to be the founder of the city of

Bucharest], *1001 Nopţi* '1001 nights', *Absinteria Sixtina*). Metaphoric or symbolic English names include *Olive Garden*, *Spice Club*, *Wings Club*, *Open Doors*, *Happy Time*, *Off the Records*, *Underworld Club*, *The Silver Church*, *Café Pink*.

c) A noticeable category of specific names meant to amuse the potential customers includes the so-called "non-trivial name" (cf. Bušs 2012). Idiomatic colloquial expressions of French origin – *Déjà vu* 'already seen', *Tête-à-tête* 'face to face', *Bouche Bée* 'great surprise [literally, mouth wide open]' – can be found as names of cafés. Ironical, malicious or even aggressive slang terms are: *Tralala*, coming from the Romanian colloquial expression *a fi tralala* 'to be crazy', *La Mitocanu* 'at the cad's'. The predicative phrase *E varză*, used in teenagers' slang with a negative figurative meaning ('devastated', 'destroyed', 'pell-mell') is the non-trivial name of a restaurant located on the campus of University Politehnica of Bucharest. As an example of an amusing blended word, one may invoke *Cafepedia* < Rom. *café[nea]* + *[Wiki]pedia*. Another amusing name resulting from intentionally created homophony is the bar name *Bal à Mouk* that can be understood by Romanian customers either as a French complex name ('*Ball at Mouk's*') or as the popular Romanian word of Turkish origin *balamuc* (with the informal and obsolete meaning of Engl. 'madhouse').

A more detailed semantic typology of NHPs may be established, based on the categorisation of hotel names proposed by Wochele (2007: 320–322).

In the group of strongly motivated NPHs, one may find, firstly, proper names evoking:

- the first name (*Silviu's Restaurant*, *Bruno Wine & Bar*) or the surname (*O'Hara Irish Pub*) of the owner;
- the surname of the Romanian founder: *Casa Vernescu* 'Vernescu house', *Casa Capşa* 'Capşa house';
- the nickname of the owner: *La Cocoşatu* 'at the hunchback's';
- the name of the street where the PH is located: *Cafeneaua Smârdan* 'Smârdan café', *La Calderon 80*) or the name of a neighbouring institution: *Bistro Opereta*, *Arena Restaurant* (by metonymical transfer);
- a domestic toponym: *Vama Veche 9*, *Bistro Jariştea*;
- a foreign toponym: *Trattoria Roma*, *Beirut* (Lebanese restaurant), *Berlin Club*;
- a foreign event or holiday: *Oktoberfest Pub*;

- the name of a famous figure from history (*Burebista, Decebal* – kings of Dacia, the ancient name of the territory which mainly corresponds to present-day Romania), art (*Da Vinci*, *Lautrec*, *Michelangelo Caffé & Gelato*), science (*Bistro Montignac*, hinting at the creator of a miraculous diet designed for losing weight very quickly), mythology (*Uranus Café*, *Thalia*, *Neptunus*), religion (*Saint George*, *St. Patrick Irish Pub & Restaurant*) and literature (*Godot Café*, *Robin Hood*, *Ali Baba*, *Gargantua*);
- the title of literary works: *1001 Nopţi* '1001 nights', *Decameron*, *Livada cu vişini* 'the cherry orchard'.

Secondly, there are common nouns onymised that are being used as proper names referring to:

- profession of the target customer (*Bankers*, *Cafeneaua Actorilor* 'the actors' café', *Paparazzi Café & Bistro*) or their hobbies, such as football (*Restaurant Golazo Sports Bar*);
- dishes and drinks: *Alioli*, *Green Tea*, *Caffé & Latte*, *Pizza and Paste*, *Caffé Frappé*, *Sangria*;
- comfort offered to the customer: *Sofa restaurant & Bistro-Café*, *La taifas* ('at a chat');
- artistic terms: *Barocco Bar*, *Dada Bistro*;
- musical terms: *Piano Café*, *Art Jazz Club*, *Hard Rock Café*;
- zoonyms: *Elephant Pub*, *Chat Noir Club*, *Cool Cat*, *Escargot Bistro*, *Piranha Club;*
- the atmosphere or the advantages offered to the customer: *Café Bohème, La Delicii* 'at the delights', *La 100 de beri* ' at the 100 beers', *Oasis Sport & Leisure.*

From the category of NPHs with a less transparent motivation, one can note abstract names (such as *Revenge*, *Traffic*, *Control*, *Tribute*) and a few names carrying pejorative connotations as a result of their being ironically associated with the clichés of the communist regime: *Fabrica* 'the factory', *Atelierul Mecanic* 'the mechanic workshop', *El Grande Comandante* ''the great commander'.

A Formal Classification of Romanian NPHs

At a formal level, the overwhelming majority of NPHs consist of more than one word. The naming patterns may be classified according to their syntactic and morphological peculiarities. Such a taxonomy is based on:

a) The number of words within NPHs:
   - a single Romanian (*Vatra* 'the fireplace') or foreign word (*Embassy*, *Heritage*, *Oasis*);
   - two words, such as: *La Mama* ('at my mother's'), *Hanul Berarilor* ('the brewers' inn'), *Old City*, *French Bakery*, *Chat Noir*;
   - three or more words, such as: *Bohemia Tea House*, *Trattoria Don Vito*, *Piranha Club & Pub*.

b) The syntactic structure of NPHs:
   - a noun phrase with a modifier placed in the postposition, according to the Romanian usual word order: *Şarpele Roz* ('the pink snake'), *Taverna Sârbului* ('the Serbian's tavern') or in anteposition (particularly in English or hybrid constructions): *White Horse*, *Vintage Pub*, *Van Gogh Grand Café*, *Cucina, the Italian Kitchen*, *De Gustibus Restaurant;*
   - preposition *la* ('at') + common noun: *La Mama* ('at my mother's'), *La Scena* ('at/ on the stage');
   - preposition *la* ('at') + first name or nickname: *La Cocoşatu* ('at the hunchback's'). The same syntactic structure is used for naming French restaurants (*Chez Marie*, *Chez Alain)* or Italian restaurants (*Da Giulio Ristorante*).

A more detailed typology of English NPHs, including acronyms (*G Point*, *OK café*, *B52 The Club*) and predicative phrases (such as *We are not angels*) can be found in Tomescu (2011: 120).

From a morphological point of view, there should be a note of a frequent pattern used to connote the "Englishness" (cf. Härmä 2000: 111) of an NPH, i.e. the English genitive: *Edgar's Pub*, *Gyuri's Pub*, *Dreamers'Pub & Restaurant.*

A Cross-cultural Approach to NPHs

Since the downfall of the totalitarian regime in December 1989, the economic, social and cultural factors influencing the naming practices of PHs have been very similar to those in other European countries. The increasingly higher amount of non-Romanian generic terms and specific names of PHs is motivated not only by the political openness towards Western Europe, the development of international tourism and of intercultural communication, but also by the persuasive function of NPHs and by subjective factors such as anglophilia and snobbish behaviour.

Foreign influences exercised upon NPHs have been discussed by Tomescu (2003 and 2011) and Felecan, O. (2011). Similar studies have been published by Härmä (2000), on Finnish names, and Kolléca (1998), on contemporary Greek names. What is noticeable in this context is the similarity between Romanian and Greek NPHs with regard to the foreign influences: English is at the top of the list, followed by Italian, French, Spanish, German and Asian languages (cf. Kolléca 1998: 179).

From the cross-cultural point of view, the most striking aspect is the huge number of English NPHs (generic, but mostly specific names, which may be seen mainly as a consequence of the globalisation process). A comprehensive approach to the complex reasons underlying the privileged status of English, as a global language and as a "language of opportunity" may be found in Crystal (2000). As pointed out by the aforementioned author, "English has penetrated deeply into the international domains of political life, business, safety, communications, entertainment, the media and education" (Crystal 2000: 25). A full picture of the impact of English on different languages is presented in Etiemble (1964) and Stoichiţoiu Ichim (2003 and 2006). Constantinescu, Popovici and Ştefănescu (2002: 186) point out that traces of English influence may also be found in the names of companies, restaurants, snack bars, shops, boutiques, sport clubs. According to Tomescu (2011), the percentage of English words in Romanian commercial names is 49.37%.

Besides international names of American origin (such as *McDonald's*, *Burger King*, *KFC*), a large number of English NPHs (mostly multicomponent words preserving their original spelling) are motivated not only by the prestige of the source-language, but also by the positive connotations and emotions associated by both owners and customers with the British and, particularly, American "lifestyle". A few examples from a very long list include: *Old City*, *Old School*, *White Horse*, *Gin Factory*, *Open Doors*, *Funky Lounge*, *Iron City*, *Guest House*, *Friends Pub*, *Four Seasons*, *The Harbour*, *The Office*, *Downtown*, *The Fifties*, *Sheriff's*.

Comparing the situation in the five large European cities referred to in this paper, one can note that Anglo-American NPs are rarely found in Paris (as a result of a purist language policy against *franglais*) and are relatively under-represented in Wien (e.g. *Point of Sale*, *Silver Bar*, *Planter's Club*). By contrast, the predominance of English NPHs is evident in Athens (e.g. *Jimmy and the Fish*, *Nick's place*, *Blue Velvet*) and in Rome (*Trinity College*, *Drunken Ship*, *Rock Castle Café*, *Stardust*).

According to a long tradition of cultural relations between France and Romania, quite a large number of NPHs are borrowed from French (*Les Bourgeois*, *La Muse*, *Légère Café*, *Café Bohème*, *Bonne Bouche*, *Bouche Bée*, *Caffé Frappé*, *Déjà-vu*, *Escargot Bistro*) or Italian (*Gallo Nero*, *Il Corso*, *Vecchio 1812*, *Pizza Forno d'Oro*, *Quattro Stagioni*). Their motivation in Romanian is quite similar to the one which is manifest in present-day Finnish: “French and Italian cultures obviously share some features which make them appealing to a Finnish audience. These features include things like elegance, ‘Southern’ quality and way of life, fashion, arts, food and wine, more or less glorious history language, etc.” (Härmä 2000: 116). The same positive associations justify the presence of Italian NPHs (*Bella Romana*, *Etrusco*, *Arlecchino*) and French NHPs (*Belle Époque*, *Renaissance*) in Athens.

German influence is illustrated in Romanian by a very small group of NPHs (*Oktoberfest Pub*, *Kulturhaus*, *Bierhaus*, *Wienerwald*). Some Spanish names that are worth mentioning include *Alioli Tapas*, *Tortilla*, *El Dictador*, *El Primer Comandante*, *Sangria*. “Exotic” cuisine is represented by Indian (*Karishma*, *Ramayana*), Japanese (*Sushi ko*) and Chinese NPHs (preserving their original name, such as *Wu Xing*, but more frequently translating it into Romanian: *Templul soarelui*, ‘the temple of the sun’, *Oraşul interzis* ‘the forbidden city’).

In Bucharest, a new, obvious trend consists of the formation of multiple-term hybrid names, incorporating words of different origins: Romanian and Italian (*Restaurant d’Amici*), English and Italian (*Trendy Pizza*, *Quattro Stagioni Events*), German and English (*Oktoberfest Pub*).

Among the main peculiarities of NPHs in these five large cities one may note: a few Romanian NPHs include the owner’s name, while in Rome, the hypocoristic forms of male first names are very frequent (*Pizzeria da Gino*, *Da Giggetto*, *Da Cesaretto*). Naming patterns including local and foreign macro- or micro-toponyms have been registered in Rome and Athens, but most frequently in Paris (*L’Alsace*, *Vallé de la Marne*, *Côté Seine*) and Bucharest (*Waterloo Tavern*, *Old Dublin*, *Trafalgar Pub*, *Santorini Greek Restaurant*). And finally, highly expressive and amusing NPHs are found in Paris (*Au Pied du Cochon*, *La Poule au Pot*, *Le Dos de la Baleine*, *Le Bœuf à la Mode*).

Concluding Remarks

The names of PHs are a subject of general interest not only for onomasticians, but also for social and cultural historians as well as for specialists in sales and marketing strategies.

The sociolinguistic approach allowed me to analyse NPHs as a special type of conventional sign in relation to their functions of individualisation and advertising. Sociolinguistics permitted a deeper understanding of the relation between the locutor-owner and the receiver-customer and of the persuasive strategies involved in commercial communication.

The onomastic analysis identified the specific formal structures and a large variety of semantic categories. From a cross-cultural perspective, special attention has been given to the motivations and to the mechanisms of the borrowing process in contemporary Romanian.

Although representing a mere preliminary analysis, the present study proves, on the one hand, the existence of a high degree of universality in the most frequent naming practices and, on the other hand, the tendency of present-day Romanian to adjust its patterns of naming PHs in accordance with the characteristics of the sociocultural Romanian environment.

References

Ainiala, T. 1998. On defining the proper name and the place name. In *Proceedings of the XIXth International Congress of Onomastic Sciences Aberdeen, August 4–11, 1996: Vol. 1*, W. F. H. Nicolaisen (ed.), 43–48. Aberdeen: University of Aberdeen.

Akselberg, G. 2005. The structure of the onomasticon and name classification. In *Proceedings of the 21st International Congress of Onomastic Sciences Uppsala, August 19–24, 2002: Vol. 1*, E. Brylla and M. Wahlberg (eds.), 67–78. Uppsala: Språk- och folkminnesinstitutet.

Avram, M. 1993. La créativité et l'«hospitalité» du roumain [Creativity and "hospitality" of the Romanian language]. *Revue roumaine de linguistique* 38 (1–3): 23–26.

Baudrillard, J. 2010. *The consumer society. Myths and structures*. Los Angeles–London–New Delhi–Singapore–Washington DC: SAGE.

Baylon, C. 2002. *Sociolinguistique. Société, langue et discours* [Sociolinguistics. Society, language and discourse]. 2nd edition. Paris: Armand Colin.

Bramblett, R. and Kennedy, J. 2007. *Roma Top 10*. Bucureşti: Litera.

Bušs, O. 2012. Non-trivial names for Latvian shops, bars, restaurants and entertainment business (unpublished communication presented at the International symposium *Names and cultures in a commercial environment. Turku, June 14–16, 2012*).

Calvet, L.-J. 2009. *La sociolinguistique* [Sociolinguistics]. 6th edition. Paris: Presses Universitaires de France.

Constantinescu, I., Popovici, V. and Ştefănescu, A. 2002. Romanian. In *English in Europe*, M. Görlach (ed.), 168–194. Oxford: Oxford University Press.

Crystal, D. 2000. *English as a global language*. Cambridge: University Press.

Davenport, C. and Foster, J. 2007. *Atena Top 10.* Bucureşti: Litera.

Doicescu, G. 2008. *Captivantul Bucureşti interbelic* [The charming interwar Bucharest]. Bucureşti: Vremea.

Etiemble, R. 1964. *Parlez-vous franglais*? [Do you speak Franglais?]. Paris: Gallimard.

Felecan, D. 2011. Observaţii referitoare la configuraţia semiotică a unor nume de firme (NF) din spaţiul public românesc actual [Observations on the semiotic configuration of certain company names (FN) in contemporary Romanian public space]. In *Limba română: ipostaze ale variaţiei lingvistice* [Romanian language: hypostases of linguistic variation]: *Vol 2*. R. Zafiu, C. Uşurelu and H. Bogdan Oprea (eds.), 63–76. Bucureşti: Editura Universităţii din Bucureşti.

Felecan, O. 2011. Tipologia numelor de firme din spaţiul public românesc actual [The typology of company names in contemporary Romanian public space]. In: *Limba română: ipostaze ale variaţiei lingvistice* [Romanian language: hypostases of linguistic variation]: *Vol 1*. R. Zafiu, C. Uşurelu and H. Bogdan Oprea (eds.), 249–258. Bucureşti: Editura Universităţii din Bucureşti.

Härmä, J. 2000. French business-names in contemporary Finnish. In: *Onomastik. Akten des 18. Internationalen Kongresses für Namenforschung, Trier, 12–17 April 1993* [Onomastics. Proceedings of the 18th international congress on names study], 110–117. Tübingen: Max Niemeyer Verlag.

Istodor, E. 2011. *Lipscani. Ghid turistic & de chefuri* [Lipscani street. A guide for tourism & parties]. Bucureşti: Art.

Kolléca, J. 1998. Appellations étrangères de salles de divertissement et d'établissements gastronomiques du Grand Athènes [Foreign appellatives for entertainment rooms and restaurants in Greater Athens]. In *Proceedings of the XIXth international congress of onomastic sciences, Aberdeen, August 4–11, 1996. Vol. 1*, W. F. H. Nicolaisen (ed.), 179–184. Aberdeen: University of Aberdeen.

Leidig, M. and Zoech, I. 2011. *Viena Top 10*. Bucureşti: Litera.

Morris, E. 2007. *Paris*. Bucureşti: Ad Libri.

NDU = Oprea, I., Pamfil C.-G., Radu, R. and Zăstroiu, V. 2009. *Noul dicţionar universal al limbii române* [The new universal dictionary of Romanian], 3rd edition. Bucureşti-Chişinău: Litera Internaţional.

NPR = *Le Nouveau Petit Robert* (sous la direction de J. Rey-Debove et A. Rey). 2004. Paris: Dictionnaires Le Robert.

OALD = Hornby, A. S. 2005. *Oxford Advanced Learner's Dictionary of Current English*, 7th editon. S. Wehmeier (chief ed.). Oxford: Oxford University Press.

Roibu, M. 2010. On Autonymy (with Reference to Romanian). *Revue roumaine de linguistique* 55 (1): 69–85.

Sjöblom, P. 2005. The problem of meaning and function related to company names. In *Proceedings of the 21st International congress of onomastic sciences. Uppsala, August 19–24, 2002. Vol. 1*, E. Brylla and M. Wahlberg (eds.), 264–276. Uppsala: Språk-och folkminnesinstitutet.

Sklyarenko, A. and Sklyarenko, O. 2002. Interrelationship between common nouns and proper nouns. In *Proceedings of the 21st International Congress of Onomastic Sciences Uppsala, August 19–24, 2002: Vol. 1*, E. Brylla and M. Wahlberg (eds.), 276–282. Uppsala: Språk-och folkminnesinstitutet.

Spolsky, B. 2008. *Sociolinguistics*. Oxford: Oxford University Press.

Stoichiţoiu Ichim, A. 2003. "Romgleza": opţiune personală sau efect al globalizării? ['Romgleza': individual option or effect of the globalization process?]. In *Identitate românească şi integrare europeană* [Romanian identity and European integration], G. Gabor (ed.). 95–103. Bucureşti: Ars Docendi.

—. 2006. *Aspecte ale influenţei engleze în româna actuală* [Aspects of English influence upon present-day Romanian]. Bucureşti: Editura Universităţii din Bucureşti.

Tomescu, D. 2003. Noms commerciaux étrangers dans l'onomastique roumaine d'aujourd'hui [Foreign commercial names in present-day Romanian onomastics]. In *La langue et les parlants / Language and its users / Limba şi vorbitorii*. T. Slama–Cazacu (ed.), 168–175. Bucharest: Arvin Press.

—. 2011. L'emprunt des noms commerciaux anglais dans l'onomastique roumaine actuelle [The loan of English commercial names in present-day-Romanian onomastics]. In *Proceedings of the international conference Applied linguistics today – between theory and practice, Novi Sad, October 29–November 1, 2009*. S. Guduric, and D. Tocanac, (eds.), 117–123.

Vauxelaire, J.-L. 2005. *Les noms propres – une analyse lexicologique et historique* [Proper names – a lexicological and historical analysis]. Paris: Honoré Champion Éditeur.

Wochele, H. 2007. Hotel names in Italy and Romania – a comparative analysis. In *Names in commerce and industry: Past and present*. L. Kremer and E. Ronneberger–Sibold (eds.), 317–329. Berlin: Logos Verlag.

Zamani, L. 2007. *Comerţ şi loisir în vechiul Bucureşti* [Trade and loisir in old Bucharest]. Bucureşti: Vremea.

List of Abbreviations

Bg. = Bulgarian; Engl. = English; Fr. = French; Germ. = German; Gr. = Greek; It. = Italian; Lat. = Latin; Rom. = Romanian; Rus. = Russian; Sl. = Old Slavonic; Srb. = Serbo-Croatian; Tk. = Turkish.

PART II

LOCAL SEPARATION AND CULTURAL IDENTITY

NAMES IN ITALIAN SLOGANS

PAOLA COTTICELLI-KURRAS
UNIVERSITY OF VERONA, ITALY
AND ENZO CAFFARELLI
UNIVERSITY OF ROMA TOR VERGATA, ITALY

Abstract

Our study aims at describing what function slogans used to have and still have in the field of advertising, what image of Italian culture they could and can provide, and how. The study has an interdisciplinary approach, taking into account language analysis, semiotics, psychology of advertising (economic marketing strategies) and cultural anthropology. In our paper, we will focus on the company names employed in the selected corpus of approximately 500 Italian slogans and we will show the interrelationship between the slogans and what these names represent. Our results confirm how general research on the formation of brand names requires a linguistic approach to succeed and to be implemented in a major industry. Through the analysis of rhetorical figures, neo-formations and special connotations found in slogans, we can conclude that most of them are created for an Italian audience because they are based on puns on the on the semantic, phonetic and lexical level: only a native speaker can decode the right message and understand the underlying pun. The connotations emerging from the slogans provide further insight into the cultural features of the Italian consumer.

Introduction

In the business world, communication and advertising are targeted to a growing interest in the role and function of an advertisement together with brand naming, its social implications and its communicative power. Studies on trends in the development of trade names (brand names) and in the language of advertising have become more and more frequent over the past two decades, increasingly using typical tools of linguistic analysis.

It has been repeatedly stressed that the study of phonology, morphology and semantics is of the utmost importance. This fact additionally confirms that research on strategies of the formation of product names also requires a linguistic approach to be successfully implemented.

The history of the language of advertising teaches us that those slogans that are created by advertisers or famous writers who worked with famous advertising agencies to produce successful campaigns have survived in the collective memory. A successful slogan can be associated with a major brand for many generations and often intensifies awareness, as in the following examples: *Fernet Branca ti digestimola* (1967–68) ('*Fernet Branca* stimulates your digestion'; *digestimola* is a blending neo-formation between *digestion* 'digestion' and *stimolare* 'to stimulate', used only in the language of advertisement); *Metti un tigre nel motore* (1962) ('Put a tiger in the engine'); *Chiamami PERONI, sarò la tua birra* (1970–71) ('Call me PERONI, I'll be your beer'); *UniCreditBANCA al servizio delle tue idee* ('UniCreditBANCA, at the service of your ideas').

In our paper, we will present a study of the interrelationship between the slogans of Italian advertising, the names employed in them, and what these names represent (see De Stefani 2004, s.v. *slogan*). The term *slogan* entered in Italy in 1930 when the producer of electric batteries Magneti Marelli gave a statement about the term itself as a *terminus technicus* of adverting language brought out its own slogan: "Magneti Marelli è la batteria che dura di più" ('*Magneti Marelli* is the longest life battery'). The definition of slogan they gave is as follows: "Con la parola slogan si indica in gergo pubblicitario il motto creato per caratterizzare un prodotto, ed al quale viene costantemente accoppiato in ogni manifestazione pubblicitaria. Lo slogan ha la funzione di ricordare il prodotto". ('The word slogan in advertising language indicates the motto created to characterise a product, and which is constantly paired in every advertising situation. The slogan has the function to remember the product'). Our study considers, for instance, commercial names, or product[1] and corporate names (for Italian commercial names see Caffarelli 2011). The analysis seeks to take into account the type of market linked to the product concerned: the international, national or regional market.

Our study aims at describing what function slogans used to have and still have in the field of advertising, what image of the Italian culture they

---

[1] We refer to product names from 1904 to 2008 from the database by Cotticelli-Kurras 2008.

could and can provide, as well as the way they convey it. The study has an interdisciplinary approach, taking into account language analysis, semiotics, psychology of advertising (economic marketing strategies) and cultural anthropology.

In the following chapters we propose a first classification and a linguistic analysis on different levels, within a selected corpus of slogans ranging from the 1930s up until the present day. We analysed the different underlying linguistic strategies used in the construction of the slogans in order to incorporate the company name, first rhetorical figures and then morphological and semantic features.

The Corpus

Because of the lack of a database or specific publications about Italian slogans[2], for the purpose of this study, we collected some slogans by consulting many websites[3] and the helpful list available in Wikiquote[4]. We analysed around 500 slogans but selected, in particular, those that incorporate the brand name of the product, because they represent a special category. In fact, if these slogans were deprived of the opportunity to "manipulate" the brand, they should be formulated in a completely different way. Consequently, the incorporation of the brand, according to the processes we shall present, makes the slogan itself a sort of pseudo-brand, one might even say a hyper-brand name compared with the hypo-brand name, that is made up by the brand or product name itself. Some of them are even registered with the Italian Patent and Trademark Office (*Ufficio Italiano di Brevetti e Marchi*, UIBM). Some of these are included in the database by Cotticelli-Kurras and collected during a jointed research project (*Programma Vigoni*) about product names together with Elke

---

[2] The only study specifically dedicated to this issue is by Manconi 1967.

[3] Here are some website addresses that we consulted even though our corpus is the product of our own research and collection which present the material in a list without internal organisation:
http://www.libello.it/Arte_Grafica/Slogan_pubblicitari.html (07 April 2013);
http://www.calendovisita.it/Simpatici_Slogan.html (07 April 2013);
http://sitomemoria.altervista.org/pubblicita/slogan/a_m.htm (07 April 2013).

[4] Here are some website addresses that we consulted even though our corpus is the product of our own research and collection which present the material in a list without internal organisation:
http://www.libello.it/Arte_Grafica/Slogan_pubblicitari.html (07 April 2013);
http://www.calendovisita.it/Simpatici_Slogan.html (07 April 2013);
http://sitomemoria.altervista.org/pubblicita/slogan/a_m.htm (07 April 2013).

Ronneberger-Sibold and Sabine Wahl. The slogans have been studied together with the product names from the linguistic perspective of morphological and semantic features. For some of the outputs of this research, see Cotticelli-Kurras (2012), Cotticelli-Kurras (forthcoming) and Ronneberger-Sibold and Wahl (forthcoming). Further on Italian brand names cf. Zardo (1997) and (2007).

If we consider the product classes the afore mentioned slogans represent, we can see that according to the Nice classification of good and services[5], the most recurring ones are the following: food (ca. 25%, class 29–31), drink (ca. 20%, class 32–33), cosmetics and cleaning products (ca. 13%, class 3), electronics, cars and telephone (ca. 13%, class 7, 9, 11–12), and finally fashion and sportswear (8%, class 25), luxury items (clocks, jewelry, 4%, class 9, 14). Some slogans could also be found in advertising spots on Youtube[6] under numerous registrations of the daily *Carosello* broadcasting (see below). In any case, our study about Italian slogans represents pioneering work because they have not yet been systematically analysed.

A Cultural Journey through Time

We start by presenting some examples of slogans which are representative of different phases of Italian history and cultural development, beginning with the years before World War II and up to present day. We have tried to choose the most representative ones for the products and trends typical of each period (about the history of advertising see Castelvecchi Ceserani 1988 and Ballardini 1994).

Before World War II:

Typical of these decades were the first electronic products that represented pure luxury in society (ex. 3). Food and beverage products or alcohol were already the most important ones in Italy (ex. 2–3).

---

[5] Here are some website addresses that we consulted even though our corpus is the product of our own research and collection which present the material in a list without internal organisation:
http://www.libello.it/Arte_Grafica/Slogan_pubblicitari.html (07 April 2013);
http://www.calendovisita.it/Simpatici_Slogan.html (07 April 2013);
http://sitomemoria.altervista.org/pubblicita/slogan/a_m.htm (07 April 2013).
[6] www.youtube.com

1) Esigete *Marsala Florio*. Ristora, Rinfranca, Rinforza (1933) ('Demand *Marsala Florio*. Restores, refreshes, strengthens').
2) Il gioiello della casa …cucine a gas *Triples* (1939) ('The jewel of the house… gas cookers *Triples*').
3) *Irradio* la voce che incanta (1939) ('*Irradio* the voice that charms').

Irradio (ex. 3) is the brand name of a radio, a luxury item of the time; the name itself is a pun because it could also be the first person singular of the verb *irradiare*, 'to broadcast by radio'. This spot also shows that at that time, some commercials were even diffused by radio for the upper class.

In the 1950s:

The attention was focused on individual needs; films, movie actors and television shows started diffusing a new life style, so that products of fashion and personal care became typical of this period.

4) Di corsa a indossarlo, è un abito *Facis* (1954) ('Rush to wear it, it is a suit by *Facis*').

Facis (ex. 4) is, in this case, a company name; it is an acronym of *Fabbrica Abiti Confezionati in Seri*e ('dresses factory packed in series'), but *Facis* has a Latin sound and shape because it is homonymous with the second person singular of the Latin verb *facere*, 'to make'.

5) *Lux* il sapone di 9 "stelle" su 10 (1955) ('The 9 starlets out of 10 use the soap *Lux*'):

The soap advertisement (ex. 5) also uses a Latin name which means 'light'. The meaning of the sentence is supposed to be: 'this soap is the light of nine stars out of ten'. Again, the classical tradition is very strong in the field of advertising, where it works as a typical marker of "Italianity".

In the 1960s:

Cars and speed as symbols of an expanding society and economy are well represented by this example 6: oil is the basic tool to reach the newly discovered feeling of life:

6) *Esso.* Metti *un tigre* nel motore (1962) ('Put a Tiger in the engine' [by refueling Esso]).

In the 1970s:

7) Chiamami *Peroni*, sarò la tua birra (1970-71) ('Call me *Peroni*, I'll be your beer').

This beer advertisement (ex. 7) is a symbol of a good economic period, in which drink has the role of a woman.

In the 1980s:

8) AIDS. I rapporti umani non trasmettono il virus (1987) ('Human relationships do not transmit the virus').

This public service announcement (ex. 8.) was typical of the 1980s, following the evolution of new health conditions. Here, the focus is on the opposition between human relationships and the dangerous consequences of sexual relations.

In the 1990s:

9) *Citroën* presenta le offerte con i piedi per terra (1996) ('*Citroën* presents offers having their feet on the ground (= solid offers)').

Through a strong financial crisis in the 1990s, advertising had to take account of a new situation: even cars no longer belonged in a dream world.

In the 2000s:

10) *Scottex,* il posto più morbido dove mettere il naso (2008) ('*Scottex,* the softest place where you can put your nose').

In recent times several daily products like *Scottex* (ex. 10) have also found their place in advertising.

"Made in Italy" in Advertising: *Carosello* 1957–1977

In the history of Italian advertising, we have to highlight a special period, during which a television show called *Carosello*, was developed, from 1957 to 1977, and had increasing importance for the Italian consumer. From 8.50 p.m. until 9 p.m., *Carosello* brought short shows (one minute each) into Italian houses with a final adjunct in which a product was mentioned (many cinemas and artists of the theatre, also directors, were involved in it). Since 1975, the *Carosello* shows became shorter (30 seconds) and they became more focussed on the products[7]. The models in advertising, coming from Great Britain and USA, became stronger and also the Italian slogan makers, based in London or New York, brought new impulses and tendencies into Italian advertising agencies. The outcome was successful both for the agencies and the consumer. Their key names include: Gavino Sanna, Franco Moretti, Emanuele Pirella, Pasquale Barbella, Marco Mignani, Annamaria Testa, Lele Panzeri; between the 1980s and 1990s, they changed the world of Italian commercials, shiftingover from *réclame* to advertising, thus creating masterpieces in the history of Italian campaigns. The agency led by Armando Testa in Torino was able to combine marketing strategies with the qualities of an artistic product "Made in Italy". Starting in the 1960s, he invented his own personal style, creating characters that, for a long time, have been favourites of the Italian public (see Codeluppi 2001). After *Carosello*, a new era of advertising had begun. (About Carosello see Falabrino 1999, especially Chapter 5, *La rivoluzione di Carosello* [The Revolution of Carosello]; Giusti 1995; Grasso 1992; Grasso 2008; Croce et al. 2008.)

Rhetorical Figures in Italian Slogans

We shall divide the rhetoric figures into three main groups according to Mortara Garavelli (2000) and to Barberi Squarotti et al., *Dizionario di Retorica e Stilistica* (2004): 1. repetition figures, 2. opposition figures and 3. substitutions (by word or part of a word and by meaning). We can note that most slogans are directed and understandable only to native speakers because language is the most important element in their creation[8].

Repetition Figures

Figures of speech based on repetition are used in advertising when the name of the product or the brand is explicitly expressed: the basic assumption is that the constant repetition of a sound, a slogan or a thought can impress upon the memory of the consumer the very product name or brand that goes with it. As any figure of speech, repetition can be achieved

[7] www.youtube.com

[8] See also Codeluppi 2002, especially on the different interpretations of rhetoric figures and the discussion with the additional literature in chapters 3 and 4.

at the level of sound, word or thought[9].

Alliterations

11) *Ava,* come lava (‘*Ava*, how it washes’).

Ava is the product name of a detergent. This slogan (ex. 11) was the sentence which was said by Calimero, an animated character in Italian advertising, a little white chick. It appears for the first time in advertising by the company Mira Lanza during “Carosello”: having fallen in the mud, it gets dirty and turns black and is no longer recognised by the mother. He has a few sad adventures, but thanks to the detergent, *Ava*, he becomes white and clean and is happy again.

12) Aaah! *Aperol*. Un nome che non si dimentica[10] (‘Ah, *Aperol!* A name nobody forgets’).

Aperol is the product name of an aperitif; *Aaahh* is the typical exclamation when one is reminded of something.

13) *Ciokito*. Buonito. Capito? (‘*Ciokito*, very good. (Have you) understood?’).

Ciokito (ex. 13) is the product name of a snack by Nestlè; *buonito* is an Italian neo-formation close to the Spanish diminutive adjective *bonito* ‘pretty, lovely’.

Anaphora/Epiphora

14) *Lavazza*. Più lo mandi giù, più ti tira su. (‘The more you drink it [lit. ‘put it down’] the better it makes you feel’ [lit. ‘the more it picks you up’]).

Lavazza, the name of the company, is also the name of its founder and owner.

---

[9] However, we can also find figures of repetition in which one of the two opposite elements is not expressed (and should be reconstructed by the receiver) but we did not quote them.

[10] After World War II, *Aperol* has experienced a great development and has spread rapidly thanks to the sentence pronounced by the actor Tino Buazzelli, who, during “Carosello”, utters it while putting his hand to his forehead.

15) *Cioccoblocco Nestlè*. Più grande è, più gusto c'è. ('Table of Chocolate Nestlè, the larger, the tastier').

Cioccoblocco (ex. 15) is an *ad hoc* formation for a bar of chocolate, moreover it is a univerbation between *cioccolato* 'chocolate' and *blocco* 'bar' (as meaning in this context, for the more usual *tavoletta*) from an underlying phrase "tavoletta (or blocco) di cioccolato". The larger the bar, the tastier the product.

Chiasm

16) Se bevi *Neri*, *ne ri*bevi ('If you drink *Neri* you drink it again').

Neri is a company name, the product name is *Chinotto*.[11] From 1949 onwards, the company Neri in Capranica (quoted in ex. 16) started, on a large scale, marketing with the slogan 'not *Chinotto*, if there is no 8' and 'if you drink *Neri*, you drink it again', and its product became very popular. In those days, it was not unusual to see large American cars, such as Cadillacs and Chryslers, roam the streets of the peninsula with giant bottles of soda pop by *Neri* on the roof, a form of "advertising" preceding *Carosello*, which was undoubtedly effective.

Opposition Figures

The opposition figure consists of the combination of two elements within the same expression that are mirror images of one another. It can happen on the sound, word or thought level. In our examples, we included only the rhetorical figures that show both the element mirrored and the reflecting element.

Paronomasia/Adnomination

A paronomasia shows an opposition in sounds: It consists of the repetition of two words with a similar sound but different meaning (*tenta* 'seduces'… *tanto* 'much') like in the following example 17. It is also used in puns. Adnomination is a particular version of paronomasia in which the same etymological root is repeated.

---

[11] Available at: http://www.cpenti.it/chinotto/chinottonellastoria.html (retrieved the last time at 7 April 2013).

17) *Fiesta* ti tenta tre volte tanto ('*Fiesta* seduces you three times as much').

Fiesta (ex. 17) is a snack by *Ferrero*. Also note the alliteration and repetition of /t/.

Isocolon

An isocolon shows an opposition of the words in the structure of a clause:

18) Sogni calmi, sogni belli, Filtrofiore *Bonomelli* ('Peaceful dreams, pretty dreams, 'flower-filtered' *Bonomelli*').

The slogan (ex. 18) is a rhyme of two octosyllabic lines, *Bonomelli* is a company name and the product is chamomile tea. (About rhymes in advertising see Afribo 2005. At Audinoeditore.it, one can find a list of slogans with rhymes.)

Aiazzone (ex. 19) is a company name for furniture.

19) *Aiazzone*. Provare per credere ('*Aiazzone*. Try to believe').

Oxymoron

An oxymoron typically shows an opposition of meaning:

20) *Un caldo inverno* (*Singapore Airlines*, 'A warm winter').

Commutatio

The proper English term for Latin *commutatio* is *antimetabole*: reversing the order of two elements in two consecutive sentences obtaining specular meanings.

21) *Sole*. Qualità senza risparmio o risparmio senza qualità? ('Quality without saving or saving without quality?').
22) Crudo o cotto? *Granbiscotto*. ('Cooked or raw? *Granbiscotto*').

Granbiscotto (ex. 22) is a product name for a cooked ham but it literally means: 'big or good cake'. The pun refers to the double meaning of *biscotto*, etymologically meaning 'twice baked', then lexicalised as 'cake' and here used as the name of a cooked ham. The slogan is an octosyllabic verse with an internal rhyme.

Synesthesia

Synesthesia is a rhetorical figure which involves the combination of two or more words belonging to two different sensory levels, like in the following example 23:

23) *Bang&Olufsen.* Chi ha occhi per toccare ascolti ('He who has eyes for touching, should listen').

Substitution Figures

We have two main types of substitutions, substitutions of word and substitutions of meaning. In this type of rhetorical figures the message is corrupted in one of its elements and the recipient need to adjust it in order to reconstruct the original intent and content. This mechanism also works proposing a mirror image of what you want to communicate without providing even the mirror element, which must be reconstructed by the viewer and replaced instead of those expressed.

Substitutions of Word

The substitutions of word are often found in sentences or phrases that imitate well-known proverbs and sayings (see for instance ex. 24, 25 below), that is, they are based on the universal knowledge of the community of the speakers.

24) *I vov you.*

'Vov' replaces 'love' for: *I love you. Vov* is a brand name for a liqueur with eggs. *Vov* is a truncated form from the Venetian dialectal form *vovo,* like Ital. *uovo* 'egg'.

25) Chi rompe *Attak* ('(The one) Who wreaks will glue').

Attak is a brand name that in its correct orthographical form in Italian (*attacca*) means 'it glues'. This is used instead of *pay* in the underlying proverb "(the one) who breaks will pay". The brand name *Attak* shows an apocope and the introduction of the non-Italian letter *k*.

26) Vivere alla *Grundig* ('Live the *Grundig* [high life]').

The electronics company name *Grundig* in ex. 26 is used instead of *grande* ('big, high') referring to the Italian saying *vivere alla grande.*

27) *Buon appeTigre* (for *buon appetito*, 'good appetite').

Tigre is a brand name for a cream cheese. The neo-formation is a contour blend between *appetito* and *Tigre*, preserving the original number of syllables.

28) *Dreher*, la birra che *birrei* ('*Dreher*, the beer I would drink').

Dreher is a company name for a beer. *Birrei* is a substitution for the correct verbal form *berrei* 'I would drink', lexicalised as neo-formation from the substantive *birra* 'beer'.

29) *Esselunga*, prezzi corti ('*Esselunga*, long S, short prizes').

Esselunga is the name of a chain of supermarkets, its logo being the letter *S* with a long line from the *S*. The slogan contains the pun realised through the logical opposite meanings.

Substitutions of Meaning

The figures of substitutions of meaning are based on the transfer of meaning from an expression to another.

Irony means to say something that means the opposite of what is meant but for making perceptible the true intention, like in the following ex. 30:

30) *Virgilio,* il bello di internet ('*Virgilio*, the best/beauty of the Internet').

Virgilio (ex. 30) is the name of an Internet provider. The phrase means that this provider is able to show the best of the internet connection. The pun results from the connected image of an old and foul looking man and from the linguistic interpretation of the phrase; *Virgilio* is also a male personal name, the phrase *il bello* can mean 'the best of…' but also 'the handsome man', used in ironic contrast to the image of the man appearing on the screen.

The *metaphor* is achieved when the word that normally would take place in the sentence is replaced by another one whose "essence" or function goes to overlap with that of the original term, thus creating images with strong emotional charge.

31) *Esso*. Metti un *Tigre* nel motore ('*Esso*. Put a tiger in the engine').

Esso (ex. 31) is a brand of gasoline that shows how powerful this type of oil is. The particular creation or adaptation of this slogan to the Italian market consists of redetermination through the undetermined masculine article *un* of the female noun *tigre* ('tiger') as a male one.

The *litotes* is passing a judgment and denying the opposite.

32) *Artsana.* La siringa niente male ('The not-bad injection').

Artsana is a company name from Latin *ars* and *sanus,-a,-um*; the phrase "la siringa niente male" is ambiguous: it can be interpreted as 'the 'not bad' injection', as well as 'the painless injection'.

The *rhetoric question* implies to ask a question that is not a request for information, but instead implies that a predetermined answer is implicit in the question itself. In this type of slogan the viewer is led to replace the question with the answer.

33) Che mondo sarebbe senza *Nutella?* ('What would the world be without *Nutella*?').

Nutella Ferrero is a brand name for the well-known nut chocolate spread.

Linguistic Features

We shall analyse some categories of linguistic strategies which are involved in the manipulation of brand and product names. On the morphological level, these include various types of lexicalisations and some neo-formations. On the semantic level, we focussed on some lexical variations, on the domains of connotation or associations, and finally, as communication strategies, on the most typical structure of utterances found in the selected slogans.

The semantic analysis implies the analysis of some typical associations of these slogans in order to draw a picture of the type of cultural image deriving from the advertising slogans.

Morphological Strategies

Within morphological strategies, we have analysed those that contain some neo-formations or substitutions aiming to modify the brand or product name.

Lexicalisations

In the category "lexicalisations", we find a number of neo-formations, namely verbs derived directly from the brand or product name, conjugated in different persons and moods. This is a particular way to integrate the brand into the slogan. The neo-formations are characterised in some slogans through capital letters, as in the case of *Vespa* (brand name and 3rd person singular from the invented verb *vespare* 'to drive a Vespa', which also has a medial variant *vespizzarsi* 'to drive/buy a Vespa for oneself'). In Italian, *Vespa* also means 'wasp'. All these lexicalisations are employed only in advertising language.

34) Chi *Vespa* mangia le mele. Chi non *Vespa* no ('who drives a *Vespa* eats apples, who doesn't drive *Vespa*, doesn't eat (them)').

The brand name *Vespa* (a scooter) is here used as a verb transcategorised from a noun. *Vespa* is here used as lexical basis for a created verbal form in the 3 sg. present in the meaning 'who drives Vespa'. It could also mean 'who (has a) Vespa", while the writing of *Vespa* with a capital letter is deliberately ambiguous, but not its second position as verb in the sentence.

35) Non correte, *vespizzatevi* ('Don't run, make yourselves *Vespa* drivers').

Vespizzatevi is clearly a verbal form, used as hortative for the 2nd person plural, but it is a neo-formation, namely a medial verb followed by a clitic pronoun (*-vi* 'for you'), which works as a dativ of interest.

36) *Yoghiamo*? ('Let us drink a Yoga?').

Yoghiamo is built as a verbal form in the 1st person plural from the brand name of the juice *Yoga* and means literally 'let's *Yoga*', that is, 'drink a *Yoga*'.

37) *Tubiamo*? ('Let us take a chocolate from the tube').

This verbal form (ex. 37) does not exist; it is created on the basis of the brand name *Perugina Tubo,* which is chocolate in a tube. The result of the lexicalisation of "tubo" as a verb "tubare" is homophonous with the verb *tubare*, like the cooing of pigeons, but only means 'to eat a chocolate in the tube' in the slogan. *Tubare* has also the metaphoric meaning of cooing of sweethearts who eat chocolate called *Baci* 'kisses' *Perugina.*

38) *Schweppati* una *Schweppes* ('drink a *Schweppes*').

The brand name *Schwepp*(*es*) is used as an imperative verb with the clitic personal/reflexive pronoun in dative (*-ti* 'for yourself') as *dativus commodi* in the meaning 'drink a Schweppes', like ex. 35. This verb doesn't exist.

39) *Snakkiamoci* con una *Fiesta Snack* ('Let's take a snack by taking *Fiesta Snack*').

Snakkiamoci is built in the same way as *vespizzarsi* (s. ex. 35, 38) in the meaning 'Let's eat a *Snack*', with a clitic pronoun as dativ of interest (*-ci*, 'for ourself'). This verb doesn't exist.

40) *Hiphopize* yourself ('buy a *Hip Hop* watch for yourself').

Hip hop is a brand name for watches. Here it is used as an English *-ize* verb derived from a noun, as an imperative reflexive form.

Neo-formations

41) *Fabello*, lucida nuovo, lucida bello ('*Fabello*, it makes (all) beautiful' (literally), but is to be understood as 'it makes everything shiny').

Fabello is the brand name. It is a writing compound from the verbal form *fa* 'it makes' and the adjective *bello* 'beautiful' with the literal meaning 'it makes (all) beautiful'. The second part explains this semantic interpretation of the brand name as follows: 'let (all) shine beautiful, let (all) shine (as) new'. The whole slogan is also constructed on the interpretation of the brand name with the rhyme *Fabello … bello.*

42) *Peperlizia*, il contorno che ti vizia; Una delizia, di più, una *Piperlizia* ('*Peperlizia*, the garnish that spoils you; A delicacy, more, a *Piperlizia*').

This slogan (ex. 42) contains two variants of the brand name, which affects the whole structure of the phrase. *Peperlizia* is a blend from *peperone* '(red) pepper' and *delizia* 'delicacy', it models the two rhymes with *vizia* and *delizia* in a sort of semantic *crescendo*.

43) *Motta Maxibon* – Il piacere da mordere ('*Motta Maxibon* – The pleasure to bite on').

Motta Maxibon is the brand name preceded by the company name. *Maxibon* is a composition with a prefixoid *maxi-* normally used for nouns, here used together with an adjective (*bon* > *buono* 'good'), in order to build a superlative "very good", even if *Maxibon* is a newly formed adjectival noun.

44) *Keglevich*, la vodka che *volevich* ('*Keglevich*, the vodka you wanted').

Volevich (ex. 44) is a pun: the correct verbal form is *volevi*, the 2nd person imperfect from *volere* 'you wanted', and at the same time a rhyming blending form between the brand name *Keglevich* and the verbal form *volevi*.

45) *Fina* ti benzina ('*Fina* provides you with oil').

The verb *benzinare*, derived from the noun *benzina*, does not exist in Italian. It is a new formation in the language of advertising. The form rhymes with the company name *Fina*.

46) *Dreher*. La birra che *birrei* ('Dreher, the beer I would drink').

The right verbal form should be *berrei* while *birrei* is a pun used for repeating the word *birra* to build a sort of etymological figure.

47) Metti *un tigre* nel motore ('Put a tiger in the engine').

From the morphological point of view, it should be noted that the word *tigre* here is masculine, while it should be feminine (see ex. 30), which is maybe meant to stress the association with the domain of power, discussed below. Semantically, the figure sets the word 'tiger' up as a metonymy for 'fuel'.

Semantic and Lexical Strategies

On the lexical level, we chose those particular formations that receive a different meaning or use in the slogans instead of regular ones. We call them generically lexical variations, to which belong reformulations (ex. 48–50) and onomatopoetic formations (ex. 51). Under the semantic strategies we will analyse the use of connotations and their related associations in selected examples (ex. 52–82).

Reformulations of the Brand Name in the Slogan

48) È arrivata. *Punto.* (*Fiat Punto*) ('It is arrived. *Punto*', literally).

The sentence is ambiguous; it means 'The new model of FIAT, called *Punto*, has arrived', but it can be also interpreted as 'It arrived. *Punto* ('Full stop', as orthographical annotation)'. This last one-word statement could mean 'I do not need to add anything'.

49) I' son *Beatrice*, che ti faccio andare ('I'm *Beatrice*, I make you go', literally).

This is an example of the personalisation of the product name for a laxative, the sentence means: 'go to the toilet'. *I' son Beatrice* is literally the same verse by Dante, but associated with another meaning: Beatrice was Dante's muse. Here, however, it is used as the name of a laxative, so the slogan is a prosaic reformulation of a verse by Dante[12].

50) Lo *Yeti* esiste. Chi lo incontra sta *fresco* ('*Yeti* exists. Whoever meets him is cool/is in danger').

Yeti is the name of a model of a Skoda car, at the same time, the denomination of the so-called Abominable Snowman. *Fresco* is ambiguous: the meaning of the slogan is based on the second given interpretation.

---

[12] We quote from *Inferno* by Dante Alighieri, from the beginning of the description of the descent into Hell: "I'son Beatrice che ti faccio andare, vegno di loco ove tornar desio, amor mi mosse, che mi fa parlare" (*Inferno* II, 70–72).

Onomatopoetic Formations

51) O fanno *Crik* o fanno *Crok* ('They either go *Crick* or *Crock*').

Crik Crok is the product name of crackers, which is used in a phraseological new construction with an onomatopoetic meaning: "to go *Crick* or *Crock*" when you bite into them.

Domains of Connotations in Italian Slogans

Based on the pioneering research by Maslow (1970), in a comparative study conducted by Cotticelli-Kurras (2011 and forthcoming) and Ronneberger-Sibold and Wahl (forthcoming), a set of fifteen typical domains of connotations for brand and product names were individuated, each relying on one or more standard association starting from the point of view of the consumer. These domains are: power; independence; curiosity; sensory perceptions; order and wealth; saving; tradition, religion, honor; progress; social contact; high quality; status; aggression; romanticism and sensuality; physical activity; tranquillity. Some of these domains are also present in the corpus of slogans we analysed in the present paper.

In the case of the *domains of physical perceptions* (such as good feelings), *(high) quality* and *social status*, the main associations are: cosmos, physical dimensions, sensory perceptions (light, hard, dark, taste...) and high quality, fun, luxury. The products like drinks and water are discussed in ex. 52–54:

52) Cin Cin *Cinzano*; Cin Cin *Cynar*; Brr *Brancamenta*.

The three drinks *Cinzano*, *Cynar* and *Brancamenta* (ex. 52) are all digestives, twice introduced by the term for 'cheers', once with an onomatopoetic exclamation to express the feeling of cold when you have a drink containing mint.

53) Il primo sorso affascina. Il secondo ... *Strega* ('The first sip is charming. The second … bewitches').

Strega (ex. 53) is a brandy. The name *Strega* here is ambiguous: it is the brand name, but at the same time it is used as the verbal form in the 3rd person singular present. Furthermore, the Italian noun *strega* also means 'witch'.

54) Altissima. Purissima. *Levissima* ('The highest, the purest, the lightest (= *Levissima*)').

The three qualities of the mineral water form a climax in order to describe the product *Levissima.*

The (high) quality domain combined with *social status* shows the following associations: luxury, wealth, enjoyment, beauty, modernity, technology, industry and hi-tech products.

The products belonging to the category of clothing and fashion are presented in the ex. 55–59 (Note also the rhyme between *debole* and the brand name *Lebole* in ex. 57):

55) Terry ti vuole in *Terital* ('Terry wants you to wear *Terital*').
56) Vesti fino vesti *Marzotto* ('Dress fine, dress *Marzotto*').
57) Ho un debole per l'uomo in *Lebole* ('I have a weakness for the man who dresses in Lebole').
58) *Fiorucci.* I migliori sapori d'Italia ('The best tastes of Italy').
59) *Stefanel.* L'amore addosso ('Dressed in love').

Domain of *social contact and fun* is often combined with *tradition.* The main associations within them are: fun, games, summer, sun, holiday, humour, parties, and communication. These may be in turn connected to antiquity, religion, esotericism, history, good times, crafts, art and home.

It is worth observing that a pun or references to literature can be found in these Italian slogans, as the examples 60–63 are showing:

60) *Buitoni*. Ed è subito *festa* ('Buitoni: it is suddenly a party').
61) Chiara, fresca, *Sprite* ('Clear, fresh, *Sprite*').
62) *Neocid* o mosche ('*Neocid* or flies').
63) L'importanza di chiamarsi *Molinari* ('The importance to bear the name *Molinari*').

The slogan in ex. 60 is based on a line by the poet Quasimodo: *Ed è subito sera*, (*sera* = evening), *Buitoni* is the name of a famous food production company.

The slogan in ex. 61 is reminiscent of the line by Petrarca *Chiare, fresche e dolci acque*; *Sprite* is a well-known soft drink.

Neocid (ex. 62) is the product name of an insect repellent, it brings to mind the famous phrase by Garibaldi *O Roma o morte*, remodelled by Mussolini to *O Roma o Mosca*.

The slogan in ex. 63 is an imitation of the Italian title of the English novel *The Importance of Being Earnest* by Oscar Wilde: 'L'importanza di chiamarsi Ernesto'. *Molinari* is a company and product name of drinks.

Furthermore, titles of songs can be found in slogans, as the examples 64–65 show:

64) Fatti mandare dalla mamma a prendere *Brio* ('Let your mother send you to buy the milk').
65) Voulez-vous *Patè* avec moi ('Do you want *Patè* with me?').

The slogan in ex. 64 is created on the title of a famous 1960s song by Gianni Morandi, originally *Fatti mandare dalla mamma a prendere il latte*: the 'milk' is here substituted by 'to buy *Brio*', which contains the brand name of a snack.

Example 65 is a pun of the song *Lady Marmalade* by Labelle, in which the substitution *Patè* instead of *coucher* stresses the product name.

The domain of *progress* is characterised by the following associations: progress, nature, comfort, convenience, organic and beauty (not sensual).

The target of the slogan is often the housewife, like in ex. 66–70:

66) *Ava*, come lava ('*Ava*, how (well) (*Ava*) washes').

The meaning of the slogan (ex. 66) is that the laundry detergent is very good. The rhyme between the product name *Ava* and the verbal form in the 3rd person singular *lava* focusses on the product name.

67) Con *Favilla* la casa brilla ('With *Favilla* the house shines').

Favilla is the name of a cleaner, but its literal meaning is 'sparkle' – so using it is a great help to the housewife.

68) *Candy* sa come si fa ('Candy knows how to do it').

Candy is a company name for household appliances, especially for washing machines. The slogan means that the know-how of the housewife is no longer needed.

69) Dove c'è *Barilla* c'è casa ('Where there's *Barilla* there's home').

Barilla is a company name and here it is used as a symbol for "home and family", because it is the most popular pasta producer in Italy and past is typical Italian food.

70) Con *Nelsen* i piatti li vuol lavare lui ('With Nelsen, it is the man who wants to wash the dishes').

Nelsen is a dishwashing detergent, which is so good that the typical role division between men and women is here reversed; *Nelsen* is also the Italianised form of a male proper name and is reminiscent of the name of the Admiral Nelson, famous for the Battle of Trafalgar.

The domain of *high quality* is combined with the domain of *progress.* Their typical associations are: scientific, high quality and technical universality.

71) *Mitsubishi* mi stupisci ('*Mitsubishi* you amaze me').

Mitsubishi (ex. 71) is a company name of cars, the slogan also shows alliteration between the company name and the verb.

72) *Rowenta*. Per chi non s'accontenta ('*Rowenta*, for those who don't just settle for anything').

Rowenta is a company name for household appliances; in this case the product is an iron.

73) Con *API* si vola ('*API*, you will fly').

API (ex. 73) is an acronym for the oil industry and sounds like the plural form of *ape* 'bee'. The slogan is also a metaphor.

74) Siete sulla retta *Kia* ('You are on the right *Kia*', literally).

Kia (ex. 74) is a name of a car company, and the slogan is a pun based on the proverb *essere sulla retta via* 'to be on the right way', in this context having the meaning 'you are on the right way in buying a car by *Kia*'. In the slogan, *Kia* replaces the original word of the proverb *via* 'way'.

Domain of *saving* is related to the associations modesty and accuracy. Slogan in ex. 75 is the Italian translation of the original English advertisement.

75) Ci sono cose che non hanno prezzo, per tutto il resto c'è *MasterCard* ('There are some things money can't buy. For everything else, there's MasterCard').

76) *Sole.* Qualità senza risparmio o risparmio senza qualità? ('Quality without saving or saving without quality?').

Sole (ex. 76) is a laundry detergent; the proper meaning is 'sun' and *Sole* as product name is a metaphor for the shining results of washing.

77) Risparmio scandaloso, ovvio, *Oviesse* ('Scandalous saving, obviously, *Oviesse*').

The adverb *ovvio* in ex. 77 is in alliteration with the company name of the market chain *Oviesse* (OVS).

To the domain of *tranquillity* belong the following associations: sensitivity, harmony, family, childhood, children's world, reliability and comfort, as the ex. 78–82 demonstrate.

78) *Orzobimbo* bim bum bam.

Orzobimbo is a malt drink for children; *bim bum bam* is a phrase in children's language.

79) *Chicco.* Dove c'è un bambino ('*Chicco*. Where there is a child').

Chicco (ex. 79) is a company name and a symbol for the children's world, saying that "where there is a child you'll always find *Chicco*".

80) Pupo chiama *Duplo*. Mami ricevuto? ('Pupo calling *Duplo*. Is Mum hearing?').

Duplo (ex. 80) is the name of a snack; the slogan is a pun for a dialogue between a child and a mother by walkie-talkie. *Pupo* is another name for child, *mami* is the variant of *mamma* 'mum' in children's language.

81) La scuola stanca. Il *Pavesino* rinfranca ('School exhausts. *Pavesino* revives').

Pavesino (ex. 81) is the singular form of *Pavesini* which are light cookies by *Pavesi*, their company name, for children but not only, which can be eaten as a snack in school.

82) *Kinder Pinguì*. Nutre come una merenda. Piace come un gelato ('*Kinder Pinguì*. It nourishes like a snack, it tastes like an ice cream').

Pinguì is the product name of a famous snack for children, *Kinder* is its company name.

Structure of Utterance

Finally, we would like to analyse the structure of the slogans as narrative utterances referring, in general, to the model of structural semantics by Greimas (1966: 246), and to the further development and applications of similar models on the language of advertising. We refer to the application of the model by Vestergaard and Schrøder (1985) by adding the corresponding figures in parentheses. (See also Codeluppi 2002: 44ff.) The model aims to describe the discourse structures by selecting the figures in which they are acting. The model by Vestergaard and Schrøder (1985: 29) also takes into account the following pairs of figures: issuer / receiver; object / subject; positive / negative circumstances:

issuer (= product)	→	object (= scope)	→	receiver (customer)
		↑		
positive circumstance (quality of the product)	→	subject (= agent) (customer)	←	negative circumstance (quality of the product)

We focalised our attention on four points within the structure of the advertisements: issuer, scope, level (register) and actors, in order to distinguish the pragmatic focus in advertising.

Issuer: The issuer may be declared or not declared. In our cases, the issuers are often declared, because of the presence of the brand names in all messages of the slogans. The brand names, the products themselves, are often subjects or agents in the utterances.

Scope: The scope may be individual, social or political. In our corpus, the scope is often individual because the message is addressed to the individual consumer (the generic "you") in their own interest. Sometimes the scope is social, but only as far as the benefits of the product are directed to a community.

Actors: In the sentences we have collected, we have identified quite a number of actors: the products themselves as personifications, the consumer referred to as "you", by the imperative verbs or (indirectly) as housewives, children, men (male human beings; but not the woman as female human being). It is interesting to scc that the different actors are associated with different domains of connotations: children are mentioned in slogans for snacks or special commodities, clothes are combined with status and quality, household appliances with progress and comfort etc.

Register: The register of the message may be secular, ideological or religious. In our material the religious level appears only as an association, not at the explicit level. The level of slogans containing brand or product names is mostly secular; the message aims at showing that the small things of everyday life can make existence easy and comfortable.

Conclusions

We have showed that brand names and slogans, together with their connotations and associations, are a good mirror of the cultural motivations for the underlying market strategies of a nation, its language and people. Slogans formulate, in a clear but interesting way, the expectations of the customer. Food and drink, taste and good feeling, clothes, household tools and technology combined with literature and rhymes, verses, metrical structures and alliterations, fashion and cleanliness, but also saving and quality, are the mainstays of Italian slogans that go along well with brand names.

The Message Behind the Language: The Point of View of Issuer or Receiver

We can sum up some characteristic markers of the communications strategies through the linguistic analysis of the slogans in this study in order to aim at a better comprehension of the intended message.

The hortatory tone occurs frequently in the slogans, sometimes it is quite imperative, sometimes it is rather seducing, friendly or even authoritative, especially when the product is the actor itself and wants to lure the target person into using the product.

The register of the utterance is mostly smooth, playful, and rarely intensive in order to create a seducing atmosphere.

The induced emotions depend on the domains of connotations that are intended: thus, the related associations could be emotions, such as serenity and contentment for the children's world, but also for the housewife. The associations of success and good feeling are typical for the domains of status, quality and progress. Fun is generally involved by the domain for social contact.

The target of the slogans is diversified: it may be people in general for clothes, but also specific individuals, in the case of special brands of clothing or drinks. The slogans are meant to segment the target: children for snacks, housewives for detergents or household appliances, men for drinks or cars.

The slogans can promote and spread creations in the form of myths or desires, because they aim at enticing the consumer. They promote positive representations of the products they present. The tools used have changed over time: in recent years, we have had a large diffusion of slogans through mass media, social events, pay tv, pay mass media and the Internet, while in the past, the only medium was radio. Television came a little later, and only for few people. As television reached all households, Italian advertising entered the phase of *Carosello*.

Names and Culture

We can conclude that the analysed corpus shows an interesting outcome of the language "manipulation" slogans use in order to highlight the brand and the product names they contain. Most of these slogans are created for an Italian audience, because they are based on puns on the meaning, sound and word levels: it is only a native speaker who can decode the right message, who can understand the underlying pun that bears the cultural premises which allow the speaker to appreciate the puns. The references to Italian literature, to songs, the use of rhymes and the personification of many brands let them be real actors in the daily life of Italian people (*Fiesta ti tenta tre volte tanto*). The lexicalisations and neo-formations create verbs and sayings in the special language of advertising that coin patterns of lifestyle (*Vespizziamoci*, or *Tubiamo*), because they invoke certain associations (fun, party, summer and so on).

We can take a look into the culture of a given nation through the associations and the connotations emerging most frequently from brand names and from slogans: in the case of the Italian language of advertising, we find a great parallel between the associations among slogans and product names, namely: tradition, quality, progress and comfort for better quality of life and social contact.

References

Afribo, A. 2005. Il poeta è un copywriter? [Is the poet a copywriter?]. In *Poesia, rime e ghiribizzi linguistici nella pubblicità, Enciclopedia Italiana*. Available at: www.treccani.it/magazine/lingua_italiana/speciali/pubblicita_00/Afribo.html (retrieved at 7 April 2013).

Audinoeditore.it = http://www.audinoeditore.it/media/books/308/cap3/1.slogan.pdf (retrieved the last time at 7 April 2013)

Ballardini, B. 1994. *La morte della pubblicità* [The death of advertising]. Roma: Castelvecchi.

Bárberi Squarotti, G. et al. 2004. *Dizionario di retorica e stilistica* (a cura della Redazione UTET) [Lexicon of Rhetoric and Stylistics]. Torino: UTET Libreria.

Caffarelli, E. 2007. Dal nome proprio al nome proprio: la transonimizzazione imperante [From proper name to proper name: process of dominating transonymisation]. *Lid'O. Lingua italiana d'oggi* 3: 219–237.

—. 2011. Voice *Nomi commerciali* [Brand names]. In *Enciclopedia dell'Italiano* [Encyclopaedia of Italian]. R. Simone (ed. in chief), 953–955. Roma: Istituto della Enciclopedia Italiana.

Castelvecchi Ceserani, G. 1988. *Storia della pubblicità in Italia* [The History of advertising in Italy]. Roma-Bari: Laterza.

Codeluppi, V. 2001. *Che cos'è la pubblicità* [What is advertising]. Roma: Carocci Editore.

—. 2002. *La pubblicità: Guida alla lettura dei messaggi* [Advertising: a guide to the interpretation of advertisements]. Milano: Franco Angeli.

Cotticelli-Kurras, P. 2007. Die Entwicklung der hybriden Wortschöpfungen bei den italienischen Markennamen [The development of hybrid neoformations in Italian brand names]. In *Names in Commerce and Industry: Past and Present*, L. Kremer and E. Ronneberger-Sibold (eds.), 167–185. Berlin: Logos.

—. 2008. La struttura morfologica dei marchionimi italiani nel XX secolo (fino agli anni '80) [The morphological structure of Italian brand names in 20th century]. In *I Nomi nel tempo e nello spazio. Atti del XXII Congresso Internazionale di Scienze Onomastiche* [Names in time and space]. *Pisa, 28 agosto–4 settembre 2005, vol. 2.* M. G. Arcamone, D. Bremer, D. De Camilli and B. Porcelli (eds.), 695–709. Pisa: ETS.

—. 2011. 'Spieglein, Spieglein an der Wand, wer ist die mächtigste, zuverlässigste, traditionsreichste Produktklasse im ganzen Land?' – Assoziationen bei italienischen Markennamen. ['Mirror, mirror on the wall, who is the most powerful, most reliable, richest in tradition product class in the country?'– Associations in Italian brand names]. In *Eichstätter Sprachgeschichten*, Ein Kolloquium zu Ehren von E. Ronneberger-Sibold, K. Kazzazi, S. Wahl, K. Luttermann, T. A. Fritz and S. Potsch-Ringeisen (eds.), 95–113. Würzburg: Verlag Königshausen & Naumann GmbH.

—. 2012. Dal *Drivecaffé* alla *Snackerina*: Neoformazioni dei marchionimi italiani: tendenze a cavallo del secolo [From *Drivecaffè* to *Snackerina*: neoformations in Italian brand names: trends at the turn of the century]. In *Il linguaggio della pubblicità italiano e tedesco: Teoria e prassi – Italienische und deutsche Werbesprache: Theorie und Praxis,* Verona, 13–15 ottobre 2011, P. Cotticelli Kurras, E. Ronneberger-Sibold, and S. Wahl (eds.), 85–103, Alessandria: Edizioni dell'Orso.

—. Forthcoming. Italian brand names through their associations: current trends. In *Proceedings of Names in daily life, International Congress of Onomastic Sciences (ICOS) XXIV, Barcelona, 5th–9th September 2011.*

Croce, G., Berselli, E. and Nove, A. 2008. *Tutto il meglio di Carosello, 1957–1977* [The Best of Carosello]. Torino: Einaudi.

De Stefani, E. 2004. La terminologia nell'onomastica [Terminology in Onomastics]. *Rivista Italiana di Onomastica* X, 1: 53–71.

Fabris, G. 1997. *La pubblicità: teorie e prassi* [Advertising: Theories and Praxis]. Milano: Franco Angeli.

Falabrino, G. L., 1999. *Pubblicità serva padrona* [Advertising maid mistress]. Milano: Il Sole 24 Ore Libri.

Giusti, M. 1995. *Il grande libro di Carosello* [The Lexicon of Carosello]. Milano: Sperling & Kupfer.

Grasso, A. 1992. *Storia della televisione italiana* [The History of Italian Television]. Milano: Garzanti.

—. 2008. *Enciclopedia della televisione* [The Encyclopaedia of Television]. Milano: Garzanti.

Greimas, A. J. 1966. *Sémantique structurale* [Structural semantics]. Paris: Larousse, [trad. it. *Semantica strutturale*. Roma: Meltemi. 2000].

Manconi, L. 1967. *Raccolta di slogans pubblicitari italiani* [Selection of italian slogans]. Quaderni dell' I.P.R, Nr 20, Editrice l'Ufficio moderno.

Mortara Garavelli, B. 2000. *Manuale di retorica* [A Handbook of Rhetoric]. Milano: Bompiani.

Ronneberger-Sibold, E. and Wahl, S. 2012. *Kinamic*, *Bolidon* und

Maikäferflufbenzin – Wortbildung und -schöpfung in deutschen Markennamen [Word formations and neoformations in German brand names]. In *Il linguaggio della pubblicità italiano e tedesco: Teoria e prassi – Italienische und deutsche Werbesprache: Theorie und Praxis,* Verona, 13–15 ottobre 2011, P. Cotticelli Kurras, E. Ronneberger-Sibold and S. Wahl (eds.), 313–334, Alessandria: Edizioni dell'Orso.

—. Forthcoming. Associations in German Brand Names: Current Trends. In *Proceedings of Names in daily life, International Congress of Onomastic Sciences (ICOS) XXIV, Barcelona 5th–9th September 2011.*

Vestergaard, T. and Schrøder, K. 1985. *The language of advertising.* Oxford: Blackwell.

Zardo, F. 1997. Marchi nominativi, nomi propri o nomi comuni? I nomi di marchio nell'italiano scritto contemporaneo [Brands from names, personal names or common nouns? The brand names in contemporary written Italian]. *Rivista Italiana di Onomastica* III, 1: 25–43.

—. 2007. Ancora sui marchionimi [About brands again]. In *Studi linguistici per Luca Serianni* [Studies in honor of Luca Serianni], V. Della Valle and P. Trifone (eds.), 253–270. Roma: Salerno Editrice.

BREAD PACKAGES AS VERBAL AND VISUAL SIGNS

IRMA SORVALI
UNIVERSITY OF OULU, FINLAND

Abstract

The aim of this study is to analyse names of bread packages, collected during the last two decades in Finland. The methodological emphasis lies on linguistics, semiotics and translation studies. It is not only the linguistic names that stand in focus, but also the visual elements, in the form of pictures and colours, are of central meaning in the semiotic analysis. The information given on the packages is interpreted and translated by the consumer. In this process, the role of the human senses is shortly discussed.

On the basis of the results obtained, it can be stated that a Finnish bread name is most often a compound with the appellative *leipä* 'bread', with more or less informative additions. There is a frequent use of verbal and pictorial grains in the material, and many of them refer to the health of the consumer. The packages also contain special features that are able to provide further information and even convey little stories. In storytelling, a comparison with small corpuses, collected in a couple of other European countries, is made.

The Objective of the Study

The aim of this study is to analyse the names of contemporary bread packages from a multidisciplinary point of view. The material consists of Finnish bread packages collected between the 1990s and 2000s. The name, the product and the package are included in the concept "package".

In this analysis, methods from linguistics, semiotics and translation studies are applied. The verbal information given on the packages is expressed in a completed chain of linguistic utterances, and the names of the packages are linguistic expressions, produced for commercial objectives

(Ainiala, Saarelma and Sjöblom 2012). The packages are also studied from a semiotic point of view, especially when the pictures and other visual features are concerned (see Peirce [1901] 2012; Nöth 1990). When buying a package, the consumer is translating and interpreting the information given on it (see Jakobson 1966). In this process, the role of the consumer's senses is also discussed. The packages contain special features that are able to provide further information and even convey little stories with human actors (see Barthes 1989; Nöth 1990). In studying the stories, a smaller number of Swedish, Estonian and Belgian packages are used for the sake of comparison. However, the study is more descriptive and qualitative than quantitative.

The present study is a part of the project *Everyday Language* at the University of Oulu, Finland (Sorvali 2001; 2008; 2009). The aim of this project is to analyse everyday materials. Finally, it is worth mentioning that all the packages in this study are authentic, and the packaged bread has been bought and consumed by someone, in many cases even by me. In this respect, I have participated in the problem I am studying. Participant observation is a way to experience consumers' decisions (cf. Morrison et al. 2012: 45–46), but how the consumers really choose their bread is not studied here. The role of the consumer is shortly highlighted in the discussion on the human senses, and in the presentation of packages for young consumers.

The Rotation of the Names

Bread is known from time immemorial, while the packages are of a later time. The names of bread packages are product names which are linguistic expressions with reference to the idea of the product produced or developed for commercial objectives (see Ainiala et al. 2012: 211–213, 247–249). Every packaged product in sales must have a name which shall be clearly written on the package. According to the European directive (see *Directive 2000/13/EC*), compulsory labelling requirements include, among others, the name under which the product is sold, the name of the manufacturer or packager, a list of ingredients, the quantity of ingredients, and the best-before date. If needed, the name can be completed by additional information, distinguishing it from other similar products (section 7 of the *Decree on the Labelling of Foodstuffs* 1084/2004).

The Finnish corpus, collected during the 1990s and 2000s, consists of a total of 140 packages. The product names of these packages follow a special principle of rotation: a short appellative is used in various combinations. This name is considered to be an archetype in this corpus.

The product name is most often a compound with the appellatives *leipä* 'bread', *reikäleipä* 'bread (with a hole)', *rieska* 'flatbread' or *sämpylä* 'roll' as the final part. The initial part of the compound is usually an appellative expressing one of the ingredients of the product. The main ingredients, i.e. the actual grain the bread is baked with, are mentioned in nearly one hundred names of the Finnish corpus. The most common appellative is *ruis* 'rye', e.g. the name *Ruisrouhesämpylä* is composed of the appellatives *ruis*, *rouhe* ('crushed grain') and *sämpylä* ('roll'). The appellatives *peruna* 'potato', *monivilja* 'multigrain' and *luomu* 'organic' are further examples. In some cases, the name of the bakery is included, e.g. *Antellin Perunalimppu* ('potato bread by Antell'). Limppu is a specific type of loaf of dense bread.

The history of bread has played a special role in giving names. In Finland, rye bread, dried on poles suspended just below the kitchen ceiling, was obviously baked as early as in the Middle Ages. Later on, soft bread, baked on the bottom of the oven, became common in the eastern parts of Finland, while the south-western parts imported the way of baking thin, hard cakes from Sweden. (*Kulturhistoriskt lexikon* 1980, s.v. *bakning*.) The difference between hard and soft bread is nowadays readable in the Finnish names *orsileipä* (*orsi* 'pole, perch, beam') and *arinaleipä* (*arina* 'grating (on the floor of a fireplace)'). In older times, bark was used as an ingredient of bread, and during the famine years, bark was a common ingredient in cereals (ibid. s.v. *nödbröd*). As a curiosity, the name *Luomupettuleipä* ('organic bark bread') appears among the modern Finnish names in this study. Needless to say, the bread in the packages studied here is industrially produced.

The texts on the packages collected in Finland, which is officially bilingual, are mostly written in Finnish and Swedish, the two national languages in Finland. Instead of Swedish, Norwegian and Danish can also be used. Moreover, products produced in Finland and purchased in monolingual communes can be labelled in the language of these communes only. (Section 5 of the *Decree on the Labelling of Foodstuffs* 1084/2004.)

The packages with texts in Finnish and Swedish form about 60 per cent of all of the packages of the Finnish corpus. The percentage of the packages with information solely in Finnish is about thirty. Sporadically, there are also shorter English translations of the informative texts. The names of the packages are normally only in Finnish, a fact which also follows legislation. However, the Finnish name is sometimes translated into Swedish, e.g. *Ruissekaleipä* 'rye bread (with other grains)' into *Rågblandsbröd*, while the proper name *Maalaisruisleipä* 'country rye bread' is left untranslated. In accordance with national regulations, some packages completely lack a Swedish translation, which is the case especially in the eastern and northern parts of Finland which are monolingual.

The Name and the Package from a Semiotic Point of View

The names as well as the whole appearance of the packages are relevant to everyday communication with the consumer, and they provide an interesting source of material for a semiotic study. The names are not dead expressions, but living exponents in everyday life, while the packages will, in most cases, become waste.

The packaging is an influential advertising medium, and advertising is an area of research lying between economics and semiotics. "For semiotics, advertising is a process of the exchange of *messages*", as Nöth (1990: 476) puts it. In studying marketing, the discipline of semiotics has often been used (e.g. Umiker-Sebeok 1987: passim; Holbrook and Hirschman 1993: 230). In the present analysis, the division of semiotic signs between icon, index and symbol by Peirce is applied. From a semiotic point of view, a proper name is a sign "denoting something having an identity consisting in continuity of existence and common to the experience of the deliverer and interpreter of the proposition of which it forms a part", as defined by Peirce ([1901] 2012). The pictures of the product on the package, representing their objects by similarity, belong to the domain of the icon in advertising. The visual image of the bread on the package, the icon of the bread, stands for any nutritive bread, while "the advertiser's attempt to draw the consumer's attention to the product implies an act of pointing, which is the sign type of an index" (Nöth 1990: 480). The name is also a symbol of the bread, while the picture of a stalk of grain symbolises the whole product, and has a function of an index in the process of baking, i.e. from "stalk of grain" to "bread".

The colours used on the packages are informative and expressive signs. Red, green and yellow, the colours of traffic lights, are used as semiotic signs (see Klarén 1996: 74–78). A red package arouses attention, and green is commonly associated with recycling in packaging. The yellow sun, a symbol of unpolluted nature and also an index of growth, is visible on many packages. The origin of the product is usually focused on the colours. Brown iconically refers to brown bread, which is especially easy to notice due to the transparent plastic packages. Green symbolises pure nature, and also indexically refers to a living organism. The dominating colour of the package *RuisAurinko* ('RyeSun') is yellow, which simultaneously symbolises a natural product. Furthermore, the picture of a landscape with a setting sun, with yellow fields and red houses, is indexically referring to naturally baked bread. The use of white and blue – the colours of the Finnish flag – on the package *Tosisuomalainen* ('real Finn') emphasises nationality. Some packages, originating from the region of North Karelia in Eastern Finland, have expressive illustrations in red and black, symbolising typical Karelian colours.

In an interview with a group of consumers consisting of Finnish academic teachers and university students, it became apparent that the informants wanted to see "pleasant" colours on the packages, such as red and yellow, green and blue, and even brown and orange, but there were also colours, especially blue, that they did not like. (Sorvali 2009: 192–194.) The aim of this interview was to find trends in the behaviour and decision making of the consumer when buying packaged bread. Nevertheless, it must be pointed out that the choice of colours may be a matter of chance.

The Senses of the Consumer

The senses, often neglected in linguistic and philosophical ethics (cf. Brady 2005: 179), belong to the external world of the consumer and cannot be ignored in the analysis of the names of bread packages. The packages with their names provide nutritional values, and when purchasing bread, the consumer may interpret and apply the information on the packages by means of the senses.

The verbal and visual materials are components which are translated in the mind of the consumer. In this mental process of translating, the human senses are needed. Here, the role of the senses is called *orbis sensualium*: the consumer is able to see, hear, feel, taste, and smell the product. When the consumer takes a look at a bread package on the shelves at market, he or she is translating the inedible outside of the package into edible food, e.g. a bread package named *Kuituinen ruisleipä* ('rye bread with fibre') can be translated into healthy food. In other words, the verbal sign is translated into something in the non-verbal system, which in Jakobson's (1966: 233) terminology means *intersemiotic translation* or *transmutation*. Consequently, the package with its name is an intersemiotic translation of bread and food.

The senses also arouse synaesthetic reactions. Primarily, the smell and taste of the bread have a key meaning. As to functionality, the packages are visual and tactile. The visual appearance is especially noticeable when the package is transparent. The concept of beauty also belongs to the sense of sight, and it depends on individual evaluation. When eating bread, the sense of hearing is more or less present, and the package can be acoustic when it is opened.

Many of the names are allusions to a few of the senses. According to the above-mentioned interview, sight was the dominating sense in buying bread. There was even mention of taste, smell, and emotions. (Sorvali 2009: 189.) The names *Tummat lounassämpylät* (*tumma* 'dark') and *Antellin vaalea rouheinen sämpylä* (*vaalea* 'light') are connected to sight, and they furthermore refer to smell and taste. The bread name *Onnenleipä* ('happiness bread') may arouse positive feelings. The name *RuisKurvikkaat* ('curvy rye (bread)') is both visual and tactile. It is not enough that the bread is edible but it must also have flavour. The addition *Hyvällä leivällä on salaisuutensa* ('good bread has its secrets'), placed after the proper name *Pomppis Patu*, does not disclose the secret, but the words may be created in order to stimulate the taste. As for the sense of hearing, the consumer may imagine the voice of the metaphoric name *Ruisromput* (*romppu* 'CD-ROM'). While eating crispbread, the noise is acoustically heard.

It can be argued that the *orbis sensualium* is important for the consumer as well as for the producer. In any case, it is primarily hunger, the basic need of the consumer that dictates the production and the marketing of bread.

Verbal and Pictorial Grains

Grains are commonly included in the names and pictures of the modern packages. Even colours and shapes may take the role of the words. The word *iso* ('*big*') is visually arranged in order to show the large size of the bread. It can be noted that an everlasting visual picture of bread, the Italian *rosetta*, can be found on the wall of a building in Pompey, which conveys the marketing of bread form about two thousand years ago. Semiotically speaking, a picture of a special type of bread can only be understood by a person who knows what this type of bread looks like (cf. Lotman 1989: 133).

In my corpuses, the verbal and pictorial grains seem to have been put to good use. The bread and/or the stalk of grain are often included in names and pictures of the Finnish packages. This is expressed by means of a grain index, which has been counted as the number of names or pictures divided by the total number of packages. Here, a smaller corpus of a later date is used for the sake of comparison. The grain indexes can be viewed in the table below:

Table 1. Grain indexes in Finnish packages.

Number of Finnish packages	Verbal grain index	Pictorial grain index
140 (1900s–2000s)	0.7	0.5
30 (2005)	0.3	0.3

In the larger corpus, the verbal grain index is higher than the pictorial one, while both grain indexes are lower in the smaller corpus. A possible explanation for the decrease could be explained by the statement by Nöth (1990: 480) that producers want to pay more attention to the packages with illustrations which differ from the product proper.

How grains are used in the names and pictures will be exemplified below, and in addition, some stylistic aspects will be highlighted. The food should contain health-promoting ingredients, and consequently, there are also many bread names clearly referring to nutrition and health. In fact, the nutritional factors are found in the names including the appellative *leipä* 'bread'.

The names have global and local allusions, a fact which can be explained as a tendency to promote healthy bread. A map showing the geographic origin of the bread is printed on some packages, e.g. *Perunaleipä* with a map of Finland, and *Hiivaleipä* with a map of the island of Hailuoto. Names such as *Aito Pälkäneen limppu*, which contains a toponym (*Pälkäne*), are seldom found in the corpus. Furthermore, pictures of rural landscapes are often motifs used to refer to healthy bread.

Stylistics is not unknown for those who are composing product names, and the information on the packages is sometimes given by using classic, stylistic figures. The most often used picture of a stalk of grain is a visual metonym, representing the whole plant, and even the whole product. The picture of the grain is, however, crossed out on the packages of gluten-free bread, and is considered a semiotic sign of "forbidden". Gluten-free products have increasing commercial functions, and there are special European regulations on these products (see *Commission Regulation* (EC) No 41/2009). The appellative *hiiva* ('yeast') in the name *Hiivaleipä* metaphorically refers to the dough, while the pictured sun is a nonverbal metaphor of naturally produced bread. A synecdoche is exemplified by the noun *täysjyvä* 'whole grain', included in the name *Täysjyvä REAL*. The name *Meikäläinen Rukiinen Reikäläinen* 'our rye hole-bread' is not only an example of rhyme and tautology, but also of alliteration. The reduplication of the short word 'rye' in *RuisRuis* has an expressive rhythmic effect. On the contrary, names including longer syntactic constructions are rare, and are regularly found in the names with an emphasis of the agricultural origin, e.g. (*Ruiskurvikkaat*) *Maalta kotoisin* ('from the countryside').

Names Expressing Features

The consumer is supposed to be able to read and interpret the information given on the packages in marketing. As suggested above, the names are intersemiotically translated (Jakobson 1966: 233) in the mind of the consumer. It is also interesting to study whether there is any correspondence between the visual appearance and the name of the package. Special components, called *features*, are studied for this purpose.

The features are of importance for the senses and may direct the consumer's choice (Sorvali 2008: 464–467.) The packages should, among other things, be attractive and give favourable consumer response (cf. Kotler 2000: 419), and they are, with reason, considered an expressive form of the consumer lifestyle (Pongrácz 1998: 8). The features offer material for interdisciplinary analyses, and are divided into three main categories, i.e. cultural, aesthetic and ecological, which, however, are more or less intermixed.

The packages create cultural contexts by reflecting the cultural specialities in the different regions in Finland, but the bread culture traditions overlap to some extent. Famous names in fiction are sometimes used in Finnish bread names. This is a process called *indexical feature transfer* by Nöth (1990: 480). The product is represented by means of desirable objects, e.g. well-known places and events as well as film stars. The well-known features of the "famous" or "desirable" entity are associated with the less well known product, and "the features transferred to the product refer to it as an index" (ibid.). The name *Pikkusieppari* ('little catcher') is an allusion to the novel *The Catcher in the Rye*, written by J. D. Salinger. This famous name in fiction is associated with the less famous bread *Pikkusieppari*. The name *Nuori Mylläri* ('young miller') refers to a Finnish film of the 1950s, based on the text by Finnish writer Maiju Lassila. The cultural allusions to fiction are not pure graphic elements, but are seen as syndromes of society.

Cultural features are also influenced by historical events, a fact that is apparent in bread names. The Finnish name *Pietarin limppu* ('bread of St Petersburg') is *Leningrads limpa* (referring to Leningrad) in the Swedish translation on the package, but after the collapse of the Soviet Union, the Swedish name of the package was changed to *St. Peterburgs limpa*. This name change also reflects changes in society. An example of patriotism is found in the name *Vaasan rautaisen isänmaallinen Panssarivanikka* ('patriotic iron artillery bread by Vaasa'). Here, the whole package is modelled after a camouflage suit in green and brown, and the text on the back side of the package gives information about the bread during the Continuation War (WW II). In addition, the famous words by Napoleon ("An army marches on its stomach"), cited on the package, give an example of an indexical feature transfer. A name may also allude to famous events in Finland. For example, *Waskileipä* ('brass bread') can be purchased in Lieksa, in eastern Finland, during the yearly Brass Festival (Fi. *Waskiviikko*). This internationally known festival is associated with *Waskileipä* in local marketing.

The aesthetic values of the names and packages are esteemed by the consumer. We must remember that esteeming aesthetic values is very subjective. A picture of a beautiful landscape is meant to give an illusion of a pure product of nature, and even nostalgic memories from childhood can be awakened. These aesthetics are often connected to harmonious autumnal colours, indexically referring to harvest time (cf. semiotics, above). Even images of music are created, e.g. the name *Hilde leipäset Adagio*.

Foodstuffs are also supposed to be ethical products offering ecological values. As presented above, grains are common in the names and pictures. They emphasise the ecological nature of the products, and give eating pleasure and wellness, providing nutritional values. Signs of nutrition and health are involved in the package *Sydänystävän leipä* ('soulmate's bread'), with the pictures of men jogging, red hearts, and an emblem that reads *Oulun Uusi Sydänyhdistys* ('New Healthy Heart Society of Oulu)'.

The bread, described as healthy, may help the consumer's choice, but even a name change may be enough to alter the perception of health, as Irmak et al. (2011) put it. Information of the origin of the product and the environmental consequences of the production is strongly ethical (cf. Puikkonen and Myllykoski 2000: 32–36), and the ethical and health-conscious features of packaging are considered as signs of a better future, especially for those who are interested in ethics and ecology. Ecological aspects are often apparent in the information of the fact that the packaging material can be recycled.

Names and Pictures in Storytelling

The visual appearance of three-dimensional packages can be able to tell stories with human actors, even without having much textual assistance (cf. Goffman 1976: 26). Calefato (2009: 236) argues that the name hosts a narrative principle that makes it live as a sign. Interestingly, narratology is also concerned with non-literary narratives (Nöth 1990: 367). According to Barthes (1989: 79), narratives are international, transhistorical and transcultural, and they are present in every age, in every place and in every society, "caring nothing for the division between good and bad literature".

The everyday reality of the consumer is expressed through a narrative structure, in more or less an unconventional form, and one of the realities is the role of people as, more or less, active agents in the stories. The above studied features help to interpret the stories. The bread packages are also supposed to reflect the connection of the names and pictures to national specialities. In order to throw light on possible national differences, a slight comparison can be made with packages collected in Sweden, Estonia and Belgium. Due to the common history of Finland and Sweden during 600 years, there are great similarities between these countries, but also differences in their bread cultures. The Finnish and the Estonian languages are related to each other, and there are also similarities in several traditions. Belgium differs in many aspects from the countries in this study, and is represented with a small corpus only (see below).

Human beings are usually included in narrative packages. Pictures of people are relatively most common in Sweden, while people are seen more seldom in Finland and in Estonia. On the whole, human individuals are pictured in a third of the packages. It is of interest to note that Finnish and Swedish packages are clearly dominated by images of males, while a dominance of female images is quite obvious on Estonian packages. This is shown in the table below:

Table 2. Human individuals in the names and pictures on the packages.

Number of packages	Female (%)	Male (%)	Individuals (%)
Fi. 140 (1990s–2000s)	21.9	78.1	22.9
Swe. 32 (2006)	16.7	83.3	37.5
Est. 86 (2000–2007)	62.5	37.5	27.9

One can naturally discuss the role of family members when buying bread, but it is not possible to give any unambiguous explanations here. In any case, the question is connected with categorisation and vocabulary referring to women and men (cf. Fairclough 1997: 27).

The names of the Finnish packages show arrangements of linguistic and visual elements that contribute to a communicative effect; both males and females are pictured as active participants in the process. For example, a grandmother in the name *Mumminrieska* ('granny's flatbread') can be seen as a way to familiarise the product. The name *Antellin Joukahainen* refers indexically to a man named *Joukahainen* in the Finnish national epic *Kalevala*, and simultaneously, it may inspire the consumer to read more about his story in this epic.

Some of the names, e.g. *Maalaisruislimppu* (*maalais-* 'country, rural'), recount agricultural life in Finland. *Ruisrouhesämpylä Maukasta maalaisleipää* ('crushed rye roll tasty country bread') shows a man who is manually harvesting in a field. This nostalgic picture of a rural landscape is a narrative form, which makes the person intelligible within the agricultural and social environment. The package named *Nätti Jussi* tells the story of Finnish forest worker and vagabond Juho Vihtori Nätti in the first half of the 20th century. This nickname is used by two bakeries, but in spite of the identity of the name, the packages have different visual appearances.

The use of photos of bakers, displaying a scene of bakery work, is typical of the Swedish packages. The photographed bakers are thus taking the role of active agents in the stories. Descriptive Swedish adjectives such as *saftig* ('juicy'), *osötad* ('unsweetened') and *ekologisk* ('ecological') are included on many packages, emphasising the quality of the product. The size of the bread is described by the noun 'giant' in the name *Fullkornsjätte* ('wholegrain giant'), and in addition to this, there is a photo of an athlete on the package.

On the Estonian packages, there are people included in stories referring to the history of Estonia. Due to EU directives, new languages in addition to Estonian are used on the Estonian packages, and due to better printing techniques, a more colourful appearance in layout can be noted. The cornflower (the national flower of Estonia), the swallow (the national bird of Estonia), and names from the Estonian national epic *Kalevipoeg* recount the history of Estonia. (Pyhtilä, e-mail correspondence 2006.) The name *Pere Rukkileib* ('family's rye bread) is completed with a picture of a rural scene with a farmyard where swallows are flying in the clear sky. It has been stated that nature and nature writing have played a central role in Estonia (Maran and Tüür 2001: 4–10), a fact that is notable in the use of nature pictures on the Estonian packages, where rural motifs, recounting fields and forests, are common.

The dominance of female images in the Estonian corpus is exemplified by the names *Seemne-Siiri* ('seed Siiri') and *Linnapiiga* ('castle maiden').

Males with names and pictures are included in the products *Naabrimehe Leib* ('neighbouring man's bread') and *Ärimehe Leib* ('businessman's bread'), and even proper names are used, e.g. *Otto Juustukuklid just sulle* ('Otto cheeseroll just for you'). On the package named *Dr. Möldri Terviseleib* ('Dr. Möldri's healthy bread'), the doctor himself is pictured on the front, emphasising a healthy life. Even happiness is included in some of the Estonian names, e.g. in *Õnne terakuklid* ('happiness health roll'). Happiness and misery are moreover universal human problems which advertising is in fact concerned with (Nöth 1990: 479).

The corpus of 50 Belgian packages, collected between 1998 and 2004, basically differs from the other corpuses in this analysis. In Belgium, bread is baked several times during the day, and immediately sold without packaging, and that is why there are only a couple of comparable bread packages in the Belgian corpus. It is also notable that none of the Belgian packages is made of plastic. Instead, all of them are made of cardboard or some other non-definable material. An exception to this is the bread *Hoevebrood*, *Pain de Ferme,* which is packaged in a paper bag, with a drawing of a couple of bakers working in an old-fashioned, probably medieval, bakery. A package of hard bread, *Parovita, Knackebrood, Craque-Pain*, contains photo of an everyday life scene of two young consumers. In any case, the Belgian corpus is able to present modern and old stories.

In conclusion, the little stories with names and pictures are especially found on the Finnish and Estonian packages, while photos are more typical of the Swedish ones. The stories are supposed to have been used as advertising media. The old, traditional stories are absent, but instead, one can find modern ones which desire to stimulate the consumer's fantasy.

Packages for Young People

The storytelling packages are aimed to be read and interpreted by all consumers, regardless of their age. The question of whether there is something on the packages especially for young people will be answered below. Young people and children play a special role in the marketing of food (cf. Koho 2012: 38). However, they are only seldom directly observed on the packages. In any case, the young consumer may find some product names rather attractive. One example is the Finnish name *Kaurakiekko* ('oat puck') with a reference to (ice)hockey (*jääkiekko*), and *Ruisromput* (*romppu* 'CD-ROM') with a reference to music. A picture of three boys playing football on a package named *Vimpulat* may also appeal to younger consumers. Furthermore, there are packages with pictures of animals, resembling old fables, one of the best known genres of narrative art. The animals, usually anthropomorphised, also behave like human beings.

The bear, well-known from fables, arouses sympathy. One can see a picture of a bear with a cub on its shoulders on a Finnish package named *Karhuntassu* ('bear paw'). It can also be mentioned that the bear is the most popular animal in old trademarks registered in Finland (Hovi 1994: 17). Moreover, a kangaroo is surprisingly pictured on a couple of Finnish packages with the name *Pomppis* ('hoppy', cf. verb *pomppia* 'hop, jump'), viz. *Ruis Pomppis* ('rye hoppy') and *Pomppis Ruisruutu* ('hoppy rye square'). This name, together with the exotic picture, characterises the lightness of the product. A German shepherd and a couple of horses are pictured in a Finnish landscape (*Antellin Riihiruis* 'Antell's rye drying barn'). It is worth pointing out that there are no cows pictured on the package *Laktoositon Sekaleipä* ('lactose-free multigrain (white) bread').

In Sweden, pictures of animals are rare. The package *Julvört* ('Christmas bread') has a picture of a straw goat, which, together with the name, tells of Father Christmas. Some pictures of animals are also found on the Estonian packages. A rabbit, well-known in children's literature, is pictured with a carrot on the package *Porgandi Sarveke* ('carrot bread'). A frog, dressed in colourful shorts, on *Piknikukukkel* ('picnic roll') and a rhinoceros on *Kliisarveke* are more exotic examples of animals on the Estonian bread packages. As for the Belgian corpus, the stories seem to be aimed at consumers of all ages.

The packages contain small visual scenes with people and animals from the young consumer's environment, but how often the texts and pictures are "read" and interpreted by them is quite another question. In any case, the stories are characterised as a popular collection aiming to awaken young people's interest, and they are also composed for the sake of pleasure.

Conclusion

Bread is of great relevance for people, their nutrition and health, and when it is sold, it must have a name. This is why I have studied the specific connection between the names of the packages and the special information embedded in pictures and other visual features on them. On the basis of the results of the analysis, it can be stated that Finnish bread names follow a special principle of rotation: the typical name is a short appellative such as *leipä* and *limppu* ('bread'), together with various characterising additions. The names are often written in Finnish and Swedish due to the official bilingualism of Finland.

The names are typographically marked and incorporated in the text and visual illustrations, often containing special features. The cultural, aesthetic and ecological features, as reported above, show, among others, that healthfulness is a strong marketing concept. Moreover, the packages intend to be useful in giving information on the product, and this information is interpreted by the consumer. The name, together with the text and illustrations included, is often able to refer to the senses of the consumer, and even to tell little stories. In this storytelling, the findings of the analysis of the smaller corpuses of Swedish, Estonian and Belgian packages are presented. The stories, with names and pictures, are especially found on the Finnish and the Estonian packages. The human beings pictured on the packages, have a clear male dominance among the Finnish and the Swedish packages, while a female dominance is quite obvious in the Estonian corpus.

The product names and visual illustrations contribute to the wholeness of the packages, and they represent our modern bread culture. Due to growing environmental awareness, the future names and packages are expected to be more and more affected by ecological tendencies. Furthermore, packages are purchased during a defined time span and new ones are continuously designed and introduced to the market. Consequently, new names are needed in their appearance. Therefore, it is important to emphasise the role of the names of packaged products in future research.

References

Ainiala, T., Saarelma, M. and Sjöblom, P. 2012. *Names in Focus. An Introduction to Finnish Onomastics*. Leonard Pearl (trans.). Helsinki: Finnish Literature Society.

Barthes, R. 1989. *Image–Music–Text*. 11th printing. Selected and translated by S. Heath. New York: The Noonday Press.

Brady, E. 2005. Sniffling and Savoring. The Aesthetics of Smells and Tastes. In *The Aesthetics of Everyday Life*. A. Light and J. M. Smith (eds.), 177–193. New York: Columbia University Press.

Calefato, P. 2009. What name are you? In *Communication: Understanding / Misunderstanding* (2009). Proceedings of the 9th Congress of the IASS/AIS–Helsinki–Imatra: 11–17 June, 2007. Acta Semiotica Fennica XXXIV. E. Tarasti (ed.), 234–244. Imatra: International Semiotics Institute. Helsinki: Semiotic Society of Finland.

Commission Regulation (EC) No 41/2009 = Commission Regulation (EC) No 41/2009 of 20 January 2009 concerning the composition and labelling of foodstuffs suitable for people intolerant to gluten. http://eur-lex.europa.eu (retrieved 18 January 2013).

Decree on the Labelling of Foodstuffs 1084/2004. Ministry of Trade and Industry (currently the Ministry of Employment and the Economy). Helsinki 2 December 2004. http://www.mmm.fi/en/index/frontpage/food_safety/labelling_nutrition /food_labelling.html (retrieved 24 April 2012).

Directive 2000/13/EC = Directive 2000/13/EC of the European Parliament and of the Council of 20 March 2000 on the approximation of the laws of the Member States relating to the labelling, presentation and advertising of foodstuffs. http://eur-lex.europa.eu (retrieved 12 February 2012).

Fairclough, N. 1997. *Media Discourse*. London, New York, Sydney, Auckland: Arnold.

Goffman, E. 1976. *Gender Advertisements*. Communications and Culture. London: The MacMillan Press Ltd.

Holbrook, M. B. and Hirschman, E. C. 1993. *The Semiotics of Consumption. Interpreting Symbolic Consumer Behavior in Popular Culture and Works of Art*. Berlin, New York: Mouton de Gruyter.

Hovi, P. 1994. *Trade Mark. Tavaramerkki*. Helsinki: TaiK-Offset.

Irmak, C., Vallen, B. and Robinson, S. R. 2011. *The Impact of Product Name on Dieters' and Nondieters' Food Evaluations and Consumption*. Available at: Gray, N. http://www.foodnavigator.com (retrieved 24 May 2011).

Jakobson, R. 1966. On Linguistic Aspects of Translation. In *On Translation*. R. A. Brower (ed.), 232–239. New York: Oxford University Press.

Klarén, U. 1996. *Vad är färg?* [What is the colour?]. Stockholm: HLS Förlag.

Koho, T. 2012. *Lapset ja markkinointi – ohjeita vastuulliseen markkinointiviestintään* [Children and marketing]. Helsinki: Mainostajien liitto.

Kotler, P. 2000. *Marketing Management*. The Millenium Edition. Upper Saddle River, New Jersey: Prentice Hall, Inc.

Kulturhistoriskt lexikon 1980 = *Kulturhistoriskt lexikon för nordisk medeltid. Från vikingatid till reformationstid* [Encyclopaedia of the Cultural history of the Scandinavian Middle Ages. From the Vikings to the Reformation]. Köpenhamn: Rosenkilde og Bagger.

Lotman, J. 1989. *Merkkien maailma. Kirjoitelmia semiotiikasta* [The world of signs. Writings on semiotics]. E. Peuranen, P. Nieminen and J. Mallinen (trans.). Helsinki: SN-kirjat.

Maran, T. and Tüür, K. 2001. On Estonian nature writing. *Estonian Literary Magazine* 13, 4–10.

Morrison, M. A., Haley, E., Sheehan, K. B. and Taylor, R. E. 2012. *Using Qualitative Research in Advertising. Strategies, Techniques, and Applications*. 2nd ed. Los Angeles, London, New Delhi, Singapore, Washington DC: Sage.

Nöth, W. 1990. *Handbook of Semiotics*. Bloomington and Indianapolis: Indiana University Press.

Peirce, C. S. [1901] 2012 = M. Bergman and S. Paavola (eds.), *The Commens Dictionary of Peirce's Terms. Peirce's Terminology in His Own Words*. http://www.helsinki.fi/science/commens/terms (retrieved 17 August 2012).

Pongrácz, E. 1998. *The Environmental Effects of Packaging*. Licentiate Thesis. Tampere: University of Technology, Department of Environmental Technology, Institute of Water and Environmental Engineering.

Puikkonen, M. and Myllykoski, L. 2000. *Onnistunut elintarvikkeiden pakkaaminen – avain markkinoille* [Successful packaging of food – a key to marketing]. Department of Process Engineering. Oulu: University of Oulu.

Pyhtilä, P. 2006. E-mail letter from Pertti Pyhtilä, Secretary for Cultural Affairs 1993–2006. Finnish Institute in Estonia, to the writer of this article. 30 December 2006.

Sorvali, I. 2001. Leipäpakkausten viestejä [Messages on bread packages]. *Puhe ja kieli. Tal och språk. Speech and Language*. 2001 (3): 103–113.

—. 2008. Analysis of Everyday Texts. In *Problems of General, Germanic and Slavic Linguistics. Papers for 70-th anniversary of Professor V. Levickij*. G. Altmann, I. Zadorozhna and Y. Matskulyak (eds.), 461–471. Chernivtsi: Books–XXI.

—. 2009. Att vara konsument i det tvåspråkiga Finland [To be a consumer in bilingual Finland]. In *Svenskan i Finland 11. Föredrag vid elfte sammankomsten för beskrivningen av svenskan i Finland. Åbo den 16–17 maj 2008*. L. Collin and S. Haapamäki (eds.), 187–196. Skrifter från svenska institutionen vid Åbo Akademi. Nr 7. Åbo: Åbo Akademi.

Umiker-Sebeok, J. 1987. *Marketing and Semiotics. New Directions in the Study of Signs for Sale*. Berlin, New York, Amsterdam: Mouton de Gruyter.

THE TOUCHY SUBJECT OF THE PLACE NAME: CONTEMPLATING MUNICIPALITY NAMES AND BRANDING IN MERGING SITUATIONS

ULLA HAKALA
AND PAULA SJÖBLOM
UNIVERSITY OF TURKU, FINLAND

Abstract

The main objective of place branding is to create positive attitudes in the target markets – in other words, to improve the welfare of the place. The crucial factors in creating a place brand are place identity and place image. Image is the sum of beliefs, ideas and impressions that people have of a place. Identity is evident on different levels: the functional, the experiential, and the symbolic level. The name of a place is not only a valuable carrier of individual and social identity but also of historical ties. People identify with places through their names.

What happens to place brands and place branding if the names change due to municipality consolidation? The purpose of this paper is to discuss the role of names in place mergers from a place branding perspective. With three illustrative case examples, we will discuss the possible impact of a name change on place branding and on various stakeholders, particularly residents and small and medium sized enterprises, and we will contemplate the challenges of place branding from two angles: identity and image. We claim that the administrative change focusing also on the municipality name has its emotive consequences, and new emphasis and appreciation are given to locality and old symbolic elements.

Introduction: Change is Inevitable – Like it or not

According to the Finnish Government's programme, Finnish municipalities will undergo extensive reforms in the coming years. The objective of the reforms is to guarantee equal services to all inhabitants and to strengthen the economy of the municipalities. The government also emphasises local democracy and self-governance. (Ministry of Finance 2012.) The Association of Finnish Local and Regional Authorities has proposed that the future municipal structure should be grounded on the concept of a financially strong municipality, taking regional differences into consideration (Local Finland 2012).

Under the new structure the number of municipalities will decrease markedly. There were 431 municipalities in Finland in 2006, falling to 320 in 2013. (Local Finland 2012.) The Government aims at much lower number – fewer than 100 have been mentioned. This will mean a tough consolidation process. Nevertheless, it is a strategic choice aimed at making the municipalities better able to face future challenges. One purpose is to control public spending and to secure a certain level of public services. There has been very little deeper discussion about the potential effects on marketing, but it has been pointed out that a bigger municipality has better opportunities to recruit people, attract enterprises and investments, and interest tourists. In the globalising world big cities will be important hubs promoting the surrounding regions and their development. (See e.g., Ohmae 1995: 46; Laamanen 2007: 91, 175.)

People have different conceptions of what the Government's programme will really mean to the residents of the affected municipalities. The discussion in the media has become livelier recently, triggered by numerous new absorption accounts (Laamanen 2007: 37). Many people are concerned about what will happen to the inhabitants of small municipalities and their businesses if they lose their own local administration. One point that has been made is that the reform will revolutionise the nomenclature. Most municipal names will disappear, just one being selected to cover the new area. More new names will appear, too. (Paikkala 2012.) All this puts place marketing and branding in a new situation.

Similar developments have been taking place in other European countries. For instance, 270 Danish municipalities were amalgamated into 98 larger units in 2007 (Municipalities of Denmark 2012). Sweden has had two major municipal reforms, the first as early as in the 1950s and the other in 1974, which reduced the number of municipalities from 2,500 to 290 (Paljakka 2012: 52). France has a huge number of municipalities – over 36,000 of which 80 per cent have less than 1,000 residents – and the need for a radical reduction has been expressed. However, mergers are very rare because residents and local councillors tend to retain a strong sense of place identity (Swift and Kervella 2003; Paljakka 2012: 53).

The purpose of this paper is to discuss the role of names in place mergers from a place-branding perspective. The opening conceptual discussion is followed by a description of three illustrative cases (cf. Siggelkow 2007: 21), two of them already realised municipal consolidations, and the third a prospective one. We discuss the role and importance of the place name in branding in a situation in which it changes for administrative reasons. Here, too, the place identity faces new challenges: the administrative change has emotional consequences, as locality and old symbolic elements are emphasised and appreciated anew (Kuntauudistus prosessina 2012: 66). *Consolidations of municipalities* are also referred to in the literature as *place mergers*. In this paper, and for the sake of variation, we use the terms interchangeably.

This article gives the background and builds up understanding for a future empirical study investigating perceptions and attitudes towards municipality names and their potential change among both managers of small and medium-sized enterprises (SMEs) and residents in the South-Western province of Finland. This paper is exploratory: we discuss the challenges of naming on a theoretical level via three case examples from the area: Salo, Parainen and Laitila. The South West has the longest history of structured municipality administration in Finland. Unlike in other parts of the country, numerous small municipalities and a dense population have been typical, which is a consequence of its history and the strong role of the established church. Close, compact and socially coherent parishes formed the basis for the later municipal development. (Laamanen 2007: 65–67.)

Earlier research on naming related to changes in municipality structure is scarce. One of the few examples is Harri Mantila's (2012) study analysing the name proposals for a new municipality based on a public competition, arranged in connection with an initiative to consolidate three municipalities in Western Finland. Mantila explored the views of residents regarding municipality names, and whether those views coincided with those expressed by onomasticians. Some corresponding folk-linguistic studies have been conducted on street names in city areas (e.g., Ainiala 2004; Päres-Schulman 2005; Yli-Kojola 2005).

With regard to research on branding, in spite of the large number of mergers and acquisitions (M&A) in markets, previous studies have focused mainly on stable organisational conditions (Kernstock and Brexendorf 2012). Moreover, the research emphasis has been on corporate and product branding, not places. Municipality names often have a long history and a lot of emotions are embedded in them. Names are words that remain through generations, and are valuable because they carry the history of the place in them (Vahtola 1999). They are also crucial elements in place branding, thus the name change affects the branding efforts. This has not been taken into account in the consolidations thus far, however, partly due to the practically non-existent research on the issue. There is thus a clear need to study place brands in relation to the changing municipality structures.

Background to the Phenomenon

Place Naming and Naming Strategies

Place names, toponyms, are both culture- and language-bound. They are built of elements of language – lexemes and affixes. However, not just any expression can be used: native speakers of a language expect the expressions to follow certain language-bound principles of naming. These principles concern the structure and the lexicon as well as the content of the name. (e.g., Kiviniemi 1975: 12; Ainiala, Saarelma and Sjöblom 2012: 63.)

Many place names in Western languages are compound expressions, made up of two parts: one part signifies the class or type of place (i.e. the generic part) and the other signifies certain special features of it, such as ownership, shape, colour, location and usage (i.e. the specific part). Examples include *Queensland*, *Long Island*, *Alice Springs*, *Östersjön*, *Nötholmen*, *Schwarzwald*. This is also the case in Finnish – the typical structure of a toponym is a two-part compound word, a generic part expressing the place itself preceded by a specific part expressing a special feature: *Helsingintie* 'Helsinki+GEN+road', *Korkeasaari* 'high+island'. Many languages also allow place names consisting of only one part, such as *London, Oslo*, *Vättern*, *Pretoria*, *Lima*, and the Finnish town of *Oulu* and Lake *Päijänne*. (Ainiala et al. 2012: 36–37, 64, 71–72.)

With regard to naming strategies, a large number of place names have spontaneously emerged in the speech of a people. People give names to places that are significant in some way and if there is good reason to speak about them, and these are called traditional place names. All the oldest names fall into this category. All traditional place names originally described the place they referred to. The language or name may have changed in the course of time so that the original content is opaque. Such names usually originated in small communities, and many became more widely known later on. Thus, traditional names do not originate in large communities. (Ainiala et al. 2012: 64–65.)

On the other hand, official and planned names have sprung up in larger communities, approved or created by someone with the right to name places. These kinds of names feature especially in urban environments in streets, parks and squares, for example, but also in rural areas. Official and planned names vary more than traditional names because urban areas are not only geographically larger but also more heterogeneous: there is a wide range of places and also a wide variety of name users with their own expectations about place names. (Ainiala et al. 2012: 65.)

Planned names emerge when authorities, companies or other public players discover a new need. Quite often names are planned in parallel, such as the street names in a new housing area. Name planners have to take many views into consideration from different perspectives and among various interest groups. Many of the names resemble traditional names, but may deviate substantially from the natural naming principles of the language. Planned names are authorised by the few people with the official right to give names. However, they are not necessarily accepted in the language community, which sometimes even spurns or opposes them.

Place Names and Identity

Interest in the socio-onomastic view of place names has grown since the 1990s. Primarily, the focus is on name use and variation in social situations. For instance, there have been Finnish studies on the toponymic competence of people from different backgrounds (e.g., Kepsu 1990; Pitkänen 1996; Ainiala et al. 2000), place-name changes in the course of time (Ainiala 1997), and so-called folk onomastics, in other words the study of people's ideas about and attitudes towards names (e.g., Ainiala and Halonen 2011).

The sociological questions of naming and name use attract the attention of onomasticians worldwide. One branch of this field of research is critical toponomastics, which concentrates on contested practices of place naming, and raises questions about naming and name use in different national and local contexts (see *Critical Toponymies* 2009). The researchers, who are not only onomasticians but also geographers and social scientists, emphasise the key role of naming in the colonial silencing of indigenous cultures, for instance, the canonisation of nationalistic ideals into nomenclature, as well as the formation of urban identities. The questions they address include the following. How do we conceptualise space through names? What, generally speaking, is the relation between a name and a place? Is it just names and the stories that are connected to them that actually make places exist? What is the relation between name and identity? How is naming connected to power?

According to the critical view, state institutions and regional authorities such as municipalities with the right to name places are privileged to select and decide on the kind of landscape elements that come into existence by making them communicable as real places in authoritative and popular discourses (Vuolteenaho and Ainiala 2010: 26). People may rise up in opposition to such a dictate from above when the authorities decide on place names that go against a thousand-year tradition of naming and do not take account of the place's significance to the local inhabitants.

Several place-name researchers discuss the question of name and identity (e.g., Helleland 2009; Særheim 2009; Konstanski 2009). Identity is a difficult concept to define: the meaning depends on what it relates to. It could be defined, for example, as the sameness of a person or thing at all times and in all circumstances, and connected to the concepts of individuality and personality (see OED, s.v. *identity*). According to Stuart Hall (1999: 16, 60), a well-known cultural theorist, all identities are located in culture, language and history. Identity accentuates both singularity and conjunction. A place is the stronghold for our identities because it is special, tangible, familiar and demarcated, and because it has social practices that mould us. Furthermore (Hall 1999: 68), globalisation can boost local identities. Globalisation in the present context could also be understood from the perspective of merging municipalities.

Botolv Helleland (2009: 502) defines landscape identity, or place identity as "oneness between self and landscape as experienced by human beings in given circumstances". He claims that a person's place identity is stronger when it is a question of a familiar landscape and when he or she knows the place names in the area. Toponyms have an important place in an individual's vocabulary, and knowing them awakens the feeling of belonging to a group in a particular area. As Terhi Ainiala (2009: 74) puts it: "Social identity and place identity are often linked with each other: identifying yourself with a place also often means identifying yourself as a member of a social group." Place names are valuable not only as bearers of individual and social identity but also as historical ties (Helleland 2009: 503).

Places as Brands

The concept of places as brands has been attracting the interest of academics and practitioners alike since the 1990s. The discussion has focused on whether places in general can be branded on the one hand (see e.g., Anholt 2008; Kerr and Balakrishnan 2012) and, assuming that the answer is 'yes', on the extent to which they can be branded on the other. First, what is a brand? In brief, a brand is indicative of value. According to Lynch and de Chernatony (2004), it represents a cluster of values that promise a unique and welcome experience between buyer and seller. What is special about branding places? According to Dinnie (2009), a place brand is a unique, multi-dimensional blend of elements that constitute culturally grounded differentiation. The incorporation of location, landscape and social relations as well as the notion of dynamic relationships connecting people to physical space and developing networks make places relational and contextual (Campelo et al. 2010). The main objectives of place branding are to attract tourism and other businesses, stimulate investments, and create positive perceptions and attitudes in the target markets (Fetscherin 2010). A recent study emphasises the importance of private companies in employing local people, bringing in taxes and enlivening the neighbourhood (Peltomäki and Mäkinen 2012). The more businesses there are in a place, the stronger they are and the less dependent on public financing. In Finland the majority of municipalities are dependent on public funding from the government, and thus their financial standing is challenging. One of the tasks of place branding is, indeed, to keep the existing businesses alive and to attract new ones.

It is generally agreed that branding improves a place's positioning and competitiveness. However, effective positioning requires evaluation of the brand's identity and image. (Del Chiappa and Bregoli 2012.) According to Crompton (1979), image is the sum of beliefs, ideas and impressions that people have of a place. Awareness is thus a necessary but not a sufficient prerequisite of a positive image.

Likewise, a place's identity, or essence, is critical to the creation of the brand. According to Kapferer (2005), its identity can be defined in response to the following four questions: What is its vision and meaning? What makes it different? What are its core values? The way people perceive its brand identity reflects their own aspirations and self-identity. When the identity is eventually realised it should help in establishing a relationship between the target and the stakeholders – in this case a city or town, its residents and entrepreneurs, and the companies operating in it. Ideally, the people will embody, live and breathe the identity in everything they do, thus affecting the image they project to others.

In general, individuals tend to classify themselves and others into social groups in order to influence the social environment and locate themselves and others within it (Kim et al. 2010). Social identification occurs when people feel they belong to a group and have a sense of oneness with it. The more people identify with the group, the more likely the group perspective is to prevail. As He and Mukherjee (2009: 5) state, identification is the degree of overlap between self-identity and communal identity: the more commonalities there are between the identities of the people and the place, the more successful the place brand will be. This assumption is based on the idea that a successful place identity is the basis of a successful place brand. Here we adopt the concept of social identification with places, and hence discuss place identification[1] via the place name. Perceived similarity between the identities of the people and the place is important in the formation of a relationship between them (Keller and Lehmann 2006). As Campelo et al. (2010) put it, place brands are driven by the identity of the people, and listening to people will therefore help in the creation and development of the brand. Identity is apparent on different levels: the functional, the experiential, and the symbolic (see Figure 1).

Symbolic	Name; flag; coat of arms; emblems; logo; slogans; colours	*Place intangibles*
Experiential	People; events	*Place relationships*
Functional	Buildings; monuments; sights; traffic connections	*Infrastructural elements of the place*

Figure 1. Three levels of identity (modified from Hakala and Lemmetyinen 2010).

The functional level relates to the core characteristics (Gnoth 2002) and the infrastructural elements of a place, in other words the social, economic and political conditions. This gives some idea of how the inhabitants perceive the fundamental aspects of the brand. People like to live in places with accessible health care, day care and schools, affordable housing, good roads and public transportation (Florida 2008).

---

[1] There is a long research tradition on place identification in geography, for instance, but the concept is not used very often in brand research.

Furthermore, the brand is bound up with the social and sensory concept of the place, in other words how people experience their place (the experiential level). This experience is often laden with feelings and emotions: people tend to connect very strongly to their place of residence or business (e.g., Laamanen 2007: 169). Their attachment, in turn, may stem from its heritage and from nostalgia, past events and episodes (Fuchs et al. 2012). According to Florida (2008), the ability to meet people and make friends is one of the most important factors in determining how happy people are with their dwelling place. Cultural offerings – creating cultural dynamism – and general openness – a communal sense of tolerance and acceptance of diversity – are also ranked high when it comes to the experiential level (ibid.). A strong place identity is an asset in this respect (Blackston 2000). According to Fuchs et al. (2012), judgement of how a place performs is an antecedent of loyalty. Preference strengthens loyalty in that satisfied people are less eager to criticise and more willing to pass the positive buzz onwards.

Finally, on the symbolic level brand intangibles – elements that have no physical, tangible attributes – play a significant role in how places are perceived (MacKay and Fesenmaier 1997) and what they mean to people (Gnoth 2002). Covering a wide range of associations including imagery and history (Keller and Lehmann 2006), they symbolise the abstract attributes of identity and affinity, and are manifest in symbols such as the place name, its coat of arms, logo, sign, or slogan, or a combination of these. According to Cai (2002), the name is the principle reference, and it is traditionally considered fixed. Sjöblom (2006) gives this a linguistic explanation. Names are special words in a language: they pick an individual out of a group of entities of the same kind, and in a way, having a name is having an identity. On the mental level, a name incorporates a great many cognitive and emotional meanings connected with its referent. Consequently, certain personal or commercial names may also shape people's images about the referent. All in all, the linguistic character of proper names fits perfectly in the goals of marketing.

In the view of de Chernatony (2007), the symbolic component is also very much about bringing the brand's values to life through association. Brand associations refer to people's ability to identify and evaluate place attributes and benefits (Fuchs et al. 2012).

Branding in Place Mergers

In the following we discuss the challenges related to branding when places merge. We use three case examples, and in accordance with the purpose of the study place emphasis on the place names. So far, the most extensive consolidation of municipalities in Finland was the creation of the new municipality of Salo in 2009.

The Case of Salo

Salo, which is located 60 km to the east of Turku, was formed from the union of ten municipalities, of which one was called *Salo*. The other nine (*Muurla*, *Pertteli*, *Kiikala*, *Suomusjärvi*, *Kisko*, *Perniö*, *Särkisalo*, *Halikko* and *Kuusjoki*) had to change their name (Figure 2). The consolidation caused a lot of controversy among the public, most of it quite negative for many reasons. One thing that made people angry was that residents were forced to accept the change of old-established place names to *Salo*.

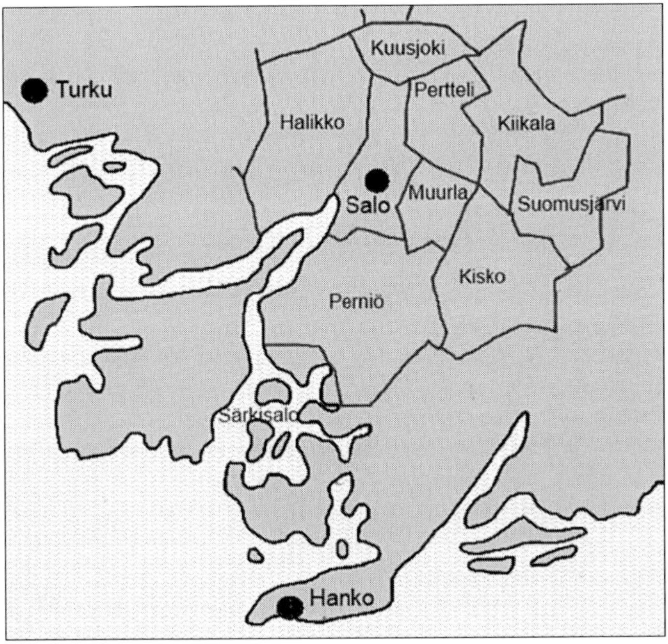

Figure 2. The area of Salo.

Interestingly, the Salo budget for 2012 alludes to the fact that the public discussion and its negative tone had an impact on the image of Salo. It is claimed that the positive effects of the consolidation were not discussed. This had fostered a negative image of the city, and would impair the attractiveness of the town of Salo as a place in which to live and do business. (Talousarvio 2012: 3.) In other words, the consolidation and the conversation had weakened the Salo brand.

In the same document is a demand to improve the conditions of entrepreneurship and encourage the setting up of new businesses in Salo by making the place better known on the one hand, and strengthening the communal spirit and residents' identification with it on the other (Talousarvio 2012: 47). It is worth mentioning that the authorities use the term identification in the budget – an influential concept in the context of place branding. How, then, should one define the identity of the residents of Salo? When the consolidation was at the planning stage the town centre was a very wealthy municipality thanks to Nokia, which was a major factor in the branding of Salo. At that time, people living in neighbouring municipalities and working in Salo were not very concerned about municipal borders, and this made the consolidation easier. Very soon afterwards the economic situation of Salo changed radically. (Kuntauudistus prosessina 2012: 17, 30.) One probable consequence of this economic downturn was a change in attitudes as people started to emphasise their place of origin instead of the focal town.

The Case of Parainen

Our second case municipality is situated in the Turku archipelago. Five island municipalities, including the town of *Parainen* and the communities of *Nauvo*, *Korppoo*, *Houtskari* and *Iniö* (*Pargas*, *Nagu*, *Korpo*, *Houtskär* and *Iniö* in Swedish[2]) accepted their consolidation in June 2007 (Figure 3).

The new town was established at the beginning of 2009 with a new name, *Länsi-Turunmaa* ('west+Turku+GEN+land'). The name choice was difficult from the very beginning. The first name the organising committee of the new town suggested was *Merikruunu* ('sea+crown'). The Institute for the Languages of Finland, which, inter alia, provides guidance on the selection of place names, did not approve of *Merikruunu* because it went against Finnish place-naming principles: traditional name models characteristic of a particular region should be followed when a new name is considered (Suomen kielen lautakunta, 13 February 2006). *Merikruunu* is a metaphorical name. Most metaphorical place names stem from the features of the place (e.g., *Siperia* 'Siberia' referring to a remote place).

[2] In addition to Finnish, Swedish is an official language of Finland, and in bilingual municipalities place names are in both languages.

However, in the case of *Merikruunu* it was the opposite: the name was meant to evoke associations, and thereby affect the image of the new municipality. This is typical in the naming of commercial brands. The Institute did not back the suggestion of *Länsi-Turunmaa* either, because it resembled an area name, not a town name. It recommended adopting the name of the focal town, *Parainen*, as the name of the new municipality. However, the residents in the other four island municipalities were strictly against this name because of their strong local identity. The arguments continued even after the official naming, and a referendum was held in 2011. *Parainen* won 58–41, and the municipality was thus renamed *Parainen* at the beginning of 2012. (Parainen 2012.) The long-lasting confusion over the name caused uncertainty, and negatively affected the locals' place identity as well as the development of the brand among stakeholders.

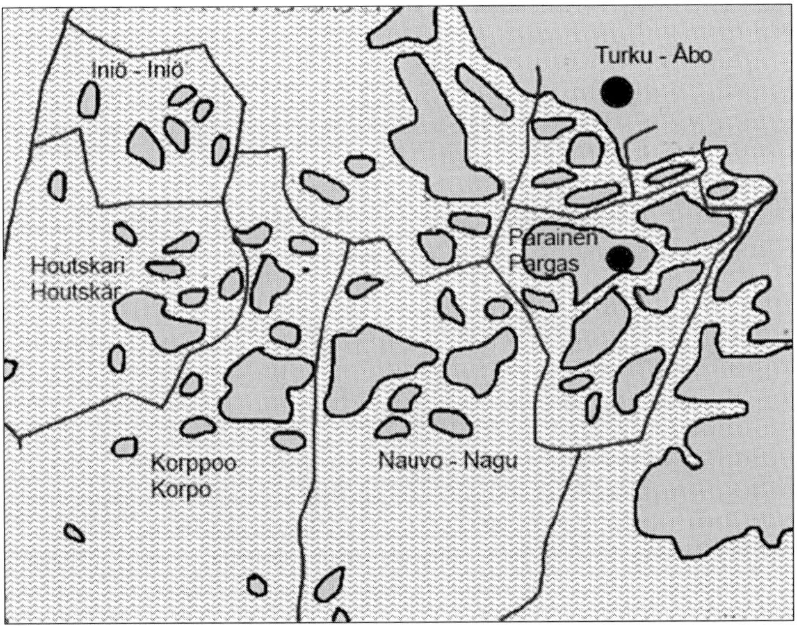

Figure 3. The area of Parainen.

The Case of Laitila

The third example concerns the potential consolidation of the town of Laitila (Figure 4). It has been proposed that Laitila and the neighbouring city of Uusikaupunki should merge. Another suggestion is for Laitila to merge with its neighbouring city to the north, Rauma (Heino 2012; Turun Sanomat 2007). Either way, the residents of this little town would have to give up the name *Laitila*[3] and accept either *Uusikaupunki* ('new+town') or *Rauma*[4]. Laitila has consistently built its own brand over the years, and this has had a positive effect on the residents' self-identity. It is a rural community that is well known for its poultry and eggs, its brewery, soft drinks and other industries, and its active cultural work. What would happen to the Laitila brand and the locals' identity in a consolidation situation?

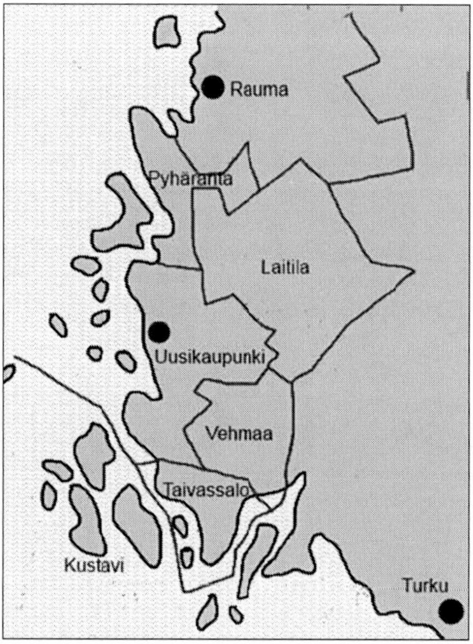

Figure 4. Laitila and its neighbourhood.

---

[3] The name is opaque. It may include a male name *Laiti,* originating from an old German male name and a derivational suffix *la*, which means 'place' (SP: 216).
[4] The name includes a dialectal word *rauma* 'narrow straits' (SP: 373).

Place Branding in the Three Cases

What, in the three above-mentioned cases, seem to be the challenges of place branding? We consider the question from two angles: identity and image. Our focus is not on the administrative level, but on the residents' and the businesses' points of view. As a phenomenon, municipal identity is ambiguous, referring to different places in different municipalities (Kuntauudistus prosessina 2012: 66). It appears that, at first, many residents of the old municipalities in the new Salo had no problem adopting the "great Salo" identity. They identified with a city that was wealthy and offered them jobs and a good standard of living. However, following the economic downturn caused by structural changes in Nokia's Salo plant the feeling of togetherness and a common spirit disappeared, and people began to reminisce about the good old days in their previous community.

In the case of Parainen the residents of the small islands had a very strong place identity, and the name of the municipality was considered extremely valuable as one of the important symbols. The residents of Laitila also have a strong place identity, and consolidation would probably mean a potential loss of roots. Businesses, on the other hand, might experience diminishing influence potential in all three cases, but the concrete loss of a place-of-origin identity may be even more significant. For instance, brand or company names that include the name of the municipality, such as *Laitilan Wirvoitusjuomatehdas* ('Laitila+GEN soft drink factory') and *Laitilan Kukko* ('Laitila+GEN cockerel', a beer brand), make use of the place-of-origin identity.

Place branding is an on-going process in which the goal is to enhance the success of the place. A consistent image is thus a critical factor. In the case of municipal consolidation there is, in terms of image, first, the risk of losing the 'local touch' – the place-of-origin image for which it is known. There is also the risk of fragmentation with regard to the image of the new municipality following the loss of heritage and the years of image-building work. This may be particularly challenging for companies operating in the place. Consumers' evaluations of a specific product may be based on the match between the product and the place of origin. For small companies a place-of-origin marketing strategy may well constitutes a competitive advantage. (cf. Kleppe, Iversen and Stensaker 2002: 62–63.) Losing the match may affect the company image.

Conclusion

A place's name is a valuable carrier of individual and social identity, and also of historical ties. People identify with places via their names. What happens, then, if the name changes as a result of municipality consolidation? The three case examples discussed here illustrate the possible impact of a name change on place branding and on various stakeholders, particularly residents and SMEs. To our knowledge, this is the first paper to discuss place branding and place names in a changing situation, in other words place mergers initiated by governmental authorities. The discussion raises several ideas for future research. In the following, therefore, we suggest propositions that should be validated in empirical studies. First, from the identity perspective, we propose that:

P1. If the place name changes, the residents experience confusion regarding

- the history of the place
- their roots
- their feeling of togetherness
- a common spirit
- individual and social identity
- their right of autonomy

Further, the place merger may cause identity challenges for companies operating in the area. Hence, we propose that:

P2. If the place name changes, businesses experience confusion regarding

- the place-of-origin identity of their company
- their influence potential

Thirdly, from the image perspective the name change may have an impact on the perceptions of residents and businesses. We therefore propose that:

P3. If the place name changes, residents and businesses experience confusion regarding

- the place-of-origin image
- the potential fragmentation of the image of the new city

In order to test the validity of the above propositions we intend to consider them in future empirical research for which the data will be gathered in two phases: first, we will conduct a large survey among residents of the South-Western province of Finland (quantitative phase), and second, we will interview managers of SMEs (qualitative phase). In the survey we will collect information about the residents' place identification, seeking answers to questions such as: What is the meaning and relevance of a municipality name? What are your attitudes towards changes of names in consolidation situations? From the image perspective, we will ask the residents if the name change will affect the image of their home town.

Our aim in the interviews is to find out the views of local businesses. We will interview representatives of SME companies operating in the area. Our choice of interviewees will be based on the company name: we are interested in firms that have the place-name adjunct. Having ascertained that, we will ask the informants to talk about the role of the place name in their business. This will bring us to the issue of place identification from the company perspective. We will also ask the company representatives about the image of the place and the potential impact of the name change on it.

This paper contributes, on the theoretical level, to the discussion on the meaning and role of a place name in a changing situation, in other words a place merger. We adopted the identification concept from the theory of social identification; we consider place identification to be a core element in place branding, and successful place identity to be the basis of a successful brand. As Freire (2009) concludes, we believe the role of local people is crucial for the evaluation of place brands, and a major asset in the branding process. We hope that the results of our empirical study, to be published in the near future, will verify these propositions.

References

Ainiala, T. 1997. *Muuttuva paikannimistö* [Change in place names]. Finnish Literature Society Publications 667. Helsinki: Finnish Literature Society.

—. 2004. Kadunnimet opastajina ja sivistäjinä. Kesän 2002 keskustelun tarkastelua [Street names as guides and educators: an investigation of a conversation in summer 2002]. *Virittäjä* 108: 106–115.

—. 2009. Place names in the construction of social identities: The uses of names of Helsinki. In *Proceedings of the 23rd International Congress of Onomastic Sciences*, W. Ahrens, S. Embleton and A. Lapierre (eds.), 67–75. York University.

Ainiala, T. and Halonen, M. 2011. Somalialaistaustaiset nuoret nimistönkäyttäjinä Itä-Helsingissä [Place names of Somali youths in Eastern Helsinki]. *Virittäjä* 115: 193–220.

Ainiala, T., Komppa, J., Mallat, K. and Pitkänen, R. L. 2000. Paikannimien käyttö ja osaaminen – nimitaito Pälkäneen Laitikkalassa [Knowledge and use of place names in Laitikkala in the parish of Pälkäne]. *Virittäjä* 104: 330–354.

Ainiala, T., Saarelma, M. and Sjöblom, P. 2012. *Names in Focus. An Introduction to Finnish Onomastics*. Leonard Pearl (trans.). Studia Fennica Linguistica. Helsinki: Finnish Literature Society.

Anholt, S. 2008. Place branding: is it marketing, or isn't it? *Place Branding and Public Diplomacy* 4: 1–6.

Berg, L. D. and Vuolteenaho, J. (eds.). 2009. *Critical Toponymies: The Contested Politics of Place Naming*. Farnham, Burlington: Ashgate.

Blackston, M. 2000. Observations: building brand equity by managing the brand's relationships. *Journal of Advertising Research* 40 (6): 101–105.

Cai, L. A. (2002) Cooperative branding for rural destinations. *Annals of Tourism Research* 29 (3): 720–742.

Campelo, A., Gnoth, J., Thyne, M. and Aitken, R. 2010. Co-creation and a sense of place. In *Proceedings of the 39th EMAC conference The six senses: The essentials of marketing,* S. C. Beckmann, T. Ringberg and T. Ritter (eds.), 143. Copenhagen Business School.

Chernatony, L. de 2007. *From brand vision to brand evaluation. The strategic process of growing and strengthening brands.* Amsterdam: Elsevier.

Crompton, J. L. 1979. Motivations for pleasure vacation. *Annals of Tourism Research* 6 (4): 408–424.

Del Chiappa G. and Bregoli, I. 2012. Destination branding development: linking supply-side and demand-side perspectives. In *Strategic marketing in tourism services,* R. H. Tsiotsou and R. E. Goldsmith (eds.), 51–61. UK: Emerald Group Publishing.

Dinnie, K. 2009. *Nation branding. Concepts, issues, practice*. Amsterdam: Elsevier.

Florida, R. 2008. *Who's Your City? How the Creative Economy Is Making Where to Live the Most Important Decision of Your Life*. New York: Basic Books.

Freire, J. R. 2009. Local people' a critical dimension for place brands. *Journal of Brand Management* 16 (7): 420–438.

Fuchs, M., Chekalina, T. and Lexhagen, M. 2012. Destination brand equity modeling and measurement – a summer tourism case from

Sweden. In *Strategic marketing in tourism services*, R. H. Tsiotsou and R. E. Goldsmith (eds.), 95–115. UK: Emerald Group Publishing.

Gnoth, J. 2002. Leveraging export brands through a tourism brand. *Journal of Brand Management* 9 (4/5): 262–280.

Hakala, U. and Lemmetyinen, A. 2010. Co-creating a nation brand "bottom up". *Tourism Review* 66 (3): 14–24.

Hall, S. 1999. *Identiteetti* [Identity]. The Finnish version translated and edited by M. Lehtonen and J. Herkman. Tampere: Vastapaino.

He, H.-W and Mukherjee, A. 2009. Corporate identity and consumer marketing: a process model and research agenda. *Journal of Marketing Communications* 15 (1): 1–16.

Heino, J. 2012. Turun seudulle rakennetaan yli 300 000 asukkaan suurkaupunkia [A massive plan to create a city of 300 000 inhabitants in Turku region]. *Turun Sanomat,* 9 February, 2012.

Helleland, B. 2009. Place names as identity markers. In *Proceedings of the 23rd International Congress of Onomastic Sciences*, W. Ahrens, S. Embleton and A. Lapierre (eds.), 501–510. York University.

Kapferer. J.-N. 2005. *The new strategic brand management. Creating and sustaining brand equity long term*. London: Kogan Page.

Keller, K. L. and Lehmann, D. R. 2006. Brands and branding: research findings and future priorities. *Marketing Science* 25 (6): 740–759.

Kepsu, S. 1990. Toponymie des Dorfes Kepsu [Toponymy of the village of Kepsu]. In *Finnish Onomastics: Namenkunde in Finnland*, H. Leskinen and E. Kiviniemi (eds.), 61–83. Studia Fennica 34. Helsinki: Finnish Literature Society.

Kernstock, J. and Brexendorf, T. O. 2012. Corporate brand integration in mergers and acquisitions – an action research-based approach. *Corporate Reputation Review* 15 (3): 169–178.

Kerr, G. and Balakrishnan, S. 2012. Challenges in managing place brands: the case of Sydney. *Place Branding and Public Diplomacy* 8 (1): 6–16.

Kim, T., Chang, K. and Ko, Y. J. 2010. Determinants of organizational identification and supportive intentions. *Journal of Marketing Management* 26: 413–427.

Kiviniemi, E. 1975. *Paikannimien rakennetyypeistä* [On structural types of place names]. Helsinki: Finnish Literature Society.

Kleppe, I. A., Iversen, N. M. and Stensaker, I. G. 2002. Country images in marketing strategies: conceptual issues and an empirical Asian illustration. *Brand Management* 10 (1): 61–74.

Konstanski, L. 2009. *What's in a Name? Place and Toponymic Attachment, Identity and Dependence. A case study of the Grampians*

(Gariwerd) National Park name restoration process. Dissertation thesis. University of Ballarat.

Kuntauudistus prosessina. Institutionaalinen johtajuus kuntamuutoksessa [Local government reform as a process. Institutional leadership in municipal change]. Valtiovarainministeriön julkaisuja 23/2012. Helsinki, http://www.vm.fi/vm/fi/04_julkaisut_ja_asiakirjat/01_julkaisut/03_kunnat/20120619Kuntau/Kuntauudistus_prosessina.pdf (retrieved 22 August 2012).

Laamanen, E. 2007. *Vapaaehtoiset pakkoliitokset? Diskurssianalyyttinen tutkimus kuntarakennetta koskevasta julkisesta keskustelusta* [Voluntary forced mergers? A discourse analysis of the public discussion on local government structures]. Acta 632. Tampere: Tampereen yliopisto & Suomen Kuntaliitto.

Local Finland 2012. *New Municipality 2017 programme*. Association of Finnish and Regional Authorities, http://www.localfinland.fi/en/authorities/newmunicipality2017/Pages/default.aspx#anchor-details (retrieved 16 August 2012).

Lynch, J. and de Chernatony, L. 2004. The power of emotion: brand communication in business to business markets. *Journal of Brand Management* 11 (5): 403–419.

MacKay, K. J. and Fesenmaier, D. R. 1997. Pictorial element of destination in image formation. *Annals of Tourism Research* 24 (3): 537–565.

Mantila, H. 2012. Kyrö, Pohjankangas vai Viltti-Hattula? Kansalaisten ehdotuksia uuden kunnan nimeksi [Citizens' proposals for a name of a new municipality]. *Virittäjä* 116: 231–253.

Ministry of Finance 2012. *Reform in Local Government Structures*. http://www.vm.fi/vm/en/05_projects/02_kuntauudistus/index.jsp (retrieved 16 August 2012).

Municipalities of Denmark 2012. http://en.wikipedia.org/wiki/Municipalities_of_Denmark (retrieved 13 September 2012).

OED = *Oxford English Dictionary*. The definitive record of the English language. http://www.oed.com/ (retrieved 3 September 2012)

Ohmea, K. 1995 *The end of the nation state*. New York: Free Press.

Paikkala, S. 2012. Kuntauudistus uhkaa mullistaa nimistön [Municipality reform threatens to revolutionise the nomenclature]. *Helsingin Sanomat,* 9 March 2012.

Paljakka, A. 2012. Näin muualla [Elsewhere like this]. *Hullunkuriset kunnat* [The absurd municipalities]. *HS Teema* 2/2012: 50–55.

Parainen 2012. = http://fi.wikipedia.org/wiki/Parainen (retrieved 13 September 2012).

Peltomäki, T. and Mäkinen, E. 2012. Kunta tarvitsee yksityistä rahaa [Municipalities need private money]. *Helsingin Sanomat,* 8 September, 2012.

Pitkänen, R. L. 1996. Viljelijän kylä – kalastajan saaristo: ammatti nimitaidon taustana [A farmer's village – a fisher's islands: profession as a backdrop to toponymic competence]. In *Kielen kannoilla: Kotimaisten kielten tutkimuskeskus 20 vuotta*, R. L. Pitkänen, H. Suni and S. Tanner (eds.), 102–118. Helsinki: Institute for the Languages of Finland.

Päres-Schulman, L. 2005. Kilpailu aluekeskuksen nimestä. Miksei Matinportti kelvannut uuden alueen etiketiksi Espoossa? [A competition of the name of a district centre in Espoo]. In *Kaupungin nimet. Kymmenen tutkielmaa kaupunkinimistöstä*, T. Ainiala (ed.), 202–220. Helsinki: Finnish Literature Society.

Siggelkow, N. 2007. Persuasion with case studies. *Academy of Management Journal* 50 (1): 20–24.

Sjöblom, P. 2006. *Toiminimen toimenkuva. Suomalaisen yritysnimistön rakenne ja funktiot* [A firm name's job description. The structure and functions of Finnish company names]. Helsinki: Finnish Literature Society.

SP = *Suomalainen paikannimikirja.* 2007 [Finnish place name book]. Helsinki: Karttakeskus & Institute for the Languages of Finland.

Suomen kielen lautakunta, 13 February 2006. *The statement of the Finnish language board for the names of merging municipalities.* http://www.kotus.fi/index.phtml?s=2643 (retrieved 9 September 2012).

Swift, N. and Kervella, K. 2003. *A complex system aims to bring French local government closer to the people*. City Mayors, Government. http://www.citymayors.com/france/france_gov.html (retrieved 9 September 2012).

Særheim, I. 2009. Street names and identity. Official naming in a European Capital of Culture. In *Proceedings of the 23rd International Congress of Onomastic Sciences*, W. Ahrens, S. Embleton and A. Lapierre (eds.), 860–865. York University.

The city of Salo 2012. = *Talousarvio vuodelle 2012* [Budget of Salo 2012]. http://www.salo.fi/attachements/2011-12-20T13-09-5486.pdf (retrieved 11 August 2012).

Turun Sanomat 2007. = Uusikaupunki haluaa jatkaa Laitilan ja Pyhärannan kanssa [Uusikaupunki wants to continue negotiations with Laitila and Pyhäranta]. Web article published on 30 January 2007, http://www.ts.fi/uutiset/kotimaa/1074177236/Uusikaupunki+haluaa+ja tkaa+Laitilan+ja+Pyharannan+kanssa (retrieved 25 January 2013).

Vahtola, J. 1999. Paikan nimi – paikan muisti [Place name – the memory of the place]. In *Euroopan rakennusperintöpäivät 11. – 12.9.1999*: 4–5. Helsinki: Suomen Kotiseutuliitto.

Vuolteenaho, J. and Ainiala, T. 2010. Naming and making places: Excavating the connection between nation-building and toponymic research. In *Language and the moulding of space. An interdisciplinary discussion*, N. Jänicke and F. Lenehan (eds.), 11–31. Magdeburg: Meine Verlag.

Yli-Kojola, M. 2005. Kurvinpussi vai Torikatu? Kouvolalaisten mielipiteitä kadunnimistä [How Kouvola residents feel about their street names]. In *Kaupungin nimet. Kymmenen tutkielmaa kaupunkinimistöstä*, T. Ainiala (ed.), 178–201. Helsinki: Finnish Literature Society.

STADI AND *HESA*: HELSINKI SLANG NAMES AS COMMERCIAL NAMES

TERHI AINIALA
UNIVERSITY OF HELSINKI, FINLAND

Abstract

This article examines the commercial use of the slang names *Hesa* and *Stadi*. These names have been used to refer to Helsinki, the capital of Finland, for over 100 years. Nowadays, *Stadi* is strongly labelled as a name variant used by native Helsinkians, whereas *Hesa* is regarded as a name variant used by non-native Helsinkians and people from the countryside. These unofficial norms regulate the names' usage and are utilised frequently in the media and in commercial use. This article examines the use of the Helsinki names *Hesa* and *Stadi* in Finnish commercial names. There are two case studies: the first discusses Helsinkian company names including the elements *Hesa* and *Stadi* and the second case deals with the name *Stara*, which is the name of the service provider of the City of Helsinki. Structural analysis and socio-onomastics are both applied. The results show that *Stadi* is used in the material more often than *Hesa* and is often connected to the use of other slang elements as well.

Research Questions

Slang names for places may be experienced as expressive and affective. The two following examples will illustrate this. The first one is an interview extract, the second one from an online discussion on the Internet. Both are English translations from the original Finnish.

(1) Interviewer: What name do you use for Helsinki?
Tuula: Hesa, of course.
Tuomas: People from the countryside say Hesa.

(2) Helsinki is either Helsinki or Stadi. Never Hesa. You should learn this.[1]

In the interview extract, the interviewer asks which name the informants use for Helsinki, their own home city. Tuula gives *Hesa* as an answer and even regards this name variant as a self-evident choice ("of course"). Tuomas replies by whispering and says that people from the countryside say *Hesa*. The whispering could be seen as an indication that Tuomas considers the use of *Hesa* somehow embarrassing. (For more about the extract, see Ainiala and Lappalainen 2010: 80–81; Ainiala and Lappalainen forthcoming.) In the second example, a native Helsinkian writes that Helsinki should be called either *Helsinki* or *Stadi* but never *Hesa*. This example reiterates the same claim Tuomas had already made in the interview: the name variant *Hesa* is not a suitable choice for a native Helsinkian. Instead, the slang name *Stadi* for Helsinki is the name used by natives.

This article will examine the use of the Helsinki names *Hesa* and *Stadi* in Finnish commercial names. I have two case studies: the first discusses Helsinkian company names, the second one discusses the name *Stara*, which is the name of the service provider of the City of Helsinki. Stara constructs and manages streets, parks and public utility services in Helsinki. Thus, both case studies comprise material from Helsinki; this is a natural choice in studying the use of slang names for Helsinki. Both the Helsinkian companies and the service provider Stara offer their products and services mainly for Helsinki customers. Thus, they aim to persuade Helsinkians to choose their particular company and give an image of a trustworthy and reliable local business. A company name with local elements (for example, with the slang names *Hesa* and *Stadi*) may be a decisive factor. In an earlier study by Reina Boerrigter (2007: 59), business names in a local dialect were regarded as a possible expression of the identity of a company and of a company's recognised relationship with a certain area. This is certainly true with company names that include *Hesa* and *Stadi*. Another reason to use these slang names lies in their potential affective nature. Accordingly, commercial names that include these slang names may be experienced as eye-catching and obtrusive. This kind of characteristic is commonly appreciated in commercial naming.

I will not only study the use of slang names *Hesa* and *Stadi* in commercial names, but I will also examine the differences between them.

---

[1] http://www.vauva.fi/keskustelut/alue/2/viestiketju/1370021/helsinki_on_joko_helsinki_tai_stadi_ei_ikina_hesa_oppikaa_tama (retrieved 13 August 2012).

As already pointed out in my two extracts, there are differences between *Hesa* and *Stadi* connected to the use and supposed user groups. I will methodologically utilise both a functional-semantic analysis (Ainiala, Saarelma and Sjöblom 2012: 233–241) in studying name formation and sosio-onomastics (Ainiala et al. 2012: 110–123) in studying name use and stances and perceptions towards names. In the following, I will first cover the history of these slang names and then present my case studies and discuss the names under investigation.

Hesa and *Stadi*: An Introduction

Hesa and *Stadi* are the most common and widespread unofficial names (or name variants) for Helsinki. They both have their origin in Helsinki slang. Helsinki slang is a unique linguistic variety that developed at the end of the 19th century and beginning of the 20th century among the working class with both Finnish and Swedish language backgrounds in their densely inhabited neighbourhoods in Helsinki. Slang was a kind of pidgin language which emerged to facilitate bilingual communication. Eventually, in its later phases, gradually from the 1950s onwards, Helsinki slang transmuted into a common street language of youth throughout the Helsinki metropolitan region. This is more or less the status of Helsinki slang today. Even though the main user groups and the function of this slang have changed, many slang expressions and slang-based place names have remained the same for over 100 years and have not changed since the creation of Helsinki slang (Paunonen 1994: 237–238; Paunonen, Vuolteenaho and Ainiala 2009).

Hesa derives from the city's official name, *Helsinki*. The official name has been shortened and a slang suffix *-sa* has been affixed to it. The variant was known in Helsinki slang as early as the beginning of the 20th century. According to the dictionary of Helsinki slang, *Hesa* belonged to the language use of native Helsinkians until the first half of the 20th century. *Hesa* was thus a common name variant used by natives when they talked about their own city (Paunonen 2000: s.v. *Hesa*).

Stadi, in turn, stems from the Swedish word *stad*, which means 'city, town'. *Stadi* has also been in use in Helsinki slang since the beginning of the 20th century. Traditionally, *Stadi* was used to refer both to a city or town generally and to Helsinki, especially the city centre, specifically. According to the dictionary of Helsinki slang, *Stadi* increasingly began to be associated with Helsinki in the second half of the 20th century, whereas *Hesa* was more explicitly a name variant used by people of the countryside and those who moved to Helsinki from elsewhere. *Stadi*, which radically deviates phonologically from the official variant (cf. *Hesa*), carries the label of a name used by "real" and native Helsinkians. (Paunonen 2000: s.v. *Hesa*, *Stadi*; Vaattovaara and Soininen-Stojanov 2006: 237). Similarly, the name for a native Helsinkian has been *stadilainen* in Helsinki slang since the 1910s (Paunonen 2000: s.v. *stadilainen*).

In practice, the use of these slang names is much more layered than what is described in slang dictionaries (Ainiala and Lappalainen 2010). However, the unofficial norms that dictate who is supposed to use *Hesa* and who should instead use or avoid *Stadi* regulate the names' usage even today. Moreover, the slang name *Hesa* seems to be a more common name for Helsinki among younger native Helsinki inhabitats. This can be seen in a study where the (reported and spontaneous) use of *Hesa* and *Stadi* was examined with the help of interview material and written questionnaire. In the interviews, a remarkable number of informants who reported using *Hesa* were under 20 years of age. In addition, most of the young informants did not justify the use of *Hesa*, but simply said that they do use it. This may indicate that these young Helsinkians do not find the use of *Hesa* unusual in any sense. Thus, the images associated with *Hesa* may be changing or neutralising. The questionnaire inquiry supports this: although there were more users of *Hesa* in the group of non-natives than in natives, the use of *Hesa* was more common among younger native Helsinkians than the older ones. While only 17% of natives that used *Hesa* were over 60 years old, the proportion in the group of natives under 20 years of age was 46% (Ainiala and Lappalainen forthcoming).

Nevertheless, the norms connected to the names *Hesa* and *Stadi* are utilised frequently in both the media and commercial use. The following case studies will shed more light on this.

Hesa and *Stadi* in Commercial Use

Hesa and *Stadi* in Company Names

How often are the slang names *Hesa* and *Stadi* used in company names in Helsinki and in what kind of names are they used? I have studied these questions with the help of comprehensive material which comes from the joint business information system of the National Board of Patents and

Registration and the Finnish Tax Administration (FBIS)[2]. According to the quantitative result of the survey, *Hesa* appears as an element in Helsinkian company names 27 times and *Stadi* 83 times; thus *Stadi* appears far more often. Should this be construed to mean that *Stadi* is regarded as a stronger symbol of Helsinkiness? I will discuss this in the following and simultaneously provide a multitude of examples of company names in question. Nevertheless, it should be pointed out that there are over 40,000 companies in Helsinki (Helsinki 2012) which means that these slang names are rather exceptional among local company names.

As previously mentioned, *Hesa* appears in Helsinkian company names 27 times. In many cases, the name refers to a company in the construction and installation industry: e.g., *Hesa asennus* (Fin. *asennus* 'installation'); *Hesa rakennus* (Fin. *rakennus* 'construction'); *Hesan Pelti ja Rakennus* (Fin. *pelti* 'metal plate', Fin. *rakennus* 'construction'); *Hesapro*; *Hesapalvelu* (Fin. *palvelu* 'service'); *Hesaservice*; *Hesatek*; *Hesa-Sähkö* (Fin. *sähkö* 'electricity'), and *Hesasbest*. Other companies are found in the businesses of cleaning (*Hesa Porrassiivous*, Fin. *porrassiivous* 'staircase cleaning'); textiles (*Hesatex*); real estate (*Asunto-Oy Hesala*, Fin. *asunto-oy* 'housing company'; *Hesa* + suffix *-la*); financial services (*Hesapurku*, Fin. *purku* 'discharge'), and with training services (*Hesarest*).

The oldest companies with *Hesa* names are over 40 years old and were established in 1965 (*Hesan St Talli ry*; car races etc.) and 1971 (*Asunto-Oy Hesala*). In addition, there are companies founded from the 1970s to present date. Altogether, 11 companies, which is more than a third of all companies, have been founded in the 2000s. Thus, it seems obvious that *Hesa* names have not gone out of fashion. One of the new companies is a firm called *Hesa inprint* which was registered in 2011. It defines itself as a "bilingual (Finnish and English) blog, web magazine and printed art magazine" (Hesainprint). It operates in the new business of internet technology and thus differentiates itself from other companies with *Hesa* names which operated in more traditional businesses.

Structurally, *Hesa* may be a part of a compound name (*Hesatex*, *Hesa-Sähkö*) or an identifying part of a company name which also usually includes a part signifying the business concept (*Hesa Porrassiivous*, Fin.

---

[2] I will give plenty of examples of these names. I use the precise form of the name under which the company is registered with one exception: I do not include the corporate identifier of the name. The corporate identifier is compulsory in Finnish company names, except for in names of private traders and general partnerships. Its form is quite standard: the part can either be a whole word signifying the form of business (for example *toiminimi* 'trade name', *osakeyhtiö* 'limited company') or its acronym (for example *tmi*, *Oy*).

porrassiivous 'staircase cleaning'). In the latter case, the name *Hesa* may be included in the name in the nominative (*Hesa asennus*) or in the genitive (*Hesan Pelti ja Rakennus*, *Hesa+n* 'of Hesa'). Forms in the nominative are as common as forms found in the genitive case. This is a bit striking, since when a place name functions as an identifying part, it is usually in the genitive. In the dissertation by Paula Sjöblom, as much as 76% of these names (total material: 3,289 company names from the cities of Helsinki and Turku) are in the genitive case (Sjöblom 2006: 169). The nominative was often used with non-Finnish names (Sjöblom 2006: 170), which is also the case with some *Hesa* names (*Hesa inprint*, *Hesa Motocross Team*). Nevertheless, the *Hesa* material is so small that any extensive comparison is not relevant.

When we study the linguistic origin of *Hesa* names, we notice that they include words and other elements in both Finnish and English (*service*, *inprint*). An interesting name with a play on words in English is *Hesasbest*; the company in question operated in the construction industry. Finnish elements seem to be far more common than English ones. Even abbreviations of Finnish words exist (*Hesarak*: *rak* < *rakennus* Fin. 'building, construction'). Some quasi-lingual words (Ainiala et al. 2012: 239–240) are also found (*pro*, *tek*, *tex*) (for more about the structure and linguistic origin of Finnish company names, see Sjöblom 2006; Ainiala et al. 2012).

Stadi appears in Helsinkian company names far more often than *Hesa*, a total of 83 times. A wide range of various businesses are represented. There are names referring to companies in the construction and installation industry: e.g. *Stadin Bygga* (slg[3] *bygga* 'construction'); *Stadin Power*; *Stadin Kattomies* (Fin. *kattomies* 'roofer'); *Stadin remonttiapu* (Fin. *remonttiapu* 'renovation help'); and *Stadirak*. There are companies in the transport industry, e.g., *Stadin Kuljetus* (Fin. *kuljetus* 'transport'); *Stadin Nopea* (Fin. *nopea* 'fast'). Companies in the restaurant industry have several different names: *Stadi Burger*; *Stadi Catering*; *Stadin Kebab*. Other companies deal with the cleaning business (*Stadinpalvelut*, Fin. *palvelut* 'services'; *Stadin Puhtis*, slg. *puhtis* 'cleansing'); with real estate (*StadiHouse Oy; Stadin Boksit*, slg. *boksit* 'apartments'; *Stadin Gosarit*, slg. *gosarit* 'caretakers'); with retail trade (*Stadin Kala Fish Factory*, Fin. *kala* 'fish'; *Stadin lahja*, Fin. *lahja* 'gift'; *Stadin Laku*, slg. *laku* 'liquorice'); with publishing (*Repro-Print Oy Stadi*; *Staditieto*, Fin. *tieto* 'information'), and with training services (*Stadin Ajostaili*, Fin. *ajo* 'driving', slg. *staili* 'style'). Even some sports clubs (e.g., *Stadi Boxing*,

---

[3] slg = slang. Word used in Helsinki slang, not in standard Finnish.

Stadi Cup, *Stadi tanssii*, Fin. *tanssii* 'dances (3rd pers. sg)', *Triathlon Stadi*) are found. In addition, there is one advertising agency (*Stadin Mainostoimisto*, Fin. *mainostoimisto* 'advertising agency') and a beauty salon (*Stadin Helmi*, Fin. *helmi* 'pearl').

The oldest company with a *Stadi* name was established – according to the current material – in 1980 (Stadin Henkilökuljettajat, Fin. *henkilö* 'person', *kuljettaja* 'driver'; a company in labour leasing). Thus, there are no companies that were established during the 1960s and 1970s, unlike companies named with *Hesa*. Furthermore, there seems to be just a few companies founded in the 1980s. More than half of the companies, a total of 53, have been founded in the 2000s. *Stadi* names have thus been fashionable in the 2000s whereas *Hesa* names were favoured more in the 1970s and 1980s. However, we should remember that the material only gives a description of companies existing in the register in August 2012, not those that have already vanished.

Structurally, just as with the *Hesa* named companies, *Stadi* may be a part of a compound company name (*Stadico*, *StadiHome*, *Stadirak*, *Staditekniikka*) or – more often – an identifying part of a company name which also includes a part signifying the business concept (*Stadi Burger*). In the latter case, the name *Stadi* may be included in the name in the nominative (*Stadi Catering*) or in the genitive (*Stadin Kattomies*, *Stadin Nopea*) case. While *Hesa* names tend to favour the nominative, the situation is quite the opposite with *Stadi* names. In the average *Stadi* name, the identifying *Stadi* part is in the genitive case, as in the majority of company names in Helsinki and Turku (Sjöblom 2006: 169).

Whilst studying the linguistic origin of the names, we find – just as with the *Hesa* named companies – words and other elements both in Finnish and English (*boxing, power, fish factory*). Finnish elements seem to be far more common than English ones. Even abbreviations of Finnish words exist (*Stadirak*: *rak* < *rakennus* Fin. 'construction'). Some universal elements (*design*, *kebab*, *pizza*) and quasi-lingual words are also found (*co*).

The most striking and, simultaneously, the most interesting phenomenon in *Stadi* names is the expansive use of slang words. *Hesa* names, in turn, do not include any slang words. In *Stadi* names, different kinds of slang words are used: from very well-known and in some cases almost colloquial words to those used and known only by "genuine" speakers of Helsinki slang. The latter words are often those that derive from the period before World War II, the "golden era" of old Helsinki slang, and they are not always well-known anymore. Most of them would not be understood by those who do not know any slang.

Out of all 83 names, as many as 18 company names include slang words. Slang words are included in names referring to companies in the construction industry: *Stadin Bygga* ('construction') and *Stadin Pläkkärit* ('sheet metal workers'). Furthermore, *Stadin Talkkari* ('caretaker'), *Stadin Gosarit* ('caretakers') and *Stadin Boksit* ('flats, apartments'), are names of real estate agencies. *Stadin Putsi* ('cleaning') is a name for a cleaning company and *Stadin Kiskat* ('kiosks') is a name for a company in the kiosk business. A special case is the name *Stadin Masa* in which *Masa* is a hypochoristic form of the Finnish male given name *Matti*. This name has been included in this group because it is stylistically similar to those names with slang words. It probably aims to have similar social and cultural functions.

Stara

The second case study diverges from the first one. While the study of company names in Helsinki gave a versatile picture about the use of *Hesa* and *Stadi* as parts of company names, this case looks in more detail at the use of *Stadi* in one particular organisation. We will now discuss *Stara*, which is the name of a service provider of the City of Helsinki.

This is how Stara describes itself on its English web pages:

> "Stara is a competent and reliable constructor that constructs and manages Helsinki's streets, parks and public utility services, repairs buildings as well as produces logistics services and technical expert services mainly for the needs of the City of Helsinki.
>
> Stara is the dedicated service provider of the City of Helsinki. We take care of Helsinki with 1,650 professionals, and in the summer our number grows to 2,000. Our turnover is approximately MEUR 250.
>
> We ensure for our part that we can all live in a clean and functional Helsinki. We maintain the streets and parks of the city – the common areas of the city residents and visitors.
>
> Let's take care of Helsinki together." (Stara 2012.)

Unlikc what is found on the English-language pages, Helsinki is usually referred to with the slang name *Stadi* on the Finnish pages of Stara. For example, the last sentence of the excerpt above is *Pidetään yhdessä Stadista huolta* which can be translated as: 'Let's take care of Stadi together'. The standard and official name *Helsinki* is used side of *Stadi*, but more seldom.

Where does the name *Stara* come from and how it is connected to the name *Stadi*? The name is relatively young, adapted in 2010. A new name was needed, since the construction office of the City of Helsinki was divided in two in 2009. There was a competition in a personnel magazine searching for a new name. The name *Stara* won the competition, which is how this service provider of the city received its name. The chief executive officer of Stara describes the name in the following way: “The name describes the experienced and skilful Helsinkian and even relates to visible role of construction services in the building of Stadi”.[4] In this description, the name *Stara* is connected to the name *Stadi*. These two names are also phonologically and morphologically very similar. Additionally, *Stara* is given an individualising function that unites company names to personal names and personifies the business, as it creates a human actor from it (Ainiala et al. 2012: 244).

Stara operates in the construction of streets, parks and other areas of Helsinki. An additional motivation for the name might be the Finnish word for construction, namely *rakentaminen*. The second syllable of the name *Stara* may thus hint at it (*ra* < *rakentaminen*) and also be an abbreviation of *Stadin rakentajat* (‘Stadi construction workers’). Moreover, it does not have a negative connotation if someone associates the name with the slang word *stara* ‘star’.

Stara utilises the name *Stadi* also in its logos. The main logo of Stara includes the Finnish sentence “Let’s take care of Stadi”. (See figure 1.)

STARA

Pidetään Stadista huolta.

Figure 1. Stara’s logo[5].

---

[4] http://www.hel.fi/hki/rakpa/fi/Ajankohtaista/Uutisarkisto?id=8759&office=rakpa&lang=fi&period=2009&path= (retrieved 13 August 2012).

[5] http://www.hel.fi/hki/rakpa/fi/Staran+esittely/Staran+ilme (retrieved 13 August 2012).

In addition, Stara has a special logo with Helsinkian slang place names. The logo includes well-known slang names of Helsinki streets (*Freda*, *Mansku*, *Bule*), neighbourhoods and other areas (*Rööperi*, *Hagis*, *Krunikka*, *Skatta*, *Kurvi*), parks and fields (*Ruttis*, *Brahis*, *Espa*, *Hietsu*) and stations (*Steissi*). This logo is highly visible in the cityscape, since it can be seen on the sides of the company's cars and vans. These names were chosen by the public. In December 2009, Stara launched a competition in which people were asked to propose slang names for Stara's logo[6]. (See figure 2.)

Figure 2. Stara's slang name logo[7].

Conclusion

As we have seen, *Stadi* and *Hesa*, the most common slang names for Helsinki, are used rather often in Helsinkian company names. In general, the slang name *Stadi* is mainly regarded as a strong indication of "genuine" Helsinkiness. Additionally, it is also a symbol of Helsinki slang, which is often described as "Stadi slang" (Ainiala and Lappalainen 2010; Ainiala and Lappalainen forthcoming). In many company names with *Stadi*, as well as in *Stara*, the name of a construction service provider of the City of Helsinki, the associations connected to the name *Stadi* are

[6] http://www.hel.fi/hki/rakpa/fi/Ajankohtaista/Uutisarkisto?id=8759&office=rakpa&lang=fi&period=2009&path= (retrieved 13 August 2012).

[7] http://www.hel.fi/hki/rakpa/fi/Staran+esittely/Staran+ilme (retrieved 13 August 2012).

utilised effectively. This is explicitly seen in the fact that slang words are often included in names with *Stadi*. Furthermore, Stara also makes good use of other slang place names. Hence, *Stadi* and other slang names and words are often found to belong together and even strengthen the Helsinkian image of a company. Thus, it may be reasonable to assume that in *Stara*, and in company names examined here, *Stadi* is associated with originality, tradition and "real" or "genuine" Helsinkiness.

Unlike *Stadi*, *Hesa* seems to represent a more or less neutral relation to Helsinki in company names. No slang words or other slang names are used together with *Hesa* names. In general, *Hesa* has been regarded as a name variant used by country people and those who moved to Helsinki from elsewhere. Nevertheless, the name is probably now becoming a bit more popular by young, native Helsinkians (Ainiala and Lappalainen 2010; Ainiala and Lappalainen forthcoming). In company names, *Hesa* names are on average older than *Stadi* names, even though some new *Hesa* names do exist. *Hesa* names are possibly becoming more fashionable and more favoured by companies, following the model using slang name *Hesa* by young Helsinkians nowadays. An indication of this might be *Hesa inprint*, the name of a new website and company established in 2011. Unlike the older and, at the same time, quite traditional *Hesa* companies, Hesa inprint operates in the new and "trendy" immaterial industry.

Stadi is – and has long been – a visible symbol of (genuine) Helsinkiness and localness. It has become enregistered with localness (see Agha 2007: 55 on the the term *enregisterment*), with (a special kind of) Helsinkiness. Many company names seem to utilise and also reinforce this symbolic meaning of *Stadi*. Even though *Hesa* does not carry the same kinds of symbolic meanings and is rather associated with non-nativeness and with the countryside, it might gain a new and more urban and local symbolic meaning. This may be seen in the future with new commercial companies named with *Hesa*.

References

Agha, A. 2007. *Language and social relations*. Cambridge: Cambridge University Press.

Ainiala, T. and Lappalainen, H. 2010. Kuinka Helsingistä puhutaan? [How do people speak about Helsinki?]. In: *Virittäjä* 114, 71–107.

—. Forthcoming. Orienting to norms: variability in the use of names for Helsinki. In: T. Ainiala and J.-O. Östman (eds.), *Names in everyday usage. Shaping social identities*.

Ainiala, T., Saarelma, M. and Sjöblom, P. 2012. *Names in Focus. An Introduction to Finnish Onomastics*. Leonard Pearl (trans.). Helsinki: Finnish Literature Society.

Boerrigter, R. 2007. Identity reflecting business names. In: E. Brylla & M. Wahlberg in collaboration with R. Rentenaar (eds.), *Proceedings of the 21st International Congress of Onomastic Sciences Uppsala 19–24 August 2002*. Vol. 3, 53–61. Uppsala: Institutet för språk och folkminnen.

FBIS. Finnish Business Information System. www.ytj.fi (retrieved 13 August 2012).

Helsinki. 2012. http://www.hel.fi/hki/elinkeinopalvelu/fi/Helsinki+ avainlukuina (retrieved 13 August 2012).

Hesainprint. http://www.hesainprint.com/about (retrieved 13 August 2012).

Paunonen, H. 1994. The Finnish Language in Helsinki. In: B. Nordberg (ed), *The Sociolinguistics of Urbanization: The Case of the Nordic Countries*, 223–245. Berlin/New York: Walter de Gruyter.

—. 2000. *Tsennaaks Stadii, bonjaaks slangii. Stadin slangin suursanakirja* [The Dictionary of Helsinki Slang]. Helsinki: WSOY.

Paunonen, H., Vuolteenaho, J. and Ainiala T. 2009. Industrial urbanization, working-class lads and slang toponyms in early twentieth-century Helsinki. In: *Urban History* 36 (3), 449–472.

Sjöblom, P. 2006. *Toiminimen toimenkuva. Suomalaisen yritysnimistön rakenne ja funktiot* [A firm name's job description. The structure and functions of Finnish company names]. Helsinki: Finnish Literature Society.

Stara. 2012. http://www.hel.fi/hki/Rakpa/en/Etusivu (retrieved 13 August 2012).

Vaattovaara, J. and Soininen-Stojanov, H. 2006. Pääkaupunkiseudulla kasvaneiden kotiseuturajaukset ja kielelliset asenteet [Defining home region and linguistic attitudes in the Helsinki region]. In *Helsinki kieliyhteisönä*, K. Juusela and K. Nisula (eds.), 223–254. Helsinki: University of Helsinki, Department of Finnish and Finnish literature.

PART III

NAMES IN THE ERA OF THE INTERNET

ABBREVIATION TENDENCIES IN COMPANY NAMES DERIVING FROM INTERNET ADDRESSES AND LOGOS

FABIAN FAHLBUSCH
JOHANNES GUTENBERG UNIVERSITY MAINZ, GERMANY

Abstract

Company names have to meet a variety of requirements. They should, for example, attract attention, be euphonic, and evoke positive associations. In particular, brevity is becoming an increasingly important criterion. Names such as *Münchener Rückversicherungs-Gesellschaft Aktiengesellschaft in München* would simply be inconceivable today, as they are too impractical and cumbersome in everyday life. The development towards simpler, more concise forms appears to be driven by their ease of use in Internet addresses and company logos. For example, the URL *munichre.com* can be remembered more easily and typed more efficiently than the full descriptive, abovementioned company name. This paper studies the names of the 160 largest German public corporations since their foundation, and explains how unofficial short forms were converted to official names over time. Future developments can be deduced from the name forms which the analysed companies use for their Internet addresses and logos today.

Introduction

Names of large companies have gradually become shorter over the past centuries. Today, nobody would name his or her business *Drogerie- und Farbwarenhandlung Gehe & Comp.*, as Franz Ludwig Gehe did in 1835. Since 2003, his "Drugstore and Dye Business" has been known as *Celesio*, a newly created artificial name. Not always do companies invent entirely new designations. Instead, they often bestow common short forms of their full name with the status of official names. Beneath this obvious transition, we can discover an underlying, more general change in society which concerns values, aesthetics, and technology alike. Outlining the process of how short forms become official names, this paper will deal with the reasons and factors of influence for this specific development, both in history and present day – from a primarily linguistic perspective. Therefore, other factors such as the impact of globalisation, or an analysis of the markets and the customers, remain subject to future research. Being the first onomastic study in this field, it will surely raise more new questions than it can answer.

Company names belong to the class of ergonyms (< Greek *ergon* 'work, product'). They are the proper names of legally independent entities seeking to deliver a sustainable and profitable performance in the form of an adequate return on capital employed. From a legal perspective, they represent the names which are recorded in the Trade Register and under which business people operate in the market (section 17 of the German Commercial Code, Handelsgesetzbuch HGB). According to the law, company names must be distinctive and not misleading (HGB, section 18). Apart from that, no other restrictive regulations exist today, at least not in Germany.

Study Design

The legal names of the 160 largest and most notable corporations, all of which are listed on the Frankfurt Stock Exchange (German DAX, MDAX, SDAX, and TecDAX stock market indices), form the basis of this study. Every name change since the foundation of each company has been recorded, resulting in 456 names. To learn more about their formation, naming motives and reasons for choice etc., we conducted a survey by sending an open e-mail questionnaire to the communications departments of all companies we analysed. More than half of them responded in a positive fashion. Their answers, some of which were very detailed, complete our research.

Our fundamental study on company names (Fahlbusch 2011) covers the years between 1850 and 2009, aggregated to eight clusters of 20 years each, and observes eight parameters, e.g. word formation, length, transparency, or associations. As a result, it reveals a significant ergonomastic change with an increasing relevance of "imaginary" names instead of personal names or objective descriptions, augmentation of irregularity, growing importance of specific graphemic characteristics as well as foreign-language elements, diminishing length, increase in sonority, reduction of transparency and amplification of international connotations. This paper, however, will only focus on the length of company names. For this special interest, we have slightly updated our aforementioned corpus concerning the length of names (see also footnote 3). More aspects, especially with regard to their development in the past and the dataset, can be found in Fahlbusch (2011) as well as Nübling, Fahlbusch and Heuser (2012: 277–283).

Length of Company Names

From *Aktien-Gesellschaft der Gerresheimer Glashüttenwerke, vorm. Ferd. Heye, Gerresheim bei Düsseldorf* (1888; 'joint-stock corporation of the Gerresheim glass foundry, formerly Ferd. Heye, Gerresheim near Düsseldorf') to *Gerresheimer*, from *Rheinisch-Westfälisches Elektrizitätswerk* (1898; 'Rhenish Westphalian electric plant') to *RWE*: long descriptive names have made room for short, concise, and internationally pronounceable forms. Company names have generally become shorter by more than one word or three syllables respectively. Today, most of them consist of one or two words with two to four syllables. The following chart (figure 1) shows the length of company names given as the average number of syllables in each time period:[1]

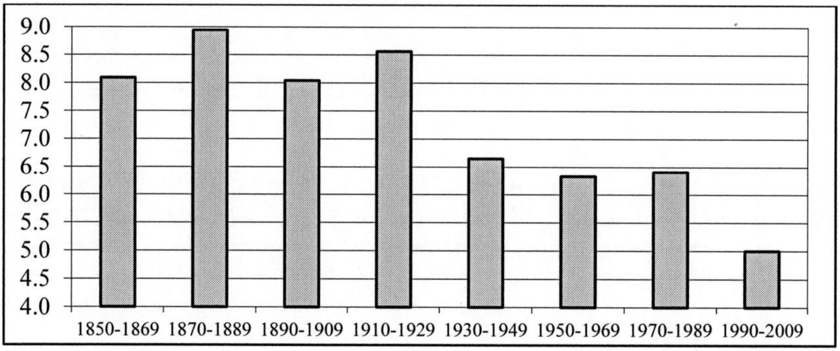

Figure 1. Average number of syllables in company names. (An analogous chart showing the number of words can be found in Fahlbusch 2011: 66.)

[1] The legal form *Aktiengesellschaft* ('joint-stock company'), its abbreviation *AG*, etc. are not taken into consideration. For better readability they are also left out in our examples (if not a necessary linguistic component, as is the case of *Bilfinger + Berger Bauaktiengesellschaft*).

In earlier years, the usually extensive description of the business activity created long (39.1% consist of ten or more syllables) and syntactically complex names. But companies slowly began to choose shorter names for practical reasons: "In 1940, the *Commerz- und Privat-Bank* adopted the name that had already often been used in public: *Commerzbank*" (quoted from the e-mail sent by Commerzbank, my translation). From the 1970s onwards, long and descriptive names have been systematically abridged. Gradually, they were no longer considered to be acronyms, but names in their own right. The abbreviation *BMW*, for example, has become prevalent over time. Used for the first time and only once in the 1937 annual report, its frequency increased steadily, showing a surge in the mid-1970s and then dominating the 1985 report with 60 appearances.[2] However, even today, the company name's official form still is *Bayerische Motoren Werke* ('Bavarian motor works'). The term *BASF* (< *Badische Anilin- & Soda-Fabrik*; 'Baden aniline and soda factory') constitutes another example – from 1972 on, this name was no longer regarded as an abbreviation, i.e. "it is not used to convey a generally understandable meaning, but is an expression of a transferred signification, the brand positioning" (quoted from the e-mail sent by BASF, my translation).

Some short forms become official names because the long version has lost its original meaning (*Gemeinnützige Aktien-Gesellschaft für Angestellten-Heimstätten* ('non-profit joint-stock corporation for employee homesteads' is no longer a non-profit company and therefore officially bears the name *Gagfah* today). The same happens if the traditional designation does not fit a company's new or enlarged business areas any longer. For example, the name *Kali und Salz* ('potash and salt'), gave a wrong impression of the altered production programme and became "too tight" (quoted from the e-mail sent by K+S, my translation), so, in 1999, the company replaced the full name by the already occasionally used abbreviation *K+S*. Even today, the names of young companies tend to be relatively long in their first years of existence so that they are more easily recognisable for clients and business partners alike. But as soon as they have gained mainstream fame in their industry, most corporations renounce explanatory additions such as their origin or range of products (1992: *Morphosys Gesellschaft für Proteinoptimierung*; 'Morphosys corporation for protein optimisation' > 1999: *MorphoSys*).

Although today's company names are the shortest in their entire history, Internet addresses and logos (or rather new requirements regarding

[2] I have to thank BMW's corporate archive for the great help they provided.

clearness, catchiness etc.) yet require (even) shorter forms. They boost the existing shortening tendencies, which have been evident since the very beginning, and gain an ever-growing influence on the length of company names. More and more corporations use short forms in both their Internet addresses and logos, which will usually also begin to dominate that company's entire corporate identity and public relations efforts (advertisements, flyers, press releases etc.). It takes just a few years before only insiders remember the actual official names, and sooner or later the abridged forms gain official status. In the following section, we will analyse the impact of Internet addresses and logos on this shortening trend in detail and shine a spotlight on this progressing development.

Internet Addresses

Long Internet addresses containing a great deal of characters and/or hyphens are far too impractical in everyday life. On the contrary, they have to be short so that every user can remember and type them easily without making any errors. The longest Internet address in our corpus consists of 20 characters: *deutsche-beteiligung.de* ('German investment').[3] For larger corporations, this length establishes something of a limit. On average, their URLs contain only 8.1 characters.[4] If the official name is much longer, companies often use short forms: *hhla.de* (Internet address) instead of *hamburger-hafen-und-logistik.de* (official name; 'Hamburg harbour and logistics'), *hlcom.ch* instead of *highlight-communications.ch* or *stada.de* instead of *stada-arzneimittel.de* ('Stada pharmaceuticals'). Acronyms with only three characters constitute the shortest URLs (*kws.de* < *KWS SAAT*).[5]

[3] For technical reasons, Internet addresses may not exceed 63 characters.
[4] We count all characters excluding *www.* and top-level domain, e.g. *.de* or *.com*. As with official company names, we do not take the legal form *AG* into consideration, which is added to some Internet addresses (*demagcranes-ag.de*). When a company has more than one homepage, we select the website for the entire corporation. Since our dataset for figure 1 ends with the year 2009, some of the companies have merged with others in the meantime or have changed their business model and thus their name completely. In these cases we analyse the Internet address used by the corporation in 2009. Three companies (*Praktiker*, *H&R*, *PUMA*) have only shortened their names, which we take into account. The research for Internet addresses and logos was conducted in May/June 2012.
[5] Today, even URLs with just one character are permissible, such as *s.de* (< *Sparkasse*; 'Savings Bank').

63.8% of all 160 corporations use their full official name on the Internet (*DOUGLAS HOLDING > douglas-holding.de*). As for the other 36.2%, the Internet address differs from the company name (*centrotherm photovoltaics > centrotherm.de*). In most of the divergent cases (91.4%), the Internet address is shorter than the official name. The largest difference is found in the case of *Münchener Rückversicherungs-Gesellschaft Aktiengesellschaft in München* ('Munich reinsurance company joint-stock company in Munich') with its URL *munichre.com*.

More than two-thirds of Internet addresses shorter than the company's official name (73.4%) leave out explanatory appellatives (mostly nouns) which indicate the products made by the corporation or its place of origin. 91.3% of such appellatives constitute the end of the name.[6] Predominantly, such adjuncts disappear that are hardly known at all today or that are no longer necessary to unambiguously identify the company (*Südzucker Aktiengesellschaft Mannheim/Ochsenfurt > suedzucker.de*). By omitting these descriptive supplements, the URLs do not only become shorter but also more opaque as their information value declines. On the other hand, an onymic or partly onymic element remains (*comdirect bank > comdirect.de*), which consequently makes the addresses look even more "name-like". This most important component forms the head of the whole company name and can be found at its beginning in 85.1% of cases.[7] Another solution to create a concise Internet address, which, however, has not yet become overly popular, given that only 11.3% of URLs shorter than the company's official name use this method, is to employ a new abbreviation altogether (*KOENIG & BAUER Aktiengesellschaft > kba.com*). An overall result of the described abridgement is that, in total, only 17.5% of the analysed Internet addresses show hyphens.

50.0% have *.de* as their top-level domain while 46.3% use *.com*. Some companies run one *.de* site for their private customers, sometimes with an online shop (*gerryweber.de*), and another one ending in *.com*, presenting the corporation in general, for shareholders, business partners etc. (*gerryweber.com*). In the latter case, the term *group* is sometimes added to indicate that this constitutes the homepage for the entire corporation (*adidas.de* vs. *adidas-group.com*).[8] As it is very difficult to find out the exact form of older, no longer existing Internet addresses, we have chosen two current examples to illustrate that the mentioned short forms are likely to become official names.

---

[6] The six new abbreviations used for the companies' Internet addresses are not taken into account.

[7] Internet addresses shorter than the official name, without abbreviations.

[8] The same trend may be observed with corporate logos.

Example: *Praktiker*

The German do-it-yourself store chain *Der Praktiker Bau- und Heimwerkermärkte* ('The practician do-it-yourself stores') was founded in 1978.[9] One year later, the masculine definite article *Der* in the company name was omitted. In 2005, the company went public as *Praktiker Bau- und Heimwerkermärkte Holding*. The Internet address for the entire company was *praktiker.com*, while the do-it-yourself stores and the online shop could be found under *praktiker.de*. From 2011 onwards, following a strategic reorientation process, the company was renamed *Praktiker* only, the same as on the Internet and in stores. The lettering in the logo changed as well so that today, the company itself and the do-it-yourself stores share the same logo. Before, the corporation's signet additionally contained the *Bau- und Heimwerkermärkte Holding AG* syntagma below the word *Praktiker*.

Example: *Bilfinger Berger*

In 1975, the two German construction companies *Grün & Bilfinger* and *Julius Berger – Bauboag* merged to form *Bilfinger + Berger Bauaktiengesellschaft*. Due to a strategic reorientation initiative, the corporation changed its name to *Bilfinger Berger* in 2001. During this process, there were discussions about whether to omit the surname *Berger* entirely. This suggestion was not implemented, however, and the management retained both halves "to emphasise the company's tradition" (quoted from the e-mail sent by Bilfinger Berger, my translation). Nonetheless, the Internet address is just *bilfinger.com*. Following a proposal by the executive board in 2012, the shareholders decided to shorten the company name to *Bilfinger*. A new logo was presented in conjunction with the name change.[10]

---

[9] The first name, *Praktikus Bau- und Heimwerkermarkt*, only lasted for one month.

[10] Paul Bilfinger was a partner and chairman of Grün & Bilfinger, which became the majority shareholder of Julius Berger – Bauboag before the two companies underwent a merger. That is probably the reason why the surname *Bilfinger* prevailed. Moreover, it is a less common name than *Berger* and, as a result, much more distinctive. The first part of a company name is usually its head and will not be removed.

Logos

In previous times, letterheads were relatively huge as well as highly ornate. Descriptive and long, like the official names, they gave all relevant information about the business. Requirements have changed, however: nowadays a logo – even more so than the official name – should be concise, clear and easily decipherable. Therefore, most of them are short and catchy, often comprising only a small number of characters apart from graphic elements, symbols or small pictures (81.9%). The longest company logo in our corpus consists of 25 characters: *GERRY WEBER INTERNATIONAL*. On average, they contain 8.7 characters, making them a little longer than the average Internet address.[11] Here, companies use short letterings as well if their official name is (too) long: *Lufthansa* (logo) instead of *Deutsche Lufthansa* (company name), *HEIDELBERG* instead of *Heidelberger Druckmaschinen* ('Heidelberg printing presses'), *infineon* instead of *Infineon Technologies*, and so forth.

Logos and URLs reveal the same trends: In 70.0% of all cases, the logo consists of the entire official company name. For the remainder, the form used in the signet is longer or shorter. In 87.5% of divergent cases, the lettering presented in the logo is abridged (*IVG Immobilien* > *iVG*). Explanatory supplements (mostly nouns) are left out in 86.5% of the logos which are shorter than the official name; nine out of ten (90.6%) of the omitted parts can be found at the end of the name. The name's head can frequently (in 83.5% of cases) be identified at its left edge, i.e. at its beginning.[12] Abbreviations are not that common (7.5% of the logos which are shorter than the official names). However, sometimes an acronym is added to the logo with the longer form in a smaller font size as an explanation, as with *BDF Beiersdorf* (< *Beiersdorf*) or *DES Deutsche EuroShop* (< *Deutsche EuroShop*). These abbreviations are likely to become official names in the future, with their meaning, i.e. what is their full form today, falling into oblivion.

Not surprisingly, logos often (81.3%) have the same form as the corresponding Internet addresses. Usually these short forms are also used for public relations (advertisements, flyers, press releases etc.) and are likely to become official one day. Two companies from our corpus belonging to different industries, the one very old, other established some ten years ago, will be used as examples to outline this process in detail.

---

[11] Only the lettering is taken into consideration, not integrated slogans or symbols. We also do not count the appearance of the legal form *AG* etc. in the logos. The information given in footnote 3 applies accordingly.

[12] Logos shorter than the official name, without abbreviations.

The absolute endpoint of the described development may be seen with *Deutsche Bank* and *Deutsche Telekom*, both of which abandon their lettering in the logo almost entirely. Only occasionally is the icon accompanied by writing at all, while the written name is normally omitted. The bank just presents its well-known square with the slash in the middle, while the telecommunications provider uses a large magenta *T* to appear in public. However, these two are fairly extreme exceptions. Usually an abbreviation consisting of three characters marks the limit.

Example: *elexis*

In 1996, *elexis Elektroholding* was formed from the bankruptcy assets of former *AEG*. The new company's logo only displayed the first part of the full name. For the initial public offering that followed three years later, the management changed the official name to *elexis*, thus bringing it into conformity with the logo, which remained unaltered.

Example: *H&R*

A syndicate around the chemist Max Bielefeldt incorporated the *Westfälisch-Anhaltische Sprengstoff-Actien-Gesellschaft Chemische Fabriken* ('Westphalian Anhaltinian blasting agent joint-stock company chemical factories') in 1891 in order to manufacture explosives for the mining industry. In 1944, the part of the production that served civilian purposes was spun off into the new *WASAG-Chemie* ('WASAG chemistry'), whose designation was an abbreviation of the long, original name. 57 years later the company merged with *SRS* to form *H&R WASAG*. The initials *H&R* stand for *Hansen & Rosenthal*, the major shareholder of *SRS*. The new logo combined parts of the former signets of the two merging companies, but only included the lettering *H&R*. Finally, this abbreviation became the official name in 2011.

Internet Addresses and Logos

So far, we have examined Internet addresses and logos separately. Sometimes, however, they are mutually dependent on each other and companies use the same short forms in their signets as well as on the Internet before they become official. The popular German sporting goods manufacturer *PUMA* constitutes a prominent example. After a serious dispute with his brother Adolf, who later founded the *Adolf Dassler adidas Sportschuhfabrik* ('Adolf Dassler adidas sports shoe factory'), Rudolf

Dassler established *PUMA Schuhfabrik Rudolf Dassler* ('PUMA shoe factory Rudolf Dassler') in 1948. Eleven years later, he changed the name to *PUMA-Sportschuhfabriken Rudolf Dassler* ('PUMA sports shoe factories Rudolf Dassler'). For the 1986 stock market launch, the name was modified once again: *PUMA Aktiengesellschaft Rudolf Dassler Sport* ('PUMA joint-stock company Rudolf Dassler sport'). As this name is far too cumbersome, the company began to call itself only *PUMA* from the mid-1990s onwards and utilised *puma.com* as its Internet address. The logo has shown the short form from a much earlier point, or more precisely since 1967. With little modifications it had stayed the same until today. In 2011, the corporation became a European company (*SE* < *Societas Europaea*) and has been officially carrying the well-known (brand) name *PUMA* from that moment on.

Press Reports

Companies utilise the observed short forms for their public appearance and communicate them in advertisements, flyers, press releases etc. Apart from that, they are self-evidently used in everyday life as well as in business contexts. The media, naturally influenced by the names employed in public, Internet addresses, logos, etc., gladly take up the common short forms which people have become accustomed to. Newspapers, magazines etc. usually apply the full names inclusive of all adjuncts only once in an article and then mostly rely on the much more practical abridged forms. These can be found in the bodies of texts as well, not just in headlines. In this context, we will provide some haphazardly selected examples (1–5) using the names discussed above from the newspaper corpus Cosmas II.[13] In all of our five major examples, the media employed the short forms (long) before they became official:

(1) *Im Jahr zuvor hatte Praktiker mit 4,4 Mio. € noch einen Gewinn verbucht* ('The year before, Praktiker had still realised a profit of €4.4 million'; Nürnberger Nachrichten, 27 March 2010).
(2) *Den detaillierten Bericht zu 2009 wird Bilfinger heute liefern* ('Bilfinger is going to deliver the detailed report for 2009 today'; Mannheimer Morgen, 11 February 2010).
(3) *Außer aus eigener Kraft will Elexis auch durch Akquisitionen expandieren* ('Apart from using its own resources, Elexis also wants

[13] This can be found at www.ids-mannheim.de/cosmas2.

to expand through acquisitions'; Frankfurter Rundschau, 25 June 1997).

(4) *Der Gewinn vor Steuern legte auf 19,5 (12,3) Millionen Euro zu, wie H&R am Mittwoch mitteilte* ('Profit before tax rose to €19.5 (12.3) million, H&R announced on Wednesday'; Hannoversche Allgemeine, 13 November 2008).

(5) *Dies sei Teil des Restrukturierungsplanes, mit dem Puma 150 Mio. € einsparen möchte* ('This was part of the restructuring plan which Puma intends to employ to save €150 million'; Nürnberger Nachrichten, 18 January 2010).

The following table 1 shows how often the (former) full official names of H&R, Bilfinger Berger, PUMA, elexis and Praktiker are used in German newspapers (dataset: Cosmas II) from the 1990s to 2011 compared with their short forms. Since H&R, PUMA and Praktiker did not officialise their short forms before 2011 and Bilfinger Berger announced the shortening as recently as 2012, the validity of the results is not affected. The only exception is *elexis*[14] because its name has been officially used in this manner since 1998:[15]

Table 1. Use of full forms compared with their short forms in German newspapers (Cosmas II).

Full form		Short form	
H&R WASAG	85.7%	14.3%	*H&R*
Bilfinger Berger	69.8%	30.2%	*Bilfinger*
PUMA AG Rudolf Dassler Sport	20.0%	80.0%	*PUMA*
elexis Elektroholding	5.3%	94.7%	*elexis*
Praktiker Bau- und Heimwerker-märkte Holding	0.0%	100.0%	*Praktiker*

[14] The first hit for the company name in Cosmas II in the year 1997 is the short form *Elexis*.

[15] Naturally, all hits which do not relate to the respective company have been left out. The use of lowercase or capital letters is not taken into consideration. There is no significant increase in the usage of short forms after the announcement of their officialisation.

As the table shows, the use of full official names decreases with their length. Thus, we can assume that journalists employ the short forms solely for reasons of space. At the same time, it might be of relevance whether the adjuncts concern personal names, "imaginary" names or descriptions of corporate purpose. Overall, these first tendencies have yet to be corroborated by analysing a larger sample of companies. In addition, a separate systematic study, which asks which forms are used at what time and how they are abridged, promises interesting results.

Outlook

In previous times, company names contained an average of 27.8 characters. Up until today, this number has declined by 57.4% to just 11.9 characters.[16] Logos and Internet addresses are even shorter (8.7 respectively 8.1 characters). The following chart (figure 2) compares the average number of characters in company names in the 19th century and today, as well as in logos and Internet addresses:

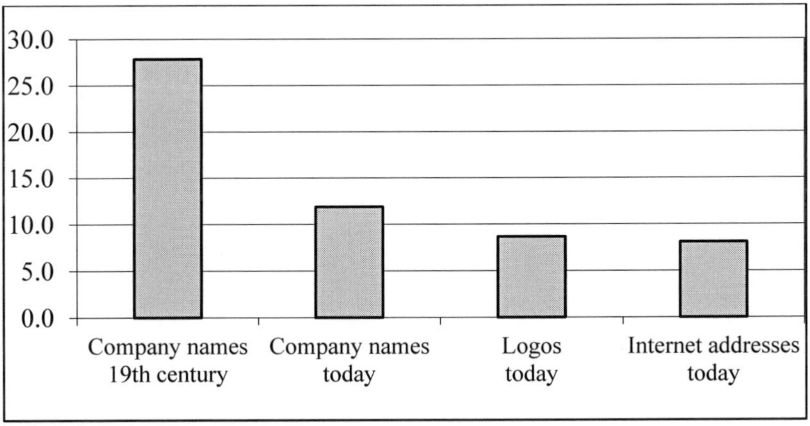

Figure 2. Average number of characters in company names, logos and Internet addresses.

As the chart shows, official company names have dramatically decreased in length. However, at present, they are still significantly longer than the lettering in logos or Internet addresses. Thus, there is room for further abridgment. From the analysed examples and the general

[16] Names from 2012. See footnote 3 for more details.

development in the past, it can be concluded that official names will continue to shrink. Sooner or later, the short forms used in Internet addresses and logos might, in most cases, turn into official names. This trend will go on even though there is a natural limit of course, which lies at one word or three letters. These abbreviations represent the absolute minimum, as a company name still has to possess a distinctive character. Furthermore, there will always be new enterprises which will have a longer name when they are first founded, and the name will be shortened later on. Two examples may illustrate this assumed future development. In the first case, a company tries to impose new branding besides its official name, which happens fairly rarely. The second corporation, and this is the rule, follows the public in adopting a common short form itself, while leaving the official version untouched (at least for the moment).

Münchener Rückversicherungs-Gesellschaft Aktiengesellschaft in München was established in 1880. As its name is far too impractical to use for customers as well as employees in everyday and business life, the company has only used the expression *Münchener Rück* (Munich Re) in public since the 1970s/1980s. In 2009, its management announced that it would globally appear as *Munich Re* from now on, using the same name on the Internet under the address *munichre.com*. The new, internationally comprehensible name was chosen to sharpen the firm's positioning as one of the world's leading companies in reinsurance. Before, the German press had widely employed *Münchener Rück* or *Münchner Rück* (Cosmas II). But from 2009 on, journalists adopted the new branding, as table 2 shows. We can see that a company has a strong influence on which name is used in the media, even if it is not its legal name. Nevertheless, the long official form *Münchener Rückversicherungs-Gesellschaft Aktiengesellschaft in München* has not changed, and time will tell which name will prevail.

Table 2. Use of *Münch(e)ner Rück* and *Munich Re* in German newspapers (Cosmas II).

year	*Münch(e)ner Rück*	*Munich Re*
2008	190	0
2009	169	19
2010	74	57
2011	46	143

In 2001 the former *Flughafen Frankfurt/Main* (Frankfurt/Main Airport) was partly privatised and changed its name to *Fraport AG Frankfurt Airport Services Worldwide* in connection with its stock market launch. The whole syntagma also appeared in the new logo, where the company omitted the adjunct *Frankfurt Airport Services Worldwide* some years later "because we are once again established in the market with our name Fraport" (quoted from the e-mail sent by Fraport, my translation). In the press, only the short form was used from the outset. While the company's Internet address is *fraport.de*, too, its official name has remained unaltered so far. At first glance, it is all but impossible to find out nowadays that *Fraport* is not the whole name. Therefore, one might presume that, at some point in the near or distant future, this short form will become the company's only and official name.

Conclusion

Company names have become much shorter during the past 160 years. In previous times, abridgments were caused by practical and/or semantic reasons. In addition, Internet addresses and logos alike require (even) shorter forms nowadays. Presumably, these unofficial variants will become official names in the future.

Once a company has achieved a relatively high level of awareness, it can easily dispense with explanatory adjuncts in its name. An Internet address and a logo require a concise form, which will then be used by the company to appear in public and in the press as well. The full name will gradually fade into the background and falls into oblivion. The short form, on the other hand, lodges in the minds of both customers and business partners. If the company undergoes a process of reorganisation the short version will quite likely be adopted as the official name. Thus, Internet addresses and logos demonstrate the trends and paths towards (very) short official names even today. It might be interesting to review developments in a few years' time in order to see how many names have changed, and in which direction.

References

Bergien, A. 2004. Image und Identität: Tendenzen der Namengebung bei regionalen Unternehmen [Image and Identity. Tendencies in the naming of regional companies]. In *"Magdeburger Namenlandschaft". Orts- und Personennamen der Stadt und Region Magdeburg*, S. Luther et al. (eds.), 253–262. Halle: druck-zuck.

Fahlbusch, F. 2011. Von *Haarmanns Vanillinfabrik* zu *Symrise*, von der *Norddeutschen Affinerie* zu *Aurubis*. Prinzipien des diachronen Wandels von Unternehmensnamen [From *Haarmanns Vanillinfabrik* to *Symrise*, from *Norddeutsche Affinerie* to *Aurubis*. Principles of the diachronic change of company names]. In *Beiträge zur Namenforschung. Neue Folge* 46 (1): 51–80.

Koss, G. 2009. Familiennamen und Firmennamen in Wirtschaft und Gesellschaft. Pioniere – Gründerväter – Aktionäre [Family names and company names in economy and society. Pioneers – Founding fathers – Shareholders]. In *Familiennamen im Deutschen. Erforschung und Nachschlagewerke. Deutsche Familiennamen im deutschen Sprachraum*, K. Hengst and D. Krüger (eds.), 537–570. Leipzig: Leipziger Universitätsverlag.

Kremer, L. 2007. Tendenzen der Namengebung bei deutschen Unternehmen [Tendencies in the naming of German companies]. In *Proceedings of the 21st International Congress of Onomastic Sciences, Uppsala 19–24 August 2002*, Vol. 3, E. Brylla and M. Wahlberg (eds.), 177–192. Uppsala: Institutet för språk och folkminnen.

Nübling, D., Fahlbusch, F. and Heuser, R. 2012. *Namen. Eine Einführung in die Onomastik* [Names. An introduction to onomastics]. Tübingen: Narr-Verlag.

THE CO-CREATION OF BRAND NAMES

NICHOLAS IND
OSLO SCHOOL OF MANAGEMENT, NORWAY

Abstract

Traditional approaches to branding stress both the organisational perspective and the concept of control. However, the emergence of a more consumer oriented and participative approach to branding is challenging this way of thinking. Increasingly, consumers and other stakeholders have the opportunity to influence the brand through their active involvement. This more participative approach can also be applied to brand naming and the development of a relevant brand language. In these contexts, managers and customers can explore meaning together over a period of time. This has the potential to increase relevance and reduce risk. However, this perspective does require a new management attitude whereby managers have sufficient humility to work productively with outsiders.

Introduction

The traditional approach to branding stresses an organisational perspective and a concept of control. In other words, it is the brand manager's task to determine the content and presentation of the brand; to decide where it will be sold and in what way. This sounds narcissistic, but the approach does not deny the importance of the consumer and other stakeholders, because brand management will typically seek to absorb insight from the market. However, just as the brand has tended to be organisationally led, so has the practice of brand naming. Typically, it is either brand managers generating new brands within an existing portfolio or organisational founders or managers (sometimes together with external consultancies) defining something new. Brand names, such as *Apple*, *Greenpeace*, *Patagonia* and *Virgin* were invented, seemingly serendipitously, by their founders. However, each of these names was chosen with the intention of communicating a set of associations that reflected the essence of these nascent brands. In this sense, such brand names are live metaphors. They provide a mental image that shapes our understanding and have the potential to re-describe reality by revealing new connections and hinting at hidden meanings: “a significant trait of living language...is the power to push the frontier of non-sense further back...the power to create new contextual meanings seems to be truly limitless” (Ricoeur 2003: 111).

As an example of a brand name as metaphor, the California-based sportswear brand, *Patagonia*, took the name of a region in South American and its connotations of extreme and elemental nature (the author and aviator, Antoine de Saint-Exupéry found his plane went backwards there because of the consistently strong winds) and (re)presented it. Our idea of Patagonia the brand and Patagonia the place are both changed because of the connection. Patagonia the brand uses a Patagonian mountain image as its logo, adopts the founder's experience of Patagonia as a key story about its identity and runs a programme in Chile that invites employees to help re-generate a national park. Patagonia, the place, is also changed because of the direct intervention of Patagonia employees donating their time and energy to the Patagonian environment, but also through the imagery of the Patagonian wilderness that the brand uses in its communications. There is a sense of fluidity here as we recognise the meaning of words evolves as they are used and re-used in the exchange between an organisation and its audiences (Eco 1999; Ronnell 2003). As Shotter (2005: 130) writes, “...if Wittgenstein is right, meanings are not hidden in people's heads, but occur out in the ceaseless flow of living language-interwoven relations between ourselves and the other and othernesses around us.”

The Growth in Participation and the Emergence of Co-creation

While the meaning of a name may change as a result of interaction, the process of constructing names still tends to be controlled. However, as our cultures become more participatory (Ind and Bjerke 2007; de Vugt 2010; Guldrandsen and Just 2011) and the way branding is practised becomes more focused on sharing, we may see greater use of participative processes in naming itself. In this context, managers will still be able to influence the brand, but both language and its meaning will arise more from conversations as experiences are shared and people learn from each other (Baker, Jensen and Kolb 2005).

The catalyst for this co-creative approach to brand building comes from two sources. First, the widespread adoption of digital communications and the emergence of online communities have enabled individuals to connect themselves with each other beyond geographic limitations and to share ideas, passions and experiences (Muniz and O'Guinn 2001; Cova et al. 2007). Additionally, people have not only seized the opportunity to talk, but also to create products and services (von Hippel 2006; Hatch and Schultz 2008). Organisations have also recognised that the emergence of participation has created the possibility of becoming closer to stakeholders by taking part in communities and sponsoring them, thereby helping to make consumers collaborators and co-developers (Prahalad and Ramaswamy 2000). The value of this is that it improves insight, reduces risk and creates value together with consumers. (Prahlad and Ramaswamy 2004; Ramaswamy and Gouillart 2010). Second, the growing emphasis on the concept of service-dominant logic within marketing thinking has shifted the emphasis from the point of purchase to the usage of products over time (Vargo and Lusch 2004). The move has changed the focus away from product features and towards experiences. Consequently, service-dominant logic means that the boundaries that denoted the separation of the consumer and the organisation are no longer explicit. The boundaries have blurred, enabling the organisation to involve itself (through the brand) to a greater degree in the life of consumers and for consumers to involve themselves with the organisation. Merz, He and Vargo (2009) note, "the logic of brand and branding is also evolving and has shifted from the conceptualization of brand as a firm-provided property of goods to brand as a collaborative, value co-creation activity of firms and all of their stakeholders."

The result of a more collaborative perspective is that brands have become social processes, in which the organisation has influence, but where meaning is co-created together in a dialogue with consumers and other stakeholders. This point is reinforced by a qualitative study of consumer attitudes towards brand names. Round and Roper (2012: 948) argue that the traditional perspective of brand equity as something determined by the organisation, needs re-thinking, to recognise that it is co-created with consumers, because "the activities of the corporation are blended with the idiosyncratic and personal associations of the individual consumer to determine the equity of the brand name."

Lego and Consumer Involvement

A good example of this consumer involvement is toy company LEGO's commitment to co-creation. In the late 1990s, LEGO was a traditionally managed company with an approach to innovation that relied on internal experts. However, the approach began to change in 1998 with the launch of a new product featuring programmable bricks, called *Mindstorms*. After the launch, it was only a short time before the software was hacked and shared. Legal action was considered, but instead, the company decided to talk to the people who had shared the code. As a consequence, LEGO discovered it had a loyal and active network of enthusiasts that it knew very little about. Company managers started attending brickfests and meeting with AFOLs (Adult Friends of LEGO) and they decided to open up their software and give users the right to hack – something that was positively received by the enthusiasts who made up the LEGO brand community. When it came to the second generation of Mindstorms, known as *NXT*, much of the work was done by four AFOLs who contributed their skills to designing the new product. Since then, the company has become actively connected with its customer base: listening, supporting but also standing back from the activities of the existing brand communities and establishing processes for bringing customers into the decision-making of the organisation. Fans have helped to co-create products such as LEGO Minecraft and every year a hundred LEGO Ambassadors are selected out of thousands of applicants to work on knowledge sharing and product innovation with LEGO employees. These brand fans, who work as company trainers, demonstrate that management is committed to encouraging real participation. (Hatch and Schultz 2008; Hatch and Schultz 2010).

A Participatory Approach to Brand Names

The underlying principle of involving consumers and employees in brand development is that it is a better method of relevant innovation, because the very people who will be the recipients of the process are involved in determining the outputs. Typifying the approach in brand naming has been the use of crowdsourcing methods, such as that used by Andersen Consulting to create *Accenture* and more recently by Kraft Foods to create *Mondelez*. These approaches are not without their merits, but they are not co-creation in the sense that they are not social, interactive and creative processes, such as one might experience in the dialogue of a community. These two examples have sensible rationalisations with the first a fusion of *Accent* and the *Future* and the second a fusion of *Monde* (world) and *Delicious*, yet they have both been criticised in the media for their obscure associations. This hints at the challenge of crowdsourcing in that it focuses on the point of conception. Given that words only acquire meaning through dialogue, a better process would be to enable discussion and usage of the name, within a community. This links to Steve Johnson'a point concerning large groups in *Where Good Ideas Come From* (2010), that it is not the crowd itself that becomes wise, but rather that connected individuals become smarter.

Vlisco's Approach to Naming

Many organisations, while recognising the value of customer closeness, are wary of ceding too much power to consumers. Control is preferred to spontaneity (Czarniawska 2003; Baumann 2001). Nonetheless, some organisations are willing to involve their customers to a larger degree. For example, the Dutch fabric producer Vlisco has been producing what is known as *Dutch Wax Print* for markets in Western and Central Africa and African consumers in metropolitan cities such as New York, Paris and London for more than 150 years (Arts 2012). The design and production take place in Helmond in Southern Holland and the fabrics are then shipped to Africa in rolls and distributed through Vlisco flagship stores, sellers and in open-air markets. Consumers buy the material and then have a tailor produce something for them. One of the interesting aspects of this whole process is the approach to naming. There is a product brand, *Vlisco*, which is an amalgamation of the name of the founder, *Van Vlissingen* and *Co*, and the endorsement of *Real Dutch Wax Print* on the product. These are the points of continuity that act as a signalling device and as a guarantee of quality, but the fabrics themselves do not have names. The designers and artists in Helmond create interesting images and patterns that they think will resonate in the market and then each produced fabric is given a number. However, the fabrics do acquire names in the markets. Whatever the original intention of the designer, it is the sellers and consumers in dialogue in the markets that baptise the fabrics. If a name resonates and people like it, it will stick and become the *de facto* name. If the name does not catch on, it will simply disappear. This is what Debray (2000) calls transmission – something distinct from communication which does not indicate longevity – as it suggests a transformation in the way people interact.

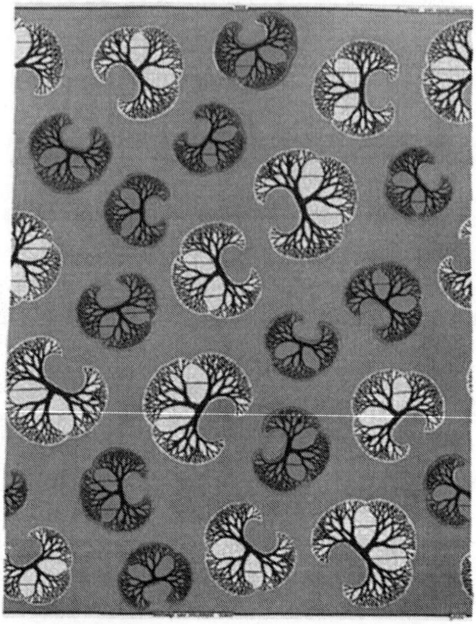

Figure 1. *Kofi Annan's Brains*.

The second aspect of the brand name – and part of the determinant of its acceptance and endurance – is the narrative that underpins it.[1] The narratives can sometimes be simple and timely, such as with an abstract pattern that some thought looked like a brain scan, which arrived in the market when Kofi Annan was making a speech at the United Nations – hence the fabric became known as *Kofi Annan's Brains* (Figure 1). Other narratives acquire more complex (and evolving) storylines that not only describe the visual aspect of the fabric, but are seen to communicate a specific message about the wearer. An enduring success of this type is a fabric known as *Six Bougies* (Figure 2). The idea for the design came from a Portuguese trader in 1940 who suggested it to the artists when he was in Helmond. The fabric features at its centre an image of Nana Benz (the name for a group of powerful women who controlled the markets) surrounded by six spark plugs (*bougies*). The design was meant to indicate that the wearer had status and wealth – enough to afford a six cylinder Mercedes Benz. However in this instance, while the name remained, the

[1] The full colour representations of the Vlisco fabrics and their stories can be viewed at www.vlisco.com and https://stories.vlisco.com.

story took on a different hue over time and came to mean that the woman in the middle is powerful enough to have six men. Arts (2012) notes that this fluidity of meaning, such that there can be multiple stories contained within one image, is partly a result of the importance of non-verbal communication within African societies.

Figure 2. *Six Bougies*.

While there is fluidity of narrative, there is also fluidity across national boundaries. Some names remain consistent as they spread across geographies, but many of the fabrics acquire different names as languages and associations vary. Consequently, a fabric that features a recurring pattern of a swallow is known in Togo as *Air Afrique* (Figure 3), because it was used in the uniform of the local airline. In Benin, the fabric is known as *Ago le fio home* and it signifies asking permission to have an audience with the king and in Ebo land it is known as *Eneke* – a reference to a bird that has learned to fly without perching. This democratised policy towards naming and the resulting diversity runs counter to the control and protect approach adopted by most organisations, but it has the virtue of enabling the stakeholders who will use the name to make their own choices and to develop meanings that resonate. This makes the point that names can acquire important emotional and symbolic meanings for consumers (Round and Roper 2012).

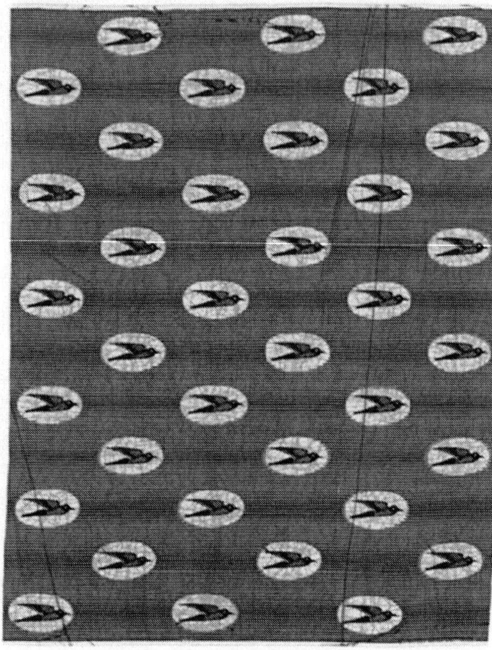

Figure 3. *Air Afrique*.

The lesson that should be absorbed from Vlisco is that naming and the underpinning narratives can be rhizomatic (Deleuze and Guattari 2004): they can be allowed to flow and connect without the imposition of rules and structure from the brand owner. This works to strengthen the identification of the consumer with the name: "By giving a design a name – and thereby endowing it with a unique meaning – the African women appropriate the cloth produced in the West and make it a part of their *own* culture. By means of naming, this foreign, European commodity is annexed and transformed into something that is truly their own." (Arts 2012: 104–105). Vlisco may be an extreme example, but its way of working creates the possibility for a strong customer connection that enhances brand identification and helps the company in its battle against counterfeits.

Organisations can adapt the Vlisco approach by bringing consumers and employees together to generate new ideas either in group events or in a larger-scale and longer term online environment such that consumers become more involved and achieve greater "perceived value and satisfaction" as they "become partial employees and employees become partial consumers." (Cova and Dalli 2009: 319). In this context, employees and consumers are given equal stature in terms of the value of their input, although the process is directed by facilitators who pose questions, provide follow-ups and share results. The key to encouraging community dialogue is the creation of a culture of trust between the participants and between the participants and the organisation. This takes time and requires the balancing of structure and freedom.

Understanding the Co-creation Process

In a community that was established to explore the concept of co-creation, 236 consumers participated over 52 days and contributed 14,130 comments during 1,935 hours (Ind, Fuller and Trevail 2012). During its existence, the community explored 21 official tasks that were defined by the facilitators, but the participants also established 146 unofficial discussion themes that were determined solely by their own interests. This supports the point that a community enables the sponsoring organisation to meet its objectives while providing a measure of freedom for its participants. The value of such a community-based approach is that it creates the opportunity to explore ideas in-depth and to contextualise brand discussions. Thus, rather than simply suggesting something, as in most crowdsourcing approaches, an idea is presented, commented on and developed. For example, in a discussion on creativity, the conversation flows between the view that creativity is the preserve of "special" people and the view that everyone can be creative. Over the course of 233 comments, there is a discussion of different aspects of creativity and suggestions that creativity can be found in many everyday activities as well as creative areas such as music or art. Furthermore, creativity is seen to be inhibited by education systems and societal pressure, but that it can be realised if people are given the opportunity to express themselves. As the conversation develops, the idea of creativity becomes more nuanced. Beyond talking about creativity, the participants also begin to feel the community makes them more creative. In response to the statement "I feel the Community allows me to be creative", 70% of respondents either agreed (49%) or strongly agreed (21%).

Barclays Bank Builds a Brand for Students (with Students)

The co-creation process, because it is conducted over time, allows for the unfolding and development of ideas and is asynchronous (at least when conducted online) and an appropriate environment for the exploration of language. If the time is taken to create a safe and trusting community, then the meaning of words can develop as employees and consumers interact. For example, Barclays Bank used such a co-creative method to develop a new approach to its student account. Within this segment in the UK, Barclays had struggled to improve its market share against a dominant competitor. Various research techniques had been used to try and generate the insight to develop a breakthrough without ever finding the key to success. Co-creation seemed to be a good way to discuss in-depth with students the component parts of the offer and to develop a viable proposition in a language that would resonate with the audience.

Students worked in small groups to develop concepts, and then they presented them to Barclays managers. Barclays recognised that many of the ideas generated linked back to concepts that had been discussed before internally, but also there were new ideas and particularly insight into the tone of communications. Partly, students had not considered Barclays as a student brand because its use of names and language was not empathetic and relevant to the audience. This suggests the distance that often exists between those inside organisations who are responsible for defining a tone to communication and the recipients. While different forms of research such as focus groups and interviews might give some sense of language, the abstraction of research does not ensure relevance. Language easily becomes misplaced, either exhorting people to do things or creating a jarring approximation of how a segment converses. Consequently Barclays understood that the tone had to be "for students by students". To deliver on this they created a student-to-student platform called *100 voices* (www.100voices.co.uk), where 100 students shared their experiences with others (Ind et al. 2012).

Using Cognitive Diversity

In a similar vein, Tata Beverages, Virgin Media and Danone have constructed online consumer communities both to generate product innovations and to determine the language and tone of communications. These are examples of what Magala (2009) calls the "Postmodern pattern of sensemaking where there is a transparent, open-ended flow of social communication built around the negotiation and renegotiation of meanings." In these instances, companies are using the cognitive diversity of community members to generate new perspectives that are hard to achieve within organisational cultures which tend to encourage cognitive unity (Ind 2009). The value of cognitive diversity, when it comes to naming, is that it opens up many more strands of thought based on the experience of participants. This broadens the network of intellectual connections when generating new names. However, as well as the opportunity for greater diversity, the exploration of names in use within an online community replicates, to a degree, the market. People not only perceive a name at the point of presentation, but rather they have the opportunity to discuss it, develop personal and collective associations and experience it over time.

The managerial implication of greater participation is that managers need to develop a leadership style that is willing to accept the input of outsiders and to demonstrate humility, empathy and transparency. This does not mean that managers abrogate their responsibility for the brand, for they still enjoy considerable powers of persuasion and the ability to influence brand direction. It still takes courage to manage the brand effectively. However, the new emphasis also involves dialogue and participation with stakeholders such that the brand is both relevant and desirable.

Conclusion

The managerial approach to branding has stressed the importance of control, but as brands become increasingly fluid due to the active involvement of consumers, the approach is becoming less viable (Kornberger 2010). Brands evolve as they adapt to new realities that are determined through continuous interactions with consumers and others. This suggests that even when approaches to name generation are organisationally determined, the meaning of the name is developed subjectively by its recipients. This is akin to the point made by Barthes in his essay on the nature of authorship and readership, The Death of the Author ('La mort de l'auteur' 1968): "a text's unity lies not in its origin but in its destination […] to give writing its future, it is necessary to overthrow the myth: the birth of the reader must be at the cost of the death of the author." However, going further, the technological and social opportunities for participation mean that consumers and other stakeholders can take a more active role in the creation of names by bringing their life experiences to name generation and development.

References

Arts, J. 2012. *Vlisco.* Arnhem, The Netherlands: WBooks.

Baker A. C., Jensen P. J. and Kolb D. A. 2005. *Conversation as Learning Experience*. Management Learning. 36: 411–427.

Barthes, R. 1977. The death of the author. (La mort de l'auteur 1968). S. Heath (trans.). In *Image-Music-Text*, 142–148. London: Fontana Press.

Bauman, Z. 2001. *Community: Seeking Safety in an Insecure World.* Cambridge: Polity Press.

Cova, B., Kozinets R. V. and Shankar A. 2007. Tribes, Inc.: the new world of tribalism. In *Consumer Tribes.* Oxford: Butterworth-Heinemann.

Cova, B. and Dalli, D. 2009. Working Consumers: The Next Step in Marketing Theory. *Marketing Theory* Vol 9 (3): 315–339.

Czarniawska, B. 2003. Forbidden Knowledge: Organization Theory in Times of Transition. *Management Learning* Vol 34 (3): 353–365.

Debray, R. 2000. *Transmitting Culture.* (Transmettre 1997). E. Rauth (trans.) New York: Columbia University Press.

Deleuze, G. and Guattari, F. 2004. *A Thousand Plateaus: Capitalism and Schizophrenia.* (Mille Plateux 1980) B. Massumi (trans.). London: Continuum.

Eco, U. 1999. *Kant and the Platypus: Essays on Language and Cognition.* (Kant e L'ornitorinco, 1997). A. McEwen (trans). London: Secker and Warburg.

Gulbrandsen I. T. and Just, S. N. 2011. The Collaborative Paradigm: towards an invitational and participatory concept of online communication. *Media, Culture and Society* 33 (7): 1095–1108.

Hatch, M. J. and Schultz, M. 2008. *Taking Brand Initiative: How Companies Align Strategy, Culture and Identity Through Corporate Branding.* San Francisco: Jossey-Bass.

—. 2010. Toward a Theory of Brand Co-Creation with Implications for Brand Governance. *Journal of Brand Management* 17: 590–604.

Hippel, E. von. 2006. *Democratizing Innovation*. Cambridge MA: The MIT Press.

Ind, N. 2009. *The Organic Organisation: freedom, creativity and the search for fulfilment.* New York: Atropos Press.

Ind, N. and Bjerke R. 2007. The concept of participatory market orientation: An organisation-wide approach to enhancing brand equity. *Journal of Brand Management* 15: 135–145.

Ind, N., Fuller, C. and Trevail, C. 2012. *Brand Together: how co-creation generates innovation and re-energizes brands.* London: Kogan Page.

Johnson, S. 2010. *Where Good Ideas Come From: the natural history of innovation*. London: Allen Lane.

Kornberger, M. 2010. *Brand Society: How Brands transform Management and Lifestyle.* Cambridge UK: Cambridge University Press.

Magala, S. 2009. *The Making of Meaning in Organizations*. Basingstoke, Hants: Palgrave.

Merz, M. A., He, Y. and Vargo, S. L. 2009. The evolving brand logic: a service dominant logic perspective. *Journal of the Academy of Marketing Science* 37: 328–344

Muniz, Jr A. M. and O'Guinn, T. C. 2001. Brand Community. *Journal of Consumer Research* 27 (4): 412–432.

Prahalad, C. K. and Ramaswamy, V. 2000. Co-opting Customer Competence. *Harvard Business Review*, January-February: 79–87.

—. 2004. *The Future of Competition: Co-creating Unique Value with Customers.* Boston, MA: Harvard Business School Press.

Ramaswamy, V. and Gouillart, F. 2010. *The Power of Co-Creation: build it with them to boost growth, productivity, and profits.* New York, NY: The Free Press.

Ricoeur, P. 2003. *The Rule of Metaphor: The creation of meaning in language.* (La Métaphore Vive, 1975). R. Czerny, K. McLaughlin and J. Costello (trans.). London: Routledge Classics.

Ronell, A. 2003 *Stupidity*. Urbana and Chicago: University of Illinois Press.

Round, D. J. G. and Roper. S. 2012. Exploring consumer brand name equity: Gaining insight through the investigation of response to name change. *European Journal of Marketing.* Vol 46 (7): 938–951.

Shotter, J. 2005. Peripheral Vision. *Organization Studies* 26 (1): 113–135.

Vargo, S. L. and Lusch R. F. 2004. Evolving to a New Dominant Logic for Marketing. *Journal of Marketing* 68: 1–17.

Vugt, G. de. 2010. Dare to edit! – the politics of Wikipedia. *Ephemera: Theory and Politics in Organization* 10 (1): 64–76.

USER NAMES IN THE ONLINE GAMING COMMUNITY PLAYFORIA

LASSE HÄMÄLÄINEN
UNIVERSITY OF HELSINKI, FINLAND

Abstract

The article examines registered personal names in online communities. The term *user name* is used when referring to these names. The research data consists of 279 user names collected from Playforia, a Finnish online gaming community.

The main research subject is the structure of user names. In the article, it is suggested that user names can be divided into two functionally different parts. The *identifying part* is the foundation of user name, usually its lingual part. A user name must be unique in the community it is registered to. Therefore, there is also a *supplementary part* in many names which sets the name apart from other user names with the same identifying part. For example, the identifying part in the name *someone44914* is *someone* and the supplementary part is *44914*.

The article also covers the capitalisation of user names. All proper names are capitalised in standard written language, but capitalisation is voluntary in user names. Only 60% of the user names in the data are capitalised, which makes the future of this orthographic rule uncertain.

Thirdly, the article examines the features of good user names. Researching good names in general is an important theme for socio-onomastics. Consequently, research methodology and collecting data is discussed in the article.

Introduction

The Internet has been an extremely remarkable cultural phenomenon for the entire 21st century. Its influence in everyday life is becoming stronger and stronger. This cultural change provides a broad new field to be researched for many sciences, including onomastics.

One new name category that has emerged amidst the rise of Internet is that of user names. The term *user name* refers to an unofficial personal name which is used in an online gaming community or service to differentiate one user from others. The primary function of user names is to identify their owners on the website, which they also do better than, for instance, personal names in the real world: every user name must be unique on the website where it is registered.

There are various kinds of websites on the Internet that require registration: discussion forums, gaming sites, webshops, dating services etc. This means that there are also various kinds of user names. For this paper, the research data is collected from a Finnish gaming community. The results cannot be generalised to the whole Internet. Obviously, there are similarities between different websites, but more likely there are also differences.

I have researched user names in my Master's thesis (Hämäläinen 2012). The most important results of this study have been compiled for this article. The main subjects include the construction of the user name, orthography and the Internet users' opinions concerning good user names: Which kinds of lingual structures user names consist of? How are they spelled? Which kinds of names are liked amongst the Internet users? These questions will, hopefully, be answered in this article.

Research Data

User names for this study are collected from the Finnish online gaming community Aapeli[1]. The community also has subsidiary websites in 14 different languages called Playforia[2]. In this article, the international name Playforia will be used when referring to any of these websites.

On a Finnish scale, Playforia is quite a remarkable Internet society. There are over 5 million registered user accounts worldwide[3]. The largest section of these accounts is Finnish, but Playforia is also popular in Germany and in the Baltic countries. The online games on the website are mainly simple short-term games such as miniature golf, billiards, chess or checkers. In addition to games, other social activities are an important part of gaming community life. There are discussion forums and game chats,

---

[1] www.aapeli.com. The name of the website is based on word play: *Aapeli* is a Finnish male name and *peli* is the Finnish word 'game'.

[2] www.playforia.com, www.playforia.de etc.

[3] It is good to be taken into account that there are not as many different users because one user can create several accounts to the website. In this research, 57% of my informants have created more than one user account.

and every user has also his or her own personal page on the website. I have selected Playforia to be the source of research data because it is popular, it has its social side and it is also the Internet society I myself am most familiar with. I have had many different user names in Playforia, perhaps the best known being *Haamukirjailija* 'ghost writer'.

Every Internet society has its own naming rules. The varying characteristics include the length of the name and special characters permitted. In Playforia, the length is limited to 3–16 characters. The characters permitted include letters, numbers, hyphen (-), underscore (_), exclamation mark (*!*) and space. Inappropriate user names are also prohibited in the Playforia rules, but in an Internet society of over 5 million user names, it is difficult to monitor these rules.

The research data was collected with an online survey in February 2012. I asked users of the Playforia discussion forums to complete a questionnaire about the meaning of their own name, possible other accounts, opinions about good user names and thoughts about naming rules in Playforia. I received 284 responses, of which 279 were usable in the study. I have used the names of these 279 users in the analysis of the functional and semantic structure of user names. The analyses are made, if possible, on the basis of what information the users have given on the background of their names. Later in this study, I will call these 279 respondents *informants*. 63% of the informants are men and 37% women. Their average year of birth is 1991. Youngest informants were born in 2002 and the oldest in 1945.

Functional and Semantic Structure

When analyzing the structure of user names, I have used the concept of Paula Sjöblom's (2006) functional-semantic analysis model. In this model, a name is divided into name parts on the basis of the parts' functions. After this, the name parts are placed into different semantic classes.

Because of the variety of different functions of user names, it is hard to find any general functional classes for them. In the end, I have divided the name parts in two. The foundation of the name is *identifying part*: it is the name's lingual part and therefore often seen as the actual name. It is in every user name, and there is only one of them in the name.

When there are more than 5 million accounts on one website, and each of them must be unique, it is obvious that most of the popular name material is already in use. For this reason, there is a *supplementary* part[4] in many names. This is the part that presumably would not be in the name if the identifying part was unique. Its function is to differentiate the name's user from other users with the same identifying part. One of the informants, a user called *Toope_79*, explains the situation as follows (translated from Finnish):

> The nickname I had come up with was taken, and so, I put my year of birth after the nickname. And even that wasn't enough, so I separated the letters and numbers with an underscore (_).

As the example shows, there can be several supplementary parts in one user name. In the name *Toope_79*, the underscore and the number *79* are two functionally different parts. Therefore, I regard them as two different supplementary parts.

I have divided the 279 identifying parts of the data into five semantic classes. Their distribution is shown in table 1.

Table 1. Identifying parts in the user names in Playforia.

Identifying part	Number (N = 279)	% (of 279 names)
Personal name	71	25
Other proper name	38	14
Word or phrase with a lexical meaning	98	35
Quasi-word	58	21
Abbreviation	14	5,1
Total	**279**	**100**

The largest class is "Word or phrase with a lexical meaning". It includes all known lingual expressions that are not proper names. Two thirds of the name parts in this class are nouns. There are also some adjectives, words from other word classes, phrases or even clauses. Some examples: *JEDI MESTARI* 'jedi master'; *Nalakuttava akka* (Finnish

[4] The term is used in Paula Sjöblom's studies concerning company names (Ainiala, Saarelma and Sjöblom 2012: 233, 237).

dialectical form for 'nagging hag'); *someone44914*; *älä naurata* 'don't make me laugh'.

In every fourth user name, there is a personal name functioning as the identifying part. Usually, they are real life forenames or nicknames, but many of them could not be recognised as nicknames without the responses to the questionnaire. For example, *Hattara* 'candyfloss', *Persikka* 'peach' and *Ykköspelle* 'number one clown' are not commonly known nicknames, but in these cases, the informants have explained that they are known by such expressions in real life.

21% of the identifying parts can be construed as quasi-words. The term *quasi-word* refers to those words that do not belong to any existing language. Many of them are derived from personal names or from other known words. However, for every third name, even the creator of the name has no idea of the origin of the quasi-word. Examples: *Apelix*; *-_AreX_-*; *perkeliina* (probably associated with the Finnish expletive 'perkele'); *Påla*; *samirr*.

In the class of other proper names, nearly half are names of fictional characters. Japanese manga and anime culture is especially well-represented. Toponyms, animal names and names of works of art appear only a couple of times. Three identifying parts are based on brand names: *CocaCola*; *Frisco*; *TheFreeWay* (*FreeWay* is a brand name of German grocery shop chain Lidl).

The smallest class of identifying parts is abbreviations. This class includes both abbreviated words and acronyms. Most of them are based on the user's real personal name. Examples: *_comp_*; *EMCi*; *Jpo*; *JU 77*; *werty213*.

Table 2. Supplementary parts in the user names found in Playforia.

Supplementary part	Number (N = 279)	% (of 145 parts)
Numeral	67	46
Special character	40	28
Letter or abbreviation	14	9,7
Lexeme or morpheme	22	15
Other	2	1,4
Total	**145**	**100**

In the data of 279 names, there is at least one supplementary part in 129 of them (46% of all names). The total count of supplementary parts is 145. They can be divided into five semantic classes.

Most often, the supplementary part is a numeral. Typically, it is either the user's year of birth (or its last two digits) or some random number. Sometimes the numbers may also have another meaning. For instance, the numbers in user name *Messi10Ronaldo7* are the playing numbers of two famous soccer players noted in the identifying parts.

Special characters are also quite popular for supplementary parts. Hyphens (in 21 names) and underscores (14) are more usual than exclamation marks (4), which are often considered irritating. Furthermore, one notable fact is that special characters are usually used symmetrically around the name's identifying part (- *Alcometer* -; -_*AreX*_-; _*comp*_).

The supplementary part can also be a morpheme or a whole word. Suffixes in particular are creatively used to turn ordinary identifying parts into totally new expressions. The Finnish feminising suffix *-tAr* is used three times (*Rauniotar* < raunio 'ruin'), the diminutive suffix *-nen* twice (*saukkonen* < saukko 'otter'; *tollonen* < tollo 'fool'). In two cases, a Finnish appellative is combined with the English article *the*: *TheSaunatakki* 'the bathrobe'; *TheSurkimus* 'the lame duck'. This kind of word play appears mostly in Finnish. User name *Loreleichen* is an exception: the German diminutive suffix *-chen* is connected to the name of a mermaid from German folk tales.

In two names, the supplementary parts cannot be placed into any of the previous classes. The spaces between the letters in user name *J a c k e* may differentiate it from other similar names. There was no comment given on the spaces when the user explained the name in the survey. In user name *EvaOnNobo* 'Eva is a nobo (noob, newcomer)', the supplementary part is the rest of the clause, while identifying part is *Eva*, person's user name in another Internet game society.

Figure 1 shows what orders the name parts can be in. IS means that the identifying part (I) is placed in front of the supplementary part (S). Consequently, SIS means that the name starts and ends with supplementary parts, the identifying part between them. For example, user name *Ventus89* represents the IS type, user name *-Crane-* the SIS type.

If there are both identifying and supplementary parts in the user name, the name usually (in 81% of cases) starts with the identifying part. Over half of the names starting with a supplementary part represent the symmetrical use of special characters. The whole supplementary part is seldom placed at the front of the name. It is interesting to analyze what causes this kind of tendency. Perhaps there is the desire to have the identifying part, which is obviously the most important part of the user name, to be in the most visible position in name. It is also possible that some kinds of name models are starting to form in this new name category.

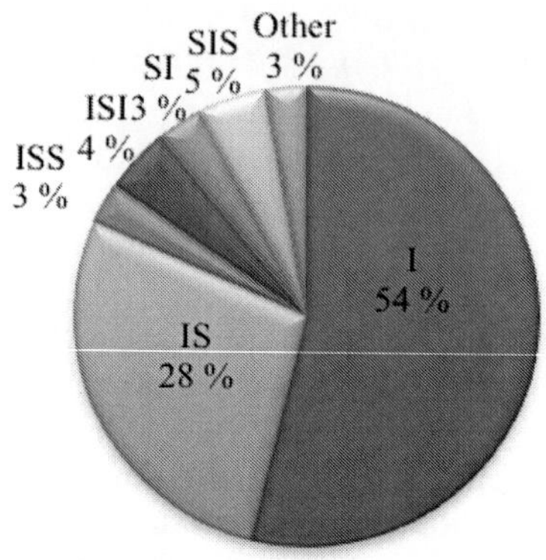

Figure 1. Order of name parts in Playforia user names.
I = Identifying part, S = Supplementary part.

Capitalisation

User names can be examined from many points of view. Perhaps the most interesting aspect for onomastics in general, is the orthography of user names. With the term orthography, I mean such structural features in user names that are not used to make the name unique. Hyphens and exclamation marks are, of course, orthographic features, but as they are used mostly as supplementary parts, I have discussed them already in analysing the structure of user names.

In this section, the main focus is in the use of letter case. Letter case cannot be used to differentiate user names. For example, if the user name *Lasse89* has already been taken, the user name *LASSE89* cannot be used. Selection of letter case only affects the visual form of user name.

A capital letter at the beginning of proper names is one of the most important orthographic norms in Finnish (as in many other languages as well). In fact, for many people, it is the easiest way to separate names from other words. User names are proper names, and therefore, according to the norm, they should begin with capital letter. However, for naming in Playforia, there are no orders given by either the authorities or naming conventions to obey the norm. Consequently, it is interesting to find out whether or not people use capital letters voluntarily.

In the data, 61% of user names begin with a capital letter. 39% are not capitalised. The result is similar to previous Finnish studies (e.g. Hämäläinen 2011; Matsi 2012): a capital letter is more common, however a lowercase letter is not rare at all. An interesting fact is that 32 names, 11% of the data, have been entered differently in the questionnaire than how they actually appear in Playforia. Mostly, the difference is in the case of the beginning letter. This can be construed as a signal of disinterest towards the capitalisation of user names.

In the questionnaire, the informants were asked whether they prefer capitalised or non-capitalised user names. 80% of informants prefer capitalised names, 20% prefer non-capitalised names. The most interesting fact considering this question is that 43% of those informants who have non-capitalised user names themselves prefer capitalised names. This seems somehow illogical. If people do like capitalised user names, why do they choose non-capitalised names for themselves? The conclusion seems to be same as above: for many website users, the capital letter of their name seems to be more or less insignificant.

These expressions of disinterest and the fact that every fifth user prefers a name beginning with lowercase letter awaken many important questions concerning the state of the orthographic rule. Could this kind of tendency affect the standard language in the future? Why should proper names be capitalised? Or should they be capitalised at all?

The most obvious reason for capitalising proper names is distinguishing them from appellatives. Sometimes the capital letter changes the meaning of the word: for instance, the Finnish city name *Lahti* also has its counterpart *lahti* 'bay'. There are plenty of appellative-based user names as well: *Cheerleader__*; *Hummeri5* 'lobster'; *Purnukka* 'jar'. Of course, a capital letter, in most cases, would not be necessary, because context is normally enough to reveal the true meaning. Therefore, this is not a probable reason for capitalising names.

The history of letter case shows that at least one of the original reasons for capitalisation was the importance of the referent. In the earliest version of the Bible in Finnish, there were three capital letters in the beginning of the word *HERra* 'Lord (God)', two capital letters in the word *JEsus*, one capital letter in religiously important words such as *Engeli* 'angel' or *Nazarethin Caupungist* 'from the city of Nazareth' and no capitalisation e.g. in the words *mailma* 'world', *sotawäen* 'the military' or *sydämesäns* 'in one's heart'. Even nowadays, capital letters are used to express respect and importance, in expressions such as *Herra Tasavallan Presidentti*

'Mister President of the Republic' or "*se oli yksi elämäni Suurista Hetkistä*" 'that was one of the Great Moments of my life'.

From the point of view of language planning, the question at hand is the future of capitalisation. Nowadays, the non-capitalisation of proper names is mainly restricted to the category of user names. Could this tendency spread to the other name categories and even to standard language? If it could, should it be regarded as a threat or problem?

This scenario is not at all impossible. At the turn of the Common Era, only one letter case was needed. Even at present, there are many languages that do not have letter cases, e. g. Arabic, Hebrew and Georgian.

Languages are in constant state of change. The directions of these changes depend mostly on the needs of language users. If a capital letter vanishes from the beginning of proper name, it can be regarded as a sign of the capital letter's redundancy. Perhaps some of my informants have already felt that capital letters are purposeless. However, this kind of well-known, long-term orthographic norm concerning Finnish capitalisation would need many, many years to change.

Capital letters can also be placed in other positions in user names. There are 44 names (16 %) in the data in which capital letters are used somewhere else than at the beginning of the name. Most of these names are not written according to orthographic norms. Exceptions include e. g. user names *Messi10Ronaldo7* and *Al Capone96* in which there are two proper names in one user name.

11 names are spelled with capital letters only, e. g. *HYMYMIELI* 'smile mind', *SHADOWALK*, *-VE-SA-* 'sapling, offspring' (also a Finnish male name). Spelling with capital letters only is often compared to yelling in the real world. In the rules of Playforia, it is prohibited if it is unnecessary. However, any user name that has been removed for the sake of its letter case has not come to my knowledge.

Many user names consist of compounds or set phrases. In such cases, every lexeme may start with a capital letter: *CrazyTiger*, *Gothic Rabbit*, *You Too*. The function of the capital letter may be to highlight the borderline between lexemes. It is not possible to use spaces in user names on many websites. That may have had an influence on the tendency to write set phrases without spaces even when it would be possible.

In some user names, there are no clear reasons for using capital letters: *-_AreX_-*; *EMCi*; *MiiZy3*. In this case, the reason presumably is not a disinterest towards orthography. Lowercase is the primary case, and every capital letter requires an additional keystroke. Consequently behind every uppercase letter there is a choice of using them. Perhaps the usage of uppercase letters can be seen as an effort to catch the other users' attention. The non-standard usage can also be some kind of protest against the present norms of standard language.

What Makes a Good User Name?

One of my greatest personal interests concerning the field of onomastics is to investigate what makes a good name. Onomastics is an important branch of science in itself, but the knowledge of good names and their creation would be very useful for many other branches of sciences and also for society and economics in general. It may also arouse the interest of the common people more than some other onomastic point of view. While making the online survey, I have noticed that most of the informants were especially interested in two themes in my study: what do the user names mean and which kinds of user names are good. The first theme has been discussed alongside the structural analysis. The second one will be covered in this section.

We must first define, of course, what we mean by the word *good.* A name can be good in many different ways, depending on its functions. User names do not have many common functions. One name may reveal something about its bearer and another user may try to have an interesting name so that other users would want to make his or her acquaintance. Because of the variety of functions, I have decided to let the informants decide, what good truly is. The informants were given some actual user names for evaluation. It was possible but not compulsory to give reasons for the answers. To understand the answers better, I have also asked the informants about some general characteristics in user names: influence of the names' meaning and length, usage of special characters etc. With all this information, I will try to create a general view of characteristics of a good user name and perhaps of a good name in general as well.

This analysis concerning good user names consists of three parts using three different methods.

In the first part, the informants got 10 actual user names from Playforia. The informants were asked to put the names in the order of how "good" they are. No instructions for defining "good" were given. This research method is called the *ranking method*.

The 10 names for ranking were (in alphabetical order): *Calopteryx*; *Clöön*; *! ixi !*; *J e s s*; *Midania*; *mies 44* ('man 44'); *pikkulutti* ('little granary'); *Riina220*; *-Sevendown-*; *tunturin tuuli* ('wind of a fell').

Figure 2 shows how the informants have ranked the 10 user names. The name's average rank is the average of all the single rankings in the data. The smaller number reveals that the name has been successful in this method and is, according to the informants, a good name. The larger number reveals that the name was not that successful. Standard deviation describes the variation in the informants' opinions. A large standard deviation shows that there has been much variation between the opinions, a small standard deviation shows that the informants have agreed with each other.

The most liked names are *Midania*, *-Sevendown-* and *Calopteryx*. These names are similar in many ways: they start with capital letter, there are not many special characters in them, they are quite long and none of them is Finnish. It is quite difficult to figure out their meanings: *Midania* is a made-up word based on *Midian*, a place name (known from the Bible) and a symphonic metal album. *-Sevendown-* is a variation of the well-known soft drink brand 7 Up. *Calopteryx* is the binomial name of a genus of dragonflies.

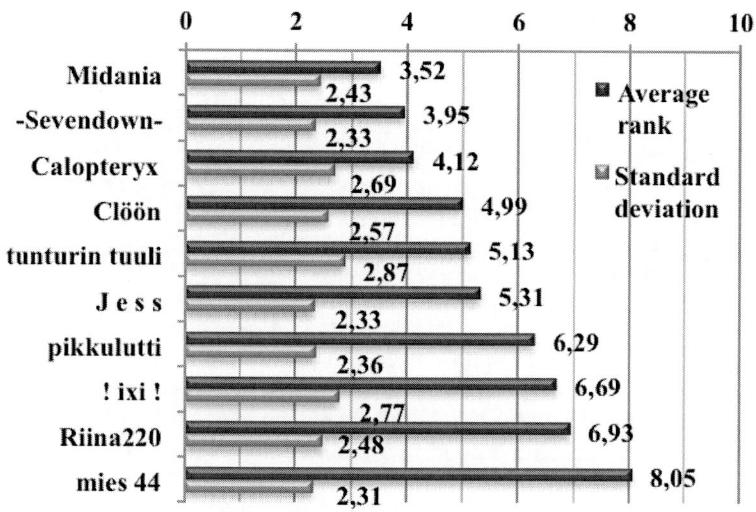

Figure 2. The results of the ranking method.

The least valued names are also quite similar. *Riina220* and *mies 44* are both semantically transparent names: *Riina* is a Finnish female name and *mies* is the Finnish word meaning 'man'. They both end with a number with no apparent meaning. Many informants stated that they dislike these names because they are very typical user names. On the basis of the results of this study and my empirical knowledge, this "name or appellative + some (random) number" is perhaps the most common construction type in user names. Most of the informants somehow prefer exceptional names. They stick out from the great mass of user names and therefore they are easier to remember.

The second method of researching good user names is called the *Likert method*. It is partly based on the Likert scale[5], which is commonly used in surveys, especially in the branch of statistics. In my Likert method, instead of statements, 10 user names were given to the informants to be rated with a five-point scale. There are no verbal counterparts for the Likert items: the informants were only told that 5 is the best score and 1 is the worst. From this point of view, this Likert method is also similar to the semantic differential scale[6].

The 10 names for rating were (in alphabetical order): *AAQQ*; *Angel 98*; *EVERTON99*; *_-Green-_*; *hupsutar*; *keksitty* 'made up'; *Leatherhead*; *maxiii*; *P4nd4*; *änglamaria*.

The most liked name, *Leatherhead*, is capitalised and has no special characters, like *Midania* and *Calopteryx* in the ranking method. The name is probably based on an animation character with the same name, but this meaning may have not been clear to all the informants. The name *hupsutar* is the most liked non-capitalised name. It is a Finnish derivative, consisting of the word *hupsu* 'silly, foolish' (in a slightly positive way) and the feminising suffix *-tAr*. User name *_-Green-_* is liked, maybe even surprisingly, because of its special characters which are mostly regarded as visually pleasant because of their symmetry.

The list of the least liked names reveals that capitalising all the letters in the name is not popular according to the informants. In the name *AAQQ*, capitalisation may be justifiable because the letters probably refer to playing card symbols (A 'ace', Q 'queen') which are often capitalised in normal online chats. Supposedly, all the informants may have not seen this meaning in the name.

---

[5] The Likert scale is a popular surveying method, used in many branches of science. In this method, there are typically some statements and the informant has to express his or her opinion by choosing one from symmetrically set, verbally coded alternatives. E.g.:
The significance of the outward appearance is overrated.
1. Definitely agree. 2. Partly agree. 3. Do not agree or disagree. 4. Partly disagree. 5. Definitely disagree. (Vehkalahti 2008: 35, 37)

[6] The semantic differential scale (sometimes called also the Osgood scale) is used similarly to the Likert scale but instead of statements, pairs of adjectives, objects or concepts in it. E.g.:
Estimate your outward experience with the following pairs of words:
Slim 1 2 3 4 5 6 7 Fat
Ugly 1 2 3 4 5 6 7 Beautiful (Vehkalahti 2008: 38–39)

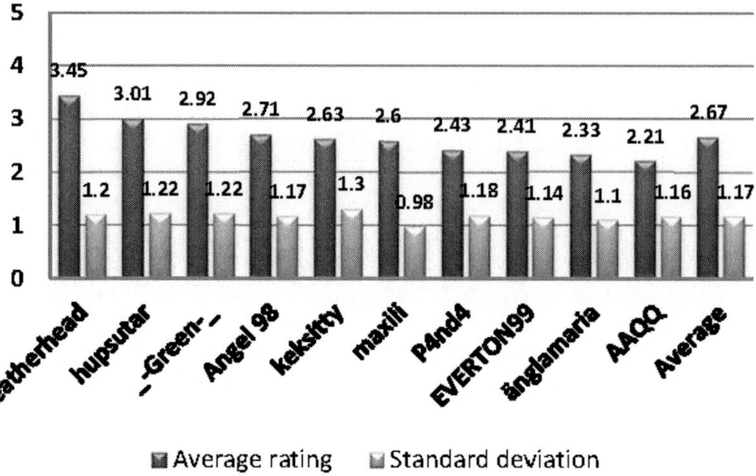

Figure 3. Results of the Likert method.

For the third method for examining good user names, the informants were asked about six general characteristics found in user names. In every section, the question was the same: "Which characteristic is better in user names?" There were only two options in each section.

The first question was about capitalisation. As noted before, four fifths of the informants prefer capitalised user names. In the second section, I asked about the length of the name: is a good user name short or long? 78% of the informants prefer short user names, which may seem unexpected. As seen in the ranking method and the Likert method, none of the most liked names (*Midania*, *-Sevendown-*, *Calopteryx*, *Leatherhead*, *hupsutar*) was extremely short. Of course, this section may have been difficult to answer because the informants probably do not know how long "short" and "long" names exactly are. The average length of the names of the informants is 8.4 characters[7] but the informants, of course, could not know about this.

The third section was about the language of the name: is a user name better in Finnish or a non-Finnish language? This question divided the informants in two. There were 271 answers given, of which 135 were in favour of Finnish names and 136 in favour of non-Finnish names. Again, we can note that the results do not agree with those of the two other methods. In these results, the most liked names have been primarily been

[7] This includes letters, numbers, special characters and spaces.

those that are non-Finnish, while the Finnish names (e. g. *Riina220*, *mies 44*) have been seen as ordinary and impractical. The reason for this may be that the examined website is Finnish and therefore the collection of names used the most is also in Finnish. Consequently, there are supplementary parts, which are most likely rather unpopular, mostly in Finnish user names, not in the more unusual non-Finnish names.

The fourth section presented the question if it is better that the name is attractive or funny. This question may have been problematic because these concepts are hard to define. A user name can be attractive or funny in many different ways. The percentages are 53–47 in favour of funny names.

In the next section, the informants were asked whether the name is better with or without special characters. 79% of the informants said that they prefer user names without special characters. The result is not particularly surprising. In the other methods, user names with special characters are quite liked, but this probably results from their symmetric usage. Asymmetric special characters and especially exclamation marks are often seen as irritating and therefore negative. Many informants also said that special characters, as well as numbers, make user names much harder to remember.

The last question was whether it is better that the user name is transparent or "mysterious". 72% of informants prefer mysterious user names. This information agrees with the earlier results. Nearly all of the popular user names in the ranking method as well as in the Likert method are somehow complicated by their meaning, if they even have one.

These results of the characteristics of good user names may seem quite trivial because creating a good user name is not necessary for enjoying time spent on the Internet. I see this part of my research partly as methodological experiments in relation to the research of good names in general. Many of the methods could be usable, for instance, in the area of commercial onomastics. It would be valuable for companies to know which kinds of company names their customers consider to be the best. Length, language and semantics are important characteristics in company names as well as in user names. With the help of the ranking method or the Likert method, interesting and practical information on good commercial names could be collected.

The major problem in this kind of a study may be how to find the informants. Collecting 279 informants for a short survey about their pastime was not too difficult, but it could be greater challenge in other kinds of studies. In Finnish onomastics, there have been other similar studies about good and bad street names, but their samples have been quite small.

Conclusion

User names found in online communities is still quite a new branch of onomastics with few wide studies carried out. Despite that, it can be considered to be an interesting, valuable topic of research. Knowledge of all kinds of names is important for onomastics in itself, but some of the results shown above can also be used for other purposes.

Researching the construction and semantics of user names is important for understanding the emergence and development of naming systems. User names as a naming system is relatively easy to research because even the oldest names are only dozens of years old and because the backgrounds of many names can be reliably understood with simple questionnaires. On many websites, including Playforia, the creation day of the name can be seen, which means that it is possible to closely investigate the rapid development of the category of user names. I have not done this kind of research in my Master's thesis but I am already working on doctoral thesis which covers also the temporal point of view to user names.

Moreover, orthography in user names and in names in general is an important aspect to discuss in onomastics in the future. The capitalisation of names is especially a very interesting orthographic rule, and it is surprisingly one of the few researched subjects thus far. A capital letter is an important part of the essence of a name in many languages, especially in European languages. Knowing the exact historical development may help us to understand how and why capitalisation started and what it reveals about names in general.

In the future I'm hoping to get even more reliable results. In my forthcoming doctoral thesis I still examine user names in Finnish online communities but the sample will be much larger and will cover several websites. However, this vast onomastic category is still quite unknown and therefore open for new researchers.

References

Ainiala, T., Saarelma M. and Sjöblom P. 2012. *Names in Focus. An Introduction to Finnish Onomastics* (trans. L. Pearl). Helsinki: Finnish Literature Society.

Hämäläinen, L. 2011. "Nimi on King Pelle": käyttäjien nimet verkkopeliyhteisö Aapelissa ["Name is King Pelle": user names in online gaming community Playforia]. Bachelor's thesis, University of Helsinki.

—. 2012. Rekisteröityneiden käyttäjien nimet verkkopeliyhteisö Aapelissa [Registered user names in online gaming community Playforia]. Master's thesis, University of Helsinki.

Matsi, J. 2012. "Nicki on nettinimi": Nettinimimerkkien muodostaminen ja käyttö ["Nick is Internet name": Creation and usage of Internet nicknames]. Master's thesis, University of Helsinki.

Sjöblom, P. 2006. *Toiminimen toimenkuva: suomalaisen yritysnimistön rakenne ja funktiot* [A firm name's job description. The structure and function of Finnish company names]. Helsinki: Suomalaisen Kirjallisuuden Seura.

Vehkalahti, K. 2008. *Kyselytutkimuksen mittarit ja menetelmät* [Survey research indicators and methods]. Helsinki: Tammi.

PART IV

CHANGING NAME USE AND NAMING PROCESSES

Preferred Sound Shapes of German Brand Names

Elke Ronneberger-Sibold and Sabine Wahl
Catholic University of Eichstätt-Ingolstadt, Germany

Abstract

Sound shapes of foreign languages are often imitated in German brand names in order to evoke certain associations in the potential consumers. For instance, the brand names *Persil* [pɛr'zi:l] (detergent) or *Veronal* [vero'na:l] (medicine) show the typical sound shape of Latin loanwords in German: two or more syllables with full vowels; main stress on the last syllable, which contains of a long vowel followed by one consonant. Because of its frequent use in scientific words such as *Medizin* [medi'tsi:n] this sound shape is associated with 'science' by German language users. Other typical foreign sound shapes evoke different associations.

The study investigates if certain sound shapes tend to signal specific product classes. For this purpose, German brand names for cosmetics and cleaning agents, pharmaceutical products, and food and drink, published in the German *Markenblatt* in 2004 and 2008, are analysed with respect to their phonological structure. A comparison with a large corpus of historical German brand names shows that some tendencies found in current German brand names are diachronically stable, whereas others are subject to historical developments. This is particularly interesting in view of recent changes in the preferred sound shapes of first names for children.

Introduction – Subject and Aims

"All the beautiful sounds of this world in a single word" – In this line from a famous song from the musical *West Side Story*[1], the word with a beautiful sound is the name of a beloved person. It could, however, just as well refer to the name of a brand such as, e.g., *Persil*. In fact, a good brand name should personalise the product: like a person, the product should be easily remembered and recognised by the customers, who should consider it to be unique and, of course, desirable. Thus, the name of a brand is an important element in a marketing strategy which aims at building a brand customers develop a deep emotional relationship with and which they remain faithful to throughout their lives.

A word or sometimes a short phrase serving as a brand name can fulfil these objectives in two ways: by its meaning and/or by its sound shape. In this paper, we are interested in the sound shape only. In order to entrench the product in the customers' memory, the sound shape of its name should be easy to pronounce, to perceive, and to recognise. Moreover, if the name is distinctive, i.e. sufficiently different from all other competing names, and if it fits its product, i.e. if it is motivated, customers will tend to consider the product to be unique. (Of course, distinctiveness is also a legal requirement.) And finally, a good brand name should evoke positive associations and be aesthetically appealing to make the product desirable for the customers.

It is difficult to meet all these requirements at the same time, for some of them contradict each other. For instance, motivated names for similar products tend to resemble each other, as do short names which are easy to pronounce and to perceive. Thus, a compromise between different needs has to be found. Our questions therefore are:

(1) Which sound shapes are preferred in German brand names?
(2) Do these preferred sound shapes represent a compromise between different needs?
(3) Are the preferences conditioned by extralinguistic, socio-cultural developments in Germany?

In the following, we will first explain some characteristic sound shapes of words in the German lexicon, which are particularly well suited for brand names, before introducing the material and method of our study.

[1] http://www.westsidestory.com/site/level2/lyrics/maria.html.

After that, we will present our statistical results, our interpretation of the data and the conclusion.

Typical Sound Shapes of Words in the German Lexicon

In phonology, we normally distinguish between two kinds of features identifying the sound shape of words: prosodic and segmental.[2] Prosodic features concern the number and shape of syllables in a word as well the place of its primary stress. Although a linguistic definition of the notion *syllable* is notoriously difficult, language users normally have a clear intuition of the number of syllables contained in a word. This intuition is sufficient for our present purpose. Thus, most Germans probably agree that the name *Twix* (for a sweet) contains one syllable, the name *Ka.ba* for a chocolate drink two, *As.pi.rin* three, and *Tho.ma.py.rin* four. Much could also be said concerning the shape of syllables, but for our purpose, a distinction between open syllables ending in a vowel versus closed syllables ending in a consonant is sufficient. Thus, both syllables in *Ka.ba* are open, both syllables in *Per.sil* closed. Finally, the syllable bearing the primary stress of a word is phonetically the most prominent one. In *Ká.ba*, it is the first one, in *Per.síl* the last, in *Ro.wén.ta* the penultimate.

Segmental features, which will play a part in this paper, concern the colour of the vowels and the sonority of the consonants: Vowels may be full (such as [a, e, i, o, u] or reduced. The only reduced vowel in German is the schwa [ə], exclusively used in unstressed syllables. E.g., *Kaba* ['ka:.ba] ends in a full vowel, but *Mampe* ['mam.pə] (a brand of alcoholic drinks) ends in [ə]. Consonants may be voiceless obstruents such as [p], [f], or voiced obstruents such as [b], [v], or resonants, which are always voiced: [r, l, m, n]. All vowels are voiced by definition. E.g., the name *Persil* [pɛr'zi:l] contains one voiceless obstruent [p], whereas all other segments are voiced: two vowels [ɛ, i:], one voiced obstruent [z], and two resonants [r, l]. Of course, the sonority of sounds can be measured in a much more finely graded manner, but for the purpose of this study, voiceless versus voiced is sufficient.

German does not allow final voiced obstruents. Therefore, underlying voiced obstruents, e.g., in *Tage* [ta:.gə] 'days', are systematically devoiced in inflectional or derivational forms where they would stand in final position, e.g., in *Tag* [ta:k] 'day'. This process, called final devoicing, is very typical of Standard German.

---

[2] See Russ (2010) for an introduction to German phonetics and phonology.

The features explained thus far allow for defining several prototypical sound shapes frequently used in German brand names.[3] They come from different languages that have shaped the German lexicon. The first two are the so-called "Germanic" sound shapes characteristic of German or English words. As far as their sound shapes are concerned, German and English, due to their close genetic relationship as West-Germanic languages, are rather similar in the fundamental syllabic, rhythmic and segmental make-up of their words: apart from a few phonemic differences such as English /θ/ and /ð/, which do not exist in German, and German /x~ç/, non-existent in English, the two languages differ more in the realisation of certain segments and most often only in their spelling conventions. Typical differences include, e.g., German [ʁ] vs. English [ɹ], final devoicing in German, but not in English etc. However, these subtleties are often not observed in the pronunciation of English brand names by German language users, and even the few loan phonemes such as /ei/ or /θ/ are often replaced by the closest German counterpart. Therefore, as far as brand names are concerned, German and English sound shapes can be subsumed under the same label "Germanic".

The prototypical "Germanic" sound shapes are a (mostly closed) monosyllable, e.g., German *Sohn* [zo:n], English *son*, and a disyllable with initial stress and a reduced vowel in the second, unstressed syllable, e.g., German *Vater* ['fa:.tɐ], English *father*. However, both types are not very frequent in German brand names, precisely because they are not exotic enough to the German ear. What is preferred are less prototypically "Germanic" sound shapes involving unstressed full vowels in different places, especially the type ending in an unstressed full vowel (as in German and English *Sófa* ['zo:.fa], German *Kólibri* ['ko:.li.bri] 'humming bird'), represented, e.g., by *Kába* ['ka:.ba], *Háribo* ['ha:.ri.bo] (sweets), *Slóggy* ['slɔ.gi] (underwear), *Quénty* ['kvɛn.ti] (cosmetics). The last two names show a popular trick for the production of an English-looking name of this type by using a *y* in the spelling of a final unstressed [-i]. Further atypical "Germanic" sound shapes used in brand names contain full vowels in closed final syllables (German *Technik* ['tɛç.nɪk], 'technology'). The least "Germanic", but still not markedly "foreign" sound shape is represented by German *Automatik* [aʊ.to.'ma:.tɪk], 'automatic': It is characterised by three or four syllables with full vowels, a closed final syllable, and penultimate stress. Its stress pattern makes it a borderline case between the "Germanic" and "Romance" sound shapes. The latter will be explained below.

---

[3] Cf. Ronneberger-Sibold (2002; 2009), Ronneberger-Sibold and Wahl (forthcoming).

As the less prototypical "Germanic" sound shapes mentioned thus far are, for the most part, characteristic of neoclassical internationalisms, creators of the respective brand names have to rely on their orthography to give them an English touch. One way to make a brand name not only look, but also sound definitely non-native, is to use one of the following three sound shapes, here called the "Latin", the "Romance" and the "French" type respectively.

The "Latin" sound shape is characterised by two or more syllables with full vowels. The final syllable is closed and bears the primary stress. In the prototype, the nucleus of this syllable is a long vowel followed by one consonant, e.g., in *Literatur* [li.te.ra.'tu:r], or, for a brand name, in *Aspirin* [as.pi.'ri:n]. In a less typical type, the final sequence consists of a short vowel + two (or more) consonants, e.g., in *Rezept* [re.'tsɛpt] 'recipe/ prescription'. It is not frequently used in brand names.

The "Latin" sound shape originated from the way in which, from the times of Humanism on, Latin and Greek words have been adapted to the German language: the original is left as intact as possible, especially with respect to the place of its primary stress. Only the inflectional endings are dropped. Thus, Latin *litteratura* results in German *Literatur*. From this origin, the "Latin" sound shape retains its associations of scientific character, reliability, and erudition. In brand names, it is therefore preferably used for scientifically prepared, especially chemical and pharmaceutical, products.

What here is called the "Romance" sound shape is characteristic of younger loans from the Mediterranean Romance languages Italian (e.g., *Mortadella, Espresso, Cappuccino, Zucchini*), Spanish (e.g., *Sombrero, Torero, Corrida*), and some Portuguese (*Veranda*). (An average German language user is unable to distinguish these languages by their sound shapes). The common features of these loans are three or more syllables with full vowels, penultimate stress and an ending in *-a, -o* or (less often) *-i.* To Germans, the "Romance" sound shape evokes associations related to its countries of origin, i.e., ease and enjoyment of life, Mediterranean flair, holidays. Therefore, it is used in brand names mainly for products which make life pleasant and easy: food, beverages, cosmetics, cleaning agents, etc. Examples include *Sanella* [za.'nɛ.la] (margarine), sounding like *Mortadella*, *Eduscho* [e.'du:.ʃo] (coffee), sharing the rhythmic and syllabic shape as well as the final vowel with *Espresso,* or *Nudossi* [nu.'dɔ.si] reminiscent of, e.g., *Grissini.*

The "French" sound shape has entered the German language via loan words such as *Allee* [a.'le:] 'alley', *Gelee* [ʒe.'le:] 'jelly' or *Büro* [by.'ro:] 'office'. It is characterised by two or more syllables and final stress on an open syllable. In brand names, it is used for products matching the associations which, for Germans, are related to Paris: elegant clothing, e.g. *Ergee* [ʔɛʁ.'ge:] (stockings), delicious food, e.g., *Ramee* [ra.'me:] (cheese), cosmetics and perfumes, e.g., *Sarabé* [za.ra.'be:], a perfume.

Material and Method

The corpus of our investigation comes from two projects on the analysis of historical German brand names, in part compared to Italian brand names.[4] The source of the German material is the periodical *Warenzeichenblatt,* today *Markenblatt*, in which all newly registered brand names have been published from 1894 on by the German Patent and Trade Mark Office, divided today into 45 product classes of the so-called Nice classification.[5] For this study, we selected the years 1904, 1924, 1954, 1974, 1994, 2004 and 2008, and within these years, the classes 3 "cleaning agents and cosmetics", 5 "pharmaceutical products", and 29–33 "food and drink". Moreover, we excluded all names containing more than one word. Among the remaining names, all of which consist of one word only, we chose those containing one to four syllables, which is the vast majority. One part of these brand names consists of previously existing words transformed into brand names; another part was directly coined as names. As far as their sound shapes are concerned, both groups are remarkably similar, which proves that the creators of brand names are unconsciously guided by the same phonetic preferences whether they select a word from the existing vocabulary or whether they actively expand it by a new name. In this paper, we treat the newly coined names only. As a result of the entire selection process, we ended up with a corpus of approximately 150 brand names per year on an average.

---

[4] We are grateful to the DFG (*Deutsche Forschungsgemeinschaft*) for subsidising the first project from 1999–2002, as well as to the DAAD (*Deutscher Akademischer Austauschdienst*), to the Ateneo Italo-Tedesco (*Programma VIGONI*) and to the University of Verona (Junior Visitor Program *COOPERINT*) for subsidising the second project in 2009–2010.

[5] Although, legally, the term *brand name* is not limited to registered product names, we confined ourselves to *Markenblatt*, because as a source, it is complete, chronologically ordered and independent of the actual economic success of the respective products.

Statistical Results and Interpretation

This section presents the statistical results of the analysis of all the brand names in our corpus according to their number of syllables, their prototypical sound shapes and their degree of sonority. As we adopt a diachronic perspective, the findings will reveal significant developments in the creation of German brand names from 1904 to 2008. For the interpretation of the findings, intra-linguistic as well as extra-linguistic factors will be taken into consideration.

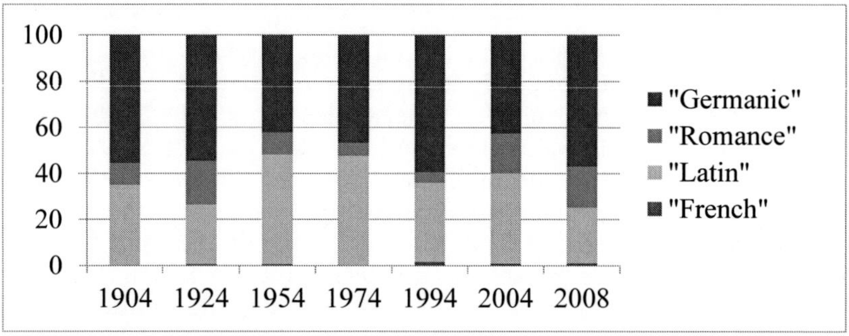

Figure 1. Number of syllables.

As far as the number of syllables is concerned, figure 1 shows that German brand names favour a trisyllabic structure throughout the entire period of investigation amounting to about 50% in each year. At the other end of the scale are names which consist of one syllable only with a minimum of 0.7% in 1924 and a maximum of 2.7% in 2008. Brand names with two or four (and more) syllables occur in varying proportions. In 1994 and 2008 there are more names with two syllables than names with four syllables, in all the other years it is the other way around.

These findings can be summed up in the following way:

most preferred				**dispreferred**
3 syllables	>	2 syllables or 4+ syllables	>	1 syllable

There may be various intra- and extra-linguistic reasons for the stable majority of the trisyllabic structure of German brand names. First, three syllables are the ideal length for the non-"Germanic" sound shapes mentioned above, because this structure is longer than and therefore markedly different from the dispreferred prototypical "Germanic" sound shapes, i.e., a monosyllable and a disyllable with initial stress and a reduced unstressed vowel. But even the less prototypical "Germanic" and therefore less dispreferred sound shapes combining initial stress with unstressed full vowels become less "Germanic" with increasing length: for instance, the well-known name *Haribo* ['ha:.ri.bo] (sweets) sounds less "Germanic" than *Kaba* ['ka:.ba]. Moreover, three syllables are the minimal length for the "Romance" sound shape, which crucially depends on its penultimate stress, and even the "Latin" sound shape sounds more scientific as the number of syllables increases: *Rhoival* appears to be a graver medication, if it is pronounced [ro.i:.'va:l] than if it is pronounced as a disyllable [ro^{I}.'va:l]. Of course, the effect of increasing length may be enhanced even further by adding a fourth syllable, e.g., in *Arutropin* [a.ru.tro.'pi:n] (medicine). This may explain the slight preference for four-syllable names over disyllabic ones, but, at the same time, four syllables make a brand name more difficult to pronounce, to perceive, and above all to memorise. According to a professional naming agency, a trisyllabic structure is considered to be a word length of brand names that can still be easily perceived and remembered by the recipients.[6]

Thus, three syllables in German brand names are an ideal compromise between the needs for shortness, ease of pronunciation and perception as well as memorability on the one hand, and the needs for phonetic motivation and for an aesthetic appeal through the marked non-"Germanic" sound shapes on the other hand: a name such as *Aspirin* for medicine is motivated by its scientific character and sounds nice to German ears without being too long and complicated. Moreover, greater length allows for more internal variation and, hence, for more distinctivity.

Figure 2 presents the results of our analysis of all one-word brand names with two to four syllables in our corpus with regard to their sound shapes.

[6] We are grateful to Nomen International Deutschland for this piece of information (personal communication).

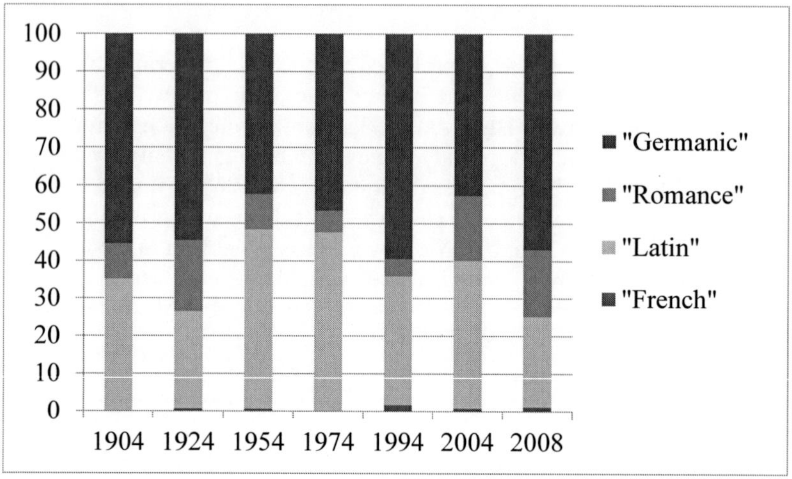

Figure 2. Sound shapes of German brand names with 2–4 syllables.

The "Germanic" sound shapes dominate from 1904 to 2008 with a percentage ranging from about 42% in 1954 and 2004 to 59% in 1994. It is only in 1954, 1974 and 2004 that all non-"Germanic" sound shapes taken together exceed the "Germanic" names.

Within the category of the non-"Germanic" sound shapes, it is the "Latin" one that is preferred in German brand names throughout the period of investigation. With a value of about 47% in 1954 and 1974, it is even more prevalent than the "Germanic" sound shapes (42% in 1954 and 46% in 1974). However, from 1994 onwards, the "Latin" sound shape has decreased considerably. Its percentage in 2008 (24%) even drops below the 1924 level (about 25%).

As the "Latin" sound shape is especially prominent in brand names for pharmaceutical products (class 5), we examined whether the remarkable decrease from 1994 onwards is simply conditioned by a corresponding drop of registered brand names for pharmaceutical products. This is shown in figure 3.

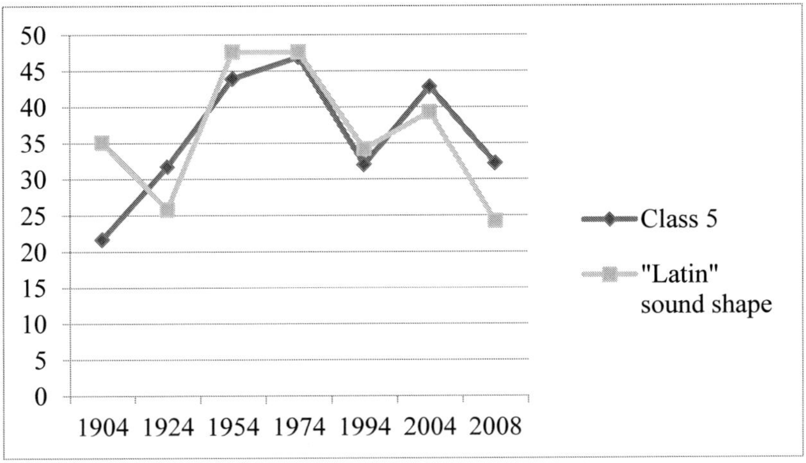

Figure 3. Relation of the "Latin" sound shape and class 5.

While the decrease of the Latin sound shape in 1994 might in fact be due to the corresponding decrease of pharmaceutical products, the subsequent development in 2004 and 2008 shows that this cannot be the only reason because, in these years, the line for the "Latin" sound shape is – even to an increasing degree – below the line for the pharmaceutical products. This means that there must be a growing number of such products which are not named with a "Latin" sound shape.

The explanation of this development may be twofold: first, the prominent association *scientific* in brand names is no longer evoked by the "Latin" sound shape only, but also by the "Germanic" sound shape with an English touch, applied to neoclassic lexical material. Examples of this English scientific nature include *Kinamic* (class 5, 2004), *Selen-Stix* (class 5, 2004), *Oxyguard* (class 5, 2004), and *Paroguard* (class 5, 2004). A second, extra-linguistic reason may be the fact that in the ecologist movement emerging from the 1970s onwards (see Schröter 2003: 403–404) the association of scientificness is no longer indisputably positive. *Scientific* is regarded as synonymous with *artificial* and thus, in this context, it stands in sharp contrast to the desired naturalness of food and drink as well as cosmetics and even environmentally friendly detergents.

In 1994 the decrease of the "Latin" sound shape is more or less compensated for by an increase in "Germanic" sounding brand names (see figure 2). However, in 2004 and 2008, there is another sound shape which seems to function as an alternative to the "Latin" sound shape: the

"Romance" one. In these two years, the "Romance" sound shape increases dramatically from about 4.5% in 1994 to about 17.2% in 2004 and 17.8% in 2008. It is remarkable that the percentage of names with a "Romance" sound shape in 2004 and 2008 almost equals that of 1924. However, in 1924, this was but a temporary development, whereas the present trend appears to be more stable.[7] Examples from our corpus include: *Lolleria* [lɔ.le.'ri:.a][8] (class 30, 2004), *Soluna* [zo.'lu:.na] (class 29, 2008), *Zitronella* [tsi.tro.'nɛ.la] (class 30, 2004), *Bratino* [bra.'ti:.no] (class 30, 2004), *Grandiso* [gran.'di:.zo] (class 30, 2004), *Nudossi* [nu.'dɔ.si] (class 3, 2004). These examples indicate that "Romance" seems to be an alternative for "Latin" as a non-"Germanic" sound shape for non-pharmaceuticals, especially in the product classes for food.

The reasons for this remarkable preference of the "Romance" sound shape at the beginning of the 21st century are manifold. If we focus on the creation of brand names as such, it is a (legal) requirement that the newly coined names are distinct. Therefore, the immense increase of "Romance" sounding names on the German market might be regarded as a reaction against the excessive preponderance of "Germanic" in 1994 with the intention of creating brand names that are distinct and at the same time more exotic than new German and English names.

Other explanations are of an extra-linguistic nature: as previously mentioned, the ecologist movement introduced a "healthy lifestyle" on the German market which placed emphasis on natural, homemade products without any artificial flavour enhancers or additives. This association may be evoked in brand names either via very traditional German names or via names which remind customers of authentic, homemade, healthy Italian food prepared by "la Mamma". Because of the high number of "Germanic" names on the market (see above), the "Romance" sound shape might have been preferred in order to add a flavour of exoticism and modernity to the associations "homemade" and "healthy". In this context, it is worth mentioning that Italy and especially Spain have always been the Germans' most popular (European) holiday destinations since the beginning of market research concerning this aspect in 1985[9].

Another extra-linguistic explanation focuses more on the second language that is subsumed under the umbrella term "Romance", namely

---

[7] A similar point can be made with respect to the decrease of the "Latin" sound shape in 1924 and from 1994 onwards.

[8] As the phoneme inventory of standard German does not contain consonantal geminates, Italian [ll] is realised as simple [l] in German brand names.

[9] Cf. www.deutsche-marktforscher.de/hilfesseite/archiv/details/article/reiseverhalten - der-deutschen.html

Spanish. It highlights the oft-cited fact that (popular) culture and advertising influence each other. From the mid 1990s onwards, Spanish has gained influence on the German music market. This development began in 1996 with the summer hit single *Macarena* by *Los del Rio*.[10] In 1997 *The Latin Academy of Recording Arts & Sciences®* was established. In 2000 this association introduced the Latin Grammy Awards for the best Latin music of the year[11]. Other representatives of Latin (dance) music whose singles are listed in the German Top 100 of the respective year include, e.g., *Ricky Martin*, *Jennifer Lopez*, *Las Ketchup*, *Juanes*, *Carlos Santana* (with a successful comeback in 2000), and *Shakira*[12]. Today, the fitness trend *Zumba* which is a Latin dance workout that has become popular worldwide in dancing schools and fitness studios with a DVD series and a video game[13] could even reinforce this development.

All these cultural influences may explain why Spanish has become one of the most popular foreign languages in Germany, even in the curricula of secondary schools. In 1970, there were only about 2,500 students taking Spanish in West Germany[14]. This number grew to 115,000 in 2000/2001 and in 2007/2008 more than 285,000 students were enrolled in Spanish language classes.[15] It has even become more popular than French as the traditional Romance language taught in German secondary schools.

---

[10] Cf. http://www.musiksampler.de/singlecharts_1996.html. Moreover, it was also during the 1990s that the work of the Spanish filmmaker Pedro Almodóvar and the Spanish actors Antonio Banderas and Penélope Cruz became known internationally, including in Germany (cf. www.imdb.com/name/nm0000264/; www.imdb.com/name/nm0004851/; www.imdb.com/name/nm0000104/). As films presented in cinemas and on television in Germany are usually dubbed so that the German audience does not hear the original Spanish language soundtrack but rather a translated one, the influence may be regarded as indirect, as a kind of incentive to study Spanish in order to be able to watch the original version. This growing interest in the language and culture of Spanish-speaking countries may also have been supported by numerous global sporting events such as the FIFA World Cup and the Olympic Games hosted by Spanish-speaking countries from 1962 onwards (cf. www.fifa.com/worldcup/archive/index.html; www.olympic.org/olympic-games).

[11] www.latingrammy.com/en/content/about-latin-academy-recording-arts-sciences

[12] Cf. www.musiksampler.de/single_charts.html.

[13] www.zumbafitness.co.uk/latin-dance-workout.aspx; www.zumba.com/de-DE/about/

[14] www.uebersetzerportal.de/nachrichten/n-archiv/2003/2003-05/2003-05-23.htm

[15] See www.focus.de/schule/lernen/lernatlas/fremdsprachen/tid-14675/schule-viva-espana_aid_399260.html. As a consequence of this growing interest in Spanish language classes, there were not enough qualified secondary school Spanish language teachers in certain parts of Germany in 2010 (cf. www.sueddeutsche.de/karriere/spanischunterricht-profesores-gesucht-1.18486).

The "French" sound shape could be another alternative to the "Latin" and the "Romance" ones as a non-"Germanic" sound shape. However, it is almost non-existent among new coinages in the product classes analysed throughout the entire period of investigation, ranging between 0% in 1904 and 1974 and 1.7% in 1994. It is only from 1994 onwards that we observe a very small increase in French-sounding brand names on the German market, e.g., *miRoo* [mi.'ro:] (class 3, 1994), *Aromee* [a.ro.'me:] (class 3, 2008), *Cocolat* [ko.ko.'la] (class 30, 2004).

It will be interesting to verify whether these developments in the creation of German brand names starting around the beginning of the 21st century – the decrease of "Latin" and the enormous increase of "Romance" – will turn out to be sustainable.

The "beautiful" name in the musical *West Side Story* mentioned in the introduction is *Maria*[16]. This first name fulfils all the characteristics of the prototypical "Romance" sound shape. It consists of three syllables with full vowels, the stress falls on the penultimate syllable, and the last syllable ends in *-a*. If we analyse this name not only with regard to its prosodic features but also to its segmental phonetic characteristics, it turns out that it is composed only of three vowels – twice [a] and once [i] – and two resonants – the nasal [m] and the liquid [r]. This limitation to vowels and resonants makes the name *Maria* extremely sonorant.

In two studies on the phonetic qualities of names in Germany, Nübling (2009) and Fahlbusch (2011) found a recent increase of sonority in first names and corporate names respectively. As sonorous sounds are associated with characteristics considered typically female, such as being soft and affectionate (Ertel 1969)[17], they used to prevail in female names. The recent extension of sonority as a preferred feature to male names is therefore interpreted as an "androgynisation" by Nübling (2009). The fact found by Fahlbusch (2011) that the same tendency also prevails in corporate names integrates the phenomenon into a broader development of aesthetic preferences. In order to find out whether this trend can also be found in brand names created for the German market, we analysed all the brand names in our corpus registered in 1904, 1954, 2004, and 2008 according to the percentage of voiced – and therefore to a higher or lower

[16] In the official lyrics, it is written without the accent on the *i* that would be required according to Spanish orthography (*María*) http://www.westsidestory.com/site/level2/lyrics/maria.html.

[17] For an application of sound symbolism to brand names cf. Shrum and Lowrey 2007.

degree sonorant – sounds in different positions.[18] The results are summarised in figure 4:

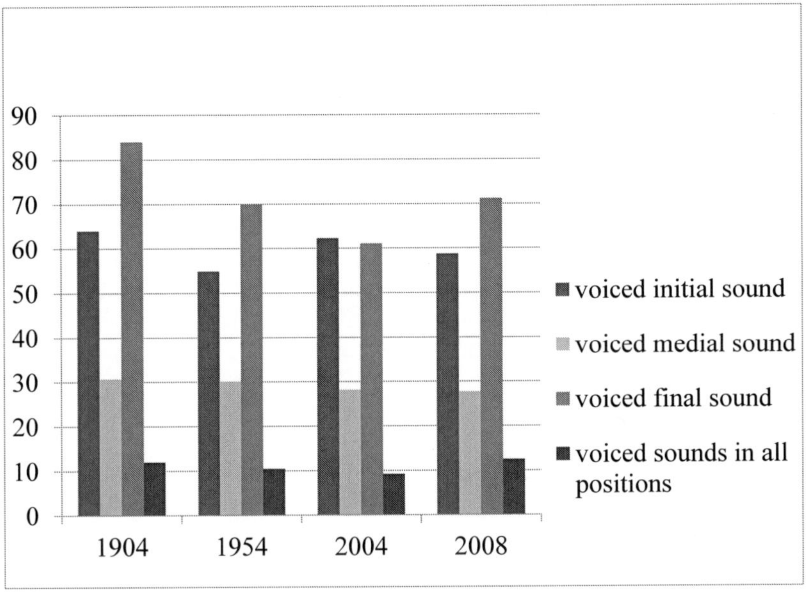

Figure 4. Percentage of names with voiced sounds in different positions.

As far as the initial sound is concerned, the majority of German brand names – between 55% in 1954 and 64% in 1904 – begin with a vowel, voiced obstruent or resonant. "Strong" voiceless onsets are in the minority throughout the entire time span. However, there is a stable preference for voiceless consonants in the medial position of brand names (about 70%). What is even more remarkable is the fact that German brand names show a strong tendency for voiced final sounds with a minimum share of 61% in 2004 and a maximum share of 84% in 1904. The main ways of achieving a voiced final sound is the use of either the prototypical "Romance" sound shape ending in the full vowels *-a* (*Soluna, Zitronella*) or *-o* (*Bratino, Grandiso*) or the prototypical "Latin" sound shape ending in a resonant (nasal or liquid), e.g., in the endings *-an*, *-al*, *-il*, *-in*, etc. (*Sanazin*, class 5,

[18] Our distinction between voiced and voiceless sounds is but a rough approximation to the far more fine-grained system for calculating different degrees of sonority applied by Nübling (2009) and Fahlbusch (2011).

2008).[19] The result of this preference is that the typically German final devoicing is circumvented – quite in line with the general tendency for avoiding typical German features in German brand names.

There are even brand names in our corpus which do not include any voiceless sound at all. These extremely sonorant names, e.g., *Soluna*, *Lolleria*, *neviolo* (class 3, 2008), *Allernil* (class 5, 2004), and *Nanosin* (class 5, 2004) have a share of 12% in 1904, 10.4% in 1954, 9.2% in 2004 and 12.5% in 2008.

These results show that voiced sounds have always been preferred in German brand names. It seems that in these names, for which an appealing sound shape is essential, the aesthetic quality of sonority has always been recognised and used, whereas, in first names, the aesthetic concern used to be superseded by the wish to emphasise the difference between the sexes. As far as companies are concerned, the deliberate creation of nice sounding names is a fairly recent phenomenon.

Conclusion

With respect to the research questions formulated in the introduction, our study has yielded the following results:

1) There is a strong and stable preference for trisyllabic brand names with a high degree of sonority. These occur in four major different sound shapes labelled "Germanic", "Latin", "Romance", and "French" respectively. Among these, "Latin" is preferred for scientifically prepared, especially pharmaceutical, products, and "Germanic" and "Romance" are primarily used for cosmetics and food and drink. In recent years, "Germanic" with an English touch has increasingly been used even for scientific products.

2) In the preferred trisyllabic and sonorant names a compromise is found between, on the one hand, the needs for shortness, ease of production and perception, as well as memorability and, on the other hand, the needs for phonetic motivation and distinctiveness through different sound shapes, as well as for an aesthetic appeal due to their non-"Germanic" sound shapes and their sonority.

---

[19] A third possibility to create brand names with voiced final sounds is the employment of the typical German endings [ə] and [ən]. This strategy, however, is only marginal in our corpus.

3) From 1994 onwards, a decrease in the “Latin” sound shape can be observed. It is mainly compensated for by the “Germanic” sound shape with an English touch due to the growth of English as a global language. Moreover, the decrease in “Latin” may be partly due to the ecologist movement, in which the scientific nature signalled by the “Latin” sound shape is no longer approved without reservation. From 2004 onwards, the “Latin” sound shape has also been replaced by a considerable increase in the “Romance” sound shape. This increase may be explained by a growing interest in Latin music and culture among young people reflected by an increasing importance of Spanish as a foreign language in the curricula of secondary schools in Germany.

To sum up, *Maria* is in fact a beautiful word – so beautiful that it could even be a brand name.

References

Ertel, S. 1969. *Psychophonetik. Untersuchungen über Lautsymbolik und Motivation* [Psychophonetics. Studies on sound symbolism and motivation]. Göttingen: Hogrefe.

Fahlbusch, F. 2011. Von *Haarmanns Vanillinfabrik* zu *Symrise*, von der *Norddeutsche Raffinerie* zu *Aurubis*. Prinzipien des diachronen Wandels von Unternehmensnamen [From *Haarmanns Vanillinfabrik* to *Symrise*, from *Norddeutschen Raffinerie* to *Aurubis*. Priciples of the diachronic change of company names]. *Beiträge zur Namenforschung* 46: 51–80.

Nübling, D. 2009. Von *Monika* zu *Mia*, von *Norbert* zu *Noah*: Zur Androgynisierung der Rufnamen seit 1945 aus prosodisch-phonologischer Perspektive [From *Monika* to *Mia*, from *Norbert* to *Noah*: On the androgynisation of first names since 1945 from a prosodic-phonological perspective]. *Beiträge zur Namenforschung* 44: 67–110.

Ronneberger-Sibold, E. 2002. On the phonostylistic function of prototypical nonnative sound shapes in contemporary German: evidence from the history of brand names. In *Future Challenges for Natural Linguistics*. K. Dziubałska and J. Weckwerth (eds.), 211–231. München: Lincom Europa.

—. 2009. *Megaflex, Dynast, Solfina*: Europäische Fremdsprachen in deutschen Markennamen aus der zweiten Hälfte des zwanzigsten Jahrhunderts [*Megaflex, Dynast, Solfina*: European foreign languages in German brand names of the second half of the tewntieth century]. In *Europäische Sprachenvielfalt und Globalisierungsprozess*. E. Ronneberger-Sibold and R. Nate (eds.), 141–169. Würzburg: Königshausen & Neumann.

Ronneberger-Sibold, E. and Wahl, S., forthcoming. Associations in German Brand Names: Current Trends. In *Proceedings of the XXIV ICOS International Congress of Onomastic Sciences: Names in Daily Life, 5.-9. September, University of Barcelona.*

Russ, C. V. J. 2010. *The Sounds of German*. Cambridge/New York: Cambridge University Press.

Schröter, H. G. 2000. Von der Teilung zur Wiedervereinigung (1945–2004) [From the division of Germany to its reunification (1945–2004)]. In *Deutsche Wirtschaftsgeschichte. Ein Jahrtausend im Überblick.* [German economic history. A millennium in overview]. Michael North (ed.), 356–426. München: Beck.

Shrum, L. J. and Lowrey, T. M. 2007. Sounds Convey Meaning: The Implications of Phonetic Symbolism for Brand Name Construction. In *Psycholinguistic Phenomena in Marketing Communications*. Tina M. Lowrey (ed.), 39–58. Mahwah/ NJ: Erlbaum.

Online Resources[20]

http://www.deutsche-marktforscher.de/hilfesseite/archiv/details/article/reiseverhalten-der-deutschen.html

http://www.fifa.com/worldcup/archive/index.html

http://www.focus.de/schule/lernen/lernatlas/fremdsprachen/tid-14675/schule-viva-espana_aid_399260.html

http://www.imdb.com/name/nm0000104/

http://www.imdb.com/name/nm0000264/

http://www.imdb.com/name/nm0004851/

http://www.latingrammy.com/en/content/about-latin-academy-recording-arts-sciences

http://www.musiksampler.de/single_charts.html

http://www.musiksampler.de/singlecharts_1996.html

http://www.olympic.org/olympic-games

http://www.sueddeutsche.de/karriere/spanischunterricht-profesores-gesucht-1.18486

http://www.uebersetzerportal.de/nachrichten/n-archiv/2003/2003-05/2003-05-23.htm

http://www.westsidestory.com/site/level2/lyrics/maria.html

[20] All internet references were last retrieved on 12 September 2012.

http://www.zumba.com/de-DE/about/
http://www.zumbafitness.co.uk/latin-dance-workout.aspx

NOTES ON THE SYNTAX OF COMMERCIAL NAMES IN ITALIAN

MARIA CHIARA JANNER
UNIVERSITY OF ZURICH, SWITZERLAND

Abstract

In everyday language, commercial names show various syntactic functions and can acquire multiple meanings depending on the morphosyntactic contexts in which they are used. This paper presents a corpus-based linguistic analysis of commercial names in Italian, focusing on their morphosyntactic features. Two common structures are considered: on one hand, nominal uses of commercial names (combined with Ø, with an article or with other determiners); on the other hand, attributive uses, where commercial names are preceded by a common noun. The group of nominal structures contains different types of commercial names traditionally referred to as company names (*la Barilla*), metonymies of the company for the product (*le Nike*) and product names (*la Vespa*). Attributive uses can be metalinguistic (such as *la ditta Migros* 'the company [called] Migros') or not (the phrase *i giubbotti Avirex* refers to 'jackets produced by the company Avirex' rather than 'jackets called *Avirex*'). Further distinctions within the two structure types are made on the basis of the combinatory properties of commercial names.

The syntactic differences that emerge both between various commercial names and within different syntactic uses of the same commercial name vouch for a complexity that goes beyond the question whether these names are proper or common nouns.

Introduction

The linguistic analysis of commercial names[1] has often concerned itself with the question of their categorical definition: are they proper or common nouns? Different answers were given (for a review, see Koss 1996: 1642; Ronneberger-Sibold 2004: 558–559). On one hand, many scholars agree on the fact that a clear distinction can be traced between product and company names (see e.g. Vaxelaire 2005: 349; Fèvre-Pernet and Roché 2005; Laurent 2007: 37; Mattioda 2008: 111, instead, distinguishes between product and brand names). For these scholars, company and product names have a different onomastic status, the latter being proper nouns and the first ones "being somewhere at the periphery of onymity" (Bergien, Kremer and Zilg 2008: 10). However, some of the works that trace well-defined boundaries between product and brand (or company) names seem to ignore how scanty this distinction might be; a linguistic account of commercial names has to describe their linguistic functioning trying not to rely (or not exclusively) on the so-called external world by saying "this name behaves so because it refers to a product and not to a company". On the other hand, Lötscher (2008: 53) claims that even product names have to be considered to be proper nouns, especially with regard to their origin: they are individual proper nouns, specifically created by marketers.

The question about the syntactic features of commercial names has received less attention than the one cited at the beginning. These nouns can frequently be found in everyday discourse, in expressions that show different patterns in each language. How can their features be described from a linguistic perspective? Which morphosyntactic peculiarities do they show?

In this paper I will draw attention toward this point, considering how commercial names appear within clauses and going beyond the onymic question. The analysis aims at describing commercial names from a linguistic point of view, based on their combinatory – that is, syntactic – features. These will vary depending on the language; this paper deals specifically with the case of Italian.

I adopt a Saussurean perspective on language as a system made up of relations and oppositions between elements (Saussure 1916; 2002). A

---

[1] I will use the term *commercial names* referring to all names that pragmatically belong to the world of commerce (see De Stefani 2007: 234; Bergien, Kremer and Zilg 2008: 10). A further classification of such names (for instance, brand names, product names, trademarks etc., either from a linguistic, economic or legal viewpoint) would require an in-depth analysis which is not the aim of this paper.

commercial name should be considered to be part of a discourse rather than an isolated entity whose features (including the lexical categorisation evoked at the beginning of this work) are destined to remain unsharp; it should be analysed and classified within the whole of its syntagmatic as well as paradigmatic relations that give it a specific value (Saussure 1916: 161–175, 2002: 28; on the *valeur linguistique* in Saussure's work see also La Fauci 2011: 81–82, 275). I shall study which elements (definite and indefinite articles, possessives) occur in combination with commercial names and what their value is: for example, which articles are compulsory in specific syntactic contexts and which can be left out without changing the global meaning of the sentence. The linguistic value of an element can be established by considering what it *is not* as well as what it is.

On Multiple Reference and Syntax

Syntax creates meanings in a dynamic way as a result of a combination process. The insertion of commercial names in discourse literally results in a name recreation; in fact, despite the almost complete lack of inflection and derivation, commercial names show a great number of syntactic functions, thereby acquiring multiple meanings depending on the morphosyntactic context in which they are used.

Based on the evidence that the same commercial name might have multiple meanings in different sentences, Van Langendonck (2007: 97) lists four principal categories of commercial names: (1) founders of companies, (2) the companies themselves, (3) brands, and (4) distinct products of the brand. The distinction between company, brand, and product names is now the result of introducing the same noun into different contexts. The English sentences Van Langendonck cites, if translated in Italian, seem to maintain the same structure and respect the classification he proposes: *Ford ha fondato una fabbrica di automobili* ('Ford founded a car industry'), *Ford è un'azienda automobilistica* ('Ford is a car company'), *Ford è una marca conosciuta* ('Ford is a familiar brand'),[2] *Ieri Maria ha acquistato una Ford* ('Jane bought a Ford yesterday').

In spite of what marketers recommend – "never use a trademark as a noun […] always use a trademark as an adjective", as Solly (2002: 228) cites –, the commercial name in these sentences enjoys nominal use, once

[2] Things would be different if one would consider this use (and maybe the previous one, too) to be a metalinguistic one since *Ford* is a brand name; "*Ford* is a familiar brand" would then be similar to "*John* is a widespread English name".

being introduced by an article and therefore appearing as a common noun. But language can go even further in terms of morphosyntactic modification. In Italian, for instance, brand names show attributive functions (*il motore Ford*, 'Ford engine'; *lo stile Ford*, 'Ford style') as well as adverbial ones (*Gianni guida Ford*, 'John drives Ford'); depending on the sort of article it is preceded by, the same brand name can refer to more than one specific product: *la Peugeot*, with a feminine article, is a car, while *il Peugeot*, with a masculine article, refers to a specific moped model of the same company.

Furthermore, not all commercial names can be used in each category Van Langendonck lists. Nouns such as *Coop* or *Nestlé* are not able to identify a specific product if they are taken as simple nouns (how can one buy *a Nestlé*?); these and other names such as *3M* or *Intimissimi* do not derive from a personal name and, thus, make the first category superfluous. Moreover, there are numerous brands that name only a product, such as *(VW) Golf* or *(3M) Post-it*; hence, they are representative of the products' and brands' category, but they lack the other two (on this point see also the critical observations of Lötscher 2008: 37–38).

Corpus and Data: an Overview

The examples considered in the previous section show one risk of creating linguistic material to support one's hypothesis (see De Stefani 2008: 714); as shown above, not all commercial names have the same syntactic features. This is the reason why I shall take examples from written sources, especially from two recent Italian novels where plenty of brands can be found: *Jack Frusciante è uscito dal gruppo*, written by Enrico Brizzi ('Jack Frusciante has left the band'; Brizzi 1995), and Federico Moccia's *Tre metri sopra il cielo* ('three meters above the sky'; Moccia 1992 and 2004).[3]

Even if the material is mostly of fictive nature, it reflects common language structures containing commercial names: nominal and attributive ones. In the nominal use – as in *le Nike* 'the Nikes (shoes)', with a feminine plural article – the commercial name can be preceded by different sorts of articles and by possessive adjectives as well. The commercial names that can be found in this sort of structure can be further distinguished according to other morphosyntactic features, as we will see in the following sections. In the attributive use, commercial names follow a common noun and have the function of an adjective, or better an

[3] Translated by the author.

attributive predication, as it is the case for *la borsa Nike* 'the Nike bag'. This structure alternates with a similar one with the same meaning, in which the commercial name is preceded by the preposition *di* 'of' or by a contraction of the preposition and the feminine definite article (*della*): *la borsa della Nike*, literally 'the bag of the Nike'.

Only the structure types described here can be found in the novel by Moccia, and they always refer to objects. Brizzi's novel, instead, sometimes shows a more original and creative use of commercial names apart from the typical ones. In fact, all commercial names found in Moccia's book, both in nominal and in attributive structures, could be substituted by or reduced to the common noun of an object (*le Nike* = *le scarpe* 'the shoes') without changing the substance of the narration or reducing the understanding of the story. This is not the case for certain expressions used by Brizzi, for instance "le facce tipo Benetton di Paulos, Ivan, Shoko e di tutti gli altri amici" ('the Benetton-like faces of Paulos, Ivan, Shoko and all other friends'; Brizzi 1995: 128). The expression refers to the well-known advertisements of Benetton during the 1980s, which showed young people of different ethnic origins, just like the friends of the novel's protagonist evoked in this passage.[4] In this case, the commercial name *Benetton* can be substituted neither by the name of a product nor by another brand name.

In the following I will concentrate on salient features of the common structures described above: nominal and attributive uses of commercial names.

Nominal Use and the Presence of Articles

Una Vespa, *i Ray-Ban*, *le Superga*: nominal uses of commercial names are the most widespread type among clauses where brand names occur, as a survey on the two aforementioned novels shows. Attributive uses of brand names, instead, both as functionally adjectival predications (immediately preceded by the common noun of the product: *uno zainetto Invicta* 'an Invicta backpack') or constructions where the commercial name is preceded by the preposition *di* (*la maglietta della Onyx* 'the Onyx T-shirt'), are far less represented.

Commercial names displaying nominal function are preceded by a definite or indefinite article, or by other forms of modification, as in the following examples:

[4] For a similar use in French, "famille-Benetton", see example 84 cited by Vaxelaire (2005: 219).

(1) Step sorride. Batte la mano affettuosamente sul serbatoio della sua **Honda**. (Moccia 2004: 95)
'Step smiles, fondly knocking on the tank of his Honda motorcycle.'

(2) Maddalena mastica una **Vigorsol** con la bocca aperta. (Moccia 2004: 141)
'Maddalena chews a piece of Vigorsol chewing gum with an open mouth.'

(3) Pallina […] corre quasi rimbalzando sulle **Nike** chiare. (Moccia 2004: 109)
'Pallina runs as if she is bouncing on her light-colored Nike sneakers.'

(4) Babi si libera della **Camomilla**. (Moccia 2004: 145)
'Babi takes off the Camomilla belt.'

(5) Quella **Marlboro** in bocca non li avrebbe salvati. Non sarebbero entrati. (Moccia 2004: 196)
'That Marlboro they were smoking would have not been enough for them to get in.'

Nominal uses constitute the less homogeneous group as far as morphosyntactic combinations are concerned.

First of all, there are commercial names preceded by a feminine and singular definite article which, at the same time, is a free variation – in other words, it can be easily left out without consequences on the general interpretation of the sentence:[5]

(6) (La) **Barilla** ha comprato (la) **Voiello** nel 1973.
'Barilla has bought Voiello in 1973.'

(7) Gianni lavora presso (la) **Peroni**.
'Gianni is working at Peroni.'

Because of this peculiarity, these names seem to have the character of a proper noun more than other brands combined with an article whose absence could be more problematic (8) or not be neutral from a stylistic point of view (9):

---

[5] For the category considered here, this type of article is the unmarked one; other articles can be found in particular structures (*Quest'anno vedremo una Fiat in grande crescita*, 'This year we are going to see a fast growing Fiat company'; *Una Barilla ha aperto vicino a casa mia*, 'A Barilla establishment just opened near my house') or, as we will see later on, they can be symptoms of belonging to another category referring to product names.

(8) Maria guida $^{?}$(la) **Mercedes** rossa.
'Maria is driving the red Mercedes.'

(9) La storia ci ha consegnato **Vespa** non come un semplice scooter ma come un "mito", un modo di essere, di pensare e di esprimere se stessi.[6] (www.vespa.com, retrieved 11 October 2012)
'History has given us Vespa not merely as a scooter but as a legend, a way of living, of thinking, of expressing oneself.'

Which of these brand names can be understood as the reduction of a nominal predication?

(6a) La ditta (chiamata) **Barilla** ha comprato la ditta (chiamata) **Voiello** nel 1973.
'The company (named) Barilla has bought the company (named) Voiello in 1973.'

(7a) Gianni lavora presso la ditta (chiamata) **Peroni**.
'Gianni is working for the company (named) Peroni.'

(8a) *Maria guida la ditta (chiamata) **Mercedes** rossa.
*'Maria is driving the company (called) red Mercedes.'

(9a) *La storia ci ha consegnato la ditta (chiamata) **Vespa** come un "mito".
*'History has given us the company (called) Vespa as a legend.'

Only in examples 6 through 7, the brand names alternate with a construction where the commercial name is an attributive predication of a common noun like *impresa*, *ditta* or *azienda* ('company', 'firm'). In clauses such as "la ditta Benetton" or "l'impresa Galbani", the brand constitutes a denominative predication, since the noun of a company results from an act of naming, an "initial baptism" (Kripke 1972: 302). This parameter allows to distinguish this type of nominal use (referring to a company, to use an approximate semantic category) from the one (9) where the same article *la* also alternates with zero without changing the meaning of the clause: *(la) Vespa*. In fact, a naming act underlies this name, too, but the noun cannot be paraphrased with "la ditta chiamata

[6] It is somewhat alienating, in this specific context, to use the noun *Vespa* without determination. On the Vespa website, though, the commercial name never appears with an article. This is an example of a common marketing strategy (see Fowler and Iwatani Kane 2011) aiming to give the brand name its character of propriality again, which it has lost in the past: *Vespa* is no longer perceived as a proper noun and belongs now to the common lexicon, being sometimes used for mopeds of other companies as well.

Vespa". While *lavorare alla Fiat* can be ambiguous, meaning 'to work for the Fiat company' as well as 'to be working on a Fiat car',[7] *lavorare alla Vespa* only means 'to be working on a Vespa'.

Another feature of commercial names like the ones seen before is that they can be the subject of verbs like *decide*, *act* and so on; they bear the feature [+ human] in virtue of a common metonymic process (the name of the company for the people who are working in the company):

(10) La **Migros** avrebbe intenzione di spendere circa 100 milioni di franchi per cambiare il suo logo e la sua immagine. (www.consumatori.ch, retrieved 11 October 2012)
'The Migros reseller is thinking of investing about hundred millions Swiss francs to change its image and logo.'

(11) «Le sostanze trovate sono effettivamente contenute in queste percentuali» ammette candidamente **Coop**, che ha deciso di prendere provvedimenti in merito. (www.consumatori.ch, retrieved 11 October 2012)
'"The product actually contains this percentage of the substances", admits Coop candidly, who has decided to take measures with regard to the problem.'

Nominal Use as the Result of Reduced Attributive Constructions

Commercial names characterised by the features listed above (feminine singular article *la* as free variation, possible paraphrase with *la ditta X* 'the company X', feature [+ human]) often occur also preceded by articles of another type (plurals, indefinites, masculine and so on) and other determiners:

(12) Lui era filato in bagno a cambiarsi la **fruit of the loom** sudata con una polo color albicocca più che rispettabile [...]. (Brizzi 1995: 130)
'He quickly disappeared into the bathroom and changed his sweaty Fruit of the Loom T-shirt with a decent apricot polo shirt.'

[7] The use of the preposition *in*, "lavorare in Fiat", a tendency of modern Italian, would clarify the sentence, relating it to the first meaning.

(13) Giuro che se vado a fare il cronista mi taglio i capelli a spazzola e compro le **Clark's** (Brizzi 1995: 21)
'I swear that if I become a reporter, I'll have a flattop and buy a pair of Clarks shoes.'

(14) Forse è l'**Heineken**, oppure anche la **Peroni**, fatto sta che si sta divertendo. (Moccia 2004: 246)
'Maybe it is because of the Heineken beer, or maybe because of the Peroni beer too; anyway, he is having fun.'

The predication inherent in these structures is not only a metalinguistic one, since the commercial name is not the name given in an "initial baptism" to the implied product (the underlying common noun: *T-shirt*, *shoes*, *beer*). It is the consumer rather than the producing company that re-baptises a pair of shoes or another product with the company name. The nominal clauses in examples 12–14 have a metonymic character, while the metalinguistic one is only indirect: *le Clark's* are 'shoes produced by *the company called Clarks*'.

In general, the article contains essential pragmatic information which hints to the product implicitly referred to, through the specific use of a commercial name that is first and foremost a company name. For the latter to become the designation of a product, it is enough to combine the commercial name with an article that recalls gender and number of the common noun of the product: if *Clark's* refers to *le scarpe* 'shoes', a name which is feminine and plural in Italian, we will have *le Clark's*, with a feminine plural article. Gender and number are relevant, as the following pairs show: *la Nike / le Nike* ('Nike company' / 'Nike shoes'), *la Rolex / il Rolex* ('Rolex company' / 'Rolex watch'), *la Levi's / i Levi's* ('Levis company' / 'Levis jeans').[8]

Structures such as 12 and 14 contain a feminine singular article and are therefore ambiguous. *La Peugeot*, for instance, can refer both to the

---

[8] Nevertheless, the presence of an article is not compulsory; suitable contexts allow a non-determined use of the brand name, though maintaining the same value and meaning of a determined one. These are mostly indefinite plurals, used e.g. in enumerations: "Nascosti dietro Ray-Ban, Web, occhiali a specchio o scuri Persol" ('Hidden behind Ray-Bans, Web, mirror glasses or dark Persols'; Moccia 2004: 309) or after the preposition *di*: "una scatola di Settebello" ('a box of Settebello condoms'; Moccia 2004: 85), "non capiscono niente di motorini o di Sony" ('they don't understand anything about mopeds or Sonys'; Moccia 2004: 194). There is also the use after the preposition *in* as for 'wearing something': "in lacoste" ('wearing a Lacoste polo shirt'; Brizzi 1995: 150); "nei panni di Signora in clark's" ('in her role as Lady wearing Clarks shoes'; Brizzi 1995: 40).

company and to its principal product. From a morphosyntactic perspective, though, the article has two different values, because only in the case of car name it shows a paradigmatic range of choices: it can be substituted by masculine articles (*il*) or indefinite ones (*un, una*), it can be combined with possessives *(la mia*), and so on. In the case of company names, however, in an unmarked context, the article *la* alternates mainly with Ø (no article) and gender is not relevant, feminine (singular) being the neutral one.

Different Types of Attributive Predications

The structure of commercial names I have examined in the previous section is traditionally seen as a very common form of metonymy in which the producer name is used for his product (see Van Langendonck 2007: 237–238; Lötscher 2008: 29–30; Bosredon and Guérin 2005: 20). This sort of nominal use often occurs with nouns of established brands, which can refer to their typical products – watches for *Swatch*, shoes for *Nike*, cigarettes for *Camel*, and so on – thus responding to an antonomastic process: the Levis product *par excellence* are not jackets or perfumes, but jeans; in Italian, by saying *i Levi's*, one normally refers to jeans. Obviously, these examples of antonomasias, or better commonplaces, are as such rooted in a specific culture; therefore, they do not occur identically in every language nor necessarily have the same referent everywhere.

Reduced examples underlie a sort of *koine* effect; in other words, only a shared knowledge of encyclopaedic nature allows us to recognise *i Levi's* as an ellipse for *i jeans Levi's*. Antonomasias, which are usual in specific sociolinguistic communities, at the same time establish a commonplace and its designation; in a family, for instance, everyone knows who "il papà" 'daddy' is, in a classroom it is clear who the referent of "il professore" 'the teacher' is (see La Fauci 2011: 216). By writing *dei crudeli Avirex* ('a too tight pair of Avirex jeans'), Moccia (1992: 20) assumes that his readers share the same knowledge and therefore know that these are jeans. There might be people who understand what is meant, and others who do not; that is why a *koine* effect ensues.

Such a group can change within time, space, and social conditions. When Moccia published a new, updated version of his novel in 2004, twelve years later, he tried to keep the pace with this evolution, because teenagers, the main addressees of his novel, were not the same as in 1992. Two dozens of commercial names were changed to keep the book up-to-date in a changed setting: the story takes place at the beginning of the new millennium and some brands had gone out of fashion. Besides, from a linguistic point of view, the substitutions allow more transparency when antonomastic uses of commercial names are concerned. *Dei crudeli Avirex* became *crudeli Miss Sixty* (Moccia 2004: 18), while an attributive construction containing the same commercial name, *giubbotti Avirex* 'Avirex jackets', was not replaced (see example 16). The author supposed that *gli Avirex* had lost its univocal reference, the possibility of being understood by young people as a paraphrase of "jeans of the Avirex brand". The problem is not just the popularity of a brand, but the diffusion of an elliptic construction whose reduced redundancy has turned to no longer be redundant because of the changed knowledge of the speakers (a linguistic implication of fashion).

The nominal use of brands is the result of an elliptic process which follows a transfer of meaning from the *appellativum* to the *proprium*. This transfer may be engendered by context, as Migliorini (1927: 93) claims. He takes the example of *l'estratto Liebig* 'Liebig meat extract'. After being introduced on the market, the referent became better known as *il Liebig* because the meaning of the first word had been transferred to the second one. Thus, the common noun had become superfluous among certain speakers; it was enough to say *il Liebig* and a reference to the meat extract was implied.

If we go back to what we have observed about company names, we can argue that both constructions, the ones referring to a company (*la Liebig*, *la Mercedes*, *la Nike*) as well as those referring to a product (*il Liebig*, *la Mercedes*, *le Nike*), can be regarded as reductions of an attributive structure: on the one hand, *la ditta Liebig* 'Liebig company', *la ditta Mercedes* 'Mercedes company', *la ditta Nike* 'Nike company', on the other hand *l'estratto Liebig* 'Liebig meat extract', *la vettura Mercedes* 'Mercedes car', *le scarpe Nike* 'Nike shoes'. Both structures are similar to so-called internal appositions such as *il dottor Bianchi* 'doctor Bianchi' or *papa Giovanni* 'pope John', where the appellative is actually the core of the noun phrase, while the proper noun is an attributive predication of a special type (a denominative one, just as in the case of company names).

However, there are some differences between the two constructions. The preposition *di*, for example, can be integrated only for product names, and in this case the definite article usually appears.[9] So we have *l'orologio di Swatch*, or better yet *della Swatch* ('Swatch watch'), but not **la ditta di/della Swatch*, literally 'the company of (the) Swatch'. This should be a consequence of the commercial name being a denominative predication of

[9] With the exception of nouns which seem to have maintained their character of properness, in particular personal names of fashion designers whose brands are not as widespread as the ones cited in these pages, both concretely and linguistically: "il mio vestito di Valentino" 'my Valentino dress' (Moccia 2004: 63); "jeans di Missoni" 'Missoni jeans' (Brizzi 1995: 30).

the common noun, considering that *il dottore di Bianchi* 'the doctor of Bianchi' or *papa di Giovanni* 'pope of John', to taking the previous examples into account, would mean something different than the original structures, losing the character of nominal predication.

Even if the use of company names to refer to their products is very frequent, not every clause including a commercial name preceded by a common noun has an elliptic equivalent, as following sentences show:

(15) Anche il consumatore più attento ha difficoltà a confrontare i prezzi dei gelati **Migros** [...]. [*dei Migros]
(www.consumatori.ch, retrieved 11 October 2012)
'Even the most careful consumer can hardly compare Migros ice cream prices.'

(16) Uno dopo l'altro, come scimmie con al posto del pelo giubbotti **Avirex**, scalano con facilità il cancello. [*con (degli) Avirex] (Moccia 2004: 22)
'One after the other, they climb up the gate like apes with Avirex jackets instead of fur.'

(17) Alex, in cambio, non avrebbe mai tentato d'introdurlo nel mondo **Fender** del punk parrocchiale. [*nel Fender...] (Brizzi 1995: 29)
'From his side, Alex would have never tried to introduce him to the Fender world of parochial punk.'

These clauses cannot be reduced for different reasons. As shown with example 15, the name of the reseller *Migros* (out of specific contexts, e.g. oppositive ones) can hardly refer to just one "typical" product of the company (there is no stable use of the construction "appellative + brand name"). In example 16, a reduced expression with the commercial name *Avirex* and a masculine plural article already exists, so that there is a risk of homonymy (in the same book, as we saw before, *gli Avirex* refers to a pair of jeans). Finally, the non-reducibility in example 17 is due to the specific nature of the predication: the brand name is used with a metaphoric or extended meaning (the whole clause "il mondo Fender del punk parrocchiale" refers to a particular musical culture and lifestyle).

Another Case of Metalinguistic Predication: Names of Specific Products

The last category I shall analyse concerns commercial names referring to products, like the ones we have just considered, but showing other morphosyntactic features:

(18) la sua vita fin lì che entrava tutta dentro un **jollinvicta**. (Brizzi 1995: 12)
'All his life until then could have been contained in a Jollinvicta backpack.'

(19) Lui, in ogni caso, era rimasto sdraiato almeno dieci ore ad ascoltare i Pixies e i Pogues col **walkman** surriscaldato e la cioccolata sciolta di fianco alla testa. (Brizzi 1995: 137)
'He had been lying at least ten hours, listening to the Pixies and the Pogues on his overheated Walkman, with slushy chocolate next to his head.'

(20) Oh, Mario, porta un po' di **Bostik**. (Moccia 1992: 385)
'Hey, Mario, bring some Bostik glue!'

(21) Le **All Star** celesti, con la piccola stella rossa che centra il rotondo di gomma sulla caviglia, scendono dalla **Vespa** e toccano agilmente terra. (Moccia 2004: 20)
'The blue All Star shoes, with the little red star in the rubber circle on the ankle, get off the Vespa and land lightly on the ground.'

(22) Mi può portare il **Viavà** per favore? (Moccia 2004: 190)
'Could you please bring me the Viavà stain remover?'

Unlike than the nouns examined in previous section, the ones here are not homonymous to a company name; even if it is sometimes possible to combine them with a feminine singular definite article, as is the case with *Vespa* in example 21, this is not a free variation (*scendono di Vespa*?).

Commercial names belonging to this category share the fact with company names that they are both metalinguistic predications: "the company named X" and "the product (backpack, personal stereo, glue…) named Y". Unlike company names which metonymically refer to an object, these product names derive from an act of naming on the part of the producer. Typically, it is the case of models of a specific product (e.g. *All Star* as a sort of Converse sneakers) or of particular (technical) innovations, as *Walkman*.

As for the case of *Vespa* (see footnote 6), these commercial names, which in everyday language are mostly used with articles or modifications of various types, normally appear in advertisements and other marketing texts without any sort of determination, most of all to reinforce the character of propriality. In fact, a typical, well-known process these names can undergo is the so-called genericisation (or "Deonymisierung": see Gabriel 2003: 39–41, 73–76), the loss of specificity of the trademark, which begins with using the commercial name as a common noun. Over time, this makes it possible for the consumer to use such a name for all sorts of the product, regardless of the company they are produced by, as it is the case with *Kleenex* 'tissue' or *Scottex*, used in Italian for 'kitchen paper'. If the expansion of the object and of the name is wide and lasting enough, the brand can eventually be added to the lexicon, thereby acquiring the status of common noun.

What could be interesting from my point of view are the similarities and differences that emerge between this category of names and the reduced nominal use of company names for their products (metonymy). Let us look at them through the figure of antonomasia, that is to say, the two-fold passage between the categories of proper and common noun.

A Lexicographic Issue

Both genericisations and elliptic expressions containing commercial names could be considered to be antonomasias in a broader sense, taking into account that they are proper nouns which appear formally as appellatives (that is, they are preceded by an article). But the process of genericisation on one side and the reductions of redundancy on the other side are of different nature. The last one underlies a reduction process which is due to a transfer of meaning from the common to the proper noun and the subsequent developing of a redundancy, while specific product names, in the first case, have their meaning extended; the original baptismal act becomes opaque and eventually can no longer be recognised as such, as is the case with appellatives that were once proper nouns and are now included in dictionaries (in Italian *mecenate* 'patron' or *cicerone* 'tourist guide'; on this see Migliorini 1927; La Fauci 2011: 218–219). The passage from proper to common noun in genericisation[10] implies a loss of specificity and in the worst case – from a marketer's perspective – the inclusion in a dictionary as generic name for the thing itself. On the other side, an expression like *i Levi's* would probably never be recorded in a dictionary as a denomination for "jeans", if not in the improbable case they would become the jeans *par excellence*. At the same time, and from another point of view, *i Levi's* is an antonomastic denomination since it refers to the Levis product *par excellence*.

Expressions like *i Levi's* or *le Nike* are unlikely to lose specificity and become a generic denomination because they still bear the uniqueness and metalinguistic character of a company name. In fact, what distinguishes *le*

[10] As a side note, the fact that the process of genericisation is defined as the developing of a proper noun into a common noun shows – as Lötscher (2008: 34) claims – that product names are originally proper nouns.

Nike from another pair of shoes of any other brand is exclusively a metalinguistic issue: the fact that they have been produced by the company *called Nike*. On the contrary, former proper names such as *K-way* or *Post-it*, as they are used today, do not necessarily say something about the company which has produced and named them (the "owner" of a product name; Lötscher 2008: 52–53) since they are losing or have already lost the specificity of belonging only to a company.

Does an article really reveal the presence of a common noun, as a traditional grammatical commonplace claims (see Vaxelaire 2005: 104)? In a certain way, the propriality of commercial names occurring in expressions such as *le Camel* 'Camel cigarettes' is greater than in other cases (see the *Vespa* example), even if they have an article – with an important function, as previously seen. These names maintain the specificity given by the original baptismal act beyond metonymy, thus remaining within the sphere of the brand. It is unthinkable to say *le Camel* to refer to cigarettes of other brands just as one can say *il Kleenex* to refer to any brand of tissue. Therefore, even if the use of company names as common nouns is not accepted by "good trademark grammar", there is not a real misuse of the brands which maintain their value and specificity.

In summary, we observe that both *Kleenex* and *(un) mecenate* share the loss of their original denominative properties. Every person with patron quality, regardless of its name, can be literally re-baptised with the former proper noun *mecenate* (a proper noun substituting a common noun, the reverse process of antonomasia); similarly, products which look like Kleenex tissues undergo a sort of (illegal) baptism when they are called *Kleenex*, and the proper (brand) name is subjected to an "illicit" meaning acquisition.

In the case of *i Levi's*, instead, a specialisation of meaning takes place and the referential extension of the commercial name becomes narrow, so that it becomes the denomination of just one type of product – as in the case of classic antonomasia where a generic expression (*il sommo Poeta* 'the Supreme Poet', *la Città eterna* 'the Eternal City') can replace a proper noun (*Dante Alighieri*, *Rome*) and refer to one (or more) specific persons or places through the use of a definite article. With commercial names too, a second baptism takes place; *i jeans di marca Levi's* are renamed *i Levi's*, an expression which refers only to jeans.

On Features and Categories – Concluding Remarks

The following section will attempt to summarise the categories of commercial names in nominal clauses that were previously distinguished based on some of their salient morphosyntactic properties. It is possible to group them around two features that I shall call (1) [company name] and (2) [product name]. As it should be clear with regard to the methodology explained above, this distinction does not derive from a mere semantic or referential consideration of the different commercial names, but refers to specific labels naming a combination of morphosyntactic features.

Given the two features [company name] and [product name], a commercial name can show syntactic properties of a company name only, a product name only, or of both company and product names. This is shown in Table 1 together with some exemplifying names occurring in the previous pages:[11]

Table 1. Classification of commercial names based on the combination of morphosyntactic features.

	[+ company name]	**[– company name]**
[+ product name]	*Avirex, Sony, Marlboro, Peugeot*	*Vespa, Post-it, Scottex, K-way*
[– product name]	*Nestlé, Benetton, 3M, Migros*	–

The two traits manifest themselves through the whole of syntagmatic and paradigmatic combinations (the "context"). Moreover, they should not be seen as ontological properties of nouns, but as phenomenal features.

Taking a look at the most faceted of these categories, the names which are both [+ product name] and [+ company name], I observed that there is a relationship between nominal constructions referring to a product (reduction of redundancy: *la Camomilla* 'Camomilla belt'; Moccia 2004: 143) and a particular extended clause where the commercial name has an attributive function (looking like an adjective: *la sua cinta Camomilla* 'her Camomilla belt'; Moccia 2004: 139), which can even be expressed as a complement of specification with the preposition *di* (*la cinta di Camomilla*

[11] The table refers only to nominal uses of commercial names, but it should be possible to find distinguishing features for other functional uses too, e.g. adverbial (*vestire Prada* 'to wear Prada') or attributive predication (*dolcificante Hermesetas* 'Hermesetas sweetener'). Some of them are supposed to belong to the fourth sector, showing neither the features of a product nor company name.

'Camomilla belt'; Moccia 2004: 133).

There can be various kinds of attributive constructions, depending, among other things, on their possibility of being reduced to commercial names. This is the reason why the expressions *la ditta Avirex* 'Avirex company', *il giubbotto Avirex* 'Avirex jacket', and *i jeans Avirex* 'Avirex jeans', even if they all contain the same commercial name in an apparently similar attributive function, are substantially different. In Italian, there is a synonymic relation between *gli Avirex* and *i jeans Avirex* that does not exist with *il giubbotto Avirex*. Therefore, *gli Avirex* is not simply "a product of the brand" because it refers to a specific product. The products of a brand or company do not share all the same types of linguistic status.

In the case of *gli Avirex*, an ellipse and a metonymic construction correspond with antonomasia. The homonymous company does not produce only jeans, but *gli Avirex* ('Avirex jeans') are the product *par excellence* of the Avirex company. Pragmatic and linguistic reasons allow this reduction with regard to shared knowledge (when this antonomastic use has become popular).

Of course, there is a relation between the three expressions. However, the passage from the company to the product name is not simply metonymic. In fact, these names are different from other metonymic expressions such as *ascolto Mozart* 'I listen to [the music of] Mozart' or *leggo Petrarca* 'I read [the poems of] Petrarch', which do not derive from an attributive construction. In Italian, it is not possible to say *concerto Mozart* ('Mozart concert') or *poesie Petrarca* ('Petrarch poems'), but *jeans Levi's* or *orologio Rolex* is possible. Simple metonymic expressions such as *vesto Prada* 'I wear Prada' or *fumo Marlboro* 'I smoke Marlboro', on the other hand, would be more similar to the case of *ascolto Mozart*.

In conclusion, some combinatory properties of commercial names and the meanings they determine have been analysed in this work, showing that investigating if they are proper or common nouns would not be sufficient to explain their linguistic nature.

The analysis I presented in this paper is not complete as other aspects could be addressed, or at least mentioned. However, my aim was to introduce a new perspective of analysis within this field of research, which might be fruitful for future studies on the linguistic aspects of commercial names.

References

Bergien, A., Kremer, L. and Zilg, A. 2008. Commercial names as indicators of innovation and change: new reflections and challenges. *Onoma* 43: 7–23.

Bosredon, B. and Guérin, O. 2005. *Le Cluny, le Champollion* : d'un emploi non prototypique de nom propre modifié [*Le Cluny, le Champollion*: on a non-prototypical use of modified proper nouns]. *Langue française* 146 (2): 9–22.

Brizzi, E. 1995. *Jack Frusciante è uscito dal gruppo* [Jack Frusciante has left the band]. Milano: Baldini & Castoldi. (1st ed. Ancona: Transeuropa, 1994.)

De Stefani, E. 2007. *Asphalttiger und Grossstadt-Gazellen*. Handelsnamen als sprachliche Ressourcen in Zeitungsberichten und im Gespräch ["Asphalt tigers and metropolis gazelles". Commercial names as linguistic resources in newspaper articles and in conversation]. In *Names in Commerce and Industry: Past and Present*, L. Kremer and E. Ronneberger-Sibold (eds.), 233–257. Berlin: Logos.

—. 2008. L'uso dei nomi commerciali nelle conversazioni spontanee [The use of commercial names in spontaneous conversations]. In *Atti del XXII Congresso Internazionale di Scienze Onomastiche, Pisa 28 agosto – 4 settembre 2005* [Proceedings of the XXII International Congress of Onomastic Sciences], Vol 2, M. G. Arcamone, D. De Camilli and B. Porcelli (eds.), 711–728. Pisa: Edizioni ETS.

Fèvre-Pernet, C. and Roché, M. 2005. Quel traitement lexicographique de l'onomastique commerciale? Pour une distinction Nom de marque/Nom de produit [How can commercial onomastics be treated lexicographically? Distinguishing brand name and product name]. (Online article.) Available through: *CORELA* corela.edel.univ-poitiers.fr (Retrieved 30 November 2011).

Fowler, G. A. and Iwatani Kane, Y. 2011. An Article of Faith for Marketers: Place No Faith in Articles. (Online article.) *The Wall Street Journal*, 12.09.2011. Available through: *The Wall Street Journal Online* online.wsj.com (retrieved 8 May 2012).

Gabriel, K. 2003. *Produktonomastik. Studien zur Wortgebildetheit, Typologie und Funktionalität italienischer Produktnamen* [Onomastics of product names. Studies on word formation, typology, and functionality of Italian product names]. Frankfurt am Main: Peter Lang.

Koss, G. 1996. Warennamen [Product names]. In *Name studies. An international handbook of onomastics*, Vol 2, E. Eichler et al. (eds.), 1642–1648. Berlin/New York: de Gruyter.

Kripke, S. A. 1972. Naming and necessity. In *Semantics of natural language*, D. Davidson and G. Harman (eds.), 253–355. Dordrecht: D. Reidel.

La Fauci, N. 2011. *Relazioni e differenze. Questioni di linguistica razionale* [Relations and differences. Issues of rational linguistics]. Palermo: Sellerio.

Laurent, B. 2007. Le nom de marque et de produit, quand la linguistique pose aussi ses marques [Brand and product name: linguistics also establishes its marks]. In *Names in Commerce and Industry: Past and Present*, L. Kremer and E. Ronneberger-Sibold (eds.), 35–44. Berlin: Logos.

Lötscher, A. 2008. Die historischen Voraussetzungen für den Eigennamenstatus von Produktnamen [Historical premises for the proper noun status of product names]. *Onoma* 43: 25–56.

Mattioda, M. M. 2008. L'«Eau d'Issey» delle marche. Migrazioni lessico-culturali nell'onomastica commerciale [The "Eau d'Issey" of brands. Lexico-cultural migrations in commercial onomastics]. *Synergies Italie* 4: 109–121.

Migliorini, B. 1927. *Dal nome proprio al nome comune* [From proper noun to common noun]. Genève: Olschki.

Moccia, F. 1992. *Tre metri sopra il cielo* [Three meters above the sky], Roma: Il Ventaglio. (Original version of the novel, republished 2005 by Feltrinelli, Milano.)

—. 2004. *Tre metri sopra il cielo* [Three meters above the sky]. Milano: Feltrinelli. (Updated version of the 1992 novel.)

Ronneberger-Sibold, E. 2004. Warennamen [Product names]. In *Namenarten und ihre Erforschung. Ein Lehrbuch für das Studium der Onomastik* [Types of names and their exploration. A textbook for onomastic studies], A. Brendler and S. Brendler (eds.), 557–603. Hamburg: Baar.

Saussure, F. de. 1916. *Cours de linguistique générale* [Course on general linguistics], Ch. Bally and A. Sechehaye (eds.). Lausanne: Payot.

—. 2002. *Écrits de linguistique générale* [Writings on general linguistics], S. Bouquet and R. Engler (eds.). Paris: Gallimard.

Solly, M. 2002. 'Once a trademark, not always a trademark': Using Language to Avoid Legal Controversy. In *Conflict and Negotiation in Specialized Texts*, M. Gotti, D. Heller and M. Dossena (eds.), 211–232. Bern: Peter Lang.

Van Langendonck, W. 2007. *Theory and Typology of Proper Names*. Berlin/New York: Mouton de Gruyter.

Vaxelaire, J.-L. 2005. *Les noms propres. Une analyse lexicologique et historique* [Proper names. A lexicological and historical analysis]. Paris: Champion.

TU Y YO: ASPECTS OF BRAND NAMES RELATED TO INTERACTION AND IDENTIFICATION

ANTJE ZILG
JUSTUS LIEBIG UNIVERSITY GIESSEN, GERMANY

Abstract

In saturated markets with interchangeable products, branding plays a key role as a means of differentiation among competitors. Brand names assume a central communication function as they serve as identifiers for what the brand has to offer, and thus help all consumers to verbally put them into words (Langner 2003: 27).

In a society characterised by a loss of interpersonal contacts, brand names can generate a tie between partners in the market. The following article focuses on the relationship between the product and the consumer, and on how this relationship is linguistically established. The occurring phenomena are described at the syntactic and lexical levels. The examination is based on a corpus of Italian, Spanish and French names of the food industry, which is the most comprehensive of all industries.

Different categories are taken into account, such as imperative forms: ***assapora*** (Ital.), ***disfruta*** (Span.), ***mangez**-moi* (Fr.). Pronouns in the first or second person play an important role when it comes to connecting the product to the consumer in an affective way: ***ti** voglio* (Ital.), ***te** cuida* (Span.), *Fait pour **moi*** (Fr.). The same holds true for possessives: ***nostro**lio* (Ital.), ***mi** primer danone* (Span.), ***ma** pause fruit* (Fr.).

Introduction

In saturated markets with interchangeable products, branding plays a key role as a means of differentiation among competitors. The brand name is the verbally reproducible, articulable part of the brand. Brand names have a central communication function as they serve as identifiers for what a brand has to offer and enable consumers to communicate about the brand (Langner 2003: 27). A suitable brand name has become the *conditio sine qua non*, a strategic success factor (Latour 1992: 140). The brand name also functions as a tie between producer and recipient in a society in which immediate, interpersonal contact is increasingly lost, and may enable the consumer to identify with the denominated product(s).

This article focuses on the relationship between the designated product and the consumer, and on how this relationship is linguistically manifested, considering syntactic and lexical aspects. The examination will be carried out using a corpus of Italian, Spanish and French brand names in the food industry. The Italian examples were taken from a corpus of 950 brand names collected in field research (Zilg 2006). The Spanish examples were collected in field research in Madrid in 2008, and taken from the *Oficina Española de Patentes y Marcas* database. The French examples were retrieved from the database of the *Institut National de la Propriété Industrielle*.[1] In the case of the names retrieved from databases, special attention has been paid to the exact identification of the designated product(s).

In the following, I will first discuss brand names with regard to their socio-economic context, and I will explain the function of brand names from a semiotic perspective followed by an outline of the aspects of brand names related to interaction and identification.

Brand Names and their Socio-economic Context

Brand names are an important element of our daily linguistic environment. They are creations of our time reflecting specific social and economic conditions. How language changes with social developments and how linguistic innovations serve to express specific social needs can rarely be seen as clearly as it is in brand names (Lötscher 1992: 323 ff.).

In saturated markets, with exhausted market potentials and fully developed products that differ only marginally in their objective and functional quality, consumers show a decreasing interest in product information. Advertisements can hardly really convince customers to buy a product with arguments such as quality facts but rather by putting the experience profile of the specific products and services into the centre of

[1] National brands in Italy must be registered with the *Ufficio Italiano Brevetti e Marchi* (www.uibm.gov.it), in Spain with the *Oficina Española de Patentes y Marcas* (www.oepm.es) and in France with the *Institut National de la Propriété Industrielle* (www.inpi.fr). Classes 29–33 of the Nice Classification are relevant for the food industry.

attention. In this context, a trend away from product competition towards communication competition has been postulated for quite some time now (Kroeber-Riel and Esch 2000: 35 ff.). In Lötscher's words: "Human beings in their complexity and diversity follow brands that have a clear signal structure." (Lötscher 1992: 12; my translation)

Within the context of social value orientation, Kroeber-Riel and Esch (2000: 45 ff.) have observed a trend towards adventure and pleasure as well as the search for individuality. Both the trend towards adventure and pleasure as well as the search for individuality are reflected in the customer's desire for emotional stimulation and experience and have a strong impact on market communication. Consequently, the success of market communication depends increasingly on the fact, whether the marketers succeed in fitting the offered products into the recipient's field of experience (Kroeber-Riel and Esch 2000: 48).

Semiotic Framework

Following Bühler (1934: 24–33), every linguistic sign has three points of reference: a speaker, a listener and the reference objects and facts (referents) they speak about (Auer 1999: 22). In the context of market communication, these components correspond to the producer, the consumer and the product referred to. The sign is constituted by the communication situation, i.e. the relationship between sender, recipient and denotation (Auer 1999: 25). As per Bühler's Organon model, each linguistic sign has three basic functions: a referential function referring to the referent, an expressive function for the sender who uses the sign as well as a conative or appealing function for the recipient (Janich 2001: 53). Usually, these three functions are intermingled in a single sign (Auer 1999: 27).

Although Bühler considers the referential function as the most important, this dominance is not relevant for brand names. According to Gabriel (2003: 33), the linguistic and non-verbal elements of a brand are always recipient-oriented in order to make the customer recognise, memorise and purchase the product. Therefore, brand names primarily have an appealing character, as Lötscher confirms:

> The use of product names in advertisements very clearly shows the appealing character of names. […] Each name, so to say, has its own exclamation mark! [...] In this sense, a name is a message to be heard. (Lötscher 1992: 356; my translation)

According to Morris, there are three functions assigned to every sign (Haseloff 1970: 167): a syntactic, a semantic and a pragmatic function. The syntactic function refers to the relations between the signs, i.e. the formal structures of signs and sign combinations. The semantic function is that of assigning a specific meaning to a sign. The pragmatic function refers to the effects signs have on the recipient and to possible reactions they can cause (Meyer and Hermanns 1981: 34–35; Haseloff 1970: 167–168), and plays a crucial role in the context of advertising.

Interaction

In the past, providers and consumers often used to know each other personally, but with the growing industrialisation and the rise of mass production this direct contact was lost. Today, producers and consumers communicate via the brand (Lötscher 1992: 11). Thus, the brand functions as a bridge between producer and consumer. As Sena puts it:

> The brand functions as a 'messenger' within the dialogue between entrepreneurs and consumers; its awareness facilitates the perception, memorizing and recognition of the brand, thus making it a particularly effective instrument of attraction and communication. (Sena 2001: 24; my translation)

Brand names are inextricably linked to the conditions of mass media communication that are characterised by the fact that a message has multiple addressees, by anonymity and distance as well as by a receptive orientation (Platen 1997: 15). Additionally, there are only limited opportunities for feedback (Schifko 1982: 987). The following examples of Italian, French and Spanish brand names in the food industry will show how the appealing function in the sense of contacting the consumer or offering him/her an opportunity for identification can be implemented linguistically. The main focus is on syntactic and lexical aspects.[2]

Syntax

At the syntactic level, the use of the imperative is a key method to contact the consumer. Myers (1994: 47) states: "Note that advertisers use commands, not because telling you to do something really makes you do

[2] In addition to the syntactic and lexical processes discussed here, it should be pointed out that on the graphic level, exclamation marks are often used to create attention: *voglia di pasta!* ('lust for pasta'), *!!guau!!!*, *t!*.

what they say, but because it will create a personal effect, a sense of one person talking to another."[3] The imperative mostly concerns different classes of verbs that refer to phases of consumption, i.e. referring to an action that is not part of the actual communicative situation, but rather following it (Calderón 1991: 41). In this context, the command to enjoy is crucial (Calderón 1991: 38). The latter finds its lexical realisation in the forms *assaporare* (Ital.), *disfrutar* (Span.), *savourer* (Fr.). Wahl (2011: 30), however, notes that the simulation of a personal contact by the use of the imperative bears the risk of this form being perceived as obtrusive by the recipient. The following tables (1–3) illustrate the use of the imperative in Italian, Spanish and French brand names:

Table 1. The imperative in Italian brand names.

Italy	Translation
assapora	*assaporare* 'enjoy'
bio ***vivisano***	*vivere* 'live'
friggi *bene*	*friggere* 'fry, roast'
prendi *e* ***vai***	*prendere* 'take', *andare* 'go'

Table 2. The imperative in Spanish brand names.

Spain	Translation
disfruta	*disfrutar* 'enjoy'
estruja *y* ***disfruta***	*estrujar* 'squeeze', *disfrutar* 'enjoy'
cuida +	*cuidar* 'care'
mix *and* ***go***[4]	
hurry *up*	

[3] See also Calderón (1991) who points out the very high frequency of the grammatical category of imperative in advertising texts, from both a perspective of communication theory as well as a semiotic perspective. Wahl (2011) examines the role of the imperative in German, English and Spanish advertising and discusses the central question to the extent of which the imperative is used in modern advertising in order to express purchase appeal. The imperative in French advertising has been examined by Kaeppel (1987).

[4] Wahl (2011: 34–35) examines the use of the imperative in English words and expressions in German and Spanish advertising. With regard to her corpus, she comes to the conclusion that 22% of the imperatives that are used in German advertising are English expressions in comparison to 12.3% of the imperatives used in Spanish advertisements.

Table 3. The imperative in French brand names.

France	Translation
***savourons** le vin, **savourons** la vie*	*savourer* 'enjoy'
***savourez** le veau de franche comté*	*savourer* 'enjoy'
***mangez**-moi*	*manger* 'eat'
***chocolatez** moi*	**chocolater*[5] '*to chocolate'

The call for action can also be expressed with the infinitive as in ***calentar** y listo* (Span. *calentar* 'warm up'). Other forms of appeal include the acronym *s.o.s.* (Span.), the prepositions *on* (Span.) and *off* (Span.), designating juice, as well as the interjection in *gluten* ***stop*** (Ital.), for gluten-free ice cream.

Besides the call for action, a brand name may include a direct request to the consumer as well as a direct product offer. Examples of this include *wuoi*? (*würstel* 'sausage', *volere* 'want'; 'do you want?') and *wulevù* (*würstel* 'sausage', Fr. *vouloir* 'want'; 'do you want?') in the Italian market. Formulaic expressions, such as the greeting *buenos días* (Span. 'hello') or *s'il te plait* (Fr. 'you're welcome'), also directly address the recipient.

Lexis

Consumers can be directly addressed by a certain choice of words in brand names, e.g. the use of personal pronouns in the first and second person singular/plural.[6] Personal pronouns can occur in the subject or object position. In this context, Latour (1996: 133–134) stresses the function of personalisation:

> The purchase of a brand by a consumer often has psychological and social components. The choice of a particular brand can in fact endorse the consumer's personality. [...] Consumers wish to identify with brands and to distinguish themselves from others. (my translation)

According to Solomon (1983: 320) products include social information the consumer often relies upon in order to shape self-image and to

[5] The derivation **chocolater* does not exist in standard French.

[6] In a 1983 study, Schuncke detected that the personal pronoun "I" is among the 30 most common words used in 100 German advertisements in the alcohol and beverage industry (Schuncke 1983: 198, 200).

maximise the quality of role performance. This is confirmed by Fritz (1994: 35):

> With the rising number of brands and their increasing differentiation, it has become more and more important for consumers to position themselves within their social environment by means of consumption decisions. (my translation)

The following tables (4–6) illustrate how personal pronouns are used in the brand names of the Italian, the Spanish and the French food industry:

Table 4. Personal pronouns in Italian brand names.

Italy	Pers. Pronoun Function	Translation
ti *voglio*[7]	2. Pers Sg - obj 1. Pers Sg - subj	'I want you'
per ***te*** *baby*	2. Pers Sg - obj	'for you, baby'
per ***noi****...? i cotti*	1. Pers Pl - obj	'for us…? the boiled ones'
pronti per ***voi***	2. Pers Pl - obj	'ready for you'

Table 5. Personal pronouns in Spanish brand names.

Spain	Pers. Pronoun Function	Translation
tu *y* ***yo***	1. Pers Sg - subj 2. Pers Sg - subj	'you and me'
cocina para ***ti***	2. Pers Sg - obj	'cooking for you'
te *cuida*	2. Pers Sg - obj	'he/she/it cares for you'
*kiére****te***[8]	2. Pers Sg - obj	'take care of you'

[7] The name *ti voglio* is ambiguous with regard to perspective. It remains uncertain whether the pronouns *io* ('I'), which is included in the verbal form, and *te* ('you') refer to the product or to the consumer.

[8] The product description reads: "Is meant for all persons who like to care for themselves."

Table 6. Personal pronouns in French brand names.

France	Pers. Pronoun Function	Translation
*thé **toi**... et embrasse **moi**!*	2. Pers Sg - obj 1. Pers Sg - obj	'stay still and kiss me'
*fait pour **moi***	1. Pers Sg - obj	'made for me'
*c'est **moi** qui cuisine*[9]	1. Pers Sg - subj	'it's me who cooks'
*savour é **nous***[10]	1. Pers Pl - subj/obj	'enjoy us'

In French, the referenced product can be found to be a part of the consumer's world by the use of the combination of preposition and personal pronoun in *chez moi/nous* 'at my/our place': *secrets de **chez nous*** ('secrets'), *saveurs de **chez nous*** ('flavours'), *les fromages de **chez nous*** ('cheese'), *les bons fruits de **chez moi*** ('good fruit').

When it comes to generating an emotional tie between product and consumer, possessives are of particular importance. They are either used pronominally and replace a noun, such as *mio* (Ital. 'mine') and ***nostran**elle* (*nostrano* Ital. 'ours'), or they accompany nouns as possessive adjectives. Calabrese writes on the use of possessive adjectives in the context of current social developments:

> The possessive adjective generates an emotional tie between producer and consumer or binds a customer in eternal adoration to a product. [...] In a depersonalized society increasingly lacking interpersonal relations, the product may even replace human beings and their emotions. (Calabrese 1989: 168–169; my translation)

Perugini concurs with this, stating: "The adjective, in particular the possessive adjective, emotionally ties the producer to the consumer and makes a product that has been created for the masses something personal." (Perugini 1994: 607; my translation). Tables 7–9 exemplify how possessive adjectives referring to the first or second person are used in brand name formation of romance languages:

[9] In this name, the subject is even emphasised by means of a cleft sentence.

[10] The name appears to be a coordination. However, the string of sounds [savurenu] corresponds to the French imperative *savourez-nous* 'enjoy us'.

Table 7. Possessive adjectives in Italian brand names.

Italy	Possessive adj.	Translation
amici ***miei***	1. Pers Sg	'my friends'
bio ***mia***	1. Pers Sg	'my bio'
il ***tuo*** *chef*	2. Pers Sg	'your boss'
ca' ***nostra***	1. Pers Pl	'our home'
nostro*lio*	1. Pers Pl	'our oil'

Table 8. Possessive adjectives in Spanish brand names.

Spain	Possessive adj.	Translation
mis *delicias*	1. Pers Sg	'my delights'
mi *primer danone*	1. Pers Sg	'my first danone'
tu *fruta fresca*	2. Pers Sg	'your fresh fruit'
tus *tentaciones*	2. Pers Sg	'your temptations'
sabores ***nuestros***	1. Pers Pl	'our flavours'
nuestro *mar*	1. Pers Pl	'our sea'

Table 9. Possessive adjectives in French brand names.

France	Possessive adj.	Translation
ma *pause fruit*	1. Pers Sg	'my fruit break'
l'océan dans ***mon*** *assiette*	1. Pers Sg	'the ocean in my plate'
les glaces de ***mon*** *enfance*	1. Pers Sg	'the ice cream of my childhood'
les recettes de ***nos*** *villages*	1. Pers Pl	'the recipes of our villages'
surprenez ***vos*** *sens*	2. Pers Pl	'surprise your senses'

Names created that include the adverb "yes" may sound like an affirmation stimulating the determination to purchase the product: *pastasì* (Ital.), *biosì* (Ital.), *les radis* ***oui****!* (Fr. 'radishes'), ***oui****! naturellement* (Fr. 'naturally'). Such affirmation is also expressed in *viva la crema!* (Ital. 'long live the cream') and *wüao!* (Ital. *würstel* 'sausage', *wow*).

Conclusion

In the context of globalised markets where there is a lack of interpersonal relations between producer and consumer, brand names can generate a tie between partners in the market. This examination has shown the syntactic and lexical methods that are used in Italian, Spanish and French brand names in the food industry. Even though the syntactic and lexical levels were treated separately, various names show that these levels may interact with one another with regard to the target audience, e.g. in *surprenez vos sens* (Fr.) and *kiérete* (Span.). In the first example, the imperative is combined with a possessive adjective, in the second, it is combined with a personal pronoun. Yet, it must be emphasised that only a customer survey can provide information on whether recipients actually feel personally addressed by the methods shown here; the same holds true for the impact of appealing names on the consumer's identification with the product and on the purchase decision.

Finally, it could be observed that brand names can even be subject to word formation processes when it comes to directly addressing the customer and encouraging identification with the product. In the May issue of the Spanish e-mail newsletter of the company Nivea, the brand name *nivea* serves as a basis for a deonomastic derivation which leads to the verb *nivearse* 'nivea oneself'. In the aforementioned newsletter, the latter is used in the following listing of verbs in the imperative form "*Diviértete, mímate, relájate, sorpréndete... nivéate!*" ('have fun, coddle yourself, relax, stagger yourself, *nivea* yourself!'). These processes deserve more detailed attention and might be interesting for further research.

References

Auer, P. 1999. *Sprachliche Interaktion. Eine Einführung anhand von 22 Klassikern* [Linguistic interaction. An introduction on the basis of 22 classics]. Tübingen: Niemeyer.

Behrens, K. C. (ed.). 1970. *Handbuch der Werbung mit programmierten Fragen und praktischen Beispielen von Werbefeldzügen* [Handbook of advertising with programmed questions and practice oriented examples of advertising campaigns]. Wiesbaden: Gabler.

Bühler, K. 1934. *Sprachtheorie: die Darstellungsfunktion der Sprache* [Theory of language: the representational function of language]. Jena: G. Fischer.

Calabrese, O. 1989. Il marinismo in serie. Una lingua tra neo-arcaismo e paleo-neologismo [Marinism in series. A language between neo-archaism and paleo-neologism]. In *Una lingua in vendita. L'italiano della pubblicità* [A language for sale. Italian in advertising], A. Chiantera (ed.), 159–178. Rome: La Nuova Italia Scientifica.

Calderón, M. 1993. Der Imperativ in spanischen Werbespots [The imperative in Spanish advertising spots]. In *Grammatikographie der romanischen Sprachen. Akten der gleichnamigen Sektion des Bamberger Romanistentages* (23.–29.9.1991) [Grammaticography of Romance languages. Proceedings of the homonymous section of the Bamberger Romanistentag], C. Schmitt (ed.), 37–59. Bonn: Romanistischer Verlag.

Chiantera, A. (ed.). 1989. *Una lingua in vendita. L'italiano della pubblicità* [A language for sale. Italian in advertising]. Rome: La Nuova Italia Scientifica.

Esch, F.-R. (ed.). 2001. *Moderne Markenführung. Grundlagen, innovative Ansätze, praktische Umsetzungen* [Modern brand management. Basic concepts, innovative approaches and practice oriented implementations]. 3rd edition. Wiesbaden: Gabler.

Fritz, T. 1994. *Die Botschaft der Markenartikel. Vertextungsstrategien in der Werbung* [The message of brands. Textualizing strategies in advertising]. Tübingen: Stauffenburg.

Gabriel, K. 2003. *Produktonomastik. Studien zur Wortgebildetheit, Typologie und Funktionalität italienischer Produktnamen* [Product onomastics. Studies on word formational aspects, the typology and functionality of Italian brand names]. Frankfurt a.M. et al.: Peter Lang.

Haseloff, O. W. 1970. Kommunikationstheoretische Probleme der Werbung [Communication theoretical problems of advertising]. In *Handbuch der Werbung mit programmierten Fragen und praktischen Beispielen von Werbefeldzügen* [Handbook of advertising with programmed questions and practice oriented examples of advertising campaigns], K. C. Behrens (ed.), 157–200. Jena: G. Fischer.

Janich, N. 2001. *Werbesprache. Ein Arbeitsbuch* [The language of advertising. A practical guide]. 2nd edition. Tübingen: Gunter Narr.

Kaeppel, E. 1987. *Der Imperativ in der französischen Anzeigenwerbung* [The imperative in French printed advertisements]. Tübingen: Gunter Narr.

Kroeber-Riel, W. and Esch, F.-R. 2000. *Strategie und Technik der Werbung. Verhaltenswissenschaftliche Ansätze* [Strategy and technique in advertising. Behavioral scientific approaches]. 5th edition. Stuttgart et al.: W. Kohlhammer.

Langner, T. 2003. *Integriertes Branding. Baupläne zur Gestaltung erfolgreicher Marken* [Integrated branding. Construction plans for the creation of successful brands]. Wiesbaden: Deutscher Universitäts-Verlag.

Latour, S. 1996. *Namen machen Marken. Handbuch zur Entwicklung von Firmen- und Produktnamen* [Names make brands. Manual for the development of company and product names]. Frankfurt a.M. and New York: Campus.

Lötscher, A. 1992. *Von Ajax bis Xerox. Ein Lexikon der Produktenamen* [From Ajax to Xerox. A lexicon of product names]. 2nd edition. Düsseldorf and Zürich: Artemis und Winkler.

Meyer, P. W. and Hermanns A. 1981. *Theorie der Wirtschaftswerbung* [Theory of commercial advertising]. Stuttgart et al.: W. Kohlhammer.

Myers, G. 1994. *Words in Ads.* London: Hodder Arnold.

Perugini, M. 1994. La lingua della pubblicità [The language of advertising]. In *Storia della lingua italiana* [History of the Italian language], Vol. 2, L. Serianni and P. Trifone (eds.), 599–615. Turin: Einaudi.

Platen, C. 1997. *«Ökonymie». Zur Produktnamen-Linguistik im Europäischen Binnenmarkt* [«Econymy[11]». On linguistics of product names in the European inland market]. Tübingen: Max Niemeyer.

Schifko, P. 1982. Die Werbetexte aus sprachwissenschaftlicher Sicht [Advertising texts from a linguistic perspective]. In *Die Werbung. Handbuch der Kommunikations- und Werbewirtschaft* [Advertising. A manual of the communication and advertising industry], Vol. 2, B. Tietz (ed.), 982–996. Landsberg am Lech: Verlag Moderne Industrie.

Schmitt, C. 1983. *Grammatikographie der romanischen Sprachen. Akten der gleichnamigen Sektion des Bamberger Romanistentages* (23.–29.9.1991) [Grammaticography of Romance languages. Proceedings of the homonymous section of the Bamberger Romanistentag]. Bonn: Romanistischer Verlag.

Schuncke, M. 1983. Sprecht die Sprache der Adressaten [Speak the recipients' language]. *Muttersprache* 93: 197–209.

Sena, G. 2001. *Il nuovo diritto dei marchi. Marchio nazionale e marchio comunitario* [The new trademark law. National brand and European brand]. 3rd edition. Mailand: Giuffrè Editore.

Serianni, L. and Trifone P. (eds.). 1994. *Storia della lingua italiana* [History of thc Italian language]. Vol. 2. Turin: Einaudi.

Solomon, M. R. 1983. The role of products as social stimuli. A symbolic interactionism perspective. *Journal of Consumer Research* 10: 319–329.

[11] The creation *Econymy* is an adaptation of the German *Ökonymie*, containing the noun *Ökonomie* 'economy' and the suffix *-onym* meaning 'name'. *Ökonymie* is thus referring to names in the economic sector.

Steinmann, C. (ed.). 2011. *Evolution der Informationsgesellschaft. Markenkommunikation im Spannungsfeld der neuen Medien* [Evolution of the information society. Brand communication in the context of new media]. Wiesbaden: Verlag für Sozialwissenschaften.

Strecker, O. et al. 1990. *Marketing für Lebensmittel. Grundlagen und praktische Entscheidungshilfen* [Marketing for food. Basic concepts and practice oriented decision guidance]. 2nd edition. Frankfurt a.M.: DLG-Verlag.

Tietz, B. (ed.). 1982. *Die Werbung. Handbuch der Kommunikations- und Werbewirtschaft* [Advertising. A manual of the communication and advertising industry]. Vol. 2. Landsberg am Lech: Verlag Moderne Industrie.

Wahl, S. 2011. Entdecken Sie…! Die Geschichte des Imperativs in der deutschen, englischen und spanischen Werbung [Discover…! The history of the imperative in German, English and Spanish advertising]. In *Evolution der Informationsgesellschaft. Markenkommunikation im Spannungsfeld der neuen Medien* [Evolution of the information society. Brand communication in the context of new media], C. Steinmann (ed.), 25–50. Wiesbaden: Verlag für Sozialwissenschaften.

Zilg, A. 2006. *Markennamen im italienischen Lebensmittelmarkt* [Brand names in the Italian food industry]. Wilhelmsfeld: Gottfried Egert Verlag.

HOW NAMES REFLECT THE CULTURE OF COMPETITION: AN EXAMPLE FROM SUGAR BEET HARVESTING TECHNOLOGY

SABINA BUCHNER
UNIVERSITY OF REGENSBURG, GERMANY

Abstract

Comparative advertising is one expression of the culture of competition. This phenomenon is known and has already been the subject of scientific research. This article focuses on the question of whether there is also such a concept as comparative naming, and additionally, if a competitive function of company and product names also exists. To answer these questions, first the main functions of company, brand and product names are listed and the options a company has when choosing a name with regard to its competitors are described. Then, to demonstrate how names can reflect the culture of competition, naming in sugar beet harvesting technology is examined as an example. Since only two companies in this field, HOLMER and ROPA, share approximately 80% of the world market equally between themselves, the names given in these companies are the main subject of this analysis. Besides the company names, the names of two different products – the sugar beet harvester and the sugar beet loader – are examined from their inception in the 1970s up to the present day.

Introduction

In an advertisement campaign from 2006, a total of four car manufacturers refer to one another. It was started by BMW with a print media advertisement reading "Congratulations to Audi for winning South African Car of the Year 2006. From the Winner of World Car of the Year 2006." Audi launched a campaign to answer this and stated:

"Congratulations to BMW for Winning World Car of the Year 2006", "From the Winner of Six Consecutive Le Mans 24 Hour Races 2000–2006". Now Subaru felt defiant and put these declarations into context by congratulating the other two car manufacturers: "Well done to Audi and BMW for winning the beauty contest. From the winner of the 2006 International Engine of the Year." Last but not least, Bentley issued its statement to these campaigns with an advertisement simply showing a stereotyped well-dressed upper-class British man on a stereotyped expensive upper-class British leather couch showing his middle finger to make it clear what Bentley thought of all those awards. (Photos via BMW-drivers.de.)

Comparative advertising – as in these campaigns – is one expression of the culture of competition in business; it is regulated by EU directives and has already been the subject of research (e.g. Danesi 2007: 22–23). Following up on this phenomenon, this article would like to answer the question: Is there also a concept such as comparative naming? The different functions of product, brand and company names have been the subject of various research projects and publications (e.g. Kremer and Ronneberger-Sibold 2007), but the competitive function of names has not yet been the very focus of scientific discussion.

To answer the question, this article first lists the main functions of company names and product names and what options a company has when choosing a name with regard to its competitors. To demonstrate how names can reflect the culture of competition, naming in sugar beet harvesting technology is examined as an example. The market for sugar beet harvesting technology lends itself to such an investigation: it is extremely limited, because sugar beet only grows under special circumstances. Just two companies, HOLMER and ROPA, share approximately 80% of the world market equally between themselves and both companies produce only two and three completely different products, which is why this article concentrates on these two companies and their names.

Functions of Company Names and Product Names

Company and product names are part of complex communication acts in a mass media environment. In order to describe the functions company names and product names fulfil, the participants in this communication – the sender and the receiver – have to be identified. According to the communication model by Stern (1994: 8–10; Janich 2010: 41–43), a company or an intermediary advertising agency or a person in a commercial acts as sender. In the example from sugar beet harvesting technology, the only senders are the respective companies, because they are two small and medium-sized companies with only a few hundred employees which consult no advertising agencies for coining new product names. The receiver in Stern's model is an implied, sponsorial or actual consumer. Implied consumers can be identified in the market of sugar beet harvesting technology as the receiver – the ideal consumers for whom the messages and names are made – and actual consumers – people who actually see an advertisement or name. In addition to this communication model, the employees of the respective company can also be identified as receivers (this is part of corporate identity, Koß 2008b: 45), as well as the people in the region and the direct business rival. This is especially the case in rural areas, where not many large companies can be found, or if factories are located very close to one another, or if only a few companies split the market; all three points apply to the market of manufacturers of sugar beet harvesting technology.

According to Stern (1994: 9–10), a message should be passed between the various senders and receivers. One part of this message constitutes the company names and product names which fulfil different functions for the different participants. Therefore, the consumer must be able to decode the sender's message (Bishara 2008: 37). The communication process is mostly unidirectional and also depends on external factors – for example, the competitor (Bishara 2008: 36–37), which plays a major role in the market of sugar beet harvesting technology.

The most important functions of product names can therefore be described as the following: Where the product is concerned, the identification function is most crucial; its main aim is the differentiation from other products. Therefore, the name should be striking and eye-catching. The aims of valorisation through positive connotation/association (these two points are not differentiated here) and passing on information can be added. For the manufacturer, the product name has primarily a deictic – so to say, an indicative – function. Important are the functions of identification (concerning the handling of products), advertising and image (names are consciously formed by people for people, Platen 1997: 33), and the legal protection of the name. The names should work according to the AIDA formula (Attention, Interest, Desire, Action; Janich 2010: 36–37). For the receiver, product names in the first instance have a recognition function: identification in terms of the recognition, signalling or appealing functions (explicit/implicit), as well as a guarantee of quality and origin (Janich 2010: 65; Ronneberger-Sibold 2004: 562–563). All these functions are fulfilled in the company and product names in sugar beet harvesting technology. However, here also lies a special emphasis on the communication with and about the competitor, which opens a wide field of connotations and associations for the names.

In order that product and company names can fulfil all these central points, numerous requirements must be made on them. They need to be inventive, expressive, valorising, if possible, informative (Platen 1997: 45–68; quotations in Danesi 2007: 62) and so on. From a linguistic perspective, a company or product name should – in addition to the aforementioned points – be not too long, euphonic, easy to perceive and easy to pronounce and also memorable (Ronneberger-Sibold 2004: 563).

Choosing a Name with Regard to the Competitor

What possibilities of naming do companies have with regard to the competitor? One possibility is the intentional or unintentional ignorance of the competitor and its names. Nevertheless, this case is extremely rare and it is not very fruitful for a linguistic analysis.

Research on company and product names has shown that especially in a competitive culture with distinct market leaders, analogies often appear: e.g., similar company names are often chosen in one market segment, such as bird names for German manufacturers of stationery with *Pelikan*, *Tukan*, *Schwan* 'swan' (Reimann 2011). They are mainly oriented on the oldest and/or most prestigious company, or in the case of paronymy (*Colgate* – *Calgete*; Platen 1997: 74) draw parallels between competitive products (Matthieu, 2009: 45[1]). Also affixoids forming paradigms are known, e.g. *-dent/-dont* with dental hygiene items, examples are *Perlodont*, *Kukident* and *Dentalux* (Matthieu 2009: 35; Koß 2008c: 81; Platen 1997: 72–83; Koß 2008d: 145–147) or *Dentagard*. This can be subsumed under the so-called "me-too" strategy. Furthermore, other similar strategies can be named here, for example, cuckoo naming. Here, companies try to mask their country of origin by using a name that evokes an association with a country that is leading in the respective sector; e.g. the name of the German luxury fashion manufacturer *Escada* (Samland 2006: 35, 68–96). With these strategies, less known or smaller companies look to profit from the fact that they adapt their product or company names to those of the branch leader and thus benefit from its image. This can lead to brand piracy. In this research area, there is a great deal of linguistic, but also legal, literature (Reimann 2011; Fritzsche 2008; Stoll 1999).

[1] The original reference: Kapferer 1992: 99.

Another possibility is the distinct differentiation of rivals in business by names which cannot be mistaken in any case. According to Gotta (1998: 18) this is an essential element of trade names. One option is to stand out in the line of suppliers of identical products by the sound shape of the product name, as is the case with *QOWAZ* in the line of numerous coke mix drinks such as *Mezzo-Mix* and so on (Samland 2006: 28). A company can also try to generate differing associations or pictures for its product: it would not be a good idea to call a new lifestyle drink *Flying Horse* with respect to *Red Bull* (Samland 2006: 73) if the unique selling point is to be stressed. The most important point here is originality (Koß 2008d: 139), which permits the perfect positioning of a name in the market.

Between the extremes of analogy and differentiation, there is a middle ground, and it should also be taken into consideration that names have to fulfil various functions for companies and consumers. The investigation of the coining of names in sugar beet harvesting technology allows an insight into how an intense culture of competition can be reflected on a linguistic level in company and product names, and the analysis of these names shows to what extent the coining of names with regard to the competitor has an impact on the main functions of company names and brand names.

Background Information on the Manufacturers

As stated in the introduction, this article focuses on the two companies HOLMER and ROPA, as they share approximately 80% of the world market equally between themselves, and the history of the two manufacturers is closely intertwined.

The headquarters of these companies lie 25 and 35 kilometres respectively south of Regensburg (Bavaria, Germany) and are located only 15 kilometres apart from each other. The ROPA company was co-f in 1986 by the former head of development of the HOLMER co Hermann Paintner. HOLMER used to be a family-owned firm, an 1973 to 1986, the founders of the two different companies, Alfons H and Hermann Paintner, worked together until Painter founded hi company in 1986 together with Rockermeier. The end of the cooperation between Holmer and Paintner, and especially the selling of the HOLMER company to a private equity firm in 2004, left a rift between the two companies which has spread to the employees and, in addition, to the population of the people in the area who work in agriculture. These factors led to very hard competition between the two market leaders.

Since only two small and medium-sized companies are concerned and these companies employ some hundred workers and the market cannot be targeted with big advertising campaigns – each year every company builds on average approximately 200 to 220 machines – no advertising agencies are involved in generating names or prospectuses. Therefore, the respective company can be identified as the only and immediate sender.

Today, both companies produce only two or three completely different products. In the following, the article will concentrate upon the company names as well as on the names of both products in which HOLMER and ROPA are direct competitors, and analyses these names especially with regard to their relation to the respective competitor. The company names and product names are written according to the orthography used by the companies. The linguistic analysis was made possible by interviews with people who have coined the names in the two companies.[2]

The Company Name

The older company is HOLMER. Here, the surname of the founder, Alfons Holmer, acts as the company name. According to Platen's classification, it can be characterised as an onomastic takeover (Platen 1997: 39–41). The name was not especially selected, but was taken over from the parental smithy of the company founder from which today's company has originated.

The name, therefore, fits in the line of company names of German agricultural technology manufacturers which are mainly named after the surnames of the founders: *Fendt, Class, Horsch, Kramer* or, though well known but no longer existent today, manufacturers such as *Schlüter* or *Eicher*. These names were selected not for advertising reasons, but are mainly taken from small crafts enterprises belonging to the family from whom the companies have arisen. When surnames are used as company names, consumers associate them with tradition, reliability, craft art, experience etc. (Danesi 2007: 57–58) – features which are much valued, especially in the agricultural sector in Germany and also in other countries, because the majority of farms have been family property for generations. Although today, there is a broader group of buyers, many people who work in the agricultural sector still come from a traditional agricultural farm.

[2] General information on the respective company history and the particular products can be found via the homepages (Holmer-maschinenbau.de; Ropa-maschinenbau.de).

Another advantage of the company name *HOLMER* is that it is also internationally recognisable as a German surname. The ending *-er* is very popular in German surnames (Kunze 2005: 167, 191, 264, 393–394) and is recognised in many countries as a mark of a German surname, which is built according to the scheme *Müller, Meier, Fischer, Reuter, Eder*. Therefore, the company name *HOLMER* can evoke all associations connected with technological products with the label *made in Germany*, and above all ‘quality’.

Here, the sender has decided unconsciously on a name, which refers appropriately to the company and is easy to decode – even if the etymological background of the surname is not understood today – and causes positive associations in the receiver. The single minor difficulty is that the company is no longer today owner-operated.

The company name *ROPA* is an acronym. It is composed of the initial letters of the surnames of both company founders *Rockermeier* and *Paintner*. It would have been possible to have a company name after the scheme *HOLMER*. Yet, the first sugar beet harvester of the HOLMER company had been delivered under the name *HOLMER System Paintner*; here, the pressure of differentiation – together with the desire for easy pronunciation – does not lead to a name which can evoke the positive associations of a German surname. The company name *ROPA* can immediately be decoded as a non-German word because German words and also surnames in general do not end with a full vowel. Moreover, the name is problematic on the international market (c.f. Ronneberger-Sibold 2004: 565) because it means e.g. ‘mineral oil’ in Czech (which might explain the low market share of the company in the Czech Republic) or ‘clothing, garment’ in Spanish.

Here, the sender has decided consciously on a modular short form, by which (whether intentionally or unintentionally) a clear differentiation to the competitor is possible. The points association and ability to be decoded by the consumer were neglected. In the culture of competition, the focus here seems to be exclusively on the point differentiation and the identification function. The other functions a company name should fulfil played a minor role in the coining of the name.

The Product Names

As already mentioned, both enterprises are direct competitors in the production of sugar beet harvesting technology. Both companies manufacture two products – the sugar beet harvester and the sugar beet loader – which can be defined in each case as perfect substitute products.

The Sugar Beet Harvester

The first products produced by both companies are self-propelled sugar beet harvesters. The early types of these machines had simple technical names, e.g. *BKSF*, which is a short form of the initial letters of *Bunkerköpfroder, selbstfahrend*, a term also used in a scientific context. Those names had originally often been used as internal project names during product development. The early HOLMER sugar beet harvesters – a technical innovation – were sold with the writing *HOLMER System Paintner* affixed to them, which led to the deonymisation of the name *HOLMER,* in that it has been used as an appellative for self-propelled sugar beet harvesters for some time. Nevertheless, the appellative function was lost when ROPA brought its own sugar beet harvester onto the market.

In 1986, ROPA was founded. The naming of the products was not initially influenced, and indeed, technically motivated names were simply given here, such as *R.6.16*: *R* stands for *Roder* 'harvester', *6* for the number of planted rows of sugar beet that could be harvested in a single passage and *16* is a reference to the volume of the bunker of the machine in metric tonnes.

Today, there are two different types of sugar beet harvesters produced by HOLMER and ROPA: machines with two axles and machines with three axles. For 18 years, HOLMER produced only sugar beet harvesters with two axles and ROPA with three axles. Since 2012, both companies produce both types of sugar beet harvesters.

From 1991 to 1996, the company HOLMER produced a sugar beet harvester named *Klassiker,* or for the international market, *Classic*. Here, the sender consciously decides on a product name for the first time. The name is semantically transparent. It is a takeover from the lexicon. Tied to this name are associations such as 'quality', 'reliability', 'tradition' etc. It is also, nevertheless, a clear signal to the receiver: this is the better product, the classic – in contrast to the new product of the competitor. The receivers were able to decode this message easily, because previously 6-row self-propelled sugar beet harvesters were a technological product only manufactured at the HOLMER company. The product name fulfils all functions listed above.

In 1996, HOLMER changed its naming strategy. The new series of sugar beet harvesters was named *Terra Dos*. Later construction series are differentiated by the additional letter *T* (for *Terra Dos*) and consecutive numbers, e.g. *T2*, *T3* (see figure 1). *Terra* was consciously selected with focus on the customer: Terra tyres – developed originally by Goodyear –

were a synonym for gentle soil treatment in the agriculture sector at that time. As soil protection is a central aim for heavy agricultural machines like sugar beet harvesters, the name was capable of causing positive associations in the receiver. *Dos* (Spanish for 'two') describes a technical innovation: the vehicle has diagonal steering (see figure 2), and is therefore capable of bringing the wheels into a position so that they run over every part of the field only once. The choice of the name is strongly customer-oriented. They should be able to decode the name easily and see the technical innovation behind it. The product is valorised by the name and its technical associations, and no longer refers to the product of the competitor. The advertising function and the transfer of information come to the foreground. With Platen (1997: 39–41) the product name can be classified as a lexical takeover with a connection between product and product name.

Figure 1. *HOLMER Terra Dos T3* (sugar beet harvester, two axles).

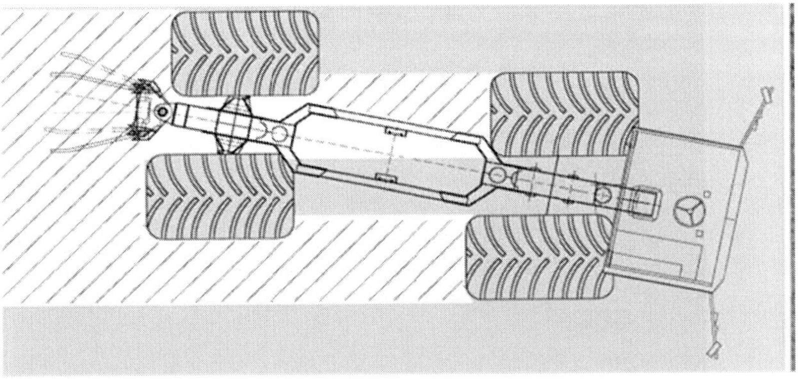

Figure 2. Diagonal steering of the HOLMER sugar beet harvester Terra Dos.

ROPA seemed to respond in 1998 with a machine called *euro-Tiger* (see figure 3). Today, all products from ROPA start with *euro*. It is a play on words between *ROPA* and *Europa*, which was used as an additional specification for a newly developed cab and refers also to the growing influence of EU regulations on the technical specification of the machines. The name element *euro* is able to create the image of a global player for consumers. Whether consumers associate it with the currency – and with what consequences – is not known. The second part of the product name is the common noun *Tiger*, with all the associations 'predator', 'jumping to overtake the other', like Asian tigers, and so on. The name is semantically transparent. It has nothing to do with sugar beet, and neither describes the product nor refers to its speed[3]. Only the black and yellow colour and the seme 'power' offer a point of contact. The name transmits a clear message not only to the consumers, but also to the competitor. The product is valorised by the name – also at a cost to the competitor. ROPA has not been able to give any reasons for the choice of the word *Tiger* as part of the product name, except that one had searched for the name of an animal as an analogy to the second, very popular product name in the portfolio.

[3] As this is the case, for example, with suggestive, metaphoric names such as the automobile *Jaguar*; or for running shoes named *Gazelle* (Koß 2008a: 13; Danesi 2007: 66).

Figure 3. *ROPA euro-Tiger V8-4* (sugar beet harvester, three axles).

Figure 4. *ROPA euro-Panther* (sugar beet harvester, two axels).

Along similar lines to these product names, the new sugar beet harvester from ROPA with two axles is named *euro-Panther* (figure 4). The common noun *Panther* was chosen as a name because it is in line with the name *Tiger* and it also represents the name of a big cat. The noun *Panther* evokes all associations that are linked to big cats – similar to *Tiger*. What is not known so far is, if the name is also associated by some receivers, especially in the Russian market, with the well known German Panther tank used in World War II. As tanks are in general associated with words like 'destruction' and 'heavy', such attributes would not be helpful in selling a harvest machine. However, so far, the product name *euro-Panther* fulfils all functions of a product name listed above. The advertising and the identification function are especially in focus, as the name clearly signals that the machine is a new type within a known product line.

Finally, an analogy can be seen in the creation of product names between the two companies, which has three parts in each case. The first element is always the same for all products from one company: *Terra* or *euro*. The second component refers to the respective product, in this case *Dos* and *Tiger/Panther* respectively, and afterwards, letter-figure combinations follow for newer series to distinguish the technical developments from each other (*T2, T3* or *V8-3, V8-4*).

Figure 5. *HOLMER Terra Dos T4-40* (sugar beet harvester, three axles).

With the development of its three axle sugar beet harvester, the HOLMER company broke this schema in 2012. The new machine was called *Terra Dos T4-40* (see figure 5). Here, the letter-figure combination *T4* is not used for a newer series of the two axle sugar beet harvester, but inconsequently for a different type of product. The product name is not differentiated enough and therefore is not able to completely fulfil the advertising function, the appealing function and the identification function. The figure *40* stands for the volume of the bunker of the machine in cubic metres. The next series of the two axle sugar beet harvester Terra Dos T3 is – according to information from the HOLMER company – going to be named *Terra Dos T4-30*, which might exacerbate especially the problem of the identification function of the product names. As the product names are in addition quite long, this already has led to a retrenchment of the original name component *Terra Dos* in the practical communication between sender and receiver, as the machines are, at the moment, called *T3* and *T4*, including the loss of all associations connected to the first part of the product name.

The Sugar Beet Loader

The second product from both companies is a self-propelled sugar beet loader. The market leader and first developer here is the company ROPA. At both companies, there were non self-propelled forerunner models which had purely technical names: HOLMER's *RRL* is an initial word for *Rübenreinigungslader,* and in ROPA's *L.8.220,* the *L* stands for *Lader* 'loader', *8* for the number of rollers in the loader and *220* is the horsepower of the engine.

Figure 6. *ROPA euro-Maus 4* (sugar beet loader).

During the development of a new, self-propelled machine, the common noun *Maus* 'mouse' was used for this product as a sort of nickname. The reason was the idea behind the machine: it would have to be able to crawl under the piles of sugar beet at the edge of the fields like a mouse, so that they would be able to be loaded without loss. The name was finally maintained as a product name. The name is semantically transparent: It was taken over from the lexicon and has a connection with the product. It informs the consumer about the functionality of the machine. The associations ‘small’, ‘grey’, ‘weak’, ‘pest’ and so on were not transferred to the machine, contrary to the association of ‘the mouse that eats its way through the pile’. The product name *Maus* was deonymised and has, up till now, been the widely used, common noun in German referring to a self-propelled sugar beet loader. The name has a strong signalling function for the consumer who can easily decode the concept: on the one hand, the machine with its pointed “nose” looks like a mouse, and on the other hand, the phenomenon of mice running out of the piles while one is loading up the sugar beet is known to farmers. The name transports the initial idea behind the product.

Today, the entire product name is *euro-Maus 4* (see figure 6). The number again shows a differentiation by technical innovations and additionally matches the numbering of the Euro Emission standard.

Figure 7. *HOLMER Terra Felis 2* (sugar beet loader).

In 2007, HOLMER also started to produce such machines. The name was founded by means of an internal company competition: an employee suggested the name *Terra Felis* (see figure 7). This fits in with the scheme of product naming at the HOLMER company. The first component is always *Terra*, the second component is a word from a Romance language, mostly Latin (*Terra Dos, Terra Variant, Terra Felis*). The name *Felis* is, according to Platen (1997: 39–41) a lexical takeover as it is identical with the Latin noun *fēlēs/fēlis* ‘cat’ (Georges 2010: 2711). The name was selected according to information given by the employees from the

HOLMER company for several reasons. It is a description of the product: the cat is a clean animal; therefore, the name befits a cleansing machine and fulfils the function of transmitting information. Nevertheless, the name was selected, above all, as a direct reference to the product of the competitor: the cat as the hunter which must catch up on the market leader – what happens to the hunted animal after a successful hunt is known. The product name has a signalling function for consumers, employees and competitors. What is problematic is the fact that the majority of receivers cannot decode the product name due to a lack of language skills. The amount of information transported by the product name *Terra Felis* can therefore vary according to the level of knowledge of the receiver (Fischer 2007: 147; Bernstein 1984: 27–32). As a result, the name remains predominantly effective with regard to the competitor.

Conclusion: Comparative Naming

This model study shows that company names and product names do not just have an advertising function or contain information about the manufacturer, the place of production, contained substances, qualities, intended purpose/field of application, mode of action and the consumer (Koß 2008b: 42 according to Lötscher 1992: 345).

Also, the naming motives reach beyond the points concerning the substance of the product, range of application covered, indicating intended effects and characterisation of the product (qualifying – distinguishing) that Schmitt (2007: 105) identified for Spanish product names.

The small market of sugar beet harvesting technology proves that names also have a competitive function and that this function plays a role in the process of naming products and companies. Product names can therefore reflect the culture of competition. Nevertheless, such a coinage of product names within the culture of competition is hardly possible in all markets. It seems to be important that there are two market leaders or rivals that are easy to identify in business. Therefore, either the market is small, or the companies are located close to each other, so that the reference object can easily be seen by employees, consumers and the addressed competitor, and the name can be decoded.

On the one hand, in a market driven by a strong culture of competition, second-rate solutions also seem to be accepted to differentiate one's own company clearly from the competitor. Probably, this would not apply to larger companies working with an advertising agency. On the other hand, a phenomenon exists in company and product naming that I would like to call comparative naming, according to comparative advertising. With the example examined here, it can be shown that the sender of such a name cultivates an active and slightly aggressive company image. Such names have a signalling function for the competitor: they show him that he is under attack. These names can moreover have an easy to decode "better than the other" message for consumers and employees. It is possible to valorise the product by attacking the competitor.

Therefore, this analysis points out that the culture of competition in a market influences the coining of names within the market, and that the product (or company – probably *Puma* vs. *Adidas* is an example here) name alone has a competitive function which allows a comparative reference to the competitor as known from comparative advertising which was shown in the introduction.

References

Bernstein, D. 1984. *Company, image and reality: A critique of corporate communications*. Eastbourne: Holt, Rinehart & Winston Ltd.

Bishara, N. 2008. *Selbstreferenzielle Werbung* [Self-referential advertising]. Konstanz: UVK.

BMW-drivers.de = www.bmw-drivers.de/forum-20/werbung-schlagabtausch - bmw-audi-subaru-und-bentley-t-39998.html (retrieved 10 September 2012).

Danesi, M. 2007. *Why it sells. Decoding the Meanings of Brand Names, Logos, Ads, and Other Marketing and Advertising Ploys.* Lanham: Rowman Littlefield.

Fischer, F. 2007. Produktnamen und Information: Cui prodest nomen? [Product names and information: Cui prodest nomen?]. In *Names in Commerce and Industry. Past and Present*, L. Kremer and E. Ronneberger-Sibold (eds.), 141–152. Berlin: Logos.

Fritzsche J. 2008. Namenkonflikte im europäischen Kennzeichenrecht [Name conflicts in European trademark legislation]. In *Namen und ihr Konfliktpotential im europäischen Kontext.* Regensburger Symposium, 11.–13. April 2007, N. Eller, St. Hackl and M. L'upták (eds.), 309–332. Regensburg: edition vulpes.

Georges, K. E. 2010. *Ausführliches Lateinisch-Deutsches Handwörterbuch. Erster Band* [Detailed Latin-German Dictionary. First volume]. Darmstadt: WBG.

Gotta, M. 1998. Die Rolle des Markennamens im Marketingmix: Global Branding und die Zukunft von Markennamen [The role of brand names in the marketing mix: Global branding and the future of brand names].

In *Brand News. Wie Namen zu Markennamen werden*, M. Gotta (ed.), 15–28. Hamburg: Spiegel-Verlagsreihe.

Holmer-maschinenbau.de = www.holmer-maschinenbau.de (retrieved 10 September 2012).

Janich, N. 2010. *Werbesprache. Ein Arbeitsbuch* [Advertising language. A workbook]. Tübingen: Narr.

Kapferer J. 1992. *Die Marke – Kapital des Unternehmens* [The brand – enterprise capital]. Landsberg/Lech: Verlag moderne Industrie.

Koß, G. 2008a. Eigennamen als Warennamen [Proper names as trade names]. In *Warennamen – Marken – Kunstnamen. Transposition und Kreation in der Wirtschaft. Ausgewählte Beiträge 1976–2006,* G. Koß, 11–22. Regensburg: edition vulpes.

—. 2008b. Warennamen: Information – Assoziation – Suggestion [Trade names: Information – association – suggestion]. In *Warennamen – Marken – Kunstnamen. Transposition und Kreation in der Wirtschaft. Ausgewählte Beiträge 1976–2006,* G. Koß, 41–48. Regensburg: edition vulpes.

—. 2008c. Warennamen [Trade names]. In *Warennamen – Marken – Kunstnamen. Transposition und Kreation in der Wirtschaft. Ausgewählte Beiträge 1976–2006,* G. Koß, 79–97. Regensburg: edition vulpes.

—. 2008d. Was ist „Ökonymie“? Vom Einzug der Globalisierung in die Onomastik [What is “econymy”? The entry of globalisation into onomastics]. In *Warennamen – Marken – Kunstnamen. Transposition und Kreation in der Wirtschaft. Ausgewählte Beiträge 1976–2006,* G. Koß, 121–178. Regensburg: edition vulpes.

Kremer, L. and Ronneberger-Sibold, E. 2007. *Names in commerce and industry: Past and present* Berlin: Logos.

Kunze, K. 2005. *Atlas Namenkunde. Vor- und Familiennamen im deutschen Sprachgebiet* [Atlas of onomastics. Forenames and surnames in the German language area]. Berlin: Directmedia Publishing.

Lötscher A. 1992. *Von Ajax bis Xerox. Ein Lexikon der Produktnamen* [From Ajax to Xerox. A lexicon of product names]. 2nd ed. Zürich: Artemis & Winkler.

Matthieu, V. 2009. *Zwischen Schokoriegel und Schaschliksoße. Linguistik im Supermarkt – Was sich hinter Produktnamen und ihrer Verwendung verbirgt* [Between chocolate bar and shashlik sauce. Linguistics in the supermarket – What is hidden behind product names and their usage]. Marburg: Tectum.

Platen, Ch. 1997. *„Ökonymie". Zur Produktnamen-Linguisitk im Europäischen Binnenmarkt* ["Econymy". On product name linguistics in the single European market]. Tübingen: Niemeyer.

Reimann, S. 2011. Der Markenname UHU im Kontext der Vogelarten-Namen bei Büro- und Schreibwaren [The brand name UHU in the context of names of bird species for office supplies and stationary]. In *Der Südwesten im Spiegel der Namen. Gedenkschrift für Lutz Reichardt,* A. Greule, St. Hackl (eds.), 253–263. Stuttgart: W. Kolhammer.

Ronneberger-Sibold E. 2004. Warennamen [Trade names]. In *Namenarten und ihre Erforschung. Ein Lehrbuch für das Studium der Onomastik*, A. Brendler and S. Brendler (eds.), 557–603, Hamburg: baar.

Ropa-maschinenbau.de = www.ropa-maschinenbau.de (retrieved 10 September 2012).

Samland, B. M. 2006. *Unverwechselbar. Name, Claim & Marke* [Unmistakable. Name, Claim & Brand]. Freiburg: Haufe.

Schmitt, Ch. 2007. Motivierte sprachliche Zeichen. Zu Formen und Funktionen spanischer und portugiesischer Firmen- und Produktnamen [Motivated linguistic signs. On forms and functions of Spanish and Portuguese company and product names]. In *Names in Commerce and Industry. Past and Present*, L. Kremer and E. Ronneberger-Sibold (eds.), 99–114. Berlin: Logos.

Stern, B. 1994. A Revised Communication Model for Advertising: Multiple Dimensions of the Source, the Message, and the Recipient. *Journal of Advertising* 23 (2): 5–15.

Stoll, K.-U. 1999. *Markennamen. Sprachliche Strukturen, Ähnlichkeit und Verwechselbarkeit. Ein Beitrag zur forensischen Linguistik des Markenrechts* [Brand names. Linguistic structures, analogies and confusability. A contribution to forensic linguistics of brand rights]. Frankfurt am Main: Peter Lang.

FROM CAR BRANDS TO THEIR LEGENDS

MARCIENNE MARTIN
UNIVERSITY OF REUNION ISLAND, FRANCE
ORACLE LABORATORY

Abstract

Brand names which define industrial artefacts or immaterial objects aim at creating the awareness of a product and to occupy the market place for it. To reach this goal (brand names), the study of the creation of brand names considers a number of different parameters, in particular, the specificity of the product, particularities of the manufacturing company or distributor, the market and customer expectations. Moreover, the development of a brand name can take various forms: antonomasia associated with a brand name may become common names, e.g. the brand name *Frigidaire* (a refrigerator) in French, or there may be various meanings for the same name e.g. *Ajax,* a cleaning product and Greek hero. The brand name can also be part of the paradigm of a legend (*Coca*).

In this article, I will present a study of two brand names, which exemplify this phenomenon. These brand names are *Citroën* (French automobile manufacturer) and *Volkswagen* (German automobile manufacturer) which have produced the legendary *2 CV* and *Beetle.*

Introduction

Naming an industrial artefact is a procedure that assigns a referent to a general lexical class, the hypernym; it subsumes brand names under hyponym classes. For example, the motor industry has launched series of vehicles which have both generic and specific features. For instance, the company Citroën has created such series as the 2 CV. The analysis of the names of this series shows that they refer to the power of the vehicles' engines. Sometimes, however, the names of these series have become legendary. The *2 CV*, which means 'two horses', is a car that was created in 1948. Designed by the Vice President Pierre-Jules Boulanger, it was code-named *TPV*, in French *Très Petit Véhicule* meaning 'very small vehicle'. Its technical characteristics were based on its convenience: four wheels under an umbrella as emphasised by the company Citroën. The relationship of customers to this car has resulted in the creation and use of an onomastic type: the hypocoristic one, such as the *deudeuche*, the *deuche*, and *la deux pattes* which means only 'the two legs'. Finally, this vehicle, created for the public at large, has involved stereotyped objects representing France in the same way as the Eiffel Tower.

In Germany, Volkswagen also created a car whose name has become legendary. It is the *Beetle,* or in French *Coccinelle* which means 'ladybug'. Before it was put on the market in 1938, it was designed by the German engineer Ferdinand Porsche and was given the code name *Type 1*. Because of its round shape, this car has inferred a nickname in relation to some form of coleopteran like ladybird or beetle. In parallel to its nominal processing, the object has also assumed the role of an actor since it has become the hero of a series of films made by Walt Disney Pictures: *The Love Bug* (1968), *Herbie Rides Again* (1974), *Herbie Goes to Monte Carlo* (1977), *Herbie Goes Bananas* (1980).

Whether the *2 CV* or the *Beetle*, their design is built around a round shape which refers to a kind of protective habitat. In this paper, I will analyze the *modus operandi* that transforms an industrial and commercial name correlated to a legend associated with a type of hypocorism feature.

The Branding of Objects of the World

Branding is a cognitive process that enables humans to develop language elements that help locate objects in the world and, thus, transform the apparent entropy of the universe into an organised system; this state refers to the concept of undifferentiated or unrealised potential (Martin 2012: 23). This procedure is performed when the undifferentiated becomes the "differential", or to put it differently, the object in itself. To exemplify this, referring to the recognition of places by the *Bembex,* which belongs to the family *Hymenoptera*, Fabre (1879: 233) an entomologist, in his works shows that an indefinable faculty, which he calls "memory", for the lack of appropriate names because the unknown cannot have one. Therefore, new technological paradigms have been given general terms (e.g. *car*), like in the case of *2 CV*. In general, taxonomy is the science of the laws and principles of the classification of living organisms (TLFi) which allows the human being at the origin of various artefacts, numbers of organisational systems and thoughts, to register in his own world.

The labelling of objects of the world is a way of mapping the latter with the help of syncretic terms: we can also mention a car, or a tree, without having a precise picture, or specific type with a more detailed picture. Such procedures will use the concepts of hypernym and hyponym, with the first term referring to the representation of a class of objects (automobiles), while the second covering the objects in their singularity (a 2 CV). In relation to lexical creations, loaning aside, the lexicon is enriched by composition and derivation, by taking new words from its own resources (Dauzat 1954: 122). Concerning the semantic field, it corresponds to the area covered in the field of meaning: a word or group of words in the language (Dubois et al. 2001: 423). Although the concept seems easy, in fact, the semantic field is crossed by other fields, such as lexical fields which results in the interpenetration of different layers. Naming presides over all sectors of human activity. This is the case of brand names.

The Brand, a Cultural Object

The creation of a brand name involves a number of phenomena, including the onomastic choice itself. As a cultural object, the brand represents professional practice, referring to the distinctive sign assigned to a referent produced by the manufacturer (*Dictionnaire historique de la langue française* 2000: 2146). As it was found on Chinese pottery, the first inscriptions on objects manufactured by humans date back to 2700 BCE. The following entries referred to the following artefacts: the name of the Emperor, or one of the artisans, or the place of manufacture. In 1634, the corporation of "vinegar and mustard in Dijon" required artisans to have their own brand (cf. Watin-Augouard 2005). A brand name or the filing of a drawing or model, is an industrial property right which represents a monopoly of exploitation (Galisson and André 1998: 10). In France, these terms are protected by the INPI, the National Institute of Industrial Property (*Institut National de la Propriété Industrielle*). The applicant is required to propose a material sign that will represent the brand, such as the following world-famous logos (Figure 1).

Club Med TOUS LES BONHEURS DU MONDE — BiC — Carrefour

Figure 1. Some examples of famous logos.

In addition, from a grammatical point of view, brand names belong to the category of proper names. They have a special status at the semantic level; indeed, they neither mark concordance in gender nor in number. However, as common names, they support the deictic. According to Gary-Prieur (1994: 20), the proper name is referred to as a designator, which designates the same referent in all possible worlds. To put it differently, this term refers to a monosemic referent, and only a specific one. For example, the *Caddy* brand, which designates a metal carriage, has protected its brand name by making the capital letter a symbol of differentiation. Moreover, to prevent its brand name from entering the common language and become a generic brand name, the company *Ateliers Réunis Caddie* spells its brand without the capital letter 'C' to refer to their *Caddie* carriage (Watin-Augouard 2005: 73). In addition, if a brand refers to the manufacturer, it also carries a number of meanings. Otherwise, the brand superposes to different levels of reality under the same name (Lewi 2003: 8). Moreover, when there is lexicalisation of a term, it is necessary that the named object (innovative artefact, new social practice, etc.) be made permanent.

From the Brand Name to the History of its Legend

The predecessor of the combustion engine corresponds to what Huygens called "a new motive force by the means of gunpowder and the pressure of the air" (Bellu 1998: 8). His experiences were recorded in *Acta Eruditorum* Liepsick, September 1688, page 497 (In *L'Industriel* 1829: 149) (for information *Acta Eruditorum*, Latin for "reports/acts of the scholars", was the first scientific journal of the German lands, published from 1682 to 1782). Subsequently, Thomas Savery, a British business man, continued this project in the late 17th century. James Watt filed a patent for a steam engine, which is known under name "fire pump" (1769). Afterwards, Nicolas-Joseph Cugnot applied this principle to the car and the predecessor of our current vehicle was born in 1769. This invention was also the basis of the railroad. The evaluation of the power of these new means of locomotion was defined by the term *horsepower* corresponding to a power unit (HP) equal to seventy-five pounds per second, that is, about 736 watts[1]. The horse tax, denoted: CV tax law, a unit of measurement of engine power, from which vehicle tax has been created[2].

---

[1] TLFi

[2] http://www.techno-science.net/?onglet=glossaire&definition=13211

In my study, I will concentrate on the 2 CV, produced by Citroën, and the Beetle manufactured by Volkswagen. To meet, or anticipate, consumer demand with low revenues, the car 2 CV was developed by the vice-president of Citroën, Pierre-Jules Boulanger, who chose the code name *TPV*, in French *Très Petit Véhicule*, meaning 'very small vehicle'. Its technical characteristics were based on its practicality: "four wheels under an umbrella", a slogan created by Citroën. As regards its specifications, the 2 CV has four seats, can carry 50kg of luggage, has front wheel drive, reaches a top speed of 60 km/h, has a three-speed box, is easy to maintain, and consumes only three litres of petrol per 100 kilometres. In Germany, Volkswagen also created a car whose name has become legendary: the *Beetle*. It was launched in 1938 and it was designed by the German engineer Ferdinand Porsche. It received the code name *Type 1*. This car was created to allow consumers with low budgets to own a car. In terms of onomastics, the meaning of the lexical unit *Volkswagen* is 'people's car' (*Volk* 'people' and *Wagen* 'car').

Although belonging to the general class of vehicles (hypernym) and the subclass of motor vehicles, names given to these two types of automobiles (hyponym) refer to specific semantic fields as we can see in table 1.

Table 1. Brand names and semantic fields.

2 CV	***Beetle***
Semantic fields: - *automotive technology* (horsepower) - *tax law*	**Semantic fields:** *entomology* The ladybug (*coccinelle* in French) is an insect, a beetle of the family *Coccinellidae*.

In addition, by integrating them into some societal objects, such as comic books[3], movies, or stamp collections, the 2 CV and the Beetle have entered the world of legends:

- *Boule and Bill* albums published by Dargaud. This editor presents this series: "The environment of this family is immediately recognizable: a charming pavilion, a garden and a car (the famous Red 2 CV)!"
- *The Adventures of Tintin - The Calculus Affair*, Hergé, Casterman, 1956;
- *Marsupilami*, Volume 10: *Rififi in Palombia*, Xavier Fauche, editions Marsu, 1996;

[3] Cf. http://passion-citroen.forum-actif.net/t33-2-cv-l-histoire-d-un-mythe

- *Spirou and Fantasio - Cider for stars*, Jean-Claude Fournier published by Dupuis, 1975, etc.

Regarding the Beetle, it became a movie star named *Herbie*. Gifted with life, this car transports the spectator into his or her many adventures. These films were produced by Walt Disney Pictures.

- *The Love Bug:* "A race car driver becomes a champion with a Volkswagen Beetle" named *Herbie* (1968)[4];
- *Herbie Rides Again:* "It is the sequel to The Love Bug" (1974) (ibid.);
- *Herbie Goes to Monte Carlo:* Herbie, "the Volkswagen Beetle with a mind of its own, is racing in the Monte Carlo Rally" (1977) (ibid.) ;
- *Herbie Goes Bananas:* The Beetle "helps its owners break up a counterfeiting ring in Mexico"[5] (1980).

When the Brand Name Becomes a Hypocorism

The 2 CV and the Beetle are vehicles that have allowed a large majority of French and German consumers to belong to a class of drivers and car users. The social practice of driving associated with these two brands has also opened up the field of imagination. Indeed, users have used different hypocoristic bynames to designate 2 CV and Beetle. Mounin (1974) defines the terms: hypocorism (noun) and hypocoristic (adjective) as terms that show an intention affectionate, loving, especially in children's language, or of its imitations; redoubling hypocoristic, use, value hypocoristic of a word. The formal processes used to create hypocoristic terms, that is affixes, such as a diminutive suffix, repetition, shortened names (Mounin 1974), or the choice of terms are conventionally referred to as hypocorisms. As we can see, this term is part of the emotional world and also refers to the living world. The brand name *2 CV* has been developed into a series of hypocoristic bynames (Table 2).

[4] cf. en.wikipedia.org/
[5] www.imdb.com/

Table 2. Brand name *2 CV* and hypocoristic bynames.

deuche	The apocope style (loss of the last syllable of the word) was used here for the lexical unit: ***cheval*** (singular), *chevaux* (plural) in French, 'horse' **deux che**vaux = **deu** (x) — **che**vaux → ***deuche***
deudeuche	Same process, but with the repetition of the first syllable.
deux pattes in French, which means 'two legs'	***deux pattes*** in French, meaning 'two legs'. In this phrase, we find the number ***deux*** 'two'. The referent to the word ***pattes*** 'legs' is part of the paradigm of the living world, especially within the mode of bipedal locomotion.

The analysis of the phrase "four wheels under an umbrella" shows the activation of two semantic fields (Table 3).

Table 3. Analysis of the slogan "four wheels under an umbrella".

roues (French) = 'wheel'	Wheel-shaped object, rotating about, an axis passing through its centre, which has many uses (TLFi)
sous (French) = 'under'	Preposition. Indicates that something (or someone) is situated below, lower position relative to another (*ibid.*)
parapluie (French) = 'umbrella'	Portable shelter consisting of a handle (sometimes folding or telescopic), with a fabric attached to the umbrella ribs and used for protection from the rain (*ibid.*)

For the lexical unit "wheel", the semantic field is that of 'locomotion'. For the term "umbrella", the semantic field is that of 'protection', enhanced by the use of the preposition of place "under".

With regard to the *Beetle*, the brand's nickname refers to the common language "bête à bon dieu" in French ('ladybird'). Its lexical analysis is presented in table 4.

Table 4. From the *Beetle* to the *ladybug* ("bête à bon dieu" in French).

beast = 'bête' in French	Belonging to the animal paradigm
good = 'bon' in French language	Concrete or abstract term; It designates people who respond positively to what is expected of them
god = 'dieu' in French	Belongs to the paradigm of spirituality
Definitions available on the website *Trésor de la Langue Française informatisé* (TLFi)	

If we do a comparative study between the two universes described with the brand names *2 CV* and *Beetle*, we notice that they are built around networks of common significance (Tables 5 and 6).

Table 5. Networks of common significance to both brands (semantic field of living beings).

2 CV	***Beetle***
With "deux pattes" in French, i.e. 'two legs' in English, it is part of the animal paradigm, and in particular that of the group of **bipeds**.	With "ladybug" it refers to the animal paradigm and in particular that of the group of **insects**.

From a symbolic point of view, these two cars have left the paradigm of transportation and they have become part of the universe of living beings. Both sentences "four wheels under an umbrella" and "bête à bon dieu" refer to a familiar language. Moreover, the semi-spherical shape of the umbrella and the elytra of the beetle are objects related to protection (Table 6).

Table 6. Networks of common significance to both brands (semantic field of protection).

2 CV	*Beetle*
Umbrella: portable shelter which consists of a handle (sometimes folding or telescopic), with a fabric attached to umbrella ribs and used for protection from rain (TLFi)	***Elytrum***: Very hard forewing that covers and protects the hind wing (ibid.)

Conclusion

In conclusion, it appears that the paradigm shift, from a symbolic point of view, has an influence on the representation of objects. Thus, the two brand names *2 CV* and *Beetle* have incorporated societal objects representing a country as well as legends, sometimes showing facts and events, more or less historical, because the reality was distorted and magnified by the popular imagination or literacy. This is exemplified in the case of the *Beetle* with the movies speaking of this car as it were human being. As mentioned above, the passage of an object from one universe (inanimate), for example, to the universe of human beings, for example, by using the process of branding, may lead to the fact that the qualities attached to the object would then be modified. In addition, the transition from one universe to another by referring to an object, considered in its general sense in a classification system, may result in its primary qualities being modified, either by amplification, or by reduction (the slave who lost his humanity to become a working tool) (Martin 2009: 15). The names: *Beetle* and *2 CV* have incorporated the paradigm of living species through hypocorism that uses the universe of movies and stories (*Herbie* which is the nickname for the *Beetle* in the movies). In this respect, Bourdieu (1982: 210) refers to his belief in the legitimacy of words and to the one who pronounces them. We may add that changing the symbolic aspects of an object through its lexical rephrasing can redefine its legitimacy and its paradigmatic quality.

References

Bellu, S. 1998. *Histoire mondiale de l'automobile* [A global history of the automobile]. Paris: Flammarion.

Bourdieu, P. 2001. *Langage et pouvoir symbolique* [Language and symbolic power]. Paris: Fayard.

Dauzat, A. 1954. *Le génie de la langue française* [The genius of French language]. Paris: Librairie Payot.

Dubois, J. et al. 2001. *Dictionnaire de linguistique* [Dictionary of linguistics]. Paris: Larousse-Bordas.

Fabre J. H. 1879. *Souvenirs entomologiques. Livre I* [Recollection of Entomology. Book I]. Paris: Ebooks libres et gratuits.

Galisson R. and André, J. C. 1998. *Dictionnaire de noms de marques courants* [Dictionary of generic trademarks]. Paris: Didier Érudition.

Gary-Prieur, M. N. 1994. *Grammaire du nom propre* [Grammar of proper nouns]. Paris: PUF.

Lewi, G. 2003. *La marque* [The brand]. Paris: Editions Vuibert.

L'illustration, Journal universel hebdomadaire [The Illustration Weekly Journal Universal], n° 3676, 9 August 1913.

L'Industriel : journal principalement destiné à répandre les connaissances utiles à l'industrie générale, ainsi que les découvertes et les perfectionnemens dont elle est journellement l'objet [The Industrial: Journal which aims to expand valuable knowledge on general industries, on discoveries, and on improvements on these areas], August 1829, Vol 7, n° 4: 146–192.

Martin, M. 2009. *Des humains quasi objets et des objets quasi humains* [The quasi-human objects and the quasi-object human]. Paris: Editions L'Harmattan.

—. 2012. *Se nommer pour exister – L'exemple du pseudonyme sur Internet* [To name yourself in order to exist – example of pseudonyms on Internet]. Paris: Editions L'Harmattan.

Mounin, G. 1974. *Dictionnaire de la linguistique* [Dictionary of linguistics]. Paris: PUF.

Rey, A. dir. 2000. *Dictionnaire historique de la langue française* [Historical dictionary of French language]. Paris: Le Robert.

Watin-Augouard, J. 2005. *Créateur de noms, Marcel Botton et l'aventure de Nomen* [Name creator Marcel Botton and the adventure of Nomen]. Paris: Dunod.

Online recources

en.wikipedia.org/ (retrieved 6 September 2011).
http://atilf.atilf.fr/dendien/scripts/tlfiv5/advanced.exe?8;s=1554225510; (retrieved 5 September 2011).
http://passion-citroen.forum-actif.net/t33-2-cv-l-histoire-d-un-mythe (retrieved 31 August 2011).
http://www.imdb.com/ (retrieved 9 September 2011).
http://www.legifrance.gouv.fr/ (retrieved 9 September 2011).
http://www.techno-science.net/?onglet=glossaire&definition=13211 (retrieved 8 September 2011).
TLFi = Trésor de la Langue Française informatisé [Electronic dictionary of French language]. http://atilf.atilf.fr/ (retrieved 5 September 2011).

AN EXTENDED TYPOLOGY FOR PRODUCT NAMES: EXAMPLES FROM YOGHURT NAMES OF THE GERMAN AND SWEDISH MARKET

DINA HEEGEN
ÅBO AKADEMI UNIVERSITY, FINLAND

Abstract

The paper introduces a new way of describing the structure of product names. A typology is developed on the basis of economic and linguistic terminology, considering legal aspects, i.e. European and national law on brand names. Besides structuring the product name into its distinctive components, the typology offers an immediate insight into the legal status of the component of the product name. Adding further criteria, it becomes clear where the component refers to, which information and effect it conveys, how valuable the component is for the overall effect of the product name and, comparing product names of different countries or economic ranges, which (cultural) differences or common aspects it conveys.

The introduced typology is applicable not only to names of dairy products, but to product names of diverse economic ranges and countries. As a result, companies gain from this model as it helps identify e.g. naming tendencies of a market which might be motivated, for instance, by a characteristic of the respective market or culture.

The paper represents an excerpt from the author's dissertation project investigating product names of the German, Swedish and Finnish dairy markets. The examples in this paper are taken from the Swedish and German corpus.

The Corpus

Products have to differentiate themselves from other products of the same company and from those of competitors in order to attract the customer's attention and to be competitive on the market. New product characteristics are therefore continually introduced by the manufacturer. As a result, product names lengthen: while *WEIHENSTEPHAN RAHMJOGHURT ERDBEERE* was sufficient in the beginning, it now seems to need *WEIHENSTEPHAN RAHMJOGHURT MILD UNSER CREMIGSTER SAISONGENUSS MANGO–PANNA COTTA* to promote the different benefits of the product (here, yoghurt) to the customer in order to stimulate a purchase decision. Traditional linguistic models, representing the structure of product names, still seem to lack this development.

Product names from the two countries Germany and Sweden are the basis of this study in order to be able to make a statement on e.g. cultural tendencies in naming traditions and to proove the applicability of the typology on product names from different countries. Product names will be investigated at the point of sale (PoS) and, thus, as they appear on the product packaging.

In addition to collecting data through field research work in German (REAL, Edeka) and Swedish (Hemköp ICA) grocery stores, information for completion is taken from the companies' respective websites on which product packages are displayed. The corpus comprises the complete assortment (spring 2011) of the manufacturer's brands for yoghurt of the German companies Ehrmann, Müller and Weihenstephan and the Swedish companies Arla[1], Skånemejerier, and Gefleortens. The paper will only concentrate on dairy products, more precisely on yoghurt, as these products are, to a large extent, not imported from other countries, but produced by native German or Swedish companies for distribution within the same country, i.e. Germany or Sweden. This is important in order to depict for instance cultural tendencies in naming traditions.

The German and Swedish Point of Sale (PoS)

It is worth to note that the structuring of the dairy market in Sweden is different from the structuring of the German dairy market. As Tienken

[1]Arla, originally Swedish, merged with the Danish dairy company MD Foods in spring 2000. Nowadays, known as Arla Foods, the cooperative is owned by Swedish, Danish and German dairy farmers (Arla.com). The corpus comprises products from the Swedish market.

(2008: 14) points out, it is only one brand of a company which is fulfilling consumer needs within one region in Sweden, whereas in Germany several brands and companies are competing for the same need. Tienken (ibid.) gives the extension of the company Milko into the Stockholm market area in spring 2006[2] as an example: although, being an old-established Swedish dairy company, Milko had to introduce itself in a brochure in order to obtain the consumer's acceptance, as then Arla was the predominant company for the area. This predominance of one or few companies within one distribution area in Sweden becomes obvious looking at the number of companies presented on a retail shelf for yoghurt at the PoS. As Fig. 1 shows, only few companies[3] (here, Arla, Milko, Skånemejerier and Valio[4]) compete for the consumer needs on a Swedish retail shelf (Fig. 1a), whereas several companies' (here, eleven) products try to attract the customers' attention on a German retail shelf (Fig. 1b).

Figure 1a) Figure 1b)
Retail shelves presenting yoghurt in a grocery store in Sweden (1a) and Germany (1b). Fig 1a: Noticeable are the large 1000 g yoghurt cartons and the small number of companies (Arla, Milko, Skånemejerier, Valio) at the Swedish store. Fig 1b: In

[2] Since November 1, 2011 Milko merged with Arla into a cooperative dairy company owned by Swedish, Danish and German dairy farmers. (Milko.se)

[3] Based on the umbrella brand.

[4] Valio is a Finnish dairy company which also can be found on the Swedish market.

Germany, small 125 g yoghurt cups are the common package size; the number of companies is larger (Berchtesgadener Land, Emmi, Danone, Andechser, Müller, Weihenstephan, Bauer, Elinas, Zott, Friesland Campina, real (private brand)). (Pictures: Dina Heegen)

The Product Name at the Point of Sale

Besides the structuring of the market, the different package sizes used for yoghurt in both respective countries is striking. In Germany, common package sizes for yoghurt comprise cups with fill quantities from 125g up to 500g. In contrast, 1000g yoghurt cartons[5], which are predominating the Swedish retail shelves, cannot be found on the German market. The package size, though, can have a significant effect on the packaging design, as the 1000g cartons offer a larger surface than a 125g cup and thus provide more space for informative elements, images, continuous texts etc. to be displayed on the package in order to attract the customers' attention and give information about the product. This advantage in space on Swedish packages may also have an effect on the length of product names. It might be worth to mention that many companies on the German market choose to enlarge the surface by offering family packs containing two to eight cups arranged in one bigger pack[6].

As a consequence of the different package sizes and shapes in both countries, the product name is printed on different elements of the respective packaging: looking at a cup, the product name can be found on the lid (Fig. 2a) and on the sides (Fig. 2b), whereas on cartons, the product name is presented on the sides (Fig. 2c)[7]. Consequently, the realisation of the product name that is analyzed in this study is taken from the sides of the product packaging, as the information given on the lid of a cup may vary and not contain all the elements as displayed on the sides, which can indicate the importance of information for the product name. The information on the lid only is used for completion to reconfirm the information given on the sides. Furthermore, the customer disposes of the lid sooner than the cup, which may be put back into the refrigerator or be used for storage purposes. As a result, the cup can function as a long-term "continuous communicator" (cf. Selame 1986: 93–94), a function with which it can comply even in the customer's home (cf. Hardt-Mautner

[5] These are comparable to cartons used for milk in Germany and Sweden.

[6] The corpus of this research does not contain this type of package.

[7] In rare cases, elements of the product name may be presented on top, e.g. the individual brand, flavor.

1994: 36) and with which an image of the product (name) can manifest itself in the mind of the customer.

Primary Surface I (Lid)

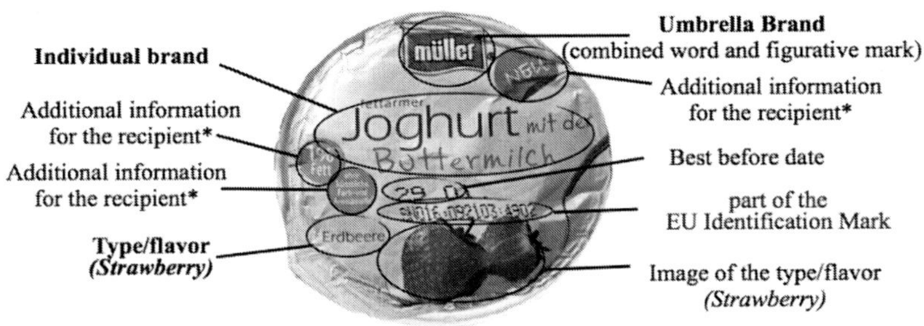

Figure 2a. The product name represented on the lid and on the sides of a yoghurt cup (German corpus) (Source/adaptation: Dina Heegen.)

Primary Surface II

Figure 2b. The product name represented on the lid and on the sides of a yoghurt cup (German corpus) (Source/adaptation: Dina Heegen.)

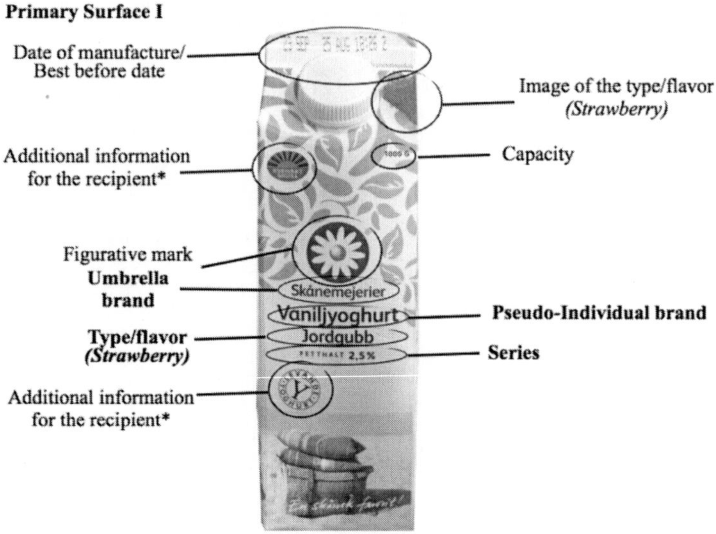

Figure 2c. The product name is displayed on the sides of the yoghurt carton (Swedish corpus) (Source/adaptation: Dina Heegen.)
*Additional information for the recipient involves information on the product which is given only temporarily (e.g. *New!*) or provides the customer with additional knowledge (e.g. capacity) which is not used as part of the product name for differentiating the respective product. The type of information may not be the crucial factor to this, as the fat content, for instance, can be both, additional information as well as core element of the product name (cf. *WEIHENSTEPHAN DER CREMIGE 0,1% FETT* 'Weihenstephan the creamy 0,1% fat') when it is used especially as unique selling proposition.

The product packaging itself not only has to fulfill the customer's but also the producer's needs: this includes, among others, the basic functions of storing and preserving the product as well as protecting it from contamination, exposure to light or damage on its various stages from the place of production to the customer's home (Schweiger and Schrattenecker 2009: 132–133; Ahlert 2007: 18–19). Moreover, lacking the presence of an advertising salesperson in today's grocery stores, the product packaging needs to attract the prospect's attention and communicate the product's benefits in order to evoke a purchase decision (Ahlert 2007: 17ff.).

Standing in front of the retail shelf at the point of sale, the prospect often sees the product for the first time or already has a notion of it because of previous advertising or product experience. Nevertheless, regarding that only approximately 2% of the information in advertising is perceived by the customer (Baumgarth 2004: 17), many purchase decisions, especially for low-involvement products, are often made emotionally and spontaneously at the PoS. Yoghurt, a Fast Moving Consumer Good (FMCG), is an inexpensive product for daily use and purchased with low involvement; in contrast to buying a high-involvement product, e.g. an expensive car, the customer is exposed to only little financial, functional, mental, or social perceived risk (Kroeber-Riel, Weinberg and Gröppel-Klein 2009: 436).[8] As a result, the product name of a low-involvement product such as yoghurt, in my opinion, needs to be significant and meaningful to the highest degree, as the customer purchases impulsively and emotionally, not giving the purchase careful, time-consuming consideration. Pointing that out, according to Langer, Esch and Kühn (2009: 287), the average time the customer spends shopping for groceries at the store is reduced from 46 minutes in 1992 to 23 minutes in 2007, and that the time spent in front of the product is only 1.6 seconds (Amann and Rippstein 1999: 202) before the purchase decision for a product is made. Thus, it becomes obvious that the role of the product name is to differentiate the product from those of competitors, make the product easily identifiable out of a mass of similar products, and show the quality of the product as well as of the company. Furthermore, the product name establishes a product identity and shall evoke positive connotations to persuade the customer to make a positive purchase decision - all in the blink of an eye (Schweiger and Schrattenecker 2009: 81ff; Ronneberger-Sibold 2004: 563–564; Kircher 2005: 589).

As figure 3 shows, the product name, as part of a branding triangle between 1) product name, 2) brand logo and 3) packaging/product design (colour, shape, haptics) (cf. Esch and Langner 2005: 578) plays an outstanding role, providing the customer with necessary information. Moreover, regarding the differences in package size and shape between Swedish and German yoghurt packages from the corpus, the product name is the essential element in the pre-purchasing process, as a German customer might regard the product inside a Swedish yoghurt carton as milk instead of yoghurt, if the essential information (a) given by the product name is missing. In addition to that, the product name adds to the basic

[8] Occasionally, low-involvement products, such as yoghurt, may for a short time become high-involvement products, if the purchase occurs due to e.g. a social reason: neighbours are coming over for dinner and the host does not want to attract attention by presenting a "wrong" brand (e.g. low-cost private brand) (Kroeber-Riel et al. 2009: 412–413).

information of the content by communicating the secondary benefits to the customer, initiating the buying process.

Figure 3a) b) c) d)

Figure 3 a–d. Lacking one of the three elements of the branding triangle has a tremendous negative effect on the overall statement of the packaging. A product packaging with a missing product name cannot be related to the correct product or leads the customer to buy the wrong product. The importance of the product name for the purchase decision cannot be denied. a) Without product name b) without umbrella brand c) without image d) original packaging design. (Source/adaptation: Dina Heegen.)

Kroeber-Riel and Esch (2004: 40) point out that especially with purchase decisions considering low-involvement products, such as yoghurt, the customer needs to be addressed emotionally, as this results in a spontaneous purchase, which is a common motivation for buying low-involvement products. The emotions, triggered by a product name, are to address the target group's needs as well as to awaken the customer's desires. Ronneberger-Sibold (2007: 136) regards "[...] brand names as a company's offer of identity to the customers [...]"[9] (my translation) and speaks in this context of "Wunschidentitäten" ('desired identities'), the customer gains from buying the product. The yoghurt *EHRMANN FIT VITAL*, for instance, adds to the customer's idea of 'vitality', 'health', 'life balance' and 'physical strength'[10] and gives the customer the notion that, when consuming the yoghurt, (s)he belongs to a group of people who are actively training their body in the style of the physical fitness and health

[9] "[...] Markennamen als Identitätsangebote der Firmen an die Verbraucher […]"
[10] Evoked associations are experienced very subjectively and can be different from customer to customer, depending e.g. on personal experience.

movement, though the yoghurt consumer might not do any sports. The primary benefit of yoghurt as a source of calcium becomes thus less important, whereas the secondary benefit turns into the unique selling proposition (USP) (Janich 2010: 56). The USP not only stimulates product perception through which the brand name as well as the brand is drawn into the customer's center of attention (Kircher 2005: 593), but awakes the customer's desire to specifically own this product of this brand – a process leading into the purchase decision (Ronneberger-Sibold 2007: 136). Especially in market segments with a high degree of product similarity and little possibility for differentiation, emphasising the secondary benefit can thus be the decisive factor for sales success. New, inventive ideas and new niches are crucial for a company's product to stick out of the mass of similar products. This need for new denominations and inventive product features becomes obvious when taking a look at yoghurt names: almost monthly, new flavors and varieties are introduced to the customer according to, for instance, seasons (e.g. Christmas) or current events (e.g. World Cup). *MÜLLER*, around Christmas, regularly introduces new types of *JOGHURT MIT DER ECKE* (literally translated: 'yoghurt with the corner') to the customer, e.g. *ECKE DES MONATS RUDI DER WEIHNACHTSELCH* ('corner of the month Rudi the christmaselk') or *ECKE DES MONATS RUDIS KNUSPERHÄUSCHEN* ('corner of the month Rudis gingerbread house').The company *WEIHENSTEPHAN* puts emphasis on the traditional cuisine and introduced its series *TRADITIONSREZEPTE* ('traditional recipes') with flavors called *À LA MÜNCHNER APFELSTRUDEL MIT BOURBON VANILLE* ('à la Munich apple strudel with bourbon vanilla') or *À LA BAYERISCH CREME MIT ERLESENEN ERDBEEREN* ('à la Bavarian crème with finest strawberries'). This trend in product differentiation through extensive naming requires reconsideration of the extent of the product name and its components.

Brand Name and Product Name

On the basis of the corpus for this study, which investigates both Swedish and German product names, it is crucial to distinguish between the terms *brand name* and *product name.*[11] Brand names, in this study,

[11] The differentiation between product name and brand name, and the definition of both, are widely discussed in onomastic research. In this article, which is part of a dissertation project, the relation between brand name and product name will only be explained in order to clarify its status in this paper and not be discussed.

comprise names which are registered[12] at the national Patent and Trademark Offices, i.e. the PRV (Patent- och Registreringsverket) in Sweden and the DPMA (Deutsches Patent- und Markenamt) in Germany. Product names are, according to Ronneberger-Sibold (2008: 130) regarded as "[…] broader term for commercial names regardless of their legal status […]" (my translation)[13]. Moreover, product names, in this study, are positioned in a hierarchy above the brand name and can include one or more brand names in its structure. Besides, the term *brand name,* in this study, always denotes the verbal realisation of a brand as word mark or combined word and figurative mark. It should be noted, that companies avoid grounds for refusal by registering a brand name as visual representation, often in combination with colours, shapes or other elements of the product name, e.g. umbrella brand, as a combined word and figurative mark, etc. Furthermore, it is necessary to describe a definition of the product name, which comprises all verbal elements of the product name (e.g. *EHRMANN ALMIGHURT ERDBEERE*; *ARLA CULTURA DOFILUS PASSION FIBER*) and allows a company-independent and cross-national comparison of the elements of the product name.

In order to ensure such comparability for this study, it is not sufficient to include only an onomastic perspective into the analysis of product names, but to integrate an economic as well as legal point of view. If, for instance, the requirements of the Swedish trademark act deviated much from the German trademark act, this could lead to decisive differences in formal aspects of the creation of a brand, which is part of the product name. As a result, the analysis of the product name would need a different onomastic approach. Moreover, considering the product name in the context of the product packaging requires a business perspective in order to get insight into the brand development, brand functions and the brand name requirements, as these influence the creation process of the product name, which is carried out by the company or an authorised agency. Private brands are common in the German food industry, but less common on the Swedish market (cf. Svensk mjölk); therefore, this study concentrates on manufacturer's brands as parts of complex brand architectures which are equally common in both dairy markets.

---

[12] Of interest are only brand names that refer to yoghurt and thus belong to class 29 of the Nizza classification.

[13] "[…] weiter gefasste[r] Begriff für kommerzielle Namen ohne Berücksichtigung des Rechtsstatus […]".

Developing a Comprehensive Naming Typology

Taking legal, economic and linguistic aspects and the complexity of the product names of the corpus into account, it seems inevitable to reconsider the dimension of the product name and its components. Product innovation and specialisation is on the rise and pushes product differentiation into more cleverly devised dimensions, not only in the food industry. This trend has also been mentioned by Brandl (2007) and Fischer (2007). Whereas Fischer (2007: 141–142) is aware of the "growing lexical complexity of product names" (ibid.) as a basis for her linguistic analysis, Brandl (2007: 87ff) identifies "various levels of brands or brand names", an approach which will be regarded later in this text.

According to the trend mentioned above, the brand name alone is no longer sufficient to distinguish and accentuate a product in a mass of similar products. As a result, I am of the opinion, that, especially in the context of a linguistic-based analysis, the product name in its complexity, as it is defined in the following, has to be considered and not only its registered components, i.e. brand names, in isolation. Therefore, due to numerous variation patterns and the creativity of the companies in coming up with new elements of the product name, it is imperative to identify and name all of these components of the product name in order to characterise them and elucidate their interaction with other components of the product name, other elements of the branding triangle or external signifiers, e.g. product names of the same company or even of competitors in order to grasp the overall message of the product name in its depth as a basis for e.g. linguistic analysis.

As illustrated in figure 4, in this work, the product name is understood as a subcategory of ergonymic names, i.e. names for objects created by humans (cf. Bauer 1985: 54–55). The brand names (shaded in grey), i.e. registered parts of the product name, display, according to the category, the umbrella brand (e.g. *EHRMANN*), family brand (e.g. *FIT VITAL*) or individual brand (e.g. *ALMIGHURT*) and are defined in line with common economic definitions in the context of brand architecture. Components of the product name which are not registered due to grounds for refusal as word mark, figurative mark[14] or combined word and figurative mark or which are for any other reasons not registered by the company, but are used in the manner of registered brands (e.g. appear in the same place and

[14] If the figurative mark is verbalised in advertising and/or product descriptions by the company and also in the mind of the customer, it is thus counted as an exception. In this corpus, only *Arla ko*, which appears as figurative mark on the package, is an established verbalisation.

design on the packaging, have the same functions), are termed *pseudo*-family brand or *pseudo*-individual brand. A pseudo-umbrella brand does not appear in the corpus. Pseudo-brands have the same function as their registered equivalents within the product name, only with the difference that pseudo-brands have never been registered at the trademark office or are, by trademark law, subject to grounds for refusal.[15] As a result, the introduced typology subdivides the product name into eight components, marks each component's position according to economic terms, as well as clarifies the component's legal status.

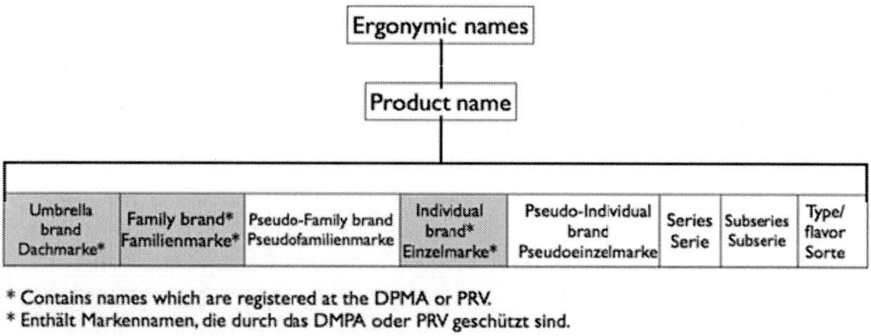

Figure 4. The product name and its components (Heegen 2011).

In this typology, the pseudo-family brand is the non-protective or not protected equivalent of the registered family brand and embraces more than one product category (e.g. yoghurt, cheese, milk; lactose-free products; organic products). In the corpus, it also appears as an addition to the family brand: *ARLA* (umbrella brand) + *ARLA KO* 'Arla cow' (family brand) + *LAKTOSFRI* 'lactose-free' (pseudo-family brand) + *FRUKTYOGHURT* 'fruit yoghurt' (pseudo-individual brand) + *JORDGUBB/SMULTRON* 'strawberry/wild strawberries' (type/flavor). The pseudo-individual brand substitutes the registered individual brand and is not registered by the company (e.g. *CREMIGHURT*, here created as analogy to the registered individual brand *ALMIGHURT*) or non-protective (e.g. *FRUKTYOGHURT*) due to grounds for refusal by trademark law. The serial name includes differentiating elements such as *SAISONGENUSS* or *DIÄT*, although these might also be used in the function of pseudo-individual brands, depending on the appearance on the packaging and its function within the product

[15] http://www.wipo.int (retrieved 3 September 2012).

name. A subseries could only be found within a product name if a serial name occurred.

It should be noted, that a classification of the elements of the product name may not be done using semantic criteria, e.g. "*DIÄT* is always the serial name", "names indicating seasonal products are always serial names", "*LAKTOSFRI* and *LAKTOSEFREI* ('lactose-free') are always pseudo-family brands". In fact, the importance of these denominations, e.g. diet, lactose-free, within the product name and for the overall message of the product name, varies from manufacturer to manufacturer and even from product to product, as figure 5 shows.

Figure 5a) Figure 5 b)

Figure 5a–b. *TRADITIONSREZEPTE* (left, highlighted) and *SAISONGENUSS* (right, highlighted) – though semantically closely related, different in position. (Source/adaptation: Dina Heegen.)

According to the introduced typology, the components of the product name (fig. 5b) are (1) *WEIHENSTEPHAN* (2) *RAHMJOGHURT MILD* (3) *UNSER CREMIGSTER* (4) *SAISONGENUSS* (5) *MANGO–PANNA COTTA* ('Weihenstephan ful-fat yoghurt our creamiest season's treat mango–panna cotta'):

(1) *WEIHENSTEPHAN* = umbrella brand

(2) *RAHMJOGHURT MILD* = pseudo-individual brand which cannot be registered as a brand as *RAHMJOGHURT MILD* is a statement to be kept free for general use

(3) *UNSER CREMIGSTER* = serial name; the series *TRADITIONSREZEPTE* ('traditional recipes') (fig. 5a), which is positioned in analogy to *UNSER CREMIGSTER* on the packaging, is also existing as subordination of the pseudo-individual brand *RAHMJOGHURT*

(4) *SAISONGENUSS* = subseries, as the serial name is already denoted by *UNSER CREMIGSTER* and *SAISONGENUSS* represents a further differentiation to the serial name

(5) *MANGO–PANNA COTTA* = flavour.

The example of *TRADITIONSREZEPTE* (serial name) and *SAISONGENUSS* (subseries) demonstrates the inconsistency in naming which occurs not only between products of several countries or companies but even within one company's product range. Semantically, *TRADITIONSREZEPTE* is closer related to *SAISONGENUSS* than it is to *UNSER CREMIGSTER* (serial name). Thus, it would be likely to call for both being either serial names or subserial names. According to the representation on the packaging, *TRADITIONSREZEPTE* is clearly positioned below the pseudo-individual brand and thus, on the packaging, put hierarchically on the same level as the serial name *UNSER CREMIGSTER* by the company. This elucidates the importance of certain components within the product name.

As product names will semantically and quantitatively be enriching, as it is already the case with *WEIHENSTEPHAN RAHMJOGHURT MILD UNSER CREMIGSTER SAISONGENUSS MANGO–PANNA COTTA*, it is therefore no longer sufficient to subsume complex structures following a construct of umbrella brand + family brand + pseudo-family brand + individual brand + pseudo-individual brand under "additions to the product name" as Matthieu (2009: 151) suggests. If done so, the addition to the product name in the example above would be *UNSER CREMIGSTER SAISONGENUSS MANGO–PANNA COTTA*. A subsumption of the family brand, pseudo-family brand, individual brand and pseudo-individual brand under the term *product name* (cf. Matthieu 2009: 151ff) is drawn too broadly and ignores the brand status of the registered, and thus protected, constituents of the name. Moreover, taking an exclusive look at the pseudo-individual brand, it becomes clear that speaking of it as a *brand name* is misleading as the pseudo-individual brand is not a registered brand and is often also subject to grounds for refusal by trademark law (e.g. *RAHMJOGHURT MILD*). Brandl (2007: 87ff), in his study including economic and linguistic aspects, identifies four levels within a product name[16]: 1) brand 2) product group 3) product description and 4) variant. For my study, this approach seems insufficient as Brandl combines several components of the analyzed product names under one superordinate term, ignoring their individual message or disguising any reference to other elements.

As a conclusion to the above, the term product name, in this study, is referred to as a superordinate to a brand name; the latter as being used as a

[16] *Product name* as defined in this study.

nonspecific term for brands, which are registered at the DPMA or PRV and thus can occur as umbrella brand, family brand or individual brand as part of the product name. As a result from the introduced constituents of the product name, as shown in figures 4 and 6, a product name is a hierarchical construct, built of several product differentiating elements, including the umbrella brand[17] as largest product distinctive element (in the scheme, in the left position) to the type/flavor name as smallest product distinctive element (in the scheme, positioned on the right).

In order to provide the reader with an overview and to avoid repetition, the following list illustrates the key benefits of the introduced typology:

1) to clearly assign a product to a manufacturer, product range, series, etc.
2) to identify inconsequent and inconsistent naming
3) the exclusive analysis of single components of the product name without isolating them from the complete product name and its overall message
4) to visualise cross references within the product name, to identify reference to parts of the branding triangle or external factors, such as events, advertisements, or even competitors
5) to add research categories, even from different disciplines
    a) to clarify structures of the name and enable cross-cultural analysis
    b) to help identify tendencies in naming traditions of a market, which companies conquering a market might follow or avoid
    c) to help identify cultural tendencies in naming traditions, such as secondary benefits, etc.
6) to visualise registered elements of the product name and, applied to several product names of a product range, can even show the necessity for brand registration within a country or give hints to the structuring of the market.

Subdivision of the Product Name into Three Units

The product name, as it is defined in this study, can be subdivided into three units:

The First Unit

The first unit of the product name is represented by the umbrella brand. Dealing with manufacturer's brands, the umbrella brand, positioned

[17] Referring to manufacturer's brands (here, in complex brand architectures).

graphically and hierarchically above the family brand, pseudo-family brand, individual brand and pseudo-individual brand on the packaging, is regarded as a vital part of the product name in complex brand architectures.

The Second Unit

The second unit of the product name is displayed by the family brand, the pseudo-family brand, the individual brand, the pseudo-individual brand and the series, respectively the subseries. Onomastically, it can be regarded as the most interesting entity, as it tends to represent the components of the product name which were mostly created for advertising reasons in order to name the product and to communicate the product's characteristics to the customer. Thus, the second unit is the core of the product name.

The Third Unit

The third unit, the type/flavor, seems to be mandatory, at least for yoghurt, as it communicates essential product characteristics: taste and even consistency. Generally, in the case of yoghurt, companies use the same names to describe the flavor and even internationally, it does not seem to be a matter of discrepancy, as mostly names, i.e. appellatives for fruits, etc. are chosen for describing the flavor. Nevertheless, the study reveals that more companies tend to create their own denominations for the type/flavor of their yoghurt, e.g. the type/flavor *SAMOA* is chosen by Arla for a combination of 'peach, kiwi, mango, pineapple, melon and passion fruit juice', which it is only obvious for the customer by taking a closer look at the ingredients. The German company Müller even refers to external public events, when it names its type/flavor *WELTMEISTER* (seasonal yoghurt *ECKE DES MONATS*). The customer learns from the list of ingredients that *WELTMEISTER* – at least during the World Cup 2010 – is the flavor for an apple-vanilla yoghurt with chocolate soccer balls.

The product name, consisting of all three units, can be referred to as a *product name in its broad sense*, whereas the second unit regarded in isolation can be referred to as a *product name in its narrow sense*. Nevertheless, as stated above, the product name should always be considered in its entirety and complexity.

Table 1. Extended structural model on the basis of the introduced typology for the product name.

	Umbrella brand	Family brand	Pseudo-Family brand	Individual brand	Pseudo-individual brand	Serial name	Subseries	Type/ flavor
Product name	WEIHEN-STEPHAN				RAHM-JOGHURT MILD	UNSER CREMIGSTER	SAISONGENUSS	MANGO PANNA-COTTA
Function	referring to sender (referring to recipient) (referring to product) originality (combined word and figurative mark) information (manufacturer), expressivness (tradition, quality u.a.), valorization				referring to product (referring to recipient) Information valorization	referring to product (referring to recipient) information expressiveness , quality valorization	referring to product (referring to recipient) information expressiveness, quality valorization	referring to product informa-tion
Naming Motives	company/ manufacturer				type of product quality taste/consistency	product characteristics (quality) consistency, referring to manufacturer	offer period (seasonal product) product characteristics (quality, exclusiveness)	taste

Applicability of the Typology to Other Products

The introduced typology (figure 4 and table 1) can be applied not only to yoghurt, but to other products as well. The example from Janich (2010: 63) *NIVEA VISAGE OPTIMALE 3* displays "[…] a product name which contains the brand name *Nivea* and the name of the product line *Nivea Visage* […]" (my translation)[18]. According to the typology introduced in this paper, *NIVEA* represents the family brand, *VISAGE* the pseudo-individual brand, *OPTIMALE* the serial name and *3* the subseries. Thus, a manufacturer-internal pattern in naming (e.g. the serial name always ends with *-ale*[19]) can become easily recognisable and the function of the element of the product name for the process of advertising becomes clear. Classifying *3* as a subserial name allows the subordination of other products to the same serial name: *NIVEA + VISAGE + OPTIMALE + CUMULATIVE CARE CREAM.* The company, in the process of naming new products, can thus, on the one hand, concentrate on the creation of this certain element of the product name and its reference to other components of the product name or the branding triangle, or, on the other hand, is aware of names too similar for products of a series, as well as too many series within one product range.

Concluding Remarks

The aim of this paper was to show that due to increasing product innovation and specialisation within one product category, manufacturers choose to differentiate a product from those of its own company or from similar products of competitors, not only by a fancy colour or shape of the packaging, but by new and innovative product features. These features are communicated to the customer through the product name, which, as a result, gains in quantity. In order to be able to analyze the product name in its entity and complexity, grasp its overall message and find a common basis for a cross-company and even an intercultural comparison, it is imperative to take economic, linguistic and legal aspects into consideration. The introduced typology and the extended structuring model strived to contribute to this approach.

[18] "ein[en] Produktname[n], in dem der Markenname *Nivea* und der Name für die Produktserie *Nivea Visage* enthalten ist."

[19] This is only an assumed result in order to point out the significance of the typology.

References

Ahlert, D. (ed.) 2007. *Bedeutung der Produktverpackung für die Markenpräferenz im Kontext internationaler Markenführung in der FMCG-Branche* [The importance of product packaging for the brand preference in the context of international brand management in the FMCG Sector]. Münster: n/a.

Amann, M. and Rippstein D. 1999. *Am POS zählt das stumme Zwiegespräch zwischen Käufer und Verpackung* [It's the silent dialogue between buyer and packaging which counts at the PoS]. *Marketing Journal* 4: 202–205.

Arla.com = http://www.arla.com/about-us/our-company/ (retrieved 28 August 2012)

Baumgarth, C. 2004. *Markenpolitik: Markenwirkungen - Markenführung - Markencontrolling* [Branding: Brand effects - brand management - brand controlling]. 2nd ed. Wiesbaden: Gabler.

Bauer, G. 1985. *Namenkunde des Deutschen* [German onomastics]. (Germanistische Lehrbuchsammlung 21) Bern: Lang.

Brandl, W. 2007. Buy English? Changes in German Product Naming -a preview. In *Names in Commerce and Industry: Past and Present.* Kremer, L. and E. Ronneberger-Sibold (eds.), 87–98. Berlin: Logos

Esch, F.-R. and Langner, T. 2005. Branding als Grundlage zum Markenaufbau [Branding as basis for brand development]. In *Moderne Markenführung. Grundlagen - Innovative Ansätze - Praktische Umsetzungen* [Modern brand management. Basics - Innovative Approaches - Practical Implementation], F.-R. Esch (ed.), 573–586. Wiesbaden: Gabler.

Fischer, F. 2007. Produktnamen und Information - cui prodest nomen? [Product names and information]. In *Names in Commerce and Industry: Past and Present.* L. Kremer and E. Ronneberger-Sibold (eds.), 141–152. Berlin: Logos.

Hardt-Mautner, G. 1994. A Case in Point. On the Interplay of Verbal and Non-Verbal Messages in Packaging Discourse. In *Rhetoric and Stylistics today.* P. Skyum-Nielsen and H. Schröder (eds.), 35–42. Frankfurt am Main: Lang.

Heegen, D. 2011. *„Nomen est tota res" Sprachwissenschaftliche Analyse deutscher und schwedischer Joghurtnamen* ["Nomen est tota res" A Linguistic Analysis of German and Swedish yoghurt names]. Unpublished Master thesis. University of Regensburg (Prof. Dr. Albrecht Greule).

Janich, N. 2010. *Werbesprache. Ein Arbeitsbuch* [Advertising language. A workbook]. 5th. ed. Tübingen: Narr.

Kircher, S. 2005, Die strategische Bedeutung des Markennamens [The strategic importance of the brand name]. In *Moderne Markenführung. Grundlagen -Innovative Ansätze -Praktische Umsetzungen* [Modern brand management. Basics - Innovative Approaches - Practical Implementation], F.-R. Esch (ed.), 587–602. Wiesbaden: Gabler

Kroeber-Riel, W. and Esch, F.-R. 2004. *Strategie und Technik der Werbung. Verhaltenswissenschaftliche Ansätze* [Strategy and technique of advertising. Behavioral Approaches]. 6th ed. Stuttgart: Verlag W. Kohlhammer.

Kroeber-Riel, W., Weinberg, P. and Gröppel-Klein, A. 2009. *Konsumen-tenverhalten* [Consumer behavior]. 9th ed. München: Verlag Franz Vahlen.

Matthieu, V. 2009. *Zwischen Schokoriegel und Schaschliksoße. Linguistik im Supermarkt. Was sich hinter Produktnamen und ihrer Verwendung verbirgt* [Between chocolate bars and Shashlik gravy. Linguistics at the supermarket. What's behind product names and their use]. Marburg: Tectum.

Milko.se = http://www.milko.se (retrieved 3 September 2012)

Langner, T., Esch, F.-R. and Kühn, J. 2009. Produktverpackung - das fünfte Element im Marketing-Mix [Product packaging -the fifth element in the marketing mix]. In *Handbuch Kommunikation. Grundlagen - Innovative Ansätze - Praktische Umsetzungen.* [Handbook of communication. Basics - Innovative Approaches - Practical implementation.] M. Bruhn et al. (eds.), 285–314. Wiesbaden: Gabler.

Ronneberger-Sibold, E. 2007. Wunschidentitäten im Wandel: deutsche Markennamen aus sieben Jahrzehnten [Desired identities in transition: German brands from seven decades]. In *Identität und Differenz. Ein interdisziplinäres Kolloquium zu Ehren von Wolfgang Huber*. [Identity and difference. An interdisciplinary colloquium in honor of Wolfgang Huber.] E. Ronneberger-Sibold and K. Kazzazi (eds.), 135–158. Tübingen: Narr.

—. 2008. Markennamen als (Zerr-)Spiegel gesellschaftlichen Wertewandels in der ersten Hälfte des 20. Jahrhunderts [Brand names as (distorting) mirror of changed values in the first half of the 20th century]. In *Werbung und Werbesprache. Eine Analyse im interdisziplinären Kontext* [Advertising and advertising language. An analysis in an interdisciplinary context], B. Dumiche, Klöden, H.

(eds.), 123–167. Wilhelmsfeld: Gottfried Egert Verlag (= Pro Lingua 40).

Schweiger, G. and Schrattenecker, G. 2009. *Werbung. Eine Einführung* [*Advertising. An introduction*]. 7th ed. UTB 1370. Stuttgart: Lucius & Lucius.

Selame, E. 1986. Effective Marketing Strategy and Package Design. In *Handbook of Modern Marketing*, Buell, V. P. (Ed.), 93/1-93/11. New York.

Svensk mjölk = http://www.svenskmjolk.se/Global/Dokument/Dokumentarkiv/Skrifter%20och%20artiklar/Milk_in_Sweden.pdf (retrieved 3 September 2012)

Tienken, S. 2008. *Alltagsgattungen und der Ort von Kultur. Sprachwissenschaftliche und kulturanalytische Studien anhand von Milchverpackungen in Deutschland und Schweden* [Communicated patterns of everyday use and the place of culture. Linguistic and culture-analytical studies based on milk cartons in Germany and Sweden]. Acta Universitatis Stockholmiensis; Stockholmer Germanistische Forschungen 71. Stockholm.

Online Resources

http://www.gefleortens.se (retrieved 15 September 2012)

http://www.milko.se/templates/SubStartGeneral.aspx?id=96 (retrieved 3 September 2012)

http://www.wipo.int/wipolex/en/text.jsp?file_id=229565 (retrieved 3 September 2012)

http://www.wipo.int/wipolex/en/text.jsp?file_id=236793 (retrieved 3 September 2012)

Databases

http://register.dpma.de/DPMAregister/uebersicht (retrieved 3 September 2012)

http://www.prv.se/sv/Varumarke/ (retrieved 3 September 2012)

The Lady Gaga Economy: How Paragons Conquer Today's Business Discourse

ANGELIKA BERGIEN
UNIVERSITY OF MAGDEBURG, GERMANY

Abstract

In cognitive linguistics, a paragon is described as an individual member of a category who represents either an ideal or its opposite. Paragons make it easier for us to identify a complex content, and we therefore have a great deal of interest in experiencing paragons. *Lady Gaga* is, for example, a paragon name in the field of pop music; *Lehman (Brothers)* is a paragon of the biggest bank failures in history and is used by many people to comprehend the unfolding of the late-2000s global financial crisis. Shared knowledge and socio-cultural backgrounds of language users are especially important when paragons from different fields or disciplines enter today's business discourse. Examples include *the Lady Gaga of the Contract Manufacturing Business*, *the Lehman of Livestock*, *the Donald Trump of sweeping up* or *the Apple of Hollywood*. The comprehension process involves metonymic and metaphoric relationships which highlight or hide particular aspects of the paragon.

The present paper attempts to show that the information conveyed by the paragon serves primarily to indicate the speaker's or writer's attitude towards the referent rather than being intended to help the hearer identify complex economic issues. It is argued that the use of a paragon leads to a somewhat bleached or reduced conceptualisation of the referent. The paper will also address theoretical and methodological challenges presented by studying paragon names in their respective discourse environments. The focus will be on qualitative rather than quantitative results. The data are all attested examples collected from the Internet, unless otherwise stated. In addition, results from a survey carried out with students at Magdeburg University will be used for comparison.

Introduction

Representations of events, activities and participants in written business communication involve a number of linguistic choices. These choices, which include appellatives and names, are significant with respect to both text organisation and comprehension.

In the literature on names, we have been confronted with a number of works wrestling with the difference between names and appellatives. In general, names can be said to have two important functions: they reflect identity and distinctiveness. Whereas identity defines who someone really is, distinctiveness mainly refers to how someone or something differs from others. Following Joseph (2004: 12) we can say that names are the "primary text of personal identity, thus occupying a privileged place within the language". Compared with nouns, the choice of names in a text is marked by additional features which result from their special linguistic status. As Nicolaisen (1995: 390) points out:

> In order to use a name precisely or rather felicitously, […] we must […] have a thorough knowledge of its content. […] The more content a name has for us, the better we know it, the richer its associations and relations in a "field" are likely to be.

This aspect of name usage deserves special consideration, since the name indicates the text producer's intention to refer to a single entity with the expectation that the recipient will be able to make a similar identification. In this way, identification, and hence recognition of the referent, needs to be seen as an outcome of producer-recipient interaction. As a prerequisite of successful communication, the producer of a given text therefore has to present the name in such a way that the recipient is able to identify and recognise the referent. Names may be described as providing unequivocal identification of their referents within a given context (Bussmann 1996: 387). The term *context* includes both the linguistic context and its broader situational or cultural framework.

This paper addresses a phenomenon that is related to the growing importance of so-called paragon names in today's business discourse. Paragons can hardly be described as *proper* names, since they lack the typical characteristics and functions of personal, product or corporate names. However, they do fulfill other functions in an economy that has become more complex, more uncertain and more indeterminate.

Paragons as Metonymic Sources

The term *paragon* can, firstly, be traced back to George Lakoff's cognitive approach to metaphor and metonymy. In the chapter entitled "Idealized Cognitive Models" , Lakoff (1987: 87–88) describes paragons (together with social stereotypes, typical examples, ideals and generators) as a kind of metonymic semantic mechanism to represent a certain category which cannot or should not be directly named: "We also comprehend categories in terms of individual members who represent either an ideal or its opposite."

This is, for example, the case when Lewis Hamilton is called *the Tiger Woods of racing*. Tiger Woods is a well-known and highly successful American golfer. The name *Tiger Woods* is a paragon or best example of the category YOUNG, DYNAMIC, GOOD-LOOKING MAN FROM AN ETHNIC GROUP THAT IS NORMALLY NOT SO WELL REPRESENTED IN THE RESPECTIVE SPORT OR FIELD IN GENERAL. In this case, we have a whole-for-part metonymy, because the personal name *Tiger Woods*, normally used to cover all our knowledge about Tiger Woods, actually comes to mean something much more precise. Which properties or parts are relevant and will be selected depends on the discourse context and "the cultural or historical significance that the entity bearing the name might have acquired at some point in the life of a group of people" (Sophia & Marmaridou 1989: 364).

Paragons have a very important role in society since they mark an area of ambition and imitation. As Holmqvist and Płuciennik (2010: 375) observe:

> Imitating paragons is based on a process of cultic identification, […]. In ancient times, objects of identification usually had a cultic or ritual status. It has however become clear that, not only in ancient times but in many different historical epochs, this type of cultic identification has played an important role in popular culture. Superman and characters in computer games as well as various religious heroes provide good examples.

But this is only one part of the answer to the question of why paragons are increasingly used in media discourse. For journalists, they are, in the first place, shortcuts for identifying referents since they provide mental access to something that is linguistically more economical and cognitively more readily accessible. In popular business discourse, which includes journalistic texts that deal with current economic and business matters or advertising, journalists address a wide range of topics and events, many of which have only been brought to their readership's attention on the day in question. They can thus not expect the reference of all linguistic choices to be part of the situational or cultural context they share with their readers. As a consequence, journalists have to decide whether the name chosen as a paragon and the context provided are adequate to identify the intended target meaning.

Naming as Framing

A more powerful argument for the increasing use of paragons can be presented when we describe this phenomenon in the context of the *Naming and Framing* theory. The concept of framing has been used, for example, within sociology, following the theories of Erving Goffman (1974), but it has also been an active component of so-called crisis communication theories.[1] According to the framing concept, the choice of names in a text helps recipients to build interpretive frames that allow them to make sense of the world. Or, as Entman (1993: 52) puts it:

> To frame is to select some aspects of a perceived reality and make them more salient in a communicating text, in such a way as to promote a particular problem definition, causal interpretation, moral evaluation, and/or treatment recommendation for the item described.

In other words, frames highlight bits of information about the paragon. So, if we put a paragon name on a particular concept, then this will reflect the meaning we attach to the concept and it certainly affects the interpretation of the nature of the concept, the influence of culture and our encyclopaedic knowledge about the paragon.

In early 2012, I came across the following phrase in a talk show on the television channel Arte: *Gadaffi – the Lady Gaga of the desert.*[2] In this example, the name *Lady Gaga* can be said to represent the category ECCENTRIC PEOPLE WITH OVER-THE-TOP CLOTHING AND THEATRICS perfectly. This knowledge is used to understand the metaphoric comparison with the name *Gadaffi*. Gadaffi's clothing is discussed, not his crimes. This shows that frames call attention to particular aspects, but simultaneously direct attention away from other aspects. In addition, the conceptual frames we use to make sense of the world can be manipulated

---

[1] For example, Timothy Coombs' Situational Crisis Communication Theory (SCCT). Coombs describes framing as a symbolic response to crises. According to this, a *frame* is the way a problem is presented, the meaning one attaches to the problem. (See Vigsø 2010: 234).

[2] Arte tv, January 29, 2012.

relatively easily, especially via repetition in the media. Their use thus gives the sender or framer enormous power to influence how the receivers will interpret the message.

Paragons in Popular Business Discourse

Paragons, which are frequent in popular culture, have conquered business discourse, and this has, in the first place, something to do with changes in business activities. Today's commercial activities and business transactions increasingly take place within the framework of a global economy or market. This means "the entire world is more and more integrated into a single economic system which is based around market exchange: labour, capital, technology, consumer products, and services move with fewer and fewer restraints across national boundaries" (Li 2007: 425[3]). In some real sense, globalisation has rendered the world smaller and geographically irrelevant. This process is paralleled by an increase in the complexity, abstractness and uncertainty of economic concepts. In addition, many business activities are too fast-moving for non-experts to comprehend. The financial crisis is a case in point for this phenomenon. The question is how to put this complexity into a language that can be understood by recipients.

In contrast to rather concrete categories such as BIRD (e.g. robin, sparrow, which are used unconsciously in reasoning), it is almost impossible to identify a typical member of the category FINANCIAL CRISIS by reasoning. But, to all of us, the name *Lehman Brothers*, which is related to the global financial services firm that declared bankruptcy in 2008, makes sense to many people.

The following examples with *Lady Gaga* and *Lehman Brothers* as paragons were collected from the Internet, using Google as the search engine. They illustrate how paragons activate frames in the comprehension process and that we frequently have to shift frames when lack of comprehension forces us to replace one frame with another. It is especially in these cases that we become aware of a certain frame. In most cases, linguistic, encyclopaedic and cultural knowledge is necessary to activate the respective frame. *Lady Gaga* is the stage name of Stefani Joanne Angelina Germanotta, who is an American singer and songwriter. The name *Lady Gaga* is used in the following examples:

[3] The original reference: Peoples, J & Baily, G. 2003. *Humanity. An Introduction to Cultural Anthropology*. 6th edn. Melbourne: Thomson, 160.

(1) Flexotronics is the Lady Gaga of the contract manufacturing business… it is the queen … I think Flexotronic is real good […].[4]
(2) The Lotus Music Candle is the Lady Gaga of candles
The Lotus Music Candle is a seriously banging birthday candle. Don't put it on a cake, but […] this is way better than low-end fireworks, way better than sparklers and just below Lady Gaga's bra in the Bad Romance video. […] See the way it splits open and all the ends are like miniature candles? […] Great way to spice up a friend's birthday party.[5]
(3) Mister Gaga
Der Twizy von Renault ist weder Auto noch Roller, sondern etwas dazwischen[6] [Twizy by Renault is neither a car nor a scooter, but something in between]
(4) The Lady Gaga economy
She reminds us that (as Say's Law in economics holds) there are no general gluts; instead there is only relative overproduction in particular sectors of the economy. Say's Law in economics is the proposition that supply creates its own demand.[7]

Table 1 lists the activated *Lady Gaga* frames and the target meanings as found in the texts.

---

4 http://seekingalpha.com/article/184660-cramer-s-lightning-round-the-lady-gaga-of-the-contract-manufacturing-business-1-26-10 8 (retrieved 22 July 2012).
5 http://www.shinyshiny.tv/2010/07/pyrotechnic_candle_lotus_bloom.html (retrieved 20 July 2012).
6 http://adacemobility.wordpress.com/2012/04/25/renault-twizy-mister-gaga/ (retrieved 22 July 2012).
7 http://dailycaller.com/2010/07/09/the-lady-gaga-economy/ (retrieved 22 July 2012).

Table 1. ***Lady Gaga*****: frames and target meanings.**

Example	Frame	Target meaning
(1)	RANK Lady gaga is a top singer	Flextronics is a top business
(2)	PERFORMANCE In her *Bad Romance* video, the ends of a bra split open and all the ends are like miniature candles	a candle with pyrotechnical and musical effects
(3)	GENDER IDENTITY Lady Gaga is claimed to be intersexual	a product name for a vehicle that is neither a car nor a scooter
(4)	METHOD Gaga's economic principle that supply creates its own demand	the need to liberate and facilitate economic activity via increased supply

Lehman Brothers Holding Inc. was a global financial services firm. Before declaring bankruptcy in 2008, Lehman was the fourth largest investment bank in the USA. The name *Lehman Brothers* is used in the following examples:

(5) St. Vincent's is the Lehman Brothers of hospitals
[…] St. Vincent's collapse is only the most visible symptom of an ongoing financial emergency facing the city's five dozen remaining hospitals and threatening those they serve. In a sense, St. Vincent's is the Lehman Brothers of the local hospital system: an institution whose dramatic disappearance, once unthinkable, raises the question about the viability of the entire system[8]

[8] http://nymag.com/news/features/68991/ (retrieved 20 July 2012).

(6) The Lehman of Livestock
[…] Thomas Gibson, Eastern's longtime owner […] is under investigation by the Justice and Agriculture departments for sham transactions and accused of passing bad checks.[9]

(7) Europe's Lehman Brothers
[…] Greece is Europe's own version of Lehman – it is simply too big to fail. It was the Lehman Brothers collapse in fall 2008 that fueled the global financial crisis.[10]

Table 2 lists the activated *Lehman Brother* frames and the target meanings as found in the texts.

Table 2. *Lehman Brothers*: frames and target meanings.

Example	Frame	Target meaning
(5)	RESULT AND SYMPTOM the dramatic disappearance of an institution	St. Vincent's collapse as the most visible symptom of ongoing financial emergency of hospitals
(6)	METHOD risky trade and sham transactions	Eastern Livestock is under investigation for unjust enrichment and aggressive trade
(7)	PERSPECTIVE the collapse of an institution fuelled the global financial crisis	The bankruptcy of Greece could have knock-on effects

Both analyses reveal that paragons like *Lady Gaga* and *Lehman Brothers* represent more than one category and thus activate different frames in different discourse contexts. This is in contrast to well-established paragons such as *Shakespeare*, which today usually represents

---

9 http://www.forbes.com/forbes/2011/0214/focus-tommy-gibson-david-rings-cattle-farming-money-trail.html (retrieved 22 July 2012).

10 http://www.spiegel.de/international/europe/europe-s-lehman-brothers-brussels-intervenes-to-slow-greece-s-plunge-a-675912.html (retrieved 22 July 2012).

the category WRITERS ENDOWED WITH IMMENSE LITERARY TALENT , as for example in the sentence *That young man is a real Shakespeare* (for a detailed discussion of this and similar examples, see Barcelona 2004). Barcelona points out that a prerequisite for the creation of such a category "is the existence of the culturally entrenched metonymic model of Shakespeare" (2004: 369). Repeated usage of such models over time may lead to paragons which are conventionally associated with specific meanings to the point where they may be said to have lost their status as paragons and become lexicalised common nouns which are preceded by an indefinite article. In other words, the more conventionalised the SOURCE name is, the more it is used in its classifying function and the less (culture-specific) context is necessary for its interpretation. This can be seen in examples like *The boss could afford to pay us all more, but he is just an old Scrooge* [a person with money who is mean; from the main character in Dickens' *A Christmas Carol*].

The Survey

In addition to the analysis of the seven text extracts, a survey with 20 MA students from the University of Magdeburg, which is part of ongoing research, was conducted to demonstrate the difficulty of comprehending paragon constructions without explicit contextual support. Students were presented with a worksheet containing the abovementioned examples and were asked to explain their meaning. The resulting answers were grouped into four categories (Figure 1):

a) intended frame fully activated
b) intended frame partly activated[11]
c) no frame activated
d) different frame activated[12]

[11] For example, one student wrote about example 3 (*Mister Gaga*): "Somebody who is ambiguous."
[12] For example, one student wrote about example 3 (*Mister Gaga*): "Somebody who shocks."

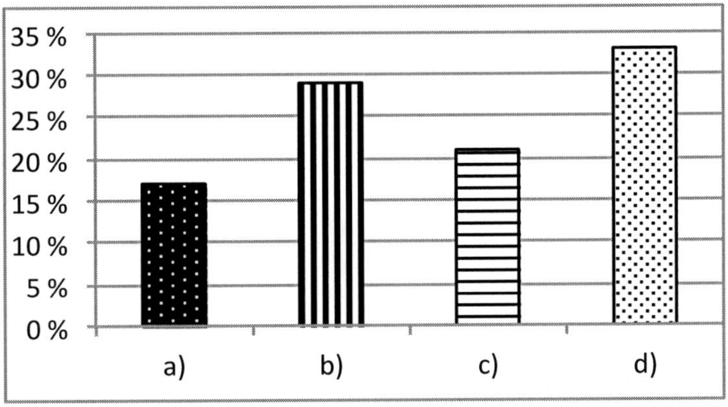

Figure 1. Categories of participants' answers.

With regard to all 140 answers, it is interesting to note (Fig. 1) that most of the answers can be found in categories d) (=33 per cent) and b) (=29 per cent). The high percentage of answers in group d) reveals that identification processes based on paragons without explicit contextual support are not always logical, but may be casual, subjective and even based on illusion.

The results also show that an activation of the frame intended by the author clearly demands explicit contextual support. However, the answers in examples 1 (*Flexotronics is the Lady Gaga of the contract manufacturing business*), 3 (*Mister Gaga*) and 7 (*Europe's Lehman Brothers*) reveal that 30 to 40 per cent of all participants activated the frames that had been intended by the text producer. It is possible that frequent repetition in the media and the fact that certain topics make more dramatised scenarios possible (for example the intersexual discussion in the case of lady Gaga) have produced strong frames which no longer need much contextual support for their activation. Against this background, it is interesting to note that in the *Lady Gaga* group the RANK (1) and SEXUAL IDENTITY (3) frames were frequently activated, whereas the PERFORMANCE (2) and the METHOD (4) frames were not. In the *Lehman Brothers* group the RESULT (5) and PERSPECTIVE (7) frames were frequently activated, whereas the METHOD (6) frame was not. It would be too early to draw conclusions from these results, but they obviously show preferences in the storage of encyclopaedic knowledge about the name functioning as paragon. The results of the detailed analysis for each of the 7 examples are illustrated in figure 2 and figure 3.

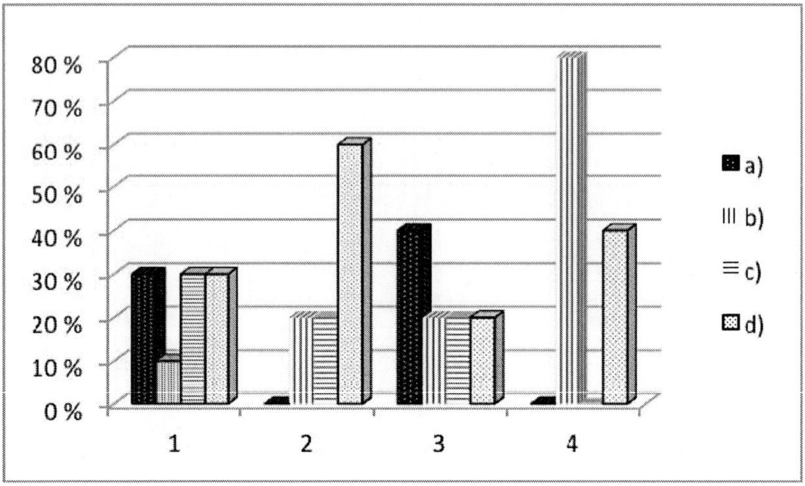

Figure 2. Categories of participants' answers for *Lady Gaga*.

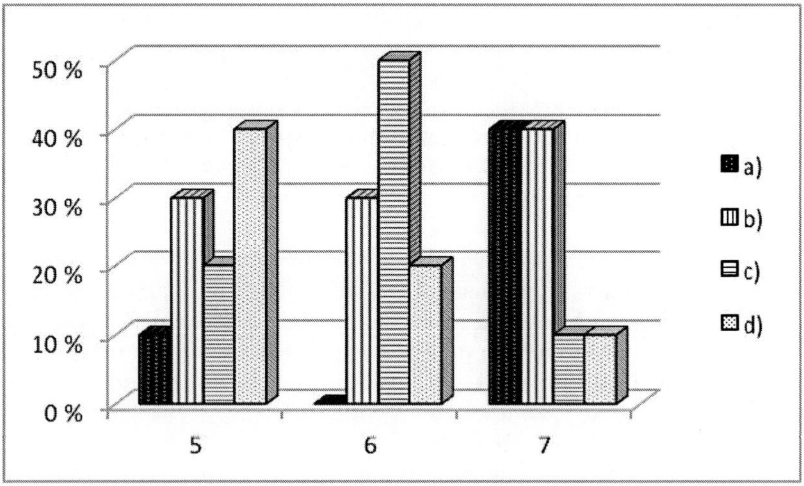

Figure 3. Categories of participants' answers for *Lehman Brothers*.

Concluding Remarks

I have attempted to show that paragons not only make target meanings accessible but also available for further elaboration and evaluation in discourse. The frame that is activated via the paragon does not only provide an adequate description, but signals the value given to the element in question. This probably explains why paragons are so effective. Space, time and other constraints prevent journalists from including all possible perspectives, and news stories, as necessary, emphasise only certain values, facts, and other considerations. Which frames will become successful to a large extent depends on the treatment of paragons in the media. They prefer concrete frames, because they foreshadow relevant information more effectively. This makes paragons and the frames they activate more adaptable to all sorts of political and business purposes since they pave the way for concrete and easily understandable solutions. However, as Vigsø (2010: 237) points out: "The question of how truthful they are does not really enter into this".

References

Barcelona, A. 2004. Metonymy behind grammar: The motivation of the seemingly "irregular" grammatical behaviour of English paragon names, In *Studies in Linguistic Motivation*, G. Radden and K. Panther (eds.), 357–374. Berlin, New York: de Gruyter,

Bussmann, H. 1996. *Routledge Dictionary of Language and Linguistics*. London: Routledge.

Entman, R. M. 1993. Framing: Toward Clarification of a Fractured Paradigm. *Journal of Communication* 43(4): 51–58.

Goffman, E. 1974. *Frame analysis*. New York: Free Press.

Holmqvist, K and Płuciennik, J. 2010. Princess Antonomasia and the Truth: Two Types of Metonymic Relations. In *Tropical Truth(s). The Epistemology of Metaphor and other Tropes*, A. Burkhardt and B. Nerlich (eds.), 372–381. Berlin, New York: de Gruyter.

Joseph J. E. 2004. *Language and Identity*. London: Palgrave Macmillan.

Lakoff, G. 1987. *Women, Fire, and Dangerous Things*. Chicago: The University of Chicago Press.

Li, D. C. S. 2007. Language and the multilingual business environment in a globalized economy. In *Handbook of multiligualism and multiligual communication*, P. Auer and L. Wei (eds.), 423–443. Berlin, New York: de Gruyter.

Nicolaisen, W. 1995. Name and appellative. In *Namenforschung – Name studies – Les noms propres. Ein internationales Handbuch zur Onomastik* [An international handbook on onomastics]: *Vol. 2*, E. Eichler, G. Hilty, H. Löffler and L. Zgusta (eds.), 384–393. Berlin, New York: de Gruyter.

Sophia, A. and Marmaridou, S. 1989. Proper names in communication. *Journal of Linguistics* 25 (2): 355–372.

Vigsø, O. 2010. Naming is Framing: Swine Flu, New Flu, and A(H1N1). *Observatorio (OBS*) Journal* 4 (3): 229–241.

CONTRIBUTORS

TERHI AINIALA, PhD, university lecturer of Finnish Language at the University of Helsinki, Finland. Her main research interests are socio-onomastics, urban place names and theoretical and methodological questions in onomastics.

ANGELIKA BERGIEN, PhD habil, professor of English Linguistics at the University of Magdeburg, Germany. Her main research interests are pragmatics, socio-onomastics, cognitive linguistics and interdisciplinary approaches to all manner of texts.

NITHAT BOONPAISARNSATIT, PhD candidate in the English as an International Language Program, Chulalongkorn University, Thailand. His research interests are brand name communication and lexical semantics and pragmatics.

SABINA BUCHNER, MA, PhD student at the University of Regensburg, Germany. She is secretary of the research group NAMEN. Her main research interests include family names, place names and database-driven onomastic internet platforms for place names.

ALINA BUGHEȘIU, PhD candidate, research assistant at the North University Center of Baia Mare (Technical University of Cluj-Napoca, Romania). Her main research interests are socio-onomastics, trade names, virtual names, and proper name theories.

ENZO CAFFARELLI, chief editor of *Rivista Italiana di Onomastica* and the scientific coordinator of the *Laboratorio Internazionale di Onomastica* at the University of Roma "Tor Vergata", Italy. His main interests in research, publications and didactics are family names, first names, odonyms, brand names, proper names in the lexicography and all the processes of lexicalisation.

PAOLA COTTICELLI, PhD, full professor in Historical Linguistics at the University of Verona, Italy; scientific and editorial member of Hethitisches Woerterbuch, Munich. Her main interest in research and didactic are Indo-European linguistics and culture, hittitology, morpho-syntax of Indo-European languages, lexicographie, onomastics and Italian advertising language, history of linguistics, old writing systems; metalinguistics.

FABIAN FAHLBUSCH, PhD student at the Johannes Gutenberg University of Mainz, Germany. Graduated in German Philology, French Philology and Economics. His main research interests are ergonomastics (company names, product names etc.), grammar of names, proprialisation, deonymisation and surname geography.

ULLA HAKALA, DSc, university lecturer in Marketing at Turku School of Economics, University of Turku, Finland. Her research interests lie in marketing communications and branding. Lately, she has carried out research on brand equity and TOMA, brand heritage and cultural heritage, city branding, country image, and cultural differences in brand perceptions.

DINA HEEGEN, MA, PhD student at Åbo Akademi University and DAAD lecturer in Turku, Finland. Her main research interests are intercultural business communication and onomastics, especially products and brand names.

LASSE HÄMÄLÄINEN, MA, PhD student of Finnish Language at the University of Helsinki. His main research interests are user names in online communities and forenames in Finland.

NICHOLAS IND, PhD, associate professor at Oslo School of Management, Norway, and a partner in Equilibrium Consulting. He is the author of eleven books and he is on the Editorial Board of the Journal of Brand Management. His main research interests are co-creation and brand building inside organisations.

MARIA CHIARA JANNER, PhD student and research assistant in Italian Linguistics at the University of Zurich, Switzerland. Her interests lie in the onomastic sciences, linguistic analysis of literary texts, and the syntax of Italian language, especially causative constructions. Her current research focuses on the morphosyntactic features of commercial names.

MARCIENNE MARTIN, PhD, associate researcher at ORACLE Laboratory, University of Reunion Island, France. Her main research interests are

NTIC, socio-onomastics and sociolinguistics. She is a member of the editorial board of NRO (Nouvelle revue d'onomastique) and she manages the "Nomino ergo sum" collection at the L'Harmattan editions.

KANAVILLIL RAJAGOPALAN, PhD, professor of Linguistics at the Institute of Language Studies, State Univesity at Campinas, Brazil. He is a senior researcher with the National Council for Scientific and Technological Development. His research interests include the philosophy of language, linguistic pragmatics and language politics.

ELKE RONNEBERGER-SIBOLD, PhD, professor of German Linguistics at the Catholic University of Eichstätt-Ingolstadt, Germany. Her main research interests in onomastics concern the interrelation between linguistic, cultural, historical, and economical aspects of German brand names.

PAULA SJÖBLOM, PhD, university lecturer of Finnish Language at the University of Turku. Her main research interests are commercial naming, theoretical and methodological questions of onomastics, cognitive linguistics and the language of economics.

IRMA SORVALI, PhD, professor emerita of Nordic Philology, University of Oulu, Finland; adjunct professor of Scandinavian languages, University of Helsinki, Finland. Her main interests are Swedish language, translation studies, semiotics and Roman literature.

JIRANTHARA SRIOUTAI, PhD, an assistant professor in the English Department of Chulalongkorn University, Bangkok, Thailand. Her research interests are semantics and pragmatics and translation studies.

ADRIANA STOICHIŢOIU ICHIM, PhD, professor of General and Romanian Linguistics at the University of Bucharest. Author of four books and 120 articles reflecting her research interests in lexicology, semantics, onomastics, sociolinguistics, language of the law and media discourse.

KYOKO TAKASHI WILKERSON, PhD, professor of Japanese and Sociolinguistics at the Nagoya University of Foreign Studies, Japan. Her research interests include language and gender, and critical discourse analysis.

SABINE WAHL, MSt, MA, lecturer and researcher for German linguistics at the Catholic University of Eichstätt-Ingolstadt, Germany. Her research interests include the phonology and morphology of German brand names as well as the multimodal design of commercials.

DOUGLAS WILKERSON, PhD, professor of Japanese Culture at the Nagoya University of Foreign Studies, Japan. His research interests include Asian drama, film, and contemporary Japanese culture.

ANTJE ZILG, PhD, university lecturer of Romance Linguistics at the Justus-Liebig-University of Giessen, Germany. Her main research interests are applied linguistics, brand names, media linguistics, and discourse analysis.

INDEX

adjective, 115, 122–123, 253–254, 267, 278, 280, 307
appellative, 6, 20, 83, 94, 136, 138, 142, 149, 220, 222, 226, 261–262, 291, 345
association, 3, 5, 44–45, 56–57, 65, 72, 80, 123, 125, 131, 161, 242–244, 286–287, 290, 297, 300
brand names, v, vi, 9–10, 15, 17–18, 20, 22–23, 25–39, 41–51, 54, 74–75, 77, 79, 81–83, 86–87, 92, 108, 111, 130–135, 202–205, 219, 233–234, 236–247, 249, 252, 254–255, 257, 271–281, 288, 299, 302, 304–305, 309–310, 312, 319, 321–322
branding, v, vi, 15–16, 22–23, 25, 54, 79, 81, 153–155, 159, 161, 163, 166, 167–170, 199, 202–204, 212, 271, 281, 299, 303, 310, 318–319, 322, 326, 329
bynames, 307–308
category, 37–39, 41, 50, 59, 82–83, 90, 97–99, 110, 121, 126, 156, 216, 221, 223, 230, 241, 254, 256–257, 262–264, 275, 305, 322–323, 329, 333, 335–337, 340
co-creation, vi, 202–205, 210–211, 214
commercial names, v, vi, 2–3, 5, 7–10, 12, 90–94, 101, 105, 109, 161, 174–176, 229, 251–256, 258, 260, 262–268, 321
common nouns, 24, 92–95, 99, 105, 135, 251–252, 265, 267, 341
company names, vi, 7–8, 13, 82, 87, 89, 94, 104–105, 108, 166, 172, 174–175, 177–185, 187–191, 198, 201, 218, 229, 231, 248, 251–252, 260–265, 284–289, 298
connotation, 25, 120, 182, 286
consolidation, 153–154, 162–163, 165–168
consumers, 3, 22, 24, 27, 29–31, 33–34, 53, 57, 78–81, 86, 92, 137, 140, 147–148, 202, 204–206, 209–212, 233, 271–272, 274, 277, 286, 288–289, 293, 298–299, 306–307
context, 7, 9, 28, 48, 65, 75–77, 80, 82–83, 85–86, 93–94, 97, 101, 116, 128, 158, 163, 196, 203, 210, 223, 242–243, 253, 257, 260–261, 266, 272–276, 278–279, 283, 285, 291, 301, 319, 321–322, 330–331, 334–336, 341
dairy products, 84, 312–313
denotation, 273
derivation, 95, 253, 276, 280, 304
derivative, 227
diminutive, 115, 220, 307
discourse, 79–80, 86, 93, 103, 130, 171, 252–253, 333–335, 337, 340, 344
ergonomastic, 188
etymological, 85, 91, 95, 96, 116, 123, 290
first name, 92, 98, 100, 163, 193, 245
food brand, 27, 34, 36–38, 41–42
food industry, 30, 271–272, 274, 277, 280, 283, 321–322
frame, 336–337, 341–342, 344
functions, 2, 10, 83, 90–91, 93, 102, 142, 172, 179, 181, 185, 217, 224, 251, 253–254, 272–274,

284–286, 288, 290, 292, 295, 301, 317, 321, 323, 334
generic component, 94–95
generic terms, 92, 95, 97, 100
glocal, 2, 4, 9, 11, 12
history, 8–9, 16, 68–69, 91, 94, 99, 102, 109, 111, 113, 126, 138, 145–146, 151, 155, 158, 161, 167, 176, 188, 190, 214, 223, 249, 283, 288, 289, 305, 310, 333
homonymous, 84, 112, 263, 267, 281–282
hypocorism, 303, 307, 310
identification, 13, 80, 83, 86, 90, 159–160, 163, 168, 170, 209, 271–272, 274, 280, 286, 290, 295, 334–335, 342
identity, 2, 4, 10–11, 21, 75, 79–82, 86, 92, 105, 107, 139, 146, 153–155, 157–161, 163–168, 170, 172, 175, 191, 203, 286, 318–319, 334, 339, 342
image, 2, 10–11, 18, 28, 32, 64, 66–67, 70, 81–82, 108, 110, 118–120, 139, 153, 159, 162, 164, 166–168, 171, 175, 184, 203, 207, 258, 276, 286–287, 293, 299, 316, 319
interaction, vi, 4, 203, 271–272, 280, 322, 334
Internet, vi, 119, 132, 174, 186–187, 190–196, 198–200, 215–217, 220, 229–230, 311, 333, 337
lexeme, 224
lexical, 25, 30, 34, 36–37, 39, 41, 43–45, 47, 49, 51, 55, 56, 82–83, 91, 95, 108, 120–121, 124, 218, 242, 253, 271–272, 274–275, 280, 292, 297, 302, 304, 306, 308, 310, 322
lexicalisation, 122
logo, 24, 32, 81, 119, 161, 182–183, 193–196, 200, 203, 258, 318
metaphor, 18, 120, 128–129, 142, 203, 335
metaphoric, 122, 141, 262, 293, 333, 336
metaphorical, 93, 163
metonym, 142
metonymic, 258–259, 267, 333, 335, 341
metonymical, 83, 98
metonymy, 124, 260, 264–265, 335
morphosyntactic, 251–254, 256, 260, 263, 266
municipality names, vi, 153, 155
names of brands, 75
naming patterns, 90, 93, 99
neo-formation, 109, 115, 119, 121
nickname, 98, 100, 146, 218, 296, 303, 308, 310
nominal constructions, 266
package, 44, 136–137, 139–141, 143–144, 146–148, 315, 318, 322
paragon, 333–336, 341–342, 344
personal name, 7–8, 82, 119, 216, 219, 254, 335
phonetic, 3, 11, 17–18, 23, 25, 28, 108, 238, 240, 245, 248
place branding, 153, 156, 159, 167
place name, vi, 103, 153, 155, 160–161, 167–168, 172, 179, 225
pragmatic, v, 27, 29, 30–31, 34, 44, 51, 76, 93, 130, 259, 274
pragmatics, 28–31, 35, 52, 55
predicative constructions, 258, 267
prestige, v, 19, 56–58, 65, 75, 79, 101
product names, vi, 7, 109, 111, 120, 125, 131–132, 137, 142, 147, 149, 238, 251–253, 256, 261, 263–264, 266, 268–269, 273, 282, 284 289, 291, 294–295, 296, 298, 300–301, 312–313, 315, 320–322, 325–326, 331
public space, 74–75, 77–81, 83, 85–88, 104
reference, 27, 34–35, 44–45, 50, 72, 76, 80, 137, 148, 161, 208, 253, 261, 273, 287, 291, 298–299, 325–326, 329, 336–337

referent, 35, 82, 94, 97, 161, 223, 260–261, 273, 302, 304–305, 308, 333–334
relation, 4, 11–12, 35, 46–48, 69, 78, 80, 82–83, 85, 95, 97, 102, 156–157, 184, 229, 267, 289, 303–304, 320
rhetorical figure, 118
semantic, v, 2, 5, 23, 27–31, 34, 44, 51, 81–82, 85, 90, 95–98, 103, 108, 110–111, 120, 122–124, 176, 200, 217–218, 220, 227, 257, 266, 274, 304–306, 308–309, 324, 335
semantics, 29–31, 52, 54, 109, 130, 134, 229–230
semiotic, 76, 82, 87, 97, 104, 136–137, 139, 142, 272, 275
slang names, vi, 174–177, 183–184
slogan, 109–111, 114–129, 133, 161, 306, 308
social, 3–4, 10, 19, 68–69, 76–77, 80, 86, 93, 95, 100, 102, 108, 125–126, 130, 132, 146, 153, 157–161, 167–168, 181, 184, 204–205, 211–212, 217, 260, 272–273, 276–278, 282, 305, 307, 318, 335
socio-onomastics, 174, 215
sound shape, 233–238, 240–243, 245, 247–248, 288
specific component, 94, 97
surname, 84, 92, 96, 98, 193, 289–290
trade names, 77–78, 83, 108, 288, 300
translation, 34, 36, 38, 53, 74–77, 81, 86–87, 92, 128, 136, 139–140, 144, 190, 193, 200, 273–274, 276–278, 319, 321, 329
user names, 215–219, 221–226, 228–230